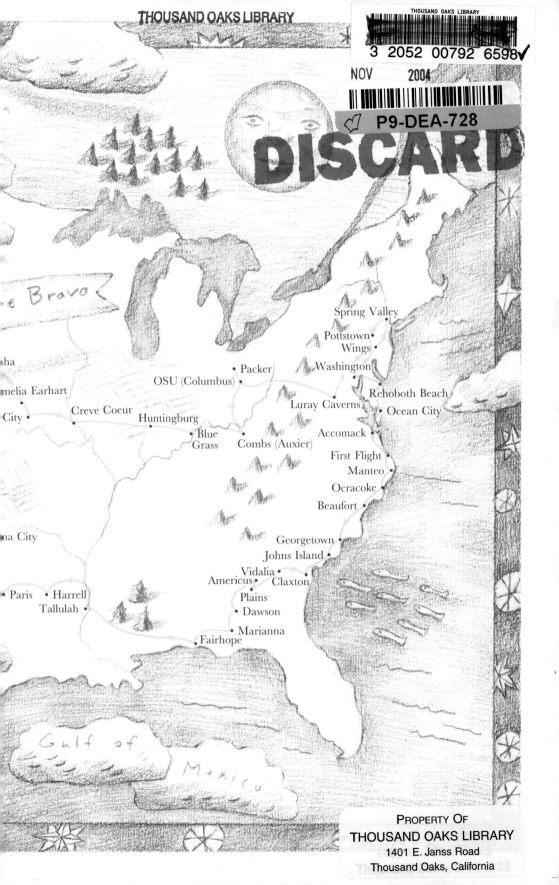

e Bravo

Spring Valley
Pottstown•
Wings
Packer • Washington
OSU (Columbus) •
melia Earhart Rehoboth Beach
City • Creve Coeur Luray Caverns Ocean City
Huntingburg
Blue Accomack •
Grass Combs (Auxier)
First Flight
Manteo •
Ocracoke •
Beaufort •

na City
Georgetown •
Johns Island •
Vidalia •
Americus • Claxton
Paris • Harrell Plains
Tallulah • Dawson
Marianna
Fairhope

Gulf of

Mexico

Collection Management

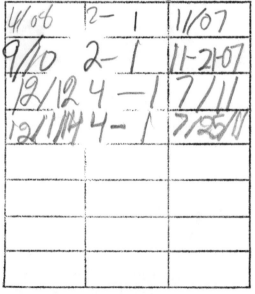

4/06	2 - 1	1/07
9/10	2 - 1	11-21-07
12/12	4 - 1	7/11
12/1/14	4 - 1	7/25/11

Zero Three Bravo

Zero Three Bravo

*Solo Across America in a
Small Plane*

Mariana Gosnell

Alfred A. Knopf · New York

1993

THIS IS A BORZOI BOOK
PUBLISHED BY ALFRED A. KNOPF, INC.

Copyright © 1993 by Mariana Gosnell
All rights reserved under International and Pan-American
Copyright Conventions. Published in the United States by
Alfred A. Knopf, Inc., New York, and simultaneously in Canada by
Random House of Canada Limited, Toronto.
Distributed by Random House, Inc., New York.

Library of Congress Cataloging-in-Publication Data
Gosnell, Mariana.
Zero three bravo / by Mariana Gosnell.—1st. ed.
p.   cm.
ISBN 0-679-40025-7
1. United States—Description and travel—1981.
2. Gosnell, Mariana—Journeys—United States.
3. Air travel—United States.
I. Title.
E169.04.G67 1993
917.304'928—dc20
92-28713   CIP

Manufactured in the United States of America

FIRST EDITION

In loving memory of my parents

•

For Bill and Molly
and for Jamie

Contents

Contents

Acknowledgments

———

To all those habitués of little airports across the country who shared advice, stories, tools, and cars with me, and to all those friends and family who encouraged and supported me in my attempt to tell the stories straight upon my return, I am profoundly grateful.

Zero Three Bravo

Spring Valley

It was a Monday and there weren't many pilots around, just a few of the regulars. Old Al Morris, who had been in the Lafayette Flying Corps in World War I and lived now in a house off the end of Runway Two-Six, was sitting with a friend in the shade of a rusty hangar. He was telling the friend that he'd seen a cancer specialist that week because he was worried about the pink spots on his nose and arms. He smiled sheepishly; the doctor said they were sunburn. Bill King walked by carrying a couple of cans of oil and said goodbye to me. Weekends Bill flew air shows in a Tiger Moth and dropped black-powder bombs on the Red Baron, who was picnicking on the grass below with a woman in a bustle; weekdays he taught high school shop. Up in the coffee shop, Helen was behind the counter, a cheerful, distracted, un-girdled woman I once saw drop a quarter pound of butter on her foot and not notice. She was cooking one of her famous square hamburgers. The fan was on in the room and the model airplanes that hung from the ceiling were bobbing around, as if struggling to fly.

From a booth just outside the coffee shop, I phoned Flight Service, which reported a scattered layer of clouds at 3,500 feet in the New York area, temperature 84 degrees, wind ten knots from 190 degrees, visibility nine miles in light haze. I looked out of the booth and made my own observations. The first wavy line of hills southeast of the airport was visible but not the second; nine miles would be about right. The grass on the field was trembling slightly and the windsock stuck out from the pole at the angle of an arm reaching for a handshake; ten knots would be about right. (Miles, knots, you had to work both scales; the wind blew in knots, the eye saw in miles.) I phoned a friend in Washington who'd be picking me up in a couple of hours and asked her what the weather was like down there. She went to the window, came back, and reported, "It's rather blue." So it would be a launch.

I wasn't sure I was ready for one. Suddenly, as I went down and stood by my plane, the cockpit seemed awfully small, the land out beyond it awfully big. In an hour or so I would be flying cross-country, which in aviation terms means taking off from one airport and landing at any other (X-C in the log book) instead of staying in the pattern or flying around the neighborhood and coming back to land at the same airport, but I'd be doing it in the general sense, going *across the country,* to the West Coast and back. I'd be flying from one little airport to another, many X-C's within the larger one. The airports would all be little ones (meaning uncontrolled, with no airplane flights in or out), since to me they were half the point of flying, often destinations in themselves, regardless of what was around them. Good airports (and there were some clunkers, dead at the stick) were at once social clubs, repositories of knowledge about the history and craft of flying, sources of inspiration for the young, and terrific places to sit and do nothing but swap stories and ogle the nubile clouds.

Usually there's love involved in running a little airport, since it's hard to make much money at it. (One manager told me his father taught him to "work for friendship," reasoning like this: "If you fly here on earth, then when you die there's a natural tendency for your wings to spread out, but if your pockets are weighed down with gold you can't rise.") It's this love—of machines that fly, the outdoor life in open, grassy settings, the beckoning sky, all shared with people drawn like you to the field—that gives the airport its sustaining quality. As you glide in, the runway spreads to meet you, wide and welcoming, and if it's the right sort of airport there's a welcome in the office too; all you need in order to belong is your own interest, your own way of caring.

I would be going in my own airplane. I owned a Luscombe Silvaire, model 8F, built in 1950 in Garland, Texas. It sounds luxurious to own your own airplane, but when I bought mine it cost less than most cars, $3,100. It had two side-by-side seats, a tail wheel, high wings, stick controls, all-metal skin and construction ("No Wood No Nails No Glue" was the company motto), and a 95-horsepower engine. It also had on the panel (aviation for "dashboard"), besides the basic instruments, a radio with whistlestop tuner (you wound a handle until you heard a whistle, then you knew—or believed—you were transmitting and receiving on the same frequency) and Wedgwood medallion depicting Aurora, the goddess of dawn, driving horses (horsepower, get it?) over a bank of clouds, given to me by a friend who knew I had trouble getting up early, as pilots often have to do ("We fly at dawn!").

The Luscombe was named after its developer, Mr. Don A. Luscombe, a dog-lover, womanizer, early pilot (one of the first hundred people in the U.S. to get a license), World War I ambulance driver but not engineer (you don't need to be an engineer to create airplanes). I called mine *Zero Three Bravo,* its registration number, or rather the part of the number I gave out as a radio identifier after the first call-in.

I bought it as a kind of getaway from New York City, where I lived and worked, a weekend cabin that moved. On days when the city seemed particularly punishing to body and spirit and the point of the job particularly well concealed, I'd sit in my mini-office halfway up the side of a 40-story building in midtown Manhattan and gaze out the window at a sliver of sky, a ribbon, a rivulet of blue, and think: There's lots more of that out there. And it's all waiting, waiting for me. From my roller chair I'd mentally zoom off into the blue and keep on going, out into a country that has the most little airports of any country in the world, over 12,000 of them, in almost every geographical niche and on almost every kind of terrain, with almost every kind of person on them (although aviation has more than its share of the tinkerers, dreamers, escapists, and leathery-faced loners).

On one such day not so very long ago, when even the leaves on the trees in Central Park had an oily film on them and there wasn't anything on the streets that didn't seem sad or hurt or tired or ugly, the gaze out my window turned into a stare. I couldn't take my eyes off that ribbon of blue. It held me as the blue of an air hole must a person trapped under the ice, whose continued breathing depends on reaching it. I asked for three months' leave from my job and got it, arranged for the daughter of a friend to stay in my apartment and hold mail, and assembled eight bags and boxes of a size that could be squeezed into the plane's baggage compartment back of the seat (almost everything in the Luscombe involves a squeeze). In them I put, for emergencies, a portable still (for making drinking water), folding saw, signaling mirror, waterproof matchbox, morphine pills (against pain after a crash), water-purification tablets, a device for trapping fish (brought without conviction that I could use it), plus wheel chocks, tiedown pegs, harmonica (I liked to picture myself in some barren place, out West preferably, sitting on a ramp, leaning against one of my tires and playing a haunting tune, never mind that I didn't know how), space blankets, clothing, cologne (Vol de Nuit, of course), cameras, food, books. I filled a whole box with books, as if I were going into semiliterate country, or a place that didn't speak my language. I planned to put the box on my right seat in place of a passenger, so that the plane's center of gravity would be well forward of the baggage compartment, and to use the top as a table for holding snacks, notepads, and charts.

With me I was taking 28 navigational charts (always "charts," as with our buddies the sailors, never "maps"), each about the size of a road map when folded but more like a table runner when unfolded, 59 by 20½ ungainly inches, representing about 400 by 150 miles per side. They weren't organized around state lines, just included whatever land and water fit onto the available paper, and were usually named for their most prominent city. Airports were shown on the charts as color-coded circles: blue for controlled, magenta for uncontrolled, solid for paved, clear for unpaved. Populated areas were yellow, railroads and power lines black, roads magenta, and water blue. I looked the charts over before I left but didn't draw any course lines. I expected that most of the time I wouldn't know where I was going until shortly before I started to go there. I had flown across the country a couple of times before, but fast, in order to get places, and this time I'd be winging it, so to speak, improvising, taking my time, getting blown about a bit by whim and events, as I imagined some of the old-time pilots did it. The only thing I knew for sure was that I'd be heading south first, along the coast, because to the west lay the Midwest and home, and home wasn't a place to begin.

I'd be going solo. Flying is an activity that allows you to indulge your passion for solitude, or society, or both. For me, society on the ground, at chummy little airports, and solitude in the air (mostly). I enjoyed taking people up flying with me, but I enjoyed even more being alone in a cockpit beyond their reach. To be sitting in some nameless cube of air or standing, an anonymous human being, on the grounds of some unidentified little airport was freedom of a different sort from just leaving the ground.

There was sure to be adventure in such a trip. Despite claims to the contrary by people who flew in more pioneering days, the time for gypsying by air is not over. The sky is bound now with electronic airways and bulging with control zones, planes are being made faster and with more instruments than ever, the land is increasingly paved, hedged, and peopled, but the *impulse* to go up and tool around the sky is the same as it was when planes were all wood, nails, and glue and aviators wore riding breeches and boots. As a pilot you still want to separate yourself from the firm ground you were born on and float among treetops and clouds, zipping over countryside that has cars only inching across it, marveling at the new view you get of your neighbors' yard, dazzled by the sight of light lying on a field, lake, or hillside in a way you've never seen it, testing yourself constantly for skill and courage, just you up there with your craft and the elements, either of which could kill you. In the last quarter of the century that began with the first powered heavier-than-air flight, there is still adventure in flying a small plane cross-country, still risk, still surprise, still sport, still fun.

Unencumbrance being the goal, I made only a few rules for the trip: Go into only small airports if possible, fly low where sensible, and don't fly at night. I once met an airline pilot who, with the great gobbets of money he got from working 12 days a month, bought Dorothy Parker's estate in eastern Pennsylvania (what he called her workroom was still painted the same bright aqua as the swimming pool just beyond it, and the pool and the study played off each other so that the study took on the quality of a pool, the most otherworldly and refreshing place to write I've ever seen) and laid in a grass strip for his Cessna 182. The pilot regularly flew thousands of miles for his airline, to Europe and Asia, many of them at night, but he absolutely would not go up in his 182 after dark. "It's one chance I won't take," he had decided. I decided too that over unknown terrain at night I wouldn't take the chance and made it a rule so I wouldn't be tempted, since flying in the light-spangled darkness can be enchanting.

I would, however, take the chance, every day if possible, of flying low, under 2,000 feet, even though it isn't as safe as flying high or as fast, usually, or as comfortable, and I'd have to do most of my navigating by chart rather than by radio. When you're high there's the grandeur of abstraction (clouds, sun, and earth-plane), but the far-off earth is a picture. Down low it's more sensual, given to texture and narrative; you see the nap on the grain field, the white dog chasing the green car, the yellow blooms deep in the swamp nobody else can see. You may even be in the picture yourself (look, there's a shadow, a bar with light shot through it, running over the hill).

So, on a day when flowering linden filled New York City with such a heartrending sweetness that it almost weakened my resolve to be off, I climbed into a rented car with eight bags and boxes, rode the 30 miles to Spring Valley airport, phoned Flight Service, told Al and Bill and Helen goodbye, went down and stood by my plane, and began to drag my (cold) feet. I asked the friend who drove me to the airport to take a photo of me standing next to the cowling of the plane, which had painted on it the outline of a goshawk (someone suggested that play on my name; to my regret it was often mistaken for a parrot or pigeon). He took six, and I did a long, careful preflight inspection, stuffed the bags and boxes into the baggage compartment, polished the windows, drank a last cup of hot tea; then there was nothing for it but to go. The friend, who never liked the idea of this trip anyway and made it clear he preferred kites, waved me off. I pulled on the starter, taxied out of my tiedown, did an engine runup by the end of Two-Six, turned onto the runway, eased in the throttle, went rolling down, lifted off, climbed away, and rocked my wings, for him.

Almost immediately the Luscombe's shadow got lost among the cars and trucks on Route 59 and the buildings on either side. A large smear of metropolitan yellow covered everything on the chart in the direction I was headed, even major roads, as far as Lincoln Park airport, my first checkpoint. Airports generally make excellent checkpoints, imprinted as they are on the landscape like tattoos, most of them simple I's (single runways) but also X's, V's, L's, T's, A's, N's, triangles, starbursts, teepees, and crosses of Lorraine. The point of checkpoints is to confirm that you're holding your course, and at Lincoln Park I knew I wasn't holding mine very well because the airport rose up on my right rather than on my nose and I realized I'd wandered, or allowed myself to be blown, left of track. I adjusted my heading, but at the next checkpoint, a tangle of highways running perpendicular to my flight path, I realized I'd drifted left of track again and had to correct again.

Meanwhile, the plane was bouncing around more than I had expected, and visibility seemed to be less than the reported nine miles.

The engine sounded uncommonly loud to me, but the radio was quiet, *too* quiet, none of the companionable weekend chatter. When I unhooked the longer hinge I'd just had installed on my left window, to give a sort of open-cockpit feeling, air rushing in, back, and around, the charts on top of the book box began unfolding on their own, expanding into the cockpit, blossoming like monster roses, and I had to bat them down, squash and refold them, and clip them to the top of the box. At my third checkpoint, a railroad crossing a road, I realized that this time I had drifted *right*.

Maybe, I thought, I should have another try at this takeoff. In Washington I'd have to do some artful dodging to get under and around the terminal control area (TCA), and I wanted to be in good shape for that. So when Pottstown-Limerick airport in eastern Pennsylvania materialized a few miles off to my right, I abandoned course and landed there to regroup, something I'd never had to do before. Pottstown happens to be the place where I spent one of the most desolate hours of my life, in a small drama involving this plane. None of the principals in the drama was around when I landed so I just stopped on the ramp, sat in the shade under one of the wings, spread the Washington charts on the asphalt, and went over my course again.

Twenty minutes later, feeling somewhat restored, I folded the charts, climbed back into the Luscombe, and took off again, with no one around to wave me off this time except maybe a couple of ghosts (one of which was probably cackling with laughter because I had to make this remedial stop). I was flying facing the sun, which gave every suspended mote a backlit glow, thickening the haze. Chesapeake Bay appeared as an enormous blank below me, a misty white prelude to the dropoff at the end of the earth; a scow on its surface seemed to hang above the general brightness like a balloon. But I felt more in charge, and the effect was almost peaceful.

Jean was waiting for me in Washington, or rather at an airport just over the district line in Maryland, and in her opinion had been waiting too long, because of that unscheduled stop, so I didn't have time to explore the place as I would have wanted. I did catch a glimpse of a long-haired white cat seated like an empress on a large desk, surveying the general untidiness of the office, and in the ladies' room came across a cup with FREDDY FUDPUCKER! printed on the side, reminding me of the subtlety of typical pilot humor. But when a man came over to my plane as I was locking up and began talking at me, about how Temco, the company that made my Luscombe, also made the F-8s he flew for the Navy, he didn't have time as he would have liked to elaborate on the fairings he told me I *should* be putting under my gear struts at the top, or the compartment for storing oil I *should* install behind my baggage compartment, or the extender I *should* get for my air-intake tube (some men can't help themselves). I was off, on my way into Washington for a couple of days of visiting art museums and ethnic restaurants, so like my life in New York that it was hard for me to think of this as the real start of my trip. In fact, I didn't think of it that way. The real start, as I saw it, would be when I took off for an airport a hundred miles east, a grass field that held a piece of my romantic past.

Rehoboth Beach

I picked Rehoboth Beach because the first time I ever went up in an airplane was on a trip to the little airport there. It was the summer after my freshman year in college (people didn't fly as easily during infancy then as they do now), and I went to visit my boyfriend, Ralph. He was staying for the summer with his parents in a house they owned near the beach (they were wealthy; his father had invented a water softener; Ralph was the first baby washed in water softened with it). He was so good-looking, I thought, that sometimes when he smiled my heart would seem to grow larger, diffuse into my chest, and my mouth would come open, in awe, like a sinner before saints. The most impressive thing about Ralph, though, I realized in later years, wasn't his good looks but his long kisses. His kisses went on for a quarter of an hour, or more. That is, during the 15 minutes, his lips would move around *on* mine but never *away* from them (those were the days when kisses carried the burden of carnality, did most of the communicating, at least in my part of the country). While he was out on the beach every day renting umbrellas and folding chairs to tourists, I was back in Ohio doing mockups for billboard ads and thinking a lot about him. Therefore, as I took off from Columbus one steamy day in early August, I had another reason to be nervous in my window seat besides the fact that it would be my first ride in an airplane. When I stepped off at the other end I'd be seeing Ralph for the first time in almost two months.

From Columbus to Washington I flew in some large liner, I didn't record what kind, just that on takeoff the thrust of the engines shoved my body hard against the seat back so I felt the speed through my own back, something that doesn't seem to happen in airliners anymore, but from Washington to Rehoboth Beach, I did notice, I flew in a DC-3. Since Rehoboth isn't far from Washington, within a short time the

DC-3 was descending to land. As it began to go down I looked around for the airport but couldn't find it. I kept on looking, in all directions, but couldn't see any sign of an airport, only cornfields and a few roads and houses. The plane kept going down anyway, drawing closer and closer to earth, and still there was no airport in sight. My God, I thought, or whatever I said in those days of timid exclamation, we're going to land in a cornfield! Lower, lower, lower the plane sank, until at last its wheels touched down . . . on *grass*, not corn. Almost as strange a choice, I thought. . . .

As the DC-3 went rolling across that wide green meadow of a field, I could see standing behind a fence at the far end of it a man with broad shoulders, dark hair, bare chest, bare legs, bare feet, a deep tan, and a bright-red bathing suit—I caught my breath. I was of course all dressed up, as people used to be whenever they took airplane trips: aqua shantung suit, high heels, matching purse, button earrings. Quickly I got out a pocket mirror and checked my cherry-red lipstick, curled eyelashes, and pin-curled hair, then looked out the window again and saw that the man was smiling—and that his smile was dazzling. I began to wonder: Will he kiss me right there, on the grass? In front of everybody? First thing, as soon as I step off? And while the other passengers are getting off and going inside the terminal and picking up their luggage and my luggage is being put someplace where I won't know where it is and other people are climbing back on the plane, will we still be out there mouth-to-mouth?

Starting my trip with Rehoboth Beach, then, suggested a sort of symmetry of motion, an already authenticated way to begin. (The symmetry would be less than precise, however. I knew from our alumni magazine that Ralph had gone on to become a lawyer in Colorado, almost as well off as his father, judging by the donations he made to the university—a real burgher, I concluded, probably run to fat, while I was still somewhat scattered, with one loose leg pulling me out of my apartment, office, and city, not yet a substantial citizen.)

Jean saw me off, for this, the real start of my trip, even shed a few tears, she told me later (''You [the plane] looked so small and brave up there''). The sky seemed to glow, and I wondered, was my excitement making everything seem brighter? There were only a few blowsy clouds in the sky and no wind. I headed south, to get out from under the Washington TCA, then turned east, which took me over farms and fields, the bay, and more farms and fields. Officially summer had just begun, so the crops were still young and I could see through them to the soil, as through hair to the scalp. In places the soil was a swirling mix of dark and light shades of brown, as if thin clouds were passing over and casting shadows. One field was so unnaturally green and neat the farmer could have been making do with AstroTurf. Before long I could make out on my right, a long way off, the pale, crystalline, upright blocks of resort hotels, standing like a fence against the sea.

At such times, flying is easier than driving. The throttle is pulled back from climb power to cruise, the compass heading is calculated and locked onto, the nose is positioned so the plane stays level except as air currents disturb it. All you have to do is hold your left hand lightly around the control stick to make small adjustments, and your right hand, relieved for the moment of working the throttle, can roam free, turning knobs, holding charts, carrying cherries from a sack to your mouth, writing, combing, scratching. Meanwhile, your feet are resting—not pressing, resting—on rudder pedals, and your eyes are directed out the windows (what on the Luscombe have rather uncharitably been called "transom-like" windows), although not every single minute. In a plane you don't have to spend as much time checking for traffic as you do in a car, since there's less of it despite what the newspapers say and you can usually see it long before it gets to you or you to it. Your scan is also different from what it is in a car, with more sweeps to the side and above and below eye level, since planes pretty much make their own roads.

The scan is one thing they don't usually get right in flying movies; the facial expressions are nearly always off. The actors look through the windshield into the middle distance without focus (you *do* focus), yet often glance away at critical moments such as during landings— crash landings they nearly always are in movies, at which times the actors sometimes yank on the controls as if they're wrestling steers and talk on the radio as if speaking to hearing-impaired foreigners.

This time when I searched for Rehoboth Beach I knew how to recognize a small airport when I saw one. By then I had learned what to look out for when trying to find an airport in open countryside: a long, narrow field without crops, ponds, or trees on it; a peculiar break in woodland foliage; buildings, often silver, too long and low to be barns; short pieces of road that went nowhere. It was easy to find Rehoboth

Beach, two miles north of a bay, three miles west of the sea. It turned out to be still grass, surrounded by corn, yet I realized as I entered the pattern for it that not everything was the same as when I flew in in my shantung suit. There had been several runways then, and I could still see the shaggy outline of three of them crossing at the center of the field to form an awkward star, but the ends of two of the runways had pastel beach houses sitting on them now. The opposite ends of the same two runways were still just grass and I could see streaks of paler grass where wheels had rolled over and over through the years, but those ends were useless now, phantom limbs.

After a bumpy landing—I promised myself I'd do better—I pulled up to the fuel pumps, got out, and walked toward the office (terminal, lounge, clubhouse, whatever). Halfway there I turned, as I often do when leaving my plane, and looked back at it, parked at its first real stop. The Luscombe has an almost human face, sweet, comic, and adenoidal. The openings for cylinder cooling are the eyes, striped with (metal) eyelashes. The prop spinner is the button nose. The vent under the prop for cooling engine accessories is the open mouth, with two fused upper teeth showing. The holes for heating the cabin and car-buretor are the dimples (probably the plane's cutest feature), and the carburetor-induction screen is the striated, gray goatee. The prop is the mustache, or maybe a bone through the nose, and the swellings on either side of the nacelle to make room for the cylinders are the plump cheeks. As I looked around, pride of ownership washed over me. You'd have to be hardhearted not to be charmed by a face like that.

I couldn't say if things were the same in the office as before—I had been too caught up in the drama of red suit and aqua suit to notice—but now it was a long metal building, like a Quonset hut except the roof was flat, with a glass display case running halfway down one side of the single room inside and a lunch counter running halfway down the other. A woman was standing behind the lunch counter, wearing a dress with flowers on it resembling clouds. The air in the room was filled with one of the world's great smells: corn on the cob cooking. On the wall behind the counter was a blackboard with white clip-on letters, spelling CHILI & BEANS, SPAGHETTI & BEEF, BEANS & FRANKS, OYSTER STEW, BOILED HAM, CORN ON THE COB, HOT CHOCOLATE, SHAKES, COFFEE, TEA.

You didn't often find lunch counters at little airports. Most airports didn't get enough pilots and passengers coming through to make a lunch counter pay. A lot of them kept coffeepots on more or less permanent perk in the office, which pilots could help themselves to and pay for on the honor system ("Make the Kitty Purr: 25 Cents"), and a fair number had vending machines which sold snacks, like potato chips, pretzels, cookies, and cheese-cracker-and-peanut-butter sandwiches. (Those peanut-butter sandwiches were my hardtack, my K-rations, my MRE's, they had pulled me through so many lean times in the field.) Some even had microwave ovens with plastic-wrapped sandwiches stacked next to them, but only a few had genuine lunch counters.

My home airport in New York was one of the few. Pilots sometimes flew in just for Helen's square hamburgers. The last time I was in there before leaving on this trip a stranger to the field had come in, a man with bad teeth, 40 or 50 years old, it was hard to say. His teeth were so gray and pitted in an otherwise well-tended-looking body that it was obvious to me he'd been living in some exotic place, out of the reach of care, for a long time. The place, I discovered when he sat at my table to drink his coffee, was the Amazon, where he spent half of the year digging for diamonds, with only a male friend and a parrot for company. The other half of the year he sold plumbing supplies in the Bronx. This was the other half of the year. He'd just flown his plane up from South America; it was sitting on the ramp in front of the coffee shop, a Cessna 182 with worn paint and lots of scratch marks. At one point he reached into his pocket and pulled out a small, cobalt-blue velvet pouch, then with great care shook diamonds from it onto the palm of his hand. We brought our faces close to the hand. About eight diamonds were in there, and he moved his palm so they sparkled. He stared for a long moment at the diamonds, apparently enthralled. They were of several different sizes, and some day soon, he said, he was going to take them in to "the city" to be cut.

At Rehoboth Beach I ordered an iced tea, one of hundreds I'd have on this trip, I hoped, and told the woman how nice it was to find a lunch counter. It was her "convenience counter," she said. "It doesn't make money but it sure is convenient!" She explained that her husband was the airport manager and worked late most nights so they just ate there. She would fix stews and soups at home and bring them in. At that her husband walked in the office, surrounded by a little aura of bluster. He was short with a dark, neat mustache and a potbelly that was putting considerable strain on a blue polo shirt. He also had on the modern version of the old flying helmet and goggles: baseball (or gimme) cap and sunglasses, what a large portion of today's pilots wear both outside and inside their cockpits. His sunglasses were the darkest ones I'd ever seen not on a blind person; they were swamp-black, impenetrable, and he never took them off, not even in the meager light of the office, not even while trying to read the raised numbers on my credit card. They could have been surgically installed and made him look oddly vulnerable.

His name, he said, was Hal Wallin, his wife's Eleanor Wallin. I told them my name and what I was up to—writing things down about my trip—and without waiting to hear more he pulled something out of a desk and laid it on the display case for me to see. It was a scrapbook. He flipped through it until he came to some pages with color photos. "You don't make money at an airport," he said, stating a theme on which others would sing variations throughout the trip, "but you sure meet a lot of notable people." The photos were of airplanes, parked, not airborne. Most of them had somebody standing next to them, looking pleased. All were airplanes that Wallin had either owned, painted, or admired.

He flipped through the scrapbook again and stopped at a page covered with newspaper articles. The articles were about a collision that had taken place at the airport a few years before. A Piper Colt had been on final approach at the same time that an Ag Cat, flying only 200 feet off the ground and twice as fast as the Colt, was doing a straight-in for the same runway. The Ag Cat slammed into the Colt from behind and both planes fell to the ground. The Ag Cat pilot wasn't hurt (spray planes are built to withstand crashes), but the Colt pilot became paralyzed from the waist down and had to have a foot amputated. A friend of Wallin's, he had been flying in for a visit. "Numbskull of a duster!" Wallin muttered, obviously still pained. "Must've been admiring his truck in the trailer park. The Colt was doing everything right . . . ."

He turned to another page and flicked at something shiny. It was a religious medal. "Our Lady of Loreto," it said. "Patroness of Aviators and Air Travelers. Protect My Flight." I'd never heard of Our

Lady of Loreto; pilots I knew who carried Catholic medals stuck with St. Christopher. Wallin told me that a Jewish pilot from Long Island had celebrated his 50th birthday and the bicentennial of the United States by flying around to all the oldest surviving public airports in the thirteen original states and giving each a medal. Later I looked Our Lady of Loreto up in *The Catholic Encyclopedia* and concluded that the only connection she might have had to flight, air, sky, or wings was that her *house* had disappeared from Nazareth, on May 10, 1291, apparently transported by angels to a site in present-day Croatia, from which, "not properly venerated," according to tradition, it vanished three and a half years later, only to reappear in an Italian woods, from which, "again not fittingly venerated," it took flight eight months later and materialized on a nearby hill. Four months after *that* it was spirited away again, to a spot close to the sea, where, presumably appreciated at last, it remains today. Perhaps it was all this levitation, rapid transit over considerable distances of a structure measuring exactly 31 by 13 feet (compare the Luscombe's 35 by 20 feet) that qualified Our Lady of Loreto for her role as patroness of those who take to the air.

I pointed out that there was nothing in the scrapbook that evoked Wallin's own flying history, so he told me about it. "I was a poor boy," he said rather soupily, "but I had a chance." During the Depression, he was working in his brother's tire store near Philadelphia, and one day a customer came in asking for a new set of tires but without the money to pay for them. The man offered airplane lessons instead. Wallin's brother wasn't interested, but Wallin was. As soon as he got his license, he started teaching other young men to fly. "It was just before World War II and everybody wanted to be a fighter pilot," he explained, "but there weren't enough military pilots to teach them." During the war he didn't become a fighter pilot himself because he was married and had a child, but he did fly on civilian patrols. One of his missions was to fly over downtown Washington at night so that antiaircraft spotters could practice getting him in their searchlights. "I'd pass right over the White House and the Capitol building, and everything would be fine until the spotlight hit me," he said. "Then I thought I was going to fall out of the sky. It was like suddenly being in a very tall building."

Another of his assignments was to search for German submarines off Long Island, where American oil tankers were docked. Once he had to make an emergency landing beside a beach, and when he waded ashore in his rubber suit the Long Island natives thought he was a Nazi. Mostly he flew open-cockpit Stearmans and Wacos, with "women's powder puffs" stuffed under his helmet over his ears to muffle the noise of the big radial engines. Nowadays he used George Shearing tapes for the same purpose, when flying the quieter Cubs and Cessnas. "Piano music goes with flying," he insisted, "except the low chords get drowned out."

I mentioned the DC-3, and Wallin scowled. He remembered the DC-3s but not fondly, as I did. "They came for about four years, then quit," he said testily. "The airlines *had* to serve the small towns to get the routes they wanted in the cities in those days, but as soon as they got the cities they dropped the towns." He pulled something else out of the desk and laid it on the case for me to see. It was a newspaper clipping. I read the headline, "NATION'S AIRLINES FACE A KEY PROBLEM, HOW TO PAY FOR NEW PLANES," but before I could get to the text he started speaking, in a state of passionate irritation, like a minister with a message he's having trouble getting through to the parishioners. His phrases had the sound of slogans, and I suspected this wasn't the first time he'd used them.

"Aviation," he said sternly, "has gone in the wrong direction. Pilots want to fly bigger and better airplanes but they can't afford to fly them. They can't even afford to keep them up! Guys with big airplanes are always trying to make a pile to justify their airplanes, but they can't justify them. Who makes money? The slowest airplanes do! Bush planes in Canada do! A Cub makes four times as much as a 411 on a charter! What's hurting aviation more than anything is *speed*. We don't need speed. We don't need radios. We don't need jets. We need airplanes we can *afford!* Airplanes don't feed themselves! Here we've got fancy saloons flying around but nobody's making a profit. I see half-million-dollar pieces of equipment sitting around that never get up in the air. People aren't realists; if you've got the money to buy a Plymouth and you buy a Duesenberg, it doesn't make sense, does it? We've got to stop this lying!"

Then the aggrieved tone evaporated, like frost off a hot cowling, and with a jaunty "Anyhooo!" Wallin laid the clipping back in the desk. His rapid recovery might have had something to do with his being forced to live for a long time with his passion unrequited (speed, jets, and radios weren't about to go away). About then the first paying customer I'd seen since I got to Rehoboth Beach walked into the office. He was an 11-year-old boy, looking for a pass-hop. (A pass-hop is a sightseeing ride, usually lasting 15 minutes.) His uncle was with him. "Been bugging me for *days*," the uncle said, making it clear that he himself had gotten lots of free rides in the Navy and found flying boring. The kid, though, had built 30 model airplanes and now wanted "the real thing." We could see that; he didn't say anything but his pale eyes shone with determination.

I never got to ask him how he liked the real thing, because he and the uncle left without passing through the office. But I did get to ask Wallin something after he came down. Behind the glass case, stacked floor to ceiling against the wall, were dozens of brightly colored boxes containing kits for making model aircraft—mini-Mustangs, Champs, Bonanzas, "EZ" trainers, Stinsons, and "stunt" planes (chances were the boy had made all of them)—plus six-foot strips of balsa for making models from scratch or else, as Mrs. Wallin shouted across the room, "doll houses!" "That's our 'hobby corner,'" she explained. In the case itself were items for sale to pilots, mostly student pilots who had yet to own one of everything: log books, plotters, hand-held computers they would probably never use again once they'd gotten their private licenses, headsets, windshield cleaner, mikes. Elsewhere around the office were placards offering DECALS FOR SALE, PENNANTS FOR SALE, BICYCLES FOR RENT, CARS FOR RENT, BICYCLES FOR SALE.

What I asked Wallin was: Since he worked at the airport 15 hours a day and his wife worked there almost that many hours, every day of the week, every week of the year except the two weeks in February when they went to her sister's in Florida, and they had done this for 22 years, selling model-airplane kits and log books, iced tea and oyster stew, renting bicycles, cars, and planes, leasing tiedowns and flying pass-hops and teaching flying, repairing and painting planes, flying charters, pumping fuel, and even, I couldn't help but notice, selling off the ends of two of the runways to developers, why hadn't they paved the runways? Why, at the oldest continually operating public airport in the state of Delaware, was there still grass? Hadn't they (or the consortium of owners) ever, in all those years, gotten enough money together so they could manage to pave the runways—or, as things stood now, runway? Was it a matter of playing it safe with a Plymouth instead of gambling on a Duesenberg? Or did they *choose* grass?

Wallin scowled again. He didn't like the question and didn't quite answer it. "Tires last three times as long on grass," he said, sounding defensive. "Brakes last twice as long." How about the mud, when it rains? "That's only a problem a couple of times a year when there's a long cold spell and the ground freezes a couple of feet down followed by a warm day with a surface thaw," he said, adding defiantly, "Some days we're open when Philadelphia's closed!" But as he kept on, in the half-belligerent, half-wistful tone he used when discussing aviation in general, he let slip, said it so fast and low it seemed to be for his own accounting, "Grass is a necessity." Meaning, I presumed, that they would have paved the runway if they could. Did it help then to stay away from fancy saloons? Did an airport with beach houses on two of its runways have long to live? Was *everybody* lying a little?

Safety Corner · Ocean City

On the beach at Rehoboth, as I lay slathered with suntan oil and was nudged repeatedly from sleep by the shouts of women in sailor hats calling out from motorboats that were passing back and forth in front of the beach, I was feeling rather vulnerable. The Colt had been doing everything right, and now the man was without a foot. The author of the book I was reading, Richard Hillary, a champion rower at Oxford before World War II and a fighter pilot during it, had been severely burned when his Spitfire was shot down by a Messerschmitt over the North Sea and he had trouble getting out because of a stuck canopy. Afterward he had to have four new eyelids and an upper lip grafted on. The lip, he wrote, was "a blow to my vanity. [It was] dead white, and thinner than its predecessor." So, despite the surf at Rehoboth lapping at the feet of small children, the women waving from motorboats strung with gay little flags (tomorrow was the Fourth of July), and brilliant sunshine falling through a clear blue sky, I couldn't get those images out of my mind, the leg without a foot, the dead-white lip, the four new eyelids.

Ordinarily I didn't dwell on such things, possible bad ends to my flying (mutilation, dismemberment, death, although now and then I did consider paralysis). However, like most pilots, I *was* drawn to stories about crashes. When the new issue of AOPA *Pilot* magazine came in the mail I turned first to the feature called "Safety Corner," with its brief accounts of real-life, always fatal crashes. Under headings like "Pea Soup," "Life of the Party Cut Short," and "Mountain Stops Plane," they began with pilot's particulars (age, occupation, ratings, hours of experience, etc.), followed by purpose of flight ("bring son home from a hunting trip to Montana," "narcotics investigation," "drop ice cream to the Boy Scouts," "tour of Alaska," "outing with friends"); known weather ("rain, snow, fog, and icing," "facing headwinds going west''); radio communications, if any (''We're in the soup pretty bad up here,'' ''How far off are we?''); witnesses' statements, if any (''Two sudden loud 'bangs' followed by silence. Moments later the ground shook and dishes rattled in the kitchen''); description of crash site (''Wreckage was strewn over a 500-foot path before the plane came to rest and burned,'' ''Pieces of the red nav light lens cover were found in a ground scar''); and probable cause of accident as decided by federal investigators (''The plane, it was determined, had made an uncontrolled descent into the ground''). Probable cause of accident, ten times out of ten, it seemed to me, was ''pilot error,'' since even if the tips of a factory-new propeller spun off in flight like those whistling fireworks or a newly overhauled engine leapt from its mounts onto a full playground, the pilot was to blame because he should have noticed something wrong during preflight inspection. He should have noticed *something*.

Still, I read ''Safety Corner'' without conjuring up final images—severed arms, smashed-in faces, and skin blackened like pork rind—as I was doing on the beach at Rehoboth. My flying fears, whether I was up flying or only thinking of going up, were more vague, took on a more lumpish form, a dread that encompassed worries not only about survival but also about performance, the suspicion that I was a fraud for being up at all, uncertainty in the face of all the things that might present themselves while I was airborne yet excitement at the possibility of success in dealing with them brilliantly. Anxiety at the thought of making a fool of myself by crashing and dying—something like stage fright. In his book, *The Last Enemy*, Hillary described what it was like sitting on the flightline in the cockpit of his Spitfire before taking off on the mission that would fry his eyelids. ''I felt the usual sick feeling in the pit of the stomach,'' he wrote, ''as though I were about to row a race.''

First blood on this trip was a couple of scalp wounds. During preflight inspection and postflight locking up, as I did walkarounds of my plane, I kept running into the trailing edges of my wings, which had metal flutes sticking up and down from them like a series of tiny arrowheads, all at about the level of the top of my head when my head was bent. I'd be looking down at something or other and whomp! a splotch of blood-dampened hair. As the trip went along and I became less of a weekend pilot and more accustomed to the dimensions of my plane—the way it displaced space on the ramp—I'd quit doing that, I hoped. I also hoped I'd get a more precise sense for the limits of the plane when I was in it, how far out the wings reached (from the cockpit I couldn't see the last foot and a half of them), how far back the tail extended, the size of my new shell. At Rehoboth I almost turned my tail into a work of origami when I pivoted the plane to get it into position for refueling. While applying power, I stepped hard on a rudder pedal and tapped the brake on the same side and swung the plane nicely around to face the pumps, but when I got out I saw that the tail had rolled to a stop mere inches from a chain-link fence. My long cross-country trip could have been very short.

My parents were thinking about more than scalp wounds. They tried not to show it. "Well, it's better than driving!" my mother would say, but she knew. I had decided to phone them often on this trip, and send postcards. The Wallins had a rack of postcards sitting on the display case—lighthouses, dunes, lifeguards on the beach. I took a long, close look at the one with the lifeguards. There were 26 guards lined up in two rows, 13 to a row. All of them were men. The ones in the first row had their right knees down in the sand and their left knees raised and their left arms resting on their raised left knees and their right hands gripping their left wrists—every single one of them. The guards in the back row were all standing with their arms akimbo and hands hidden behind their backs. The sun must have been strong because their muscles were defined by deep chiaroscuro, and the sand was wavy with footprints. In the distance I could just make out two tiny beach umbrellas, one red and one yellow. None of the guards was smiling. The kiss, I was thinking, had been brief, Ralph uncharacteristically shy.

"Happy landings!" Mrs. Wallin called out on the radio as I took off and passed over the beach houses that sat, gull-like, on the ends of her old runways. (People in aviation do say things like "happy landings" to each other. I've heard "Tail winds to ya" and once got a letter signed "Keep all your rivets in fairly close formation." A man wanting to wish me well in my non-flying life advised, "Don't get on the back side of the power curve!") This was the Fourth of July, and the Wallins had told me that the best fireworks anywhere along the coast would be at Ocean City, Maryland, so I was headed down there. It was a short run, only 30 miles along the beach, but one full of stunning views, down onto the ziggurat-, arrowhead-, and octagon-shaped roofs of the high-rise hotels, the beryl-blue of the swimming pools, the rainbow glitter of the parking lots. Sunbathers seemed to be lying, locust-like, on every surface, even (a few of them) on top of the waterless and featureless roofs, from which (the roofs being walled and they lying down) they were unable to see anything except the hazy sky, maybe a bird or two, and my airplane.

Which made me feel better about the noise I was making. I was offering them diversion, movement on a blank screen. At times when flying around I felt like a dog with tin cans tied to its tail, wishing I could shake the noise I carried with me but of course unable to, if I wanted to stay *up*. Even when throttled back the engine droned on, although in a lower key, when what I wanted was to be surrounded by a sweet, unobjectionable silence, to slip in close to things, unobserved. That was the spirit in which I flew, as a wraith-like spy. Sometimes I tried to achieve a roar, relished one, as when ''strafing'' hills near the Hudson River or making a flyby at the airport in front of pilots whose planes were bigger than mine, plus every time I took off, wanting the surge, the sound and feel of horsepower at work.

As I got closer to Ocean City, Maryland, I thought about noise again. The airstrip was on the mainland across the bay from Assateague Island, where the famous herd of wild ponies roamed, and as I entered the landing pattern I looked for them. A pilot told me when I was at Ocean City one other time that the horses sometimes grazed along the beach on Assateague directly across from the airport, which would put them under final approach for runway Three-Two and take-off slope for One-Four. (One physical runway is two operational ones.) ''We eyeball-to-eyeball 'em,'' the pilot said. Yet the horses never bolted or even lifted their heads from the dune grass they were munching as hundreds of horsepower ground up the air over their heads. Apparently they were indifferent to engine noise once they figured out it wasn't a growl attached to something that would eat them.

I didn't see any horses on Assateague, so I looked for them on the airport itself. The same pilot told me they occasionally grazed beside the runway (having swum across the bay? galloped over the nearest bridge?). I didn't see any by the runway either but did spot something on the field that was out of the ordinary: what looked from above (although I knew better) like large Chinese characters, huge red ideograms set out in long lines on the grass, to form sayings or proverbs. After landing and pulling into a tiedown spot next to an Aero Commander with European registration (no numbers, as American planes have, only letters)—out of which a half dozen men and women were climbing, all speaking German, several already stripped to bikinis, with skin white as pillows, leading me to wonder whether the word about the fireworks had crossed the Atlantic and made its way to Munich or Ulm or St. Goarshausen—I crossed the runway to the other side, where I'd seen the characters. As I got closer to them the characters began to change and slowly, ingeniously resolve themselves into ordinary letters of the Western alphabet, just made wavy, distorted, by the uneven ground (grass clumps and chopped-off roots) on which they were lying. Several young men without shirts on were kneeling or bending down beside the letters, buckling them onto long white cords—five cords laid parallel to each other, like a musical staff. When the men stood to check on their work, a message about 100 feet long stretched across the grass, a proverb of sorts. TUES LADIES NITE HURRICANE LADIES' DRINKS 75¢, it said.

Banners at the source. Ocean City was one of the airports where this form of required reading matter at the beach was assembled for presentation. A young woman was standing near the men, watching them closely. She was frowning and had her hands on her hips. "We just ripped a C," she said peevishly, as soon as I was within earshot. "That's eleven dollars!" At that moment a plane approached from the far end of the field, as if it was about to land. The plane was a Citabria. It wasn't bearing down on the runway, though; it was bearing down on us. Between it and us stood a pair of narrow metal poles about ten feet high with a rope strung between them attached by clothespins, a sort of flimsy goalpost. From the top of one pole the rope ran down to the ground and across it to a line of letters. The Citabria kept coming toward us and looked as if it were about to pass over the goalpost when suddenly it dived at it, as if to grind up the rope with its prop, then swung violently upward again, causing a hook on the end of a rope that hung from the tail to swing forward and snag the goalpost rope and—as the Citabria kept on climbing, at an extremely nose-high angle—to yank the rope from the poles, after which, with a loud breathy whoosh, the letters on the grass began peeling from it and lifted into the air, outlined dark against the sky and undulating lightly: TRADER LEE'S FREE BEER LIVE BLUEGRASS.

After the Citabria disappeared in the direction of the beach, another Citabria flew overhead and reversed the process: It let a banner go. This one floated down, rippling but readable to the ground: ENGLISH'S STEAK AND CHICKEN. Immediately the bucklers pounced on it and began tearing it apart. The woman spoke again. "Three days ago we lost two and a half banners in an afternoon." What, whole banners? I thought. Why had she bothered to mention one little C? "The knots slipped off of BILLY'S and it fell in the water. FENWICK INN snapped in two and the back half fell in . . .

"Then," she said, motioning toward the end of the runway nearest the bay, where there was a yellow spot I hadn't noticed on the way in, "we lost a tow plane." What, a whole plane? Could that possibly be an afterthought? "Then *another* tow plane nosed over on its prop when the pilot was taxiing down the runway in too much of a hurry to see if his buddy was hurt in the crash. He didn't see a truck pulling out of the taxiway and had to stand on his brakes to keep from hitting it." She sighed heavily. Her father owned the airport operation, she said, and was letting her run the banner-towing part of it for the summer, but the pressure was getting to her. "What we take in here keeps the airport going for the rest of the year, so it's go go go all the time. For three months we just *pound* away. Today alone we're carrying 44 banners." She kept her eyes on the bucklers, but the sight of them working hard for her, muscular backs glistening with sweat, seemed to give her no pleasure. She heaved another sigh, feeling the terrible burden of her father's trust.

The other time I was in Ocean City the weather had been lousy so I didn't get to see any banner-towing, but I did get to meet a tow pilot. His name was Chris Keenan; I remembered that because it sounded like a comic-strip detective's name, or Nancy Drew's boy-friend's, or otherwise made up. He was 19. On the Sunday before I arrived, another tow pilot, a friend of his, had crashed and died while making a banner pickup. "The problem is," Keenan explained, "if you hold the stick back too long you stall out, but if you don't hold it back long enough the banner drags on the ground and catches on something and rips." The death of his friend didn't seem to alter his attitude about his own job. "Being this young," he said respectfully, "I know it's going to help me in the future." By future he meant working as a bush pilot in Canada, something he'd always wanted to do. He was towing banners to build up his flying hours so he'd have a better chance of being hired as a bush pilot some day. His friend, who was 18, had wanted to be a cropduster.

I asked Keenan how his parents felt about his job, if they worried that it was high-risk. "My mother's an old-fashioned person," he answered. "She's a romantic. She *likes* heroes." (Oh, one of those.) And his father? "He's a private, World War Two–type person," was all he said. By which I didn't know if he meant that his father was a hero himself (in the war), or that he approved of his *son* being a hero, or that he didn't approve of his son being a hero, and for some reason I didn't ask.

I wished the woman better luck and went to take a look at the wrecked tow plane. It was lying past the end of the runway, by a shallow slope, on the last firm ground before a stand of marsh grass, a yellow-and-white Citabria, upside down. Its legs were sticking up in the air but they didn't have any wheels on them. The fabric of its belly had been ripped open and metal struts were showing through. Its propeller was missing and so was a rectangular piece of cloth cut from the side of the fuselage where the registration numbers would have been (the insurance game had begun already). Its wings were twisted and a wad of mud and grass was stuck to the top of the tail.

With the crushed cabin roof as a fulcrum, the plane was rocking back and forth in the wind, slowly, rhythmically, rocking to and fro, and creaking as it rocked, like a widow grieving, a ritual rocking and a keening. In the air all around gulls were cawing lugubriously. How, I wondered, would I feel about flying again if ever I had crawled out of an airplane altered like this one? The pilot hadn't been killed in the crash, the woman told me; he hadn't even been hurt except for hitting his head when he undid his seat belt while hanging upside down. He was in fact up flying now, and it occurred to me while looking at that plane to ask him how he felt about flying again. So I went to the office to wait for him to come down.

I wasn't the only one waiting. A reporter for the *Eastern Shore Times* was there with a camera around his neck, pacing. "I'm on deadline," he said importantly. I waited at a flight-planning table and went through a large stack of FAA circulars sitting there. The usual horrifying warnings. "FURY ALOFT THUNDERSTORMS" was the heading of one. "Thunderstorms are bad business," went the text. "Experts conservatively estimate the kinetic energy roiling around in even a moderate size thunderstorm packs more of a wallop than the atomic bomb that flattened Nagasaki in 1945." It noted that with "some 44,000 thunderstorms occurring daily over the world, almost every active pilot can expect to face them occasionally." Heroes, I thought. Maybe we're *all* heroes.

An hour or so later, after four o'clock, when the audience for the banners had presumably either gone home or become too zonked out to read with retention, the pilot of the wrecked Citabria showed up. Perhaps I was projecting the awesome strangeness of a crash on him, but he struck me as the quintessential aviator, tall, lanky, taciturn, and of stout nerve. Maybe not straight-arrow enough, with mouth a bit too full, eyes a bit too slanted. Quickly it became clear that he didn't want to talk to the *Times* reporter, but somebody was making him do it. He sat but kept squirming in his chair and toying with his Coke cup, never looking at the reporter, who was asking him questions. By body and voice the pilot was asking his own questions. Why make such a big deal about this? What's the deal about a plane crash? *Go away.* The reporter kept on plugging, though, and gradually a story emerged.

The pilot's name was Marc Osmer, and he was from Pullman, Michigan. A couple of days earlier he had been flying over the airport with the power back so he could yell down to the ground crew and ask if there were any more banners to pick up. The crew said no and he came around to land. Since he was low he added power. The engine coughed. He applied full power, and the engine backfired, then quit altogether. He tried to start the engine again but couldn't, tried to stretch his glide to the runway but couldn't. The plane went down in marsh grass. Still, everything would have been all right if there hadn't been a ditch running through the grass. The wheels got caught in the ditch and flipped the plane into a foot of water.

Wasn't this a pretty dangerous business he was in? the reporter wanted to know. Osmer, giving his longest answer, said, "There are risks whatever you do. You get killed just breathing. You get killed crossing the road. [Sounded like a confirmed smoker to me.] You cross the road, you get run over. You work in a factory, you get your hand cut off.'' All of which sort of answered my question, but once the reporter left, I asked Osmer some other questions, which, since I didn't have the means to embarrass him in the local paper, he put up with. I found out, for instance, that he knew a lot about factories and getting hands cut off, had in fact been working in an iron factory in Michigan when he got this job. One day he had been on his coffee break, leafing through a new issue of *Trade-A-Plane,* when he saw an ad asking for pilots to tow banners. Being from inland Michigan, he didn't know what a banner was, he said, ''but I was willing to tow one.''

About then another tow pilot showed up, the one who'd gone up on his prop taxiing too fast down the runway. He seemed younger than Osmer, despite having a beard, which was red and traced his jawline, forming a narrow frame around the fresh, eager look on his face. Osmer introduced him as Hugh Patrick James Mason, but he said his name was ''Rocket Man'' Mason. He laughed at his bragging but kept on bragging nevertheless. ''That's because I go straight up! There's less chance of snagging that way. My record is *twenty pickups without a miss.* '' His manner, I was thinking, was amazingly blithe and bouncy for someone who had just spent hours towing banners in typical Fourth of July heat. I couldn't help thinking of those plucky boy-heroes in the old flying novels, Frank and Harry in *Wing for Wing,* Billy Barry from Bangor in *Our Young Aeroplane Scouts,* laughing as they leapt into their rickety aircraft and wobbled off with their chums to fight the foe.

Also, I was thinking: There have been times in my life when I felt that, deep down, I too was a boy-hero, an 11- or 12-year-old boy (a boy of my own childhood, when girls had it stricter). Struggling with naïveté, just figuring stuff out, hoping the world was good, running amok with discoveries, excited to find even a paw print in the woods. An innocent, eager, hopeful 12-year-old boy. At airports, I've realized, I particularly liked the company of young men (few young women at airports), all older than 12, of course, yet still young in their longings and at least partly innocent, their eyes easily lit up by thoughts of the wide world they would discover through flying, if only they could make a career of it. Aviation had more than its share of eager young men, and they lent the whole enterprise a certain buoyancy, helped recycle the romance of the sky. How they hoped and dreamed and yearned! What they wouldn't do to be flying for a living!

Also, I was thinking: Banner-towing was an extreme test for anybody to have to pass through to get somewhere else. "Rocket Man" was towing banners to build up his hours so he might get a job some day as biologist-pilot for the National Park Service, taking wildlife censuses from the air, etc., and Osmer was building up his hours so he might be hired as a cropduster. Banner-towing was what pilots did when they were raw and had no history and wanted to go on and make a living in aviation. (That, and teach flying.) But towing banners wasn't really just like crossing the road, or even working in a factory. In the spirit of "Safety Corner," I asked Osmer and Mason what sorts of things could go wrong while towing banners. The worst, they agreed, was stalling during a pickup (stalling means not that the engine quits providing power but that the wing quits providing lift, as for instance when the plane is making a three-point landing or is climbing very steeply). That was what happened to the 18-year-old who died on a Sunday—and it happened to Mason. "I was lucky," he said, chipper as ever. "I recovered at windsock level."

Stalling was the worst, but there were other things that could happen. The banner could get snagged on the ground by something during pickup and be stretched tight, then snap loose, "like rubber on a slingshot," and shoot up and wrap around the plane's tail, freezing the controls. (That happened to Osmer once.) The tailwheel instead of the hook could catch the crossrope, forcing the pilot to land with a banner dangling behind him, or the tail hook could swing too far forward and slice the belly fabric open, or it could (I found this hard to imagine) pick up two banners at once, the combined weight dragging the plane down. Even one banner if it was long enough, such as "PLAYLAND," which had 52 letters and produced 150 to 200 pounds of drag, could pull a plane down on a hot day.

In addition, fog could form offshore in minutes (Osmer was once forced to fly "down between condominiums" to get back to the airport) and air currents spill off high-rises. "If a strong breeze blows offshore," said Mason, "you get this terrible rotor, like in the mountains, with different rotors from different buildings. They can roll you right into the water."

Before having to face these things on their own, they got only one hour of instruction each. A tow pilot took them up, demonstrated one pickup, watched while they did one, then flew with them to the beach, told them how high above the water to fly (200 to 300 feet) and how far from shore (200 to 500 feet), then outlined ditching procedures. " 'Pop the door, grab a vest, drop the banner,' " recited Mason, who after several weeks on his own had decided not to do exactly as he was told. "Now," he said, "I think I'd hang on to the banner so when it hit the water the drag would keep the plane from nosing over. Also, I'd stick my wallet in my mouth. My father's a cropduster and he told me to do that."

A wallet in the mouth, I was thinking, would at least keep me from screaming. I couldn't imagine adding the complications of a 200-pound-drag banner to the delicate aeronautical balance I tried to achieve in my plane. Rocket Men! It didn't seem to be a question of daredevilry, though. The boys had made a hard contract. Still uncomplaining but looking a bit bushed, they rose from the table to go home—which turned out to be a couple of hundred feet away. They shared an old farmhouse with several guys in the ground crew and the maintenance shop. (Not surprisingly, many small airports were farms first, and at some airports the farmhouse survived and became the office or the owner's family house, or was rented to a fishing club, or something. At some airports there was even a barn still standing, or at least an old baler left sitting, rusting, at the edge of the field.)

Politely, they offered to show me the house. A big brown dog wearing an aqua kerchief tied around his neck Tom Mix–style blocked the front hallway. "Out of the way, Rex," said Osmer, nudging him aside. Rex belonged to a member of the ground crew who had been a tow pilot last year but was not this year. One day last summer the guy went up in a Piper Cub with a friend who had just flown his first solo. The friend was at the controls. They were drinking beer, celebrating. The Cub crashed in the surf and the tow pilot was pulled out with a crushed foot. The friend was never found.

In the living room bookshelves lined two walls from floor to ceiling, and they were filled with . . . beer bottles. Three hundred and seventy-five empty beer bottles, 360 of them the same brand, National Bohemian, Osmer's favorite. The bottles were lined up neatly, labels out, like a matching set of brown books. Upstairs the guys showed me with perverse pride the rusty-brown shower water in the bathroom, then the electrician's room, where everything that wasn't electronic was purple—drapes, pillows, bedspreads, rug. Osmer and Mason said I could stay in the electrician's room that night if I wanted to, since he was going to be with his girlfriend for the Fourth. It seemed very much in the fraternity-house spirit for them to make me the offer without bothering to ask him first. I was delighted, one of the boys.

By the time I brought my sleeping bag from the plane, Osmer was in the living room, preparing another "book" for display. Mason was in the kitchen, passing a hot iron over the wing of a large model airplane, heat-shrinking the plastic. His face glowed in concentration. I would have thought he'd had enough of aircraft for one day, but no. A couple of hours later I went with them and several of their buddies to a pier to see the fireworks. While we waited for the sky to get dark enough, we had drinks in a bar. They had beer and I had piña coladas (not so much one of the boys after all). Despite the darkness of the bar, the flesh-quivering throb of the music, and the girls slipping around the room like fish bait, a dozen or so guys sat together around a big table and talked mostly about banner towing—how to get people on the beach to "really sit up and take notice."

"Wouldn't it look great if we could use different-colored letters instead of just red?" one asked. The rest agreed it would look great.

"How about fluorescent letters?" somebody else asked. "You could train a spotlight on them at night."

"We did that." (A veteran from last summer.) "Nobody liked it."

"How about upside down in a Stearman?"

"How about in a helicopter?"

"Have you seen the guy with a chute they pull with a boat and when he gets up to 200 feet he lets out a banner?"

"Yeah, I almost hit him once."

"I saw this pilot in Miami who tows banners with a Rawdon—only 36 of those ever made. His has one purple wing and one orange wing and he wears a white scarf and goggles when he flies it. It looks terrific."

"Sounds terrific."

"Any of you know the guy from Long Island who flies the wrong way [left to right as seen from the beach] carrying a BLUE NUN banner?" It was Greg, one of the other new tow pilots, talking. "Well, he can fly five hours without refueling—he's got a 20-gallon tank in his back seat. He just goes as far down the coast as he can, lands, folds up the banner, and flies home.'' Osmer and Mason had mentioned Greg when they were in the office, and a look had passed between them. "Different," they said. It seemed that Greg would rather fly large planes than small ones, rather fly nosewheel planes than tailwheel planes, rather carry passengers than banners. To these two, tailwheel planes—bush planes, cropdusting planes, planes to count animals from, even planes to pull banners with—were the essence of the flying experience, its most satisfying form.

(Being a tailwheel pilot myself, I agreed with them, though I must confess to some snobbery about it. Tailwheel planes—and for a long, long time almost all planes were tailwheel, or tailskid, for so long a time, in fact, that they are still called "conventional-gear," although they make up only a small portion of aircraft still flying—tend to be harder to land than nosewheel planes and therefore require more skillful handling. With the third wheel back of the paired main ones, the center of gravity is also well back and if the paired wheels veer to one side on landing, the tailwheel can whip around, like a ball at the end of a rope, and if nothing is done to stop it, by timely depression of opposite rudder pedal and brake, the tailwheel will keep on going around, leading the plane into an ever-tightening, skidding turn and that most embarrassing of finales to a landing, a ground loop. By contrast, the nosewheel, being closer to and forward of the center of gravity, tends to *stop* an incipient turn when the main wheels swerve and to bring them back toward center line.

(However, taildraggers do redeem themselves in other ways. They can stop in shorter distances, since the wings are angled farther up during landing and lift is therefore spilled more quickly. Also, like the top end of a seesaw, the prop sits higher off the ground, so tailwheel planes perform better on rough fields and are thus naturals for bush work. Aerobatic planes nearly always have tailwheels, since maneuvers are better done without something big sticking out in front. And tailwheel planes tend to be cheaper than nosewheel ones since most are old, either "classic" (manufactured in the first decade after World War II) or "antique" (manufactured before that), thus appealing to poor as well as nostalgic pilots. Back when Luscombes were being built, so were lots of other tailwheel planes—Cubs, Chiefs, Champs, Pacers, Cessna 120s, Cessna 140s, Swifts, Taylorcrafts—and many of them are still flying, their owners working hard to keep them straight on land-ing, and maybe a little snobbish about what that takes.)

Five hours was a long time, someone told Greg, to be just pulling a banner. "Well, at least he's going somewhere," said Greg huffily. Greg desperately wanted to go somewhere. Tow pilots flew the same two-mile stretch of beach every day, over and over, two miles out and two miles back, which was a bit too much, or too little, even for the bush pilots. "You can space out up there," Osmer admitted. "Some-times I hop from the front seat to the back to keep from falling asleep. Or I pretend an insane person in a high-rise is shooting at me." "Me too!" cried Mason, amazed to hear they had been playing the same game. He told us what he planned to do when the bullets started coming: "I'll drop the banner and put my tail to the high-rise to make the smallest target possible and zigzag out to sea. With my wallet in my mouth." Mason's face had a look of such determination as he told us this I thought he just might actually wish to have an insane person in a high-rise shoot at him so he could try it out.

When the fireworks finally started, I thought of the kid on the ground crew I'd heard mention he was going to rent an airplane and take a friend up flying during the show. As the sky filled with great globes and streaks of color, I hoped he was where he could see them not only in the air around him but shining up from the surface of the bay, sparking the tips of ocean waves, and making the undersides of clouds glow.

That night I had trouble getting to sleep in the electrician's room. The wall by the head of his bed was pulsing with light. The light didn't come from any of the electronic devices in the room but from some-where outside. It was passing through the venetian blinds, green (pause) white (pause) green (pause) white. A rotating beacon, some-where on the airport grounds. Lying there, I felt as if I were in a sort of lighthouse, which in a sense I was. Airport beacons too guide trav-elers through the dark, offering them safe passage as they sail their particular seas, although they beckon pilots in instead of warning them off.

When I got up the house was empty, so I ate breakfast in the office. I brought a can of orange juice in from my plane and got two packages of cheese-cracker-and-peanut-butter sandwiches out of the vending ma-chine. There was a pot of hot coffee on a counter in the office, but coffee made me too jangly to fly so I didn't have any. I did, however, take the time to read a framed poem on the wall above the coffeepot, which someone had carefully typed, illustrated with little ink drawings, and hung in that popular spot. It was written in the mystical vein so beloved of aviators:

> When the last long flight is over,
> And the happy landings past
> And my altimeter tells me
> That the crack-up's come at last
> I'll swing her nose for the ceiling
> And I'll give my crate the gun
> I'll open her up, and let her zoom
> For the airport of the sun.
> And the great God of flying men [sic]
> Will smile at me sort of slow
> As I stow my crate in the hangar
> On the field where flyers go
> Then I'll look upon his face
> The Almighty Flying Boss
> Whose Wingspread fills the Heavens
> From Orion to the Cross.

As I taxied to One-Four the Heavens were cloudless but hazy, a muted, washed-out blue. Several shirtless men were out on the grass already, buckling red letters to white cords. Mason was jogging around the runway, which he did every day, a mile and a half each circuit. Rex was running with him, a yellow kerchief around his neck this time. I pulled the plane onto the threshhold, eased in the throttle, started moving, pulled back on the stick, rose, and looked out the window to see the red letters growing smaller and smaller, twisting out of shape, becoming unrecognizable—Chinese characters again. Several lines of them had already been laid out on the field, and as I flew off I imagined them reading, all together like that, as a fortune I once got in a Chinese fortune cookie did, satisfying me so much that I memorized it: "You are going on a voyage, go before the wind, whenever and wherever, satisfactorily return with treasures full of equipage."

Africa · Accomack

I learned to fly in Africa. When I arrived in Kenya on vacation I had never given any thought to piloting a plane, had never as a child looked at the sky except to see the color blue, the sun, moon, stars, clouds, and an occasional bat, never made the *nyaaaaa* engine noises my older brother Bill did. As an adult if I flew commercially I was one of those who'd spend the whole of a rough flight with her eyes on the rubbery wing. Yet when I left Africa at the end of my vacation, I was aching to fly.

The way it happened was that a friend and I flew in a small charter plane to Samburu, a game park in the northern part of Kenya where there were different kinds of giraffes from those we'd seen (spots set closer together, like paving stones), different kinds of zebras (bigger, with rounder ears and narrower stripes), plus crocodiles and gerenuks, those antelopes with swan necks and jelly-bean eyes. We flew rather than drove up there because bandits were stopping cars on the roads to Samburu and robbing passengers. The park itself was safe, but tourists stayed away anyhow so Cynthia and I had the lodge, cabins, river, and wildlife all to ourselves. She left a day ahead of time to go back to Nairobi, for a date with a wildlife scientist she'd just discovered, so when it came my turn the charter company sent a small plane up just for me, a four-seat Cessna 172.

The pilot, it turned out, was a woman, an American, from Mississippi, in her early twenties, with the kind of blond hair we used to call platinum. She was wearing loafers and a red sweater and skirt. She had me sit in the right front seat, next to her, and we took off from Samburu's red-dirt strip, to the east. She seemed casual, relaxed at the controls. We made a right turn, over the muddy Ewaso Ng'iro River, where Cynthia and I had watched the frenzied splashing of many crocodiles ripping apart a female waterbuck who'd made the mistake of coming to the water's edge to drink; then we headed south-west, toward Nanyuki. On our right was a red tabletop mountain, on our left rusty-brown cliffs, and below the barren, rocky scrubland of Samburu National Park. The plane was bouncing around on the same thermals that carried vultures to their scouting altitudes, and after a few minutes the pilot said, "We could fly above the clouds where it isn't so bumpy. Or we can fly below the clouds and see more. It's up to you." "Below the clouds," I said.

After a while she pointed at the ground. "There's an elephant herd," she said. "Do you want to see it?" "Yes," I said. *Nyaaaaa,* we banked right and dropped toward the elephants, walking at their usual stately pace, like bridesmaids down an aisle. When they were behind us we crossed an escarpment and began to see the green patches of small farms and the tin roofs of settlements. We made a left turn, toward Nairobi, and not long afterward the pilot pointed again. "There's the Mount Kenya Safari Club," she said. "Do you want to see it?" I said, "Yes," and over and down we went. The peak of Mount Kenya was in cloud but not its slopes, and we could see partway up the slope, between a rain forest higher up and wheat farms lower down, several cottages, a pond, a swimming pool, and a half circle of brilliant green lawn. That was when the idea entered my brain with the abruptness of a hyrax's scream and the force of a hammerkop's blow and split my life in two, already rearranging the second part. *"She* is sitting over there," I said to myself. *"I* am sitting over here. *She* is an American woman. *I* am an American woman. *She* is flying. I . . ."

"Do you think," I asked, in a voice that seemed a lot younger than my own, "that I could learn to fly?" "Shewer," she said, in her drawl. "How long would it take me to solo?" I asked. "Oh a week, ten days," she said. When I saw Cynthia in Nairobi I was very excited. "I have something to tell you!" I said. Before I could tell her she said, "I've got something to tell *you!* He's asked me to his camp in Tanzania! I'm going to have to stay in Africa longer than we planned." "I'm going to stay longer too!" I said. "I'm going to learn to *fly!"* But before either of us could do what we were dying to do, we took the sightseeing trip to the coast we'd already arranged. We flew in a commercial plane to Dar es Salaam, and sometime in mid-flight the pilot cut power so drastically and lowered the plane's nose so sharply that glassware and crockery shot out of the galley and crashed to the floor and chunks of them went sliding and tinkling down the aisle next to our seats. The stewardess hardly looked up. I reached over and clutched the window curtains so hard they sprang out of their sprockets. Brave pilot-to-be!

My flight instructor at the Aero Club of East Africa was named Jimmy Stewart. The Aero Club was at Wilson airport, a large general-aviation field on the outskirts of Nairobi, and it still had a strong colonial feel to it, with worn easy chairs, dozens of cups laid out for afternoon tea, odes to dead airmen on the walls, Pimm's at the bar. My first hour with Mr. Stewart included taxiing the airplane, a two-seat Cessna 150, but to my great embarrassment I kept pushing the rudder pedal opposite to the way I wanted to go, which I realized and tried to explain to him was the way you did it when you were skiing, the only other occasion when I had to use my feet for the same purpose—that is, directional control—but he wasn't buying any excuses. He was very, very British, meticulous, mordantly witty, exceedingly demanding, and passionate about flying. When he came down after doing aerobatics he was silent for a while, out of the depth of his feeling for what he had just experienced.

My second hour of instruction included stalls and spins, and the only way I got through them, that sickening failure of the wings' ability to hold the plane up, was to accept the fact that I was going to die. After we landed I had to sign a flight log, and Mr. Stewart watched closely to see whether my hand trembled; I was interested to see that it didn't. During the next five hours of lessons I mostly practiced take-offs and landings; then one morning as I was rolling out after what must have been an okay landing, Mr. Stewart told me to stop the plane, although we were still only a short way down the runway. He opened the door, climbed out, and without saying a word to me or looking back started hiking across the field in the direction of the Aero Club. I stared at his white shirt back, then ahead at the rest of the runway, pushed the throttle in, went up and around the "circuit," hearing his voice as before and even feeling his weight, though I had been told that I wouldn't, and only realized fully what I'd done after I'd bounced onto the asphalt alone and a voice from the tower told me in a lovely African cadence, as I started to taxi across a runway which I had failed to ask for permission to cross, "Five Yankee Alfa Echo Romeo. Cleared to cross One-Four. *Congratulations!*"

Your first solo is a big deal, even pilots with thousands of hours assured me, so when I got to the Aero Club I allowed myself to feel puffed up, bought drinks all around, as I was supposed to do (better than being doused with a hose, as some people in the States used to do). A couple of hours later, as I was standing outside by the club fence, wrapped in the glory of my achievement, watching other pilots' takeoffs and landings, and talking with a club member, I had the strange feeling that I knew the man. There was no reason to think I should. He was a Kenyan citizen, had grown up in India, the son of a missionary doctor, spoke with a British accent, said un-American things like "tough titty," and wore a mustache of a shape you'd never see outside the Empire. Yet I couldn't shake the feeling. I mentioned it to him. It turned out that the only four complete years he'd spent in the U.S. (and most miserably) were at a college his father had sent him to in the Midwest—my college! We figured out that he had been a senior while I was a freshman, so we didn't go to any of the same classes and almost certainly never spoke to each other, but I must have seen his unhappy face, decades younger and minus the mustache, floating by on some campus street. I took this very accurate perception of a stranger's much-altered face many miles away and many years later, on the basis of something as ephemeral as a few passing glimpses, as a sign that much about my flying was going to be extraordinary.

Doug figured slightly in the next stage of my flight training. He had flown a couple of times out of a small airport north of New York City and suggested it would be a good place for me to finish my lessons. So, once I got home, the very first weekend, I hopped on a bus, hopped off an hour and a half later, walked along a highway, turned right past a trailer park, headed up a street with small houses on either side, and there it was, the airport where I was to go for my license, across the street from a Russian Orthodox church with a blue cupola and its own graveyard. I was shocked to discover, after the fastidiousness of the British-based aviation scene in East Africa and the beauty of the landscape there, a general sloppiness and unsightliness at the airport: oil puddles on the ramp, ramshackle hangars, a pilot hot-dogging it up to the pumps and stopping at the last minute, a slovenly dressed instructor (not mine) who answered questions with jokes, views out onto shopping malls and freeways. In time, however, I became fond of Spring Valley airport and came to see that the flying done there was serious in its way. More important, I became fond of small American airports in general. In East Africa, except for Wilson and the international jetports, airfields by and large were nothing more than strips of dirt or grass with fences around them to keep off the zebra and wildebeest.

One thing that did not change in time: The way that I first flew when the idea of flying hit me with such force that I never recovered was the way I kept wanting to fly, underneath the clouds so I could always look at the ground, swooping down from time to time to get an even closer look at the elephant herds and safari clubs.

From Ocean City I could have found my way holding one eye closed and squinting with the other. Assateague was a long narrow bone of an island, 35 miles end to end but only a quarter mile wide in places; the ocean side was straight and bordered by a pencil line of surf, so navigation couldn't have been easier. It was like following a light-brown highway with a white side stripe. The air was so still at that hour of the morning I was flying with only my knees on the control stick. All I had to do to make corrections was press inward with one leg or the other. With my hands and eyes thus freed up, almost idle, I felt almost like a passenger riding along, able to give myself over more than usual to the distractions of the shoreline. One distraction that was missing was horses. Where the wild ponies went was a mystery to me, since I flew the length of Assateague, which had nothing on it higher than scrubby bushes, and never did see one of them.

Or *almost* the length of Assateague. Two miles from the southern tip of the island a chunk of restricted airspace blocked my way like an invisible mountain. Called R-6604 on the chart, it consisted of an 80-square-mile notched wedge covering ten miles of shore and extending three and a half miles out to sea. It "belonged" to the NASA air station at Wallops Island, Virginia, and was off-limits to all civilian aircraft from the ground up to, as the chart put it, "unlimited"—the stratosphere, jet stream, Van Allen belt, moon, stars. When I got to the edge I detoured 35 miles around it plus two Marine air bases, and when I got back to shore, the shore was no longer a highway. It was shaggy with inlets and lacy with islets and covered with grass, not sand. Also, it was no longer an island but a peninsula, Accomack, shaped vaguely like lower Sweden. I radioed an airport in the middle of it on

122.8, or Unicom, a frequency uncontrolled airports shared. "Acco-mack. Luscombe Eight Zero Three Bravo. Active, please," I said, expecting someone in the office to tell me which runway was being used, or should be used, because the wind favored it. Silence. "Active, please," I called again. Silence. I flew over the field at a safe 2,000 feet so I could look down at the orange windsock and figure out myself which way to land. The sock was hanging straight down, as limp as a month-old carrot, and about as useful to me. So in the end I chose the runway whose downwind leg was easiest for me to get into from where I happened to be and spent a large part of my time in the pattern looking around to make sure nobody else was doing the same thing on the other downwind leg. I had no interest in eyeball-to-eyeballing an-other pilot from the opposite end of the same runway.

No sooner had I shut down than a man stepped out of the office and walked briskly toward my plane, looking eager to be of service. Was he deaf, then, but not blind? He had thin white hair, light eyes, and pink squirrel cheeks. I asked if he would top both fuel tanks and he dragged a stepladder over, then a hose, climbed the ladder with the hose, and started pumping. While he was waiting for my tank to fill, we got to talking. He happened to mention in the course of things that his name was Orville Wright.

"Wha-a-a-at!?!" He must have seen my expression before. "Well, you got to be named *something*," he said. "My Aunt Lulu gave me this name, in 1914. I never did like the idea of it. Only about two people ever got it right. It's supposed to be Or-*ville*, not *Or*-ville. I like to be called O.J." As he carried the stepladder and hose around to the other side I began to wonder if any of the dreams Aunt Lulu had for little Orville, soaring on life's heady currents and all that, had come to pass, if her high aim had put any spin on his life. So I asked him what he'd done before coming to the airport. He told me he'd stayed home and looked after his paralyzed father for years, then when his father died tried farming ("no luck"). After that he worked for a "fur-niture lady," a friend of Aunt Lulu's, then tried farming again ("no luck"). During World War II he had a job (and this was the closest he'd come to aviation so far) with a contracting company that fur-nished the sand the Navy used to build this very runway. After the war, he worked in a hardware store, then bought his own hardware store and ran that for 20 years. A year ago he lost his store and one day showed up at the county unemployment office. It sent him to Accomack airport to apply for the job of assistant manager.

You would think it was only fitting, a soul come home, the end of a journey Orville Wright didn't know he was making, but he burst that bubble just as I was blowing it up. "Oh flying's o-*kay,*" he said, "but I don't really crave it. I've never even flown an airplane. I didn't go up in one until I was 43, and when I finally got up nerve enough I made the pilot promise, 'No fancy stuff!' " However, it was clear that he got benefits from being at an airport he wouldn't have gotten any-place else. For instance, when students on solo cross-country flights landed at Accomack and asked for someone to sign their log books, as they were supposed to do to let their instructors back home know they'd made it to their destination airports, Wright would dutifully write his name in their log books, then watch with glee as they checked the entry. Suspicion would creep over their faces. "Ah, come on!" they'd say. "What are you trying to *pull?*"

I knew it was ridiculous but still I felt . . . something and asked Wright if I could take a photo of him. He agreed in such a way that it seemed he thought there might be something there, too. He stood formally beside the oversized prop of an Ag Cat, his arms straight to his sides, hands in half-fists, chin high, mouth set in a dignified little smile. After I took the photo he offered me his card. I asked him to sign it, then watched while he did. The script was careful but not without flourish, the large O doubling back on itself, in a sort of mill-er's knot, and the g trailing a long, open tail.

A nice, conjunctive touch, I thought: Using gas that Orville Wright had just pumped, I'd be flying that very day to Kitty Hawk, North Carolina (or Kill Devil Hill, it actually was). To get there I'd be pass-ing over the wide-open mouth of Chesapeake Bay, 25 miles of water with a low bridge running across it, which I intended to follow. Ac-cording to the chart, the bridge zigzagged across, tunneling below the surface a couple of times, then reemerging, like a sea serpent, several miles farther on. The bridge turned out to be a poor match for the mix of sun, haze, and water, appearing as no more than a vague, spectral line, and I had trouble keeping my attention on it. My con-centration kept wandering to the sharper, clearer images inside my cockpit. I noticed for the first time for instance that my shoelaces and the flesh of my calves shook with the engine's vibrations as they came through the rudder pedals to my sneakers and up my legs, stared, fascinated for a while, then forced my gaze outside and down again, and began tracking a floater, one of those clumps of eyeball jelly you don't notice ordinarily, the so-called spots before your eyes, as it moved from left to right across my windscreen, looking like a distant plane, then dragged my attention back to the bridge, where I spotted an orange VW going my way, focused on it, and when it fell behind looked for something else to give the bridge substance. I tried a blue car, a gray car, a white fishing boat, and by that time was over land, which had a lot of substance for about 15 miles, then split and formed another barrier island, which in places was almost as narrow as the bridge.

At that point I began dropping toward the beach, the better to see it through the haze, losing altitude slowly yet steadily, as if on a greased slide. Three thousand feet, 2,000, 1,800, 600, 400, leveled off when I was at about the height of a chimneytop. Nobody was on the beach; I was buzzing sand. Something flashed past: a large, dark rock. Thoom! Something else—a wad of wet clothing. Thoom! A rubber tire—gone, gone. With a couple of fingers I pressed the front of the stick lightly, and the plane shot up, doubling its altitude. I relaxed pressure and the plane sank to where it had been. At cruise altitude the difference would hardly have been noticeable, but since I was low, with the stationary earth as foil, even a small upward motion seemed a bound.

Next, I pressed the left side of the stick and went sliding over to the dunes, pressed the right side and slid back to the beach, then out to sea. Left side again and over to the dunes, right side back to the beach and out to sea. Back to the beach up to the dunes back to the beach out to sea, beach, dunes, beach, sea, in long fluid strokes, right, left, right, left; it was like ice skating. Oh the joy of it! The uncomplicated *joy* of it! There I was, almost on the earth but not quite, close enough to see some of its treasures (ominous dark tangles of seaweed, the delicate lace-edge of foam), yet able to ride smoothly above them all, slide equally over sand, driftwood, and dune grass, move upon earth and water as if upon a single polished element. The joy of it! As I glided along at that low yet majestic height, I found my sense of myself rising, building like a song in the throat: How like a goddess I am! Was this, then, the purest form of flying? Or, as many would argue, was being high up, among the clouds, and nearly out of sight of earth?

Up ahead, I saw a man standing, fishing in the surf. I swung out to sea, then when he was behind me went back to the beach. Minutes later I saw two more figures ahead, women this time. I swung out to sea but began to feel less like a god and more like a dog, with tin cans tied to its tail. As I drew even with them, both women waved at me, using their whole arms to do it, as if I were giving them a big treat. Maybe, I thought, an airplane still had the power to charm, if it were small, slow, low, and maybe old enough. Or maybe they just guessed how splendid it was to be up flying that day, close to the earth yet not confined to it. Besides, I soon realized, they had tin cans of their own. A little way past where they were standing I spotted a car parked beside a dune, with tire tracks leading a long way down the beach.

First Flight · Beaufort

At the start of any long airplane trip, I've always thought, it's a good idea to do something to evoke the strangeness of it. Remind yourself how odd it is to be actually *up in the air*. Sometimes when flying along I stare out the window at my left tire, look down at the dark curve of the top of it and the narrow tread, just like an auto tire except smaller and with a few extra grooves, obviously made for pressing on land, bearing great weight, and yet there it is, tooling along with nothing under it but a breathy mix of gas, a thin stew of molecules, and solid fields more than half a mile below, while above, three-quarters of a ton of metal, petroleum, bone, flesh, Plexiglas, chrome, and carpet pass through the air as surely as a scrap of rice paper, a wind-blown seed. At such times I often think of the Wright brothers and say something to them in gratitude, for their having believed flying was possible before they flew, while I can hardly believe it now myself. A couple of times at the beginning of cross-country flights I've stopped at the Wright museum at Kill Devil Hill, to pay homage to them, and remind myself of the extraordinary nature of what I was doing.

This time I had trouble getting into a grateful frame of mind, despite the joy ride I'd just had. When I landed on First Flight, the museum's 4,000-foot paved strip, the thermometer on my right window, which was shaded by the wing, read 100 degrees. I was already hot and sweaty after my flight (there were trade-offs to flying low in summer, since for every 1,000 feet of increased altitude air cools about three and a half degrees), and my own sweat was making me itch. The tiedown area of First Flight was at least a half mile from the museum, and the only way to cover that distance was to walk, across a field with little to cast shade. The air was torpid—none of those strong, reliable winds that made the Wright brothers choose that stretch of shoreline to kick off the aviation era. Setting out in the direction of the museum, with flies

circling my head and limbs like attack planes, I quickly became bogged
down in my own discomfort, had to push myself along, tell myself to
keep going. Repeatedly I tried to rise to the occasion, give the Wright
brothers their due, but my thoughts wouldn't, so to speak, soar. Instead I found myself looking almost obsessively at the ground cover
(heat and fatigue pulling my head down?), studying the low stuff at
my feet—short-stemmed grasses, mini-cacti, tiny flowering weeds, with
dragonflies and bees crisscrossing over them. All seemed imbued with
an extraordinary clarity, their details positively riveting.

As I was thus moving along, ignoring almost entirely the upper
world the brothers had opened for me, I nearly stepped on a cluster of
small, white, star-shaped flowers. I slid my foot away just in time. The
flowers reminded me of a story a botanist once told me. In 1912, the
year Wilbur died of typhoid, some botany students from the University
of Chicago went on a field trip to study prairie grasses. While on their
hands and knees they spotted, half buried in the dirt, a couple of tiny,
stemless plants with bright, orchid-like flowers no more than half an
inch across. They dug the plants up and showed them to their professor, who had never seen plants like those before; the professor showed
them to other professors back at the university, who had never seen
plants like those before either. The plants were put in vials of formal-
dehyde, classified, and proclaimed a new species, *Thismia americana,* the
all-American plant. In the years following their discovery, botanists
searched for other specimens, first in the place where the originals were
found, then farther and farther afield. They looked for months, years.
The original site became developed, covered over. None of the little
plants was ever found again. Once the nation's rarest plant, *Thismia
americana* had gone extinct in a day.

As I slid my foot away from the tiny white flowers on the slog to the
museum I began to wonder: Had *I* seen a rare thing at some moment
in my life and, having no idea of it, crushed the thing? Or witnessed
a rare event, like the hatching of a ghost moth or a pebble rising off
the ground from the combined force of most of the molecules in it
lining up toward one pole at the same instant, and passed right by,
assumed that the hatching was sunlight on a leaf or that somebody
kicked the stone? With Nature being so stealthy, what a responsibility
for vigilance we all had!

Once in the museum I deep-breathed the air-conditioning and recovered somewhat, then headed for my favorite exhibit, a remark Orville made in 1940 to an interviewer who asked what was the biggest kick he got out of inventing the airplane. "I got more thrill out of flying before I had ever been in the air at all," said Orville, "by lying in bed thinking how exciting it would be to fly." Which raised the question: Was the first flight in any way a letdown for him? What had he dreamed flying would be like, different from what it actually was? And Wilbur, what were his dreams of flying? My own dream as I went around the museum was that Leonardo da Vinci was going around with me. I pictured him wearing white robes, for some reason, and speaking English. I'd explain a few things to him, from my vantage point of over 400 years. His face would be wise and radiant. "So that's it," he'd keep saying. "So that's it!," not at all let down.

Somebody else for whom the reality of heavier-than-air flight was no letdown whatever was Amos I. Root, the Ohio beekeeper who witnessed "the world's first circle by an aeroplane," made by Wilbur Wright above a field near Dayton, Ohio, in 1904. He described what he saw in a 1905 issue of *Gleanings in Bee Culture,* which he edited and which the museum sold reprints of. "Imagine," Root wrote, "a locomotive that has left its track and is climbing up in the air right toward you—a locomotive without any wheels, we will say, but with white wings instead. Well, now, imagine this white locomotive, with wings that spread 20 feet each way, coming right toward you with a tremendous flap of its propellers, and you will have something like what I saw . . . one of the grandest sights, if not the grandest sight, of my life."

Flap of its propellers! That evoked well enough the strangeness of what I was doing. From First Flight, I took off, flapping at 2,475 rpm— and ten minutes later landed again. First Flight didn't have fuel so I went to Manteo, an old Army air base on an island seven miles out in the sound, to get some. There the FBO (or Fixed Base Operator, one of the less happy terms in aviation, an FBO being, the way the term is commonly used, both a business at an airport and the person who runs it; *"it's* an FBO," *"he's* an FBO") not only gave me fuel and helped me get a motel room, he also arranged a ride for me to my motel, no small matter. One of the big drawbacks to flying cross-country is that once you've landed at a little airport there's often no way for you to get around on the ground. Airports tend to be located outside of towns, or at least at the edge of towns, and from there you can't walk much of any place. Buses and trains don't usually run nearby, and rental cars cost too much to use routinely if you're a pilot of typical means. So do taxis. Some pilots carry such things as folding bicycles and even folding motorcycles in their baggage compartments, but most can't fit in anything bigger than roller skates.

So all too often you find yourself in places you've gotten to in a hurry but can't get out of. It's a situation that has led many people to dream about air-cars, and a few actually to make them. At the end of World War II, Robert Edison Fulton, Jr., a descendant of the inventor of the steamboat, hand-built eight ''Airphibians'' and flew one of them thousands of miles around the country. The front of the Airphibian was the car part, with windshield wipers, horn, and fourth wheel added, which pilots could drive around on streets while the rear, or airplane, part (fuselage, wings, and tail) stayed back on the ramp, resting on stilts. By contrast, Dewey Bryan's Bryan III left nothing behind at the airport, since it was meant to hit the road entire, with the same 175-hp pusher engine forcing a prop around (''kicks up a little dust on the road,'' went one report) and the same three wheels supporting the frame (''a bit tricky especially with a crosswind,'' admitted the inventor). However, it had retractable license plates and headlights on its wings, which were hinged to swing up vertically when the pilot wanted to become a driver.

Other people designed other air-cars, including the Aerocar, the Aero Car, the Aerauto, and the Flying Pinto, but despite the inventors' ingenuity and hard work and the importance of the niche they were trying to fill, such hybrids do not crowd our skies and highways today. It seems that the features needed for a vehicle to be ground-worthy as well as airworthy, particularly with all the recently mandated pollution-control and safety devices, produce so much weight and drag that any air-car is an inefficient performer in the sky, and not always great on the ground either.

Therefore, to help them get where they want to go, pilots often rely on people already at the airport where they've just landed. An office manager may see a guy standing uncertainly around, hand him the keys to her pickup truck, and tell him he can drive it to a diner for lunch. Or a mechanic may offer the use of the Airport Car, usually a dinged-up Chevy with oil cans on the floor and rags on the seats. Or a pilot based at the airport, remembering the times he himself has been

stranded, may ask, "You got wheels?" and, if the answer is no, drive
the stranger somewhere. Or an FBO may cast about for somebody to
give her a lift. "Murray," the one at Manteo said to a pilot hanging
around the office, "mind taking this little lady to the Fin 'n'
Feather?"

The pilot didn't much have the look of one. In general, aviators are
mainstream if not retrograde in appearance, with probably more crew
cuts per capita than any other population group. This pilot, though,
had a long, narrow, red, drooping mustache with ends twirled to points
like rodents' tails—Dali with a license to enter his own dreamy,
butter-yellow skies. He dropped me off at my motel on the way to his,
and the next morning I got a ride back to Manteo with one of the
managers of the Fin 'n' Feather. Her son, Artie, about nine, offered
me a ride in his father's inboard motorboat just before I left. He seemed
small for his age and had buck teeth. As we were about to leave, his
sister, Laura, about eight, ran up and asked if she could come along.
She was wearing her mother's lipstick, a heavy layer of it, in a brilliant
shade of pink.

Artie started the motor, backed the boat around, and headed into
the sound (the Fin 'n' Feather was on a causeway). The ride was
refreshing, for about a minute. Then I realized we were heading full
power for a stand of tall grasses and Artie had a funny smile on his
teeny face. In a way that I thought conveyed quiet authority, I said,
"Turn, Artie, turn," but the boat kept on going, speed undiminished,
toward the grass wall. "TURN, ARTIE, *TURN!*" I yelled, but Artie
never wavered, and neither did the boat until, just as it would have
slammed into the vegetation, it slid around in a sharp 180 which sent
water sloshing over our arms and legs; then we were off again, full tilt
across the bay, bouncing on waves we'd stirred up on the way over,
and aiming for yet another clump of high reeds. *"Tu-u-u-rn,* Artie!" I
screamed, but Artie, face twisted into an evil grin, held firm until the
last nanosecond, when the boat skidded and the stern kissed the fronds
and we zoomed off again, our bodies flung this way and that as we
tacked across the bay, with me shouting "Slow down, Artie!" and
"DON'T!" and holding onto the sides of the boat as if to the saddle
of a horse that would surely throw me—what? a grownup pilot nervous
in a motorboat driven by a child?—*yes!* And little Artie whipping the
wheel of the boat around wildly and grinning hideously, when all of a

sudden relief came in the form of an odor, as I became aware more than anything else of the sweet, cheap, Jell-O-like, boudoir scent of little Laura's lipstick, a cloying, treacly smell which took me by an olfactory route into another dimension so that the hard facts of water and sun and boat in my clenched hands became mostly backdrop, unreal and alien, rather than the other way around.

On our way to the airport I mentioned Artie's performance to his mother, but she just smiled sweetly. By way of conversation she told me she was a midget. I was taken aback. Like Artie and Laura, she was small, but not all that small. "Oh," she said, surprised I hadn't heard of them. "Midgetts are famous. Midgett men are *all* Coast Guard. Have been for generations. My father and uncle and two brothers are *all* Midgetts and they're *all* Coast Guard. Every year we have a picnic and *hundreds* of Midgetts come. It's in *all* the papers." Was mad Artie then destined to be in the Coast Guard someday, a mini-Midgett patrolling our shores and rendering them unsafe for swimmers and boaters?

On my way out of Manteo, I flew over a pair of sunken ships. They were opposite the Wright brothers' memorial obelisk, not far from shore, in shallow water, yet were barely discernible from the air, two dim almond shapes lying close to each other and almost parallel except turned slightly outward at the tips, like a pair of narrow shoes someone had just stepped out of. By nature wrecked ships are mysterious, but these were particularly so because there were two of them. Had they collided? I wondered. If so, why here, beside a beach, far from port? And why two so much alike? Had they run aground? But why together? Were they scuttled, maybe? Then why side by side? Could they have been sister ships that tried to help each other through some dark and stormy night and perished on the same ocean roll?

I took a photo of them, then turned and flew south along the beach, toward Beaufort, North Carolina. There weren't many people on the beach that day, just some sunbathers scattered around, in small groups. From the altitude I was flying at, 1,000 feet, they looked sweet, lying on their handkerchief-size towels, beneath party-favor umbrellas, on rafts no bigger than soap cakes. "It looks like a Toyland down there!" passengers often say during their first ride in a small plane, and it does. It's this miniaturization, this *cutening* of the world, that endears small-plane flying to so many people. A few hundred feet can make all the difference, turn things on the ground wholesome and clean. The sunbathers on the beach that day weren't ordinary human beings but adorable figurines, darling little creatures. All seemed well formed from where I was, the objects they brought with them to the beach new and saturated with color. Some were lying in pairs on their towels, legs apart, like little scissors. Others had set their toy chairs at the edge of the surf and were letting their doll feet dangle, splash in the foam . . .

It occurred to me as I was making the turn at Cape Hatteras (bent elbow of the long line of bones) that I could be a sunbather myself, and soon. The next island west was Ocracoke, and according to the chart it had an airstrip on it. Since Ocracoke was as narrow as the other islands, I figured the airstrip had to be near a beach. When I flew over I didn't see anything near the airstrip *except* a beach, no motels, restaurants, or piers which might explain why it was there, only a road that didn't run even the length of the island. Could the airstrip have been built for just this, I asked myself, so that pilots in their overheated cockpits could swoop down from the sky like kingfishers, hit the water, and come up cool and dripping?

A half dozen planes were parked beside the strip already, and I pulled in beside one of them and shut down. Several children of an impressionable age plus a couple of adults were standing between it and my plane, close enough for all of them to see into my cockpit, so when I changed into my bathing suit I ducked below window level. It wasn't easy maneuvering my body and clothes around the control stick and throttle, not to mention having the foot pedals exactly where I wanted a flat surface to give purchase, but I finally managed and crawled out carrying beach equipment (towel, tea, tuna fish, crackers, peach, hat, book) and climbed the sandbank that lay between the airstrip and the ocean, then stood at the top looking out. Before me lay a long, wide, pale, sparkling, unblemished, nearly empty beach, so lovely and bright and fresh that I almost blushed at the privilege, my airplane becoming for the moment a luxury in the category of a Rolls-Royce, a villa on the Riviera, a yacht that slept ten. I walked out onto the beach. It was pitted with the holes of ghost crabs. Black skimmers flew along the surf line. The sea oats shone. For two hours I swam, slept, read, and ate my lunch on the beach, then climbed back over the sandbank, threw my gear in the plane again, and took off without bothering to change out of my wet suit. I waited until I was airborne to do that. No one to see me topless at 1,000 feet. No need to be shy in the sky. Perfect privacy, between walls of blue.

The next island west, Core Bank, didn't have even a road for the first 25 miles. Empty sound lay to my right, open ocean to my left, and underneath a strip of unpeopled sand; this was sure getting away from it all, I thought. After a while the plane crossed a line, a neat hard edge of shadow, as if it were entering a closet, and several large drops of rain hit the windscreen. Rain hadn't been predicted; what *was* this? More drops fell, pelting the roof and cowling, and I considered turning around. Then, as suddenly as the rain had started, it stopped, and the plane flew out of the closet. Everywhere ahead the sky was bright and utterly cloudless, and it stayed like that, all the way to Beaufort, sunshine blanketing the sand, water, birds, the first fisherman, first road, first billboard, farm, horse, house. What, I wondered, accounted for that stray fragment of weather back there? That fleck of storm? For, if one unstable pocket developed somewhere in conditions that brought forth a rain cloud, then as the world turned, and the sun shone, and the breezes blew, why not another? . . . and another? . . . and another?

For dinner that night, in a seafood restaurant beside my motel, I took my own vodka in a paper bag. I never wanted a drink, or felt I needed and deserved one, nearly as much at any other time in my life as I did at the end of a day spent flying, not even as much as at the end of a day spent working, or so it seemed. Maybe it was the constant engine noise and vibration, or the prolonged crouch I was forced into if I wanted to have a good view out, or the stabs of anxiety that penetrated my general pleasure, I didn't know, but when the last leg was flown and my plane, like a cowboy's horse, looked after first, I hankered for a slug or two of the old red-eye. Since Beaufort was dry I brought my own, in a paper bag. The 15-year-old granddaughter of the restaurant owner waited on me and told me to keep the bag on the bench beside me while she brought orange-juice setups, leaving it to me to choose between sneaking the bottle up or the orange juice down. She was carrying a flask herself, in her apron pocket, and when her grandmother wasn't looking she'd take a swig. She told me she was getting in the mood to go dancing on the boardwalk that night. Already she was pinwheel-eyed and giggly, and I began to worry about her, with all those Marines out there on the boardwalk looking for a little quick R&R. I reasoned that it was one thing for a grownup pilot like me—in a watered-down version of the brandy-drinking that World War I aviators indulged in after their terrible adventures in the sky— to drink to relax, and quite another for a 15-year-old to drink to relax *before* her (possibly terrible) adventures on the ground.

Yet on the beach the next day, I decided I needn't have worried. Some young Marines were horsing around near where I put my towel and I got a good look at them. Their haircuts were so short and their bathing suits so small that their developed bodies looked grotesquely large, almost sinister with muscle, yet they played like tykes, romping and squealing. They didn't look ready for seduction, I thought, or at least very good at it. Their spirits seemed not at all diminished by the bleak aspect of the beach, which lay under a viscid layer of haze. People standing only a short way down the shoreline were no more than pale-blue cutouts. The sky and the sea were one steamy curtain. That morning a briefer had told me a warm front was stalled in the Smoky Mountains and was keeping the old, stale air in Beaufort. It would be keeping me in Beaufort too, I realized, since visibility was down to a mile and I needed three miles to be legal. I would have to wait on weather.

I hated waiting on weather, even when I had no place in particular to go. Waiting well was an essential flying skill, I knew, as important sometimes as laying out a good course. I believed all those signs in airport offices that said GET-HOME-ITIS CAN KILL YOU, and I believed that get-home-itis could kill you whether you were headed for home or not. But waiting on weather made me feel restless, cranky, full of longing; somebody else was in charge.

On the other hand, not much could be said in favor of flying in haze that was legal but barely so. In heavy haze you had to do without most of the things you took up flying for in the first place: the sense of being in big, booming spaces, under the great vault of heaven, in poetic contact with distant hills. Also, you couldn't let your thoughts bounce around the landscape as you usually did since you had to concentrate so hard on finding your checkpoints, which tended to slide off into the peripheral sludge, or to present themselves faintly and parsimoniously. ''Contact flying,'' what navigating by reference to the ground is called, became almost real contact, you held objects so fast with your eyes (the railroad, the river, the bridge—no, not the right bridge!—the lake—is that the right shape?), you became almost fused with the object—the power line, the bridge, the highway that told you you were safe, you knew where you were.

On one trip I flew in sludgy skies for eight straight days, managing only about two hours of flying a day between the time the morning fog lifted and the afternoon thundershowers began, intently studying the clogged yellowish air mass ahead for the signs of thickening. or darkening that might mean embedded thunderstorms. On a couple of those days I woke up feeling as if I were about to cross the Atlantic alone and it had never been done before; dread mixed miserably with desire. (There they were, aviation's twin watchbirds, dread and desire. A vulture sitting on one wingtip, a sweetly singing thrush on the other.)

At Beaufort the first day I waited I passed the time washing my clothes and hanging them on a line back of the motel. My flying clothes: T-shirts, short-sleeved buttoned shirts, shorts, and sneakers. That was it, the wardrobe. In Washington I saw an exhibit at the National Air and Space Museum of the outfits women pilots wore in the early days of aviation and felt not a little envious. Harriet Quimby, the first American woman to get a pilot's license, in 1911, designed her own plum-colored satin flying suits, one of which featured a blouse with monk's hood and knickers that converted to a skirt by means of buttons on the inside leg seams. Matilde Moisant, the second American woman to get a pilot's license, preferred a heavy tweed flying suit, which not only kept off the chill of air flowing through the open cockpit of her Bleriot but once, when the plane crashed and burned, literally saved her skin; the flames couldn't make it through the thick weave.

As for the first American female to fly as a *passenger,* in 1908, she apparently had an influence that went far beyond the sphere of aviation. Before Wilbur Wright took her up in his Wright Flyer, Mrs. Hart O. Berg tied her skirt about her ankles so it wouldn't blow around indecorously and dangerously aloft, and after landing she left the skirt like that, just walked away from the plane with her ankles tied together, prompting a French couturier in the crowd (ever open to inspiration) to proclaim a new fashion: the hobble skirt.

After hanging my clothes on the line, near a canal with fishing boats drawn up to the edges (the *Anny Fanny,* the *Old John D),* I watched a duck walk around in a chicken-wire cage. The airport manager's Aunt Mabel, who owned the motel, had found the duck somewhere without its mother and was keeping it in the cage until it was big and strong enough to survive on the canal alone. The duck would strut around, stopping now and then to peck at seeds on the floor of the cage, then stand stock-still with a look that seemed to be directed at the *Anny Fanny.* At one point ducks somewhere in the distance that it couldn't see started squawking and it ran frantically around the cage and gave a piteous squawk back. At that age its wings were still quite small, even considering the small size of the rest of it, and they lay on its pale yellow body like two dark moths, or little feathered epaulets. The day when it would join the other ducks on the canal seemed woefully far away.

My second day of waiting I went to the airport, not to fly out but to check on my plane, although I had no reason to think anything had happened to it. I wasn't the only pilot drawn to the scene of his frustration. A barefoot man was sitting on a sofa in the lounge, a glum look on his face. On the coffee table in front of him was spread a tempting array of flying magazines—*Rotor & Wing, A/C Flyer, Private Pilot, Air Progress, Professional Pilot, Airport, General Aviation News,* and *Sport Aviation*—but apparently he wasn't interested in any of them. His gaze was directed out into the room. I asked him what was going on. When it was hot like this, he answered, fish stayed low in the water and he couldn't see them. Which was important because he was a fishspotter, and if he didn't spot fish he didn't get paid. The problem wasn't haze but heat. Over the ocean one-mile visibility was legal since there wasn't much out there to run into, on the surface of the water or just above it, in the air.

Before long another fishspotter showed up, unable to stay away either. The first (Pat Smith) was young, with a face that was round, pink, and puffed as a baby's. The second (Dick Rodd) was older, darker, and leaner. Smith and Rodd were competitors, spotted for different companies. If the day hadn't been so hot, the fish they'd have been spotting was menhaden, also known as bunker, mossback, shad, and mamashad. Ships netted it by the ton to be ground up and sold as animal feed. In order to spot fish, Smith and Rodd flew along the coastline, part of the time over the ocean, part of the time over the bay, usually within a half mile of shore, looking for patches of color in the water. The patches were schools of fish. Said Rodd, ''The patches can be every color of the rainbow. I've seen light shades of red, light shades of pink, light shades of brown, dark shades of brown, and dark shades of black. It depends on how close together the fish are and how big. Some patches even show *blue*. Usually the darker and redder the patch, the larger the catch. If they're blue they're not worth messing with.'' Smith added, ''Sometimes the fish play and whip in the water so you can tell where they are by the foam. If your motor's not running, you can even hear them. I know a guy who swore he could *smell* them.''

The spotters usually took off a half hour before sunrise since the schools the menhaden formed at night broke up gradually during the day as the sharks got to them. ''Everything I see,'' said Rodd, ''I write down. What I saw. Where I saw it. How fast it was moving (fish can run faster than a boat can get to them). How big it was. Was it net-size, half-boat-size, or steamer-size? If you see a patch as big as a steamer, you've got 100,000, maybe 400,000 fish. It depends. As soon as you've got a million fish, you send three boats out.''

The boats left port at 2 or 3 a.m. the following day, to be in a position to drop their nets at sunrise. The planes went with them. ''The boats can't see down there so we orbit and tell them to 'open up,' 'close up,' 'give speed,' 'stay out a little the fish are spreading,' that sort of thing,'' said Smith. ''Meanwhile, we've got to keep our eyes out for other planes. Seven or eight other guys could be out there circling their boats at the same time that we're circling ours. Separation is usually 300 or 500 vertical feet but sometimes it's less because of clouds, so if a pilot goofs off and doesn't hold his altitude it can get real dangerous. We lose about two spotters a year, mostly from midairs. That's with 125 spotters in the country, including the tuna boys and the swordfish boys.''

For at least one of the menhaden boys, competition presented other hazards besides midairs. One day Rodd was ready to take off from Beaufort when his engine froze up; a minute later and it would have frozen in the air. He checked the engine and discovered that someone had put ''high-grade sugar'' in his oil tank. On another occasion he was flying at night and when he looked out his window toward the runway lights that had been there only a moment before he could no longer see them. He looked again and realized a flap of fabric from the underside of his wing was hanging loose, covering the window. When he got down he determined that someone had sliced a rectangle from his wing and left the corners attached so they would be torn loose in the slipstream. While doing a preflight inspection in the dark he hadn't noticed, nor had he been meant to.

Time on all our hands, we wandered down to Rodd's hangar, where he kept his Skyhawk. Whenever he went spotting in it, he took four radios along, one just for eavesdropping on other spotters. He owned a Luscombe once, he told me, but one day he dropped a lit cigarette on the cockpit floor and when he bent down to retrieve it he leaned on the stick and got his belt caught on it, and by the time he came up with the cigarette the Luscombe was in a 200-mile-an-hour power dive. Pulling out he popped several tail rivets and bent both ailerons into V's. He blamed the Luscombe, for instability, and couldn't get rid of it quickly enough. But what plane *wouldn't* dive if the pilot leaned on the stick? I thought. Still, I didn't say anything—Rodd seemed so sour about the whole episode that I was afraid if I defended Luscombes he'd find something even worse to say about them.

Right in front of his hangar door was a pile of large, torpedo-shaped metal objects. They were F-4 wing fuel tanks Rodd got from the Air Force and sold to neighborhood kids as pontoons for their homemade rafts ("They love 'em," he said). Near the tanks was a vegetable garden he made no attempt to hide. Squash, corn, tomatoes, and cantaloupe "big as quarters" were growing in the garden, and I asked him if he ever took any of the produce up with him. No, he said, he was on a "rather strict" diet, then told us what it was. "Just after takeoff, around 6 a.m., I eat a banana. It's my first bite of the day. Then I have a salt-free-bread and jelly sandwich. At 10 o'clock I eat an apple. I try to pace myself. At 1 o'clock I have some other fruit. At 2 I have a pack of Melba toast. That's it until I get home at 7 or 8 p.m. and toss back a couple of martinis. I used to bring a ten-pound bag of peanuts with me and eat them all day long, but when I threw the shells out the window they blew back in and the cockpit looked like a zoo."

Takeoff at 6 a.m., home at 7 or 8 p.m. added up to a 13- or 14-hour day, which sounded altogether too gruelling to me. But Rodd called fishspotting "the best" and Smith declared it "fun." "You laugh every day when you're up there," said Rodd. Smith agreed. "It's as nice and easy a job as there ever has been. I don't like dealing with people." For Rodd it was the same. "When I was a kid I'd go out in the woods looking for arrowheads to get away from my three sisters," he said. "I flew single-seat fighters in the Marines. I guess I like being alone."

At one point it came out that they were both part American Indian. Rodd looked it, but Smith looked more like Custer's mother. Neither of them belonged to the tribe with a genius for heights, the Mohawks, who built skyscrapers and suspension bridges and climbed higher than these guys flew. They descended instead from the Cherokees, a tribe that now lived mostly on the Great Plains, where the land is open and flat as the sea. I thought their forebears might have approved of the life they were leading: hunting all day from the sky, for fish, with great skill, patience, and stamina, looking for signs on the water, rainbow patches of color, and always alone, happy in their aloneness.

My third day I didn't wait; visibility was up, though not much. Aunt Mabel gave me a ride to the airport, telling me she wanted to see her nephew. He had mentioned shortly after I landed that he was retired Air Force, had taken the airport manager's job "almost as a hobby," and lived mostly on his retirement pay. "Nobody can make money running an airport," he declared. "The county gives us $3,500 a year and that's not enough to cut the grass." He was at the airport because he loved flying. "Flying just gets in your blood and you can't get it out," he explained. Unfortunately, flying never got in his wife's blood. "I'd like to buy a little plane like yours and go around the country someday, like you're doing," he said, "but she won't do it. She says when she's up she feels like she's in a little cup."

He was sitting in the office when Aunt Mabel and I walked in, behind a radio, mike in hand, looking professionally engaged. A voice came in over the radio. It was a male voice, sort of. "Turkey!" it went. "Turkey doo doo dah. Turrrrrr- [some mouth noises] *key!*" The nephew lifted the mike and spoke in an official manner. "Turkey, come back in. Come back, Turkey!" He waited. We waited. No answer. He lifted the mike again. "Turkey," he called. "Come back in, Turkey!" Nothing. Well, Turkey wasn't dumb. *Turkeys* was more like it. A couple of boys in worn-out jeans sitting in some unlocked airplane in some unlocked hangar somewhere, whipping control wheels around like car steering wheels, pulling panel buttons and flipping switches, stomping on floor pedals with dirty sneakers, bouncing on adjustable Naugahyde seats, wearing headphones and making mouth noises into a mike. But in which airplane, in which hangar, at which airport? the nephew wanted to know. "Turkey!" he called again. *"Come back!"* Turkey never did.

Georgetown · Charleston

Starting about 15 miles south of Beaufort, military restricted areas blocked passage along the coast for 25 more miles, an arrangement so inconvenient for private pilots on the Atlantic flyway that the Marines had installed a special phone in the Beaufort office. If the areas weren't going to be "hot" that day—bombed or shelled or otherwise abused—Marine controllers could give pilots permission to cut through. The phone didn't look at all modern-military to me, more like Hello Central, with a black bugle mouthpiece, a hand crank, and a high wooden base like the ones on old sewing machines. When I got ready to go, I gave the handle a few cranks, not sure how many was the right number to attract attention without being naggy, brought my mouth close to the bugle, and told the man who answered that I'd like to fly south along the coast starting in about 15 minutes. He didn't say yes, he didn't say no. "We won't even see you," he said. His voice was soft and languid. "It's Sunday."

Not only south of Beaufort but north of it, over the bay and mainland back of the bay, there were military areas, so many, in fact, that that part of the chart resembled a sewing pattern for a dress, with all the strangely shaped and numbered blocks thereon—R-5311-A; R-5306-A, -B, -C, -D, and -E; R-5313; R-5314-A, -B, -C, -D, -E, -F, -G, -H, and -J; E-2 MCA, on pentagons, squares, trapezoids, and a couple of small, button-like circles. Elsewhere around the country, there were other such areas, some 800 of them assigned to one branch or another of the armed services (plus NASA, which had two), rendering around a million square miles of American countryside off-limits or reduced- or shared-access to the rest of the flying community—often the lovelier square miles, too, since they tended to be the less developed ones. In all, at least a third of the airspace above the continental U.S. was designated, either part-time or full-time, partway up or all the way up or only high up, as prohibited areas, restricted areas, alert areas, military operations areas, and military training routes, some so small they covered only a single target ship at anchor in some bay (one of the buttons, probably), others as large as whole countries (Lebanon, Kuwait). With about 25,000 square miles being added to the total every year, and many thousands of square miles of civilian control zones—veils, airport radar service areas, terminal control areas—being added on a regular basis to the military ones, we small, low-tech users are being herded, for better or worse, like so many Indians or buffalo, into steadily shrinking reserves of air, the range we roam in the old frontier spirit growing smaller and smaller year by year.

But on this lazy Sunday, the military and I shared a quiet beach. The beach looked just like the others I'd seen so far on this coast, except the sand had more depressions in it through which water could flow between the ocean and the bay according to the tides. The tide must have been on its way out then, I figured, because on the ocean side of each depression was spread a large fan of foam; in one place the foam reached so far out it looked like a lace curtain billowing over the sea. Rodd had told me that the best place to land a plane if you have to go down on a beach is the wettest part *without water actually on it.* If the sand has water on it, presumably, it's soft and the wheels will sink in and nose the plane over. If the sand is dry, it's soft in a different way (loose), and the wheels will grab and nose the plane over. Damp, like the third bowl of porridge, is just about right. With the tide on its way out now, most of the beach appeared to be wet without water actually on it and looked from above like an ideal natural runway: wide, smooth, long, brown, straight, and, if Rodd was right, firm. I was tempted to try it, just set the wheels down on the sand, roll out, see if it *was* right, and take off again, but Rodd had also told me that along that entire stretch of coast he flew every day, two or three times a day, there were only two beaches he would land on voluntarily, Figure Eight and Diamond Shoals. To those two places he even took picnics, but every other beach he considered too risky to land on. "Even a small incline will turn your airplane into the sea," he warned. "One conch shell and you're upside down."

Since I forgot to ask him where the two beaches were and the chart didn't show them, I had to content myself with just staring at the sand, and the things around it. A couple of dozen surfers were bobbing in the water near a long pier, waiting for a wave. They were wearing brightly colored T-shirts and, all together like that, looked like a bunch of tropical fish come up to feed. Beyond them a stretch of ocean caught the sun in a way that appeared to flatten and harden its surface, so that for a moment the water became a giant paving stone, an impenetrable slab of textured slate. Meanwhile, on the bay side, a row of islands came into view, all of them about the same size and same (round) shape and same distance from each other. Lined up that way, parallel with the beach, they looked for all the world like giant cowpies some great beast had dropped, in the act of walking. Sometimes when you're flying along, it's hard not to believe that there are larger creatures on earth than we, coming and going without our knowing it (at night perhaps?), leaving gulleys of footprint, piles of offal, tail streaks, and claw marks on the grass.

I left the beach to refuel at Georgetown County, ten miles inland. Refueling a plane isn't much different from gassing up a car: you go down (pull over), stretch your legs, drink a Coke, go to the toilet, make a phone call, chat with the guy who fills your tanks (tank), get back in your vehicle, and fly (drive) on. Except the gas costs nearly twice as much, and you check your own oil. Also, air stations are set up to encourage lingering on the part of customers. Georgetown was uncomfortably hot, muggy, and close when I landed, those ten miles being apparently enough to protect it from any refreshing influences, such as sea breezes, but the office was hospitable according to the tropical theme. Besides the standard prints of dogfighting Spads and Fokkers on the walls, the usual fly-in trophy named for a dead aerobatic champ on a shelf, the Snoopy jewelry (what did we do before we had that dog to express so benignly our love of pose?) in the display case, the office had two armchairs of woven rattan with high backs shaped like lotus leaves, a chaise longue also of rattan, a coffee table the size and shape of a dugout canoe, five bamboo-handled brooms— or were some of them fans?—propped decoratively against one wall, and a glass case with nothing in it but beautiful pink, brown, and white seashells.

As soon as I stepped in, a man behind the counter offered me a lemonade. He had red hair and eyebrows and the body of a defensive tackle. He told me the lemonade was homemade, as if I had to be talked into it, then went to another room and came back with two glasses, one for him and one for me. He drank his lemonade while standing behind the counter and I had mine on the chaise longue while fanning myself with an aviation magazine, like any tourist in old Malay. I asked about the furniture. He said he'd been stationed with the Navy in the Philippines for 15 years, and when he traveled around to different islands he'd pick things up. Last year he retired from the Navy and was offered the airport job and decided to put the furniture in the office. He thought it would give the place a lift. He thought customers would like it.

Clearly he had been betrayed by his hopes. His face grew flushed as he spoke. "Twelve hours a day, seven days a week, I put in here and so do my boys—one's 18 and one's 20—and still we don't make half what I made by myself in the Navy." He spat the words out. "You'll never get rich in *this* business." He left the room again and came back with two more lemonades. From where I lay on the chaise I could see his rosy face and hair through the glass case with the seashells. "Why do you stay?" I asked, expecting him to say he *wasn't* going to stay, not one minute longer than he absolutely had to. But he just looked pensive. I could see he was taking the question seriously. It was hard to believe he hadn't thought about it before. When he finally answered his voice had been altered by something—the same old love?—and he said quietly but firmly, "Travel." No longer asking for sympathy, from me or anybody, accepting the difficult compromise, "Because with aviation you get to travel."

. . . So are we all caught in the undertow. Another time when I was at Georgetown, a couple of years before when the office had nothing of the South Pacific to it, I had flown in through light rain and haze beneath a thousand-foot ceiling and crossed paths in the office with a man who had been flying up from Charleston, through the same stuff. He had a woman and baby with him. As he talked on the phone to Flight Service, getting the weather ahead, the woman stood a few feet away from him, in a pale print dress, leaning on a wall, a dreamy look on her face, maybe listening to him and maybe not, holding the sleeping child in her arms. Together she and the baby presented a picture of such trust and vulnerability that it occurred to me what a burden it must be to carry passengers in weather like this. How much easier to be flying alone! The man handled his briefing well enough, asking questions and taking notes, but his mouth gave him away; it was dry with fear, made little ticking sounds whenever he spoke and his tongue pulled away from his gums and teeth. The weather wasn't really dire (after all, we were both going on), but it wasn't great either, and what was more, the land we'd be flying over wasn't great—mostly mush, miles of salt marsh and uninhabited boggy islands.

I didn't see anything about the little family on TV that night, so I assume they made it through all right. *I* made it through all right, but on the way became a little dry-mouthed myself. About midway between Georgetown and Charleston (rather Johns Island, a field 15 miles south of the main Charleston airport), when I was over nothing firmer than a grackle's nest and the rain was falling in a light and steady spray, I became aware that the sound of my engine had coarsened. Pulling carburetor heat (drawing hot air into the carburetor throat in order to melt ice formed there by the rapid cooling of water vapor, which could block air intake even on days so warm that the only ice you're thinking about is in your lemonade) didn't help. There weren't any airstrips around then to go into, so all I could do was sit and listen and hope the sound didn't get worse. I was listening so hard that I was probably picking up the rapping of the valve lifters, usually subsumed by the pulses of the engine firing and the prop blades slapping the air.

At Johns Island, I asked some pilots who were hanging around what they thought might be wrong, after describing the sound to them. Despite the rain, there were quite a few pilots around to ask. A couple were inside the office, a trailer at the end of a line of small hangars, but several more were outdoors, without umbrellas, looking quite at their ease, glad to be where they were, getting sprinkled on, in the company of other pilots. Several gathered cheerfully around my cowling, took their time poking at the engine and making their diagnosis: a fouled spark plug, which is what I had been thinking.

This time on the Georgetown-to-Charleston leg everything seemed different, as if it were a new route to a new place. The sky was cloudless if hazy, the cockpit cozy yet buoyant, floating in light. The engine thrummed with the steadiness of a high-mountain stream. On the ground at Johns Island, too, everything seemed different, but not better. Gone was the little trailer and the T and lean-to hangars the pilots were hanging around. Gone, too, were the pilots. Instead there was a ramp the size of a shopping-mall parking lot, a terminal the size of a warehouse, three hangars each of which could hold several of the old hangars, plus two hangars only slightly less huge. Surveying the inflated scene, I felt a strong sense of loss: another old-style human-scale bullshitting little airport gone. Sacrificed to upgrading, a better business image. I tried to be adult about it, telling myself that not everyone could be expected to run an airport for the love of it, for the Flying in his Blood or the Seashells on his Mind. But I couldn't forget those pilots, how contentedly they'd been milling around, how at home they'd seemed, as if the airport belonged at least half to them.

There was one pilot in the office, with its unscarred wood paneling, bare flight-planning table, and new, empty chairs. The man at the desk introduced him as Frank Garcia, a customs officer on narcotics duty, former sky marshal from Puerto Rico. What, I asked, was a customs officer doing at Johns Island? "Looking for suspicious airplanes," said Garcia. What, I asked, was a suspicious airplane? Garcia opened his briefcase, took out a sheet of paper, and handed it to me. It was a list with a lead-in paragraph.

> The following activities and circumstances when coupled with abnormal behavior of the aircraft operator may indicate smuggling activity
> Unusual odors about aircraft . . .
> Arrival extremely low on fuel . . .
> Closed curtains, remote parking . . .
> Display of large sums of cash by aircrew . . .
> Maps and charts of foreign countries, especially in the Caribbean or South American areas.
> Pilot reluctance to discuss destination . . .
> Numerous cardboard boxes, duffel bags, plastic bags etc. inside aircraft.

Only the last one, or maybe two, applied to me, but they weren't yet coupled with abnormal behavior, whatever that was. Garcia said he had to go out looking for suspicious airplanes because nobody called and gave him leads or tips in time. "They always call after the fact," he complained. "By the time we reach the airport it's too late." For example, a few weeks before, an FBO at nearby Walterboro airport called to report that a DC-4 had landed four days earlier, but the pilot didn't check in or come back for his plane. When agents arrived at Walterboro they found marijuana seeds all over the floor of the DC-4 (good example of suspicious airplane), seized it (and the seeds), but never did find the leaves or the person who could afford to abandon a $300,000 aircraft.

Garcia was leaving for Charleston and gave me a lift into town, in an old car with handcuffs dangling from the air-conditioner knob. He told me on the drive in that a couple of times a month he rented a Cessna 172 from Johns Island so he could fly along the coast looking for suspicious boats. What, I asked, was a suspicious boat? "A shrimp boat without nets," he said. "Or a boat with excessive electronic equipment. Or a large boat with small boats meeting it." He talked about his work the whole ride, always in a manner that suggested lots of risk-taking and intrigue. By word and tone he gave the impression that there were dangerous thrills at every turn. But in the course of listening to him, I figured out that in his two years on narcotics duty he hadn't caught a single person doing anything wrong. He hadn't made one arrest yet. Which didn't curb his impulse for melodrama a bit. When he let me off on a street corner in Old Charleston and started to drive away, he leaned out and shouted, as if he were heading into a fiery ambush set especially for him, "Never a dull moment!"

Old Charleston seemed to be deserted that day. A few dogged tourists were dragging themselves from restored house to restored house in the excoriating heat, but that was about it. I took one house tour myself but otherwise stayed outdoors, wandering up and down the streets and marveling at the lovely houses with their front and side verandas, often two or three stories high, wrought-iron balconies, courtyards, and gardens, all those places meant to refresh the inhabitants of Charleston and allow them to take the air while enjoying the sight of their flowers and neighbors. In not one of those places, though, did I see a single human being. Not one woman, man, or child sitting in the shade so artfully arranged for them and sipping a mint julep, waving a funeral fan, munching on a praline, playing poker, shelling black-eyed peas, or whistling Dixie. Air-conditioning, I guessed, had changed all that, if any of it ever was.

After dark, I went back to Johns Island to sleep. So far on the trip I hadn't slept out under my wing, that ultimate expression of the plane-pilot partnership, because the days had been so hot that I was going to motels not so much to sleep as to shower. Earlier that day, though, two linemen had offered to let me sleep in a hangar that night, and the hangar they had in mind was the plane-wash, since it had a hose, water, and floor drain. One lineman was still around when I got back from Charleston and together we rolled the Luscombe into the hangar. He told me I'd have to stay inside with the doors closed since the airport owner didn't like people staying on the field overnight and I couldn't let him see me.

While I made up my bed on the hangar floor—space blanket down first, to keep everything else clean, then cushions from the cockpit laid end to end as a fairly hard, excessively contoured mattress, then sleeping bag zipped up as a second, softer mattress, then, as topsheet, a flowered cloth which often tripled as tablecloth and sarong—the lineman was trying to slide the hangar doors shut. Even with the doors open, however, the air in the hangar was suffocatingly hot, the metal hangar making for a perfect solar oven. That must have been the kind of air mosquitoes loved, because most of them on the island (voting with their wings) had come to take advantage of it. Sweating, slapping, swatting, and scratching, I began to get the idea that my chances of going to bed refreshed by a mere shower were not good. The lineman, a tall, sweet-natured young man named Ray, must have been thinking along the same lines because, after informing me that one of the doors kept coming off track and therefore he couldn't shut them, he said I could stay the night at his parents' house if I wanted. Poor kid; each good deed he did seemed to oblige him to another.

As we walked in their front door, I wondered what his parents would think of their son bringing home a sweaty, mosquito-bitten, bedraggled older woman he didn't know who had been trying to sleep and shower on a hangar floor that night, but they just looked up politely from the TV they were watching, and his mother went off to the kitchen to make iced tea and his father to the bedroom to put on a shirt. Afterward the four of us sat around drinking the tea and talking about Ray. How as a boy he would run out of the house every time he heard an airplane overhead and stand looking up. How he had a great library of flying books; they were the only books he'd buy, or read. How he had worked after school and on weekends to earn money to take flight lessons and after graduation worked to put himself through flight school in Florida and earn his advanced ratings. How for two years he'd been trying to get a job as a pilot, had applied to airlines, charter companies, and corporations, kept applying and reapplying, but still hadn't been hired. You had to know somebody, the mother said, sounding sad but accepting, or have experience, a job already, that was how it was. Recently, Ray had applied to United Airlines for training—as a flight attendant. I felt sad myself. It seemed to me that handing out drinks while other people were piloting a plane you desperately wanted to fly yourself would be more painful than not being in a plane at all.

The next morning, as I was taxiing out of my spot, another tall, dark, good-looking man (only older) ran up to my plane and started shouting above the engine noise. *Where are you from? Did you enjoy your stay in Charleston? What did you see while you were here? Where are you going now?* A persistent friendliness. "Oh, just flying around," I said. *Where to?* "Different airports. Just looking around." *What are you looking for?* "Interesting things." *There are some interesting things right here; maybe you should see.*

The man had dark eyes that seemed a bit too wide open all the time, giving him a faintly mad look. Still, I chopped the power, and in the quiet that followed he introduced himself—George Marion Reid, the airport manager. I climbed out of the plane and into his truck, and he drove far out on the field, over several hundred yards of grass, up to the edge of a woods. We got out and walked into the woods. There was no path but the going was easy. The trees were mostly pine, white and loblolly, Reid pointed out, sounding like a field guide. After a few minutes he turned and said, in a way that showed he was sure of the effect it would have on me, "There it is." Just beyond him was something as large as an airplane (a Spad perhaps), metal like an airplane, with two "wings," a "fuselage," and a "tail" rounded on top like a Parnall Pixie III's. It appeared to be intact, although the bottom third of the tail was sunk in dirt and pine needles. Clearly it couldn't have fallen in there, because it wasn't smashed up, and it couldn't have been carried in, because trees were standing close around it. Like a ship in a bottle: How did it get there?

Reid explained. During World War II Johns Island was a "bogie" field, which meant that soldiers were flown in for short periods to practice setting up their tents, getting the field operational, etc., as if it were an invaded country, and there had been nothing but grass here then, no trees to keep the thing from swinging in the breezes. The breezes: It was a wind tee (a sort of ground-based weathervane), the largest wind tee I had ever seen, maybe as large as they got, and it was built, as many tees were, to look like an airplane landing nose to the wind (pilot see, pilot do). "This thing guided B-25s in here," Reid said, sounding impressed himself. After the war, when the airport was deeded to the county, as dozens of military airports across the country were deeded to the counties they were in as part of the War Powers Act of 1946, nobody bothered to cut the seedlings that sprouted around the big tee. They grew until they stopped the tee's free swing, kept growing until they cast shade on it, grew until they'd hidden it from the sight of pilots flying overhead, then from the sight of pilots taxiing on the airport grounds. It was an eerie thing to behold, a "plane" among trees, quite out of its element, like a sofa at the bottom of a lake.

"Something else you should see," Reid said, and started walking again. We exited the woods at a different place from where we entered, emerging onto a field of soybeans. The airport, he explained, leased land around the runways to farmers so the staff wouldn't have so much grass to mow. We picked our way across the field, trying not to step on any of the soybean plants, but the rows were set awkwardly far apart and we crunched a few, uttering little cries of apology. On the other side of the field we entered another woods, denser than the first, with more understory, a greater mix of trees, black oaks and nut trees along with the pines. Vines were everywhere, on branches, tree trunks, and rocks. The ground was covered with a mat of creepers, weeds, and dead leaves. Birdsong, from phoebes and mockingbirds mostly (Reid pointed out), mingled with the light that made its way through the tangled canopy and fell in broken shafts about us. The whole layered, intricate, webbed scene suggested to me, oddly enough, *human* history. What trysts, rituals, and hideouts must have been here! I vowed that if ever I came this way again I'd sleep in these woods and forget the shower. Dreams would enter the head by osmosis.

Reid was waving a branch of a sassafras tree in front of his face as he walked, to brush away spiderwebs; they caught on his face anyhow. After a while the trees thinned and the ground swelled to form a large, inverted bowl of grass and Reid stopped and looked around as if satisfied. "Four or five thousand Confederate soldiers camped here when they were guarding the Stono River from the Yankees," he said. He pointed. *"This* is probably where they pitched their tents." He pointed again. *"This* was a revetment. The guns were probably *here.* And *this"*—he stood at the top of a shallow slope, where the grass was a brighter green than any of the other grass around—"was the moat." He told me the Confederate soldiers had built the fort entirely of dirt, and they built it themselves. "Charleston," he added, "has never forgiven Savannah for surrendering its big brick fort so easily."

We came out of the woods into another clearing, one not planted in anything except watermelons. Six people in the office took home one watermelon each almost every night from that one patch, Reid said. "Watermelons grow like crazy in newly cleared land. The minerals haven't been used up yet." Another indication that this was newly cleared land was a nightmarish pile of trees, large, twisted, and fireblackened, lying on their sides at one edge of the clearing. They were live oaks, cut down to clear the runway approaches. "Live oak's hard to cut down," he said, "but it's hell to burn. Very tough and ungiving."

He took me on a little natural-history tour of the clearing, pointing out pokeberry bushes ("We boil the leaves or put 'em in salad"), rabbit tobacco ("We smoked it when we were kids"), wild fennel ("It takes over everything"), a katydid shell, a raccoon jawbone, and raccoon droppings ("Been eating pokeberries, I see"). He shifted to military history. A gully full of weeds had been "a Yankee dump"; he found old bottles there once. He stood on the lip of the gully, looking down into it, seeing something else. "Southerners should have been like the Italians," he mused. "Friendly. *Welcomed* the Yankees. We're still trying to get out of that slump." I'd never heard a Southerner talk that way before.

We made our way back to the truck, and Reid drove it down a dirt road into yet another woods. Like many small airports, Johns Island was actually pretty large, 1,200 acres in all—300 acres planted in soybeans, 300 used for shrimp-breeding (being too low and too wet to be used for anything else), 100 or so underneath airport structures, runways, and taxiways, and 500 left in grass and trees. The road was bumpy and dead-ended in front of a live oak, still alive. It was the kind of broad-crowned, sheltering tree you could picture children growing up under, men gathering to go off to war under, teenagers courting under. Those things could really have happened. This used to be a plantation, Reid said, whether cotton or potatoes he didn't know (a *potato* plantation?). He showed me all that was left of the plantation buildings. The base of four "tabby" walls, about a foot high, from an old smokehouse, with dirty-gray fans of oyster shells still sticking up out of the homemade cement.

Claxton · Vidalia · Peterson

Once I started flying, I realized that there were other things that made it a congenial thing for me to do—that maybe what happened on the way back from Samburu wasn't fortuitous. For instance, I had always liked the vertical view of things, gazing down from my old fifth-floor apartment in Manhattan at people on the sidewalk (heads abnormally close to feet), or from the fourth ring at the opera, up by the chandelier, at singers onstage. Also, I was brought up in a preppie WASP suburb of a Midwestern city of medium size in the 1950s (can't get more white-bread than that) and, although quite happy there, I never got over wanting to be lifted into a wider, more diverse world. I was a journalist by trade and therefore nosy (or nosy and therefore a journalist), and pilots are well placed to indulge their curiosity. I liked being alone a lot, chose to live by myself in a one-bedroom apartment, even bought a one-slice toaster once, out of a concern that owning a major appliance would make me feel too tied down (the thing made my friends sad so I got rid of it). When they weren't looking I sketched people on the subway and considered the visual my main channel for response to the world. I had had a few minor attacks of claustrophobia in my life, once heard a whimper coming out of my mouth when the only way to leave a very small room I was in was to descend through a very small hole in the floor . . .

On the next legs of my trip, nosiness, of a kind that could best be satisfied on the ground, was most indulged. I planned to end the day's flight at an airport that had become a peculiar, short footnote in U.S. political history. The flight would take me inland for the first time on this trip (as before, forget Washington). Navigation would now be more complicated than remembering to keep an ocean on my left. Still, it wouldn't be all that complicated. From Johns Island, I drew a straight line on the chart, in pencil, to Claxton airport, 115 air miles away, then made marks at the 50- and 100-mile points. Next to the line, with arrows pointing in appropriate directions, I wrote the compass heading I'd be following if I stuck to the line (250 degrees), as well as the reciprocal of that heading, in case I had to beat a hasty retreat (070 degrees). Then I looked on the chart for landmarks to use as checkpoints. There were plenty of choices. About 35 miles out, for instance, Saint Helena Sound would appear off to my left; at 45 miles, Beaufort airport (BYEW-furt, South Carolina, not BOW-fort, North Carolina, home of the fishspotters) would be pretty much on my nose; at 60 miles, Route 95 would bisect my route with a bulge to my right I should be able to recognize; at 72 miles the Savannah River, doubling as the South Carolina–Georgia border, would flow by; at 80 miles a railroad would run into a town; at 85 miles a railroad would leave a town; at 105 miles there would be a conspicuous X where two highways met; and at 115 miles, *Voilà! Ecco!* and *Eureka!* Claxton would materialize on the other side of my prop.

From Johns Island I did turn inland, but the ocean was slow to let go. Waterways cut through miles and miles of marshland, weaving back and forth in long, deep curves, great, unfinished loops, as if the sea were killing time, dragging its wet feet, putting off as long as possible the moment when it would reach high ground and disappear. Every turn the waterways took, every combination of turns, seemed graceful and felicitous, the way paths traced by paper caught in eddies of wind on city streets are graceful, spiraling up and gliding down, the line of their rise and fall nearly always curved and never anything but lovely.

High ground when it did appear looked pretty unremarkable, dry and mostly flat with scrubby vegetation and a few houses and roads. There were some things on it that I found intriguing, however. I called them ''strips'' since I couldn't think of what else to call them. They appeared over the course of many miles, usually one at a time but occasionally in a rough grouping. They never took up all the space that would seem to be available to them, as you'd expect if they were under cultivation, and there was never anything near them that I could see, such as a house or road, which might shed light on what they were there for. Also, they weren't lined up in any way, for example along the same axis, and although they were all rectangles their sizes and proportions varied. Still, they seemed to be related. So what were they?

Some of them were pale brown, like unpaved roads, yet were too short to be roads. Others had a bit of greenery on them, like truck farms, yet were too small to be farms. Others were a bright green, brighter than any of the other greenery around, like lawns, yet were too isolated to be lawns. What *were* they?

Puzzles like these popped up now and then on the American landscape, tantalizing pilots overhead. What, for instance, were the four white posts with connecting white fences arranged in the shape of a clover with a white box in the center of each ''leaf'' that I once saw in central Pennsylvania? The ten pinkish-purple ridges I flew over someplace out West, which were almost straight but not quite, almost parallel but not quite, the ones on the ends shorter than the others, all set on a hilltop stripped to dirt but not quite? Or the bunker-like bumps in the middle of the desert? Always I tried to guess what the things were even though there was usually no way of finding out if I was right or wrong—the plane carried on. As for the ''strips'' I saw on a 250-degree compass heading out of Johns Island, my guess was . . . sod plots. That is, sod being grown for transplantation to suburban lawns, with the bright-green strips being the mature grass ready to be peeled off and shipped out, the pale-brown strips being the dirt exposed after the grass was dug up, and the pale-green strips being the new grass starting to grow after reseeding. But no, I thought, those small, scattered, unconnected rectangles were an inefficient way to grow anything, even grass. What *were* they?

For almost an hour; the checkpoints rolled obediently by, in the proper order; then I switched fuel tanks. Since my fuel gauges weren't accurate I calculated consumption by the clock; one hour equaled six gallons gone. I made the switch over a straight, paved road with no light poles, parked cars, or trees alongside it, since it might serve as a runway in case something went wrong in the changeover. You never knew . . .

One time my friend John had his fuel tanks filled by a lineman who was trying to chew gum at the same time and apparently couldn't manage because he let his jaw go slack at the very instant that he was peering into the mouth of a tank to check the level of the fuel. *Plunk!* Being honest as well as brave, he confessed to his boss, who asked the lineman what brand of gum he'd been chewing, bought a pack himself and chewed a piece, dropped the wad in a jar of aviation fuel, and gave the jar to John to keep an eye on. Fuel lines are generally no wider than soda straws and a sticky pellet sucked into one of them could, well, gum up the works. From time to time over the next several days John shook the bottle and skeptically eyed the diaphanous filaments forming in it. After a week all he had was a "beautiful, clean bottle of fuel." Still skeptical, however, the next time he went flying he took off on the gumless tank and "only switched to the other one at a nice altitude."

At mile 115, *Ecco!* Claxton airport in Claxton, Georgia, "home of the Claxton fruitcake." The one other time I was in Claxton I didn't eat a Claxton fruitcake, but I did eat one once. A New York friend whose mother had given it to him for Christmas—the *previous* Christmas—gave it to me; he didn't like fruitcake and kept it in his refrigerator for a year until he met someone who did. The time I was there before, Claxton didn't seem to me a very fruitcake kind of place, or rather I didn't have a fruitcake kind of time; it had nothing sweet or celebratory to it. I hadn't even wanted to go there. The day had been hot and hazy and I was on my way to Savannah when lightning flashed somewhere in the clogged air mass ahead and I took a new compass heading to get around it, then saw lightning flash on my new heading and decided to go down and figure out what to do next. The nearest airport happened to be Claxton.

Two men were standing by the fuel pumps talking as I taxied in, sturdy middle-aged men with roomy bellies, looking as if they'd settled into something comfortable, bodies angled back a bit, hands in overall pockets. They kept talking even after I approached them, clearly business, a customer wanting fuel. I stood listening to them, waiting my turn. They were discussing an airplane crash that had taken place the previous February, although they talked about it as if it were fresh news. A man had been flying alone, at night, near Claxton, in a Cessna 310, and got caught in a thunderstorm.

"The wings fell off," one of the men said, with a satisfied look on his face. The other man looked pleased in his own way. As hangar stories went, it wasn't bad, I had to admit. It took place close enough to Claxton that the men could share in the glamour of violence (which airplane crashes provide about as well as anything), yet not near enough that they would be likely to know the pilot and be grieving. It encouraged a sense of superiority in the tellers: The pilot had been overconfident (*I* wouldn't have gone up in that stuff, one man implied by his tone) and been given the ultimate reprimand for his arrogance (died immediately), thus reconfirming the moral force of Nature.

The hangar story was pleasing to them because they were on the ground, but to me, hoping to fly on once I'd figured out the best way to do it: The wings fell off! I decided to sort things out over lunch and borrowed a car so I could drive to a restaurant down the road from the airport. As I stepped into the restaurant, the chairs and tables heaved slightly, as if I were on a boat (something that happened occasionally when I'd flown for a long time in haze). A waitress asked if I'd mind sitting at a table instead of a booth since the floor around the booths was wet from mopping, and I had to tell her I *would* mind. I realized even as she asked that I couldn't sit as upright as a chair demanded for as long as it took to eat a meal, or endure the knobs of the chair rungs pressing into my back, which suddenly seemed tender, as if the skin were stretched too tight. I took a seat in a booth next to a window overlooking a highway, and as I was reading the menu I became aware that something was going on outside—a landing! I jerked my head around and saw a car moving down the highway, at about the speed of an airplane on rollout. Time to quit flying for the day, I thought. No matter what was lying in wait for me out there in the haze, the haze itself had already done me in.

One of the men who had been standing, rocking at the pumps was the manager of Claxton airport. Also the father of the young man who'd loaned me his car. Father and son, as well as wife and daughter, worked at the airport. "Everybody's got to help," said the father. "It's a 24-hour-a-day job." They were from Texas. "Transplants," the father called them. They lived together in a trailer back of the office. This time when I landed at Claxton, I didn't find any of them. The trailer was gone. The office door was locked and I could see through a window that the furniture was gone too. Only two planes were tied down on the ramp. I walked around looking for signs of life but didn't discover any. The hangar was closed and the concrete picnic table someone had built beside the ramp, probably with high hopes for jolly times, was empty. All I could hear as I wandered around was the clank of a bare flagpole wire being blown against a flagpole, clank clank, tolling the end of something. I felt bad for the Texans, having to give it all up, after working so hard, everybody helping out.

I left not knowing if Claxton airport was dead, dying, or just resting, waiting for another manager to show up, believing he could make a go of it. I was afraid it was one of the dead ones. Little airports come and go, but nowadays they mostly go. In a period of just over ten years I'd seen 15 small airports within 50 miles of my airport disappear. The runways X'd out, plowed under, paved over, and built upon. One of the nightmares we have as pilots is that someday we'll get airborne and have no place to land except the place we started out from—and if we don't hurry back, it will be gone too.

Once I read an elegy in "Luscombe Talk" for Hales Corners, a dying airport in Wisconsin. There, the grieving author wrote, he had learned to fly, brought his first airplane to be tied down, flown in and out for many happy years on the way to and from picnics, fly-ins, and family outings. Recently the airport was zoned for condominiums, over the objections of about everybody connected with it, but nothing could be done to save it from the demolition crews. He compared a trip to the airport in its last days to "a visit to a friend suffering from terminal cancer. The only things that will be real will be the condominiums . . . and the memories."

Claxton, surrounded by pine woods and tobacco farms, didn't seem a candidate for condos or malls, so the airport might have been suffering from starvation, not enough business. Whichever, there was no question of getting fuel, so I got back in my plane, batted a wasp out of the cockpit, and took off for the next airport west, which happened to be in Vidalia, Georgia—home of the sweet Vidalia onions, I presumed, counterpart to the sweet Claxton fruitcake. There I saw signs of life, if not very active life, as soon as I taxied in. A man and woman were sitting immobile on folding chairs in the shade of a large gray hangar. There was only about a foot of shade but they were pressed into it; it was noon and that's all there was. When I stopped at the pumps the man got up and slowly made his way over. He chatted for a while before getting around to giving me fuel. I noticed that his face resembled Gerald Ford's in some ways and Archie Bunker's in some ways and as he talked and the angle of his face changed so did his likeness; it slid from one to the other, like those postcards of Christ's mournful face with eyes that open and shut and open as you tip the card, he became first one man, then the other, Ford, Bunker, Ford, Bunker. It was fascinating to watch.

We had Pepsis together in the terminal, and Bunkford told me his real name was B. E. Nobles but everybody called him "Kin." "There weren't any boys in our family and my father wanted a boy so when I came along they called me 'Kin,' " he said. Later, another boy was born to the clan, a cousin named "Flournoy," or "Floogie," but everybody kept calling him "Kin" anyway. I noticed he kept calling the woman he'd been sitting in the shade with "Mama," although I couldn't tell from looking at her closely whenever she passed through the terminal if she was his own mother or the mother of his children.

Fordkin followed me out to my plane (there wasn't a lot else to do) and sent me off with a couple of pleasantries. "Have you drained your water?" he asked slyly, referring to the practice pilots have of taking samples of fuel from their tanks during preflight inspections to check for condensed water. Then, giggling at his raunchiness, he added, "I don't mean that *personally.*" When I started the engine and called out the window to ask, "Which runway are you using?" he laid his hand upon his heart and intoned, as if to confess a new infatuation, "Two-Four. It's my *fay*-vorite runway!"

From Kinford's beloved I flew west, over woods, mostly, with only a few scraggly-edged farms scraped out of the nap and an occasional small, still pond set into it. Tiny clouds were reflected on the surfaces of the ponds and, since I was low, as I flew by, the clouds whipped across them. At one point I passed what I was sure was a field of watermelons; from above it looked like the night sky, studded with pale green stars. The airport I was aiming for was 115 miles farther on—the closest one to the peanut farm, the Southern White House, the red-white-and-blue-striped water tower in downtown Plains, Georgia. The grass runway there had probably experienced more high-level traffic than any other grass runway in world history. In little more than two years, its 4,410 feet had felt the weight of countless U.S. senators and congressmen, heads of federal agencies, foreign ambassadors, cabinet members, cabinet hopefuls, Secret Servicemen, Democratic party officials, journalists, photographers, aides to the candidate for President, and the candidate himself. By the time I arrived to take a look at it, however, the airport was so peaceful that all I could hear after shutdown was the rustle of dry husks in the cornfields on either side of the runway.

At first it seemed to be an airport like the others. A Skyhawk sat on the ramp, stripped to its silver aluminum skin for spray-painting, with an even brighter silver strip of kitchen foil taped across its windscreen. An Ag Truck was parked on the grass, with its cowling up and a semicircle of tools and oily engine parts spread neatly on the ground beside it, as if prepped for surgery. A collie was lying on the floor just inside the hangar door, asleep. In the office, though, there was a poster on the wall with a winged peanut on it. SEE JIMMY CARTER's HOUSE & PLAINS BY AIR, it said. $5 PER PERSON. As I was looking at it, a man walked in, and I recognized him, from a photo I'd seen in an aviation magazine. He was tall and thin with a long, thin face, long, thin nose, thin lips but broad smile. (Yet another smile, I thought, for yet another tourist?) He was the man the airport was named after, or rather the man who'd named the airport after himself, Tom Peterson. He said he was on his way to his house to get some iced tea, and did I want some? (Yet another iced tea, I thought, for yet another visitor?) The house was a few yards from the office, a white bungalow with black shutters and yellow marigolds by the front steps. Lest he forget for a moment where he was, the living room had a picture window in it looking out onto the runway. Peterson fixed the iced tea himself, explaining that his wife was away at her mother's. "The campaign was traumatic for her," he confided. There was no privacy. Newsmen would come knocking on the side of the house at two o'clock in the morning and just *beg* me to fly some film or piece of copy to Atlanta, which just *had* to get there by four. Well, I saw what it all was, the old free enterprise, and I'd go fly and get my money, but she hated it. She said it gave her headaches."

While drinking my tea, I sat on the living-room sofa, which was where "priority people" sat during the campaign, Peterson said. "Interviewing was allowed on the porch and the parking lot but not in here; the truce was to come into the house." He explained how it all started. One day a black limousine pulled into the airport parking lot and a man got out. He walked over to Peterson, held out his hand, and said, "I'm Jimmy Carter and we're going to do a lot of flying together." They did, at first in a Cessna 172—"it was all he'd pay for." Carter would sit in the front seat next to Peterson and fiddle with the radio dials, sometimes speaking to the tower himself. As his political position improved, however, Secret Servicemen began urging him to fly in something with more than one engine, as they were already doing themselves. He stayed with the 172 for a while longer, then gave in and moved up to a Cessna 310, by which time the Secret Servicemen themselves had moved up to Learjets and Citations.

If eyes can be said to sparkle, Peterson's did now. "We'd *still* beat them to Atlanta some days," he said. "We'd stay low after takeoff and not talk to Center and we'd hear them ask the tower to ask us if we'd mind slowing down and Carter would get on the radio and say we *would* mind and we'd go right in. The Secret Service would be furious." The satisfaction of making the Secret Service furious was one of the few compensations he got for the hardships of a Presidential primary campaign as visited upon his airport. On days when Carter was in Plains the field was often jammed with people, all needing a ride somewhere or a meeting with someone or papers flown someplace, the use of a telephone, a toilet, something. On a single day in June, Peterson and the crew he'd pulled together from the local pilot supply flew 24 round trips to Atlanta, in planes he'd scraped together from the local supply too, including a Citabria belonging to a neighboring farmer. The den of his house was turned into a "control room" from which Peterson dispatched his little fleet and assigned seats to those clamoring for them.

Meanwhile the Secret Service seemed to consider the whole enterprise—small airport (grass runway, for God's sake), small-town pilot, small airplanes—about as safe as cape-jumping from a spinning Finch. (Carter himself seemed never to be afraid.) In Peterson's view, the agents objected to the wrong things and made a tough job tougher. They didn't know anything about general aviation to start with and rotated in and out of "Carter duty" so fast they didn't have time to learn. For example, an agent once ordered Peterson to set aside for himself and six other agents the first seven seats on a Cessna 172, which has four seats in all. Another time an agent demanded the first 17 seats on a Cessna 310, which has a total of six seats. Then there was the time Peterson got a call from a Secret Serviceman who'd seen a pilot spraying insecticide on Billy Carter's peanuts and screamed into the phone, "An *idiot* is bombing the house!"

After he became President, Carter traveled to and from Plains in a Marine helicopter, so he didn't need Peterson to fly him around anymore. Once in a while, when there was a Carter "activity" such as a funeral or delegation of farmers, the airport would get busy and Peterson might set up a hot-dog stand outside the office to take advantage of the crowd, but mostly it was history. He went back to doing what he'd done before, testing, repairing, and selling airplanes, towing gliders, teaching flying, and flying charters. The charters were mostly ferry trips from the Atlanta airport to neighboring plantation strips, to bring guests in for weekend quail hunts. "We do a lot with their dogs too," Peterson said. "There's a man who calls us from Cleveland where he has a house and tells us to pick up his hunting dogs and wife in DelRay Beach [Florida], where he has a house, and fly them to Albany [Georgia], where he has a plantation." He also flew plantation owners off their own strips to the Bahamas for weekends. When I raised my eyebrows at this, he said, "In this country, you're either rich or you're poor."

Peterson turned out to be far closer to the latter than to the former, despite his high-level connection and having turned his airport, not to mention his home, over to a major American event for a couple of years. He wasn't much better off than the day the limousine pulled into the parking lot. "Plenty of money has flowed through here since Carter showed up," he admitted. "I just haven't been able to keep much of it. I made some mistakes." He said this without apparent resentment or even regret, in as matter-of-fact a manner as if he were telling me hens lay brown eggs or the sun rises behind the hangar in winter. "I'll just keep on here," he said, a serene look on his narrow face. "I've been flying since I was ten years old. Flying is all I've ever done, and it is all I'll ever do." Whether or not he made much money in the flying game seemed not to change the essential fact: He was in it.

I made him $4 richer that night by renting his pickup truck—one the Secret Serviceman had had to ride in the back of, much to their dismay and Peterson's delight—so I could see Plains the next morning. There were two restaurants in Plains, but neither one was open for breakfast that day, so I went to a souvenir store and bought a peanut-butter ice-cream cone and a bag of "Georgia peanuts" and had those. The peanuts were so small that I felt embarrassed for Carter, as if their dinkiness reflected on him. The clerk in the store told me eagerly that her son lived next door to Miss Lillian. Then, sounding contrite, she added, "He didn't get to see her much, though."

After breakfast, I had to take the truck back to the airport, briefly, so someone there could run an errand with it. She turned out to be a female mechanic Peterson had hired for the summer, and her errand was to buy food for a flight he was making that night to Guatemala to deliver a spray plane to a farmer who'd just bought it. Would he have sent a male mechanic to buy food for him? I wondered. The woman had red hair that hung straight to her waist and called herself Carrot Top. She asked me to come to the supermarket with her while she picked out the food. The food she picked out, after much walking up and down the aisles, was a jar of peanut butter (small), a box of Ritz crackers, a bag of dried peaches, and a box of animal crackers. The animal crackers were "for a treat, when he's over the Gulf of Mexico," she said, but even with them thrown in there didn't seem to be enough there to keep a pilot's strength up past Galveston.

Carrot Top had come to Peterson's that summer, she told me as we took the food back to the airport, to repair some of his planes, but her specialty was restoring *old* planes, preferably *historic* old planes. Originally she had planned to be a schoolteacher, but she fell in love with an aerobatic pilot and "it messed up my head. I didn't care if the sun came up or the dog got fed." She started going to competitions with her boyfriend and helping tend his plane, waxing it, polishing it, fetching oil, etc. At one meet an official of an air museum in the Midwest saw her working and asked if she'd like to work for the museum instead. She decided she would but didn't intend to stay long: It would only be a matter of time before the aerobatic pilot would ask her to marry him.

She began by varnishing bookshelves at the museum, moved on to varnishing airplane wings, then to "making fittings no one else wanted to make." She became "a pro, one of the best workers there," she said, and stayed longer than she'd expected. The pilot wrote her that he didn't want to get married. Hurt, angry, she decided to build herself an airplane of the same make and model as the one he flew, an Akro Sport. "I'll show *him,*" she said, and never stopped trying.

For two whole years, every morning from 6 to 8:30 before she went to work at the museum and every evening from 6 to 10 after she came home, plus all day both days of every weekend and every holiday including Christmas and Easter, Carrot Top worked on the plane. "No dates, no going out, no nothing," she said. She built it in her living room. "My goals had to be small. I'd do one little thing at a time. I could never look at the whole. I couldn't even put a picture of the plane in my room." When it was finished, after 2,000 hours of work, she painted it blue and gold and christened it Scott—*not* the name of her boyfriend. "I think of my plane as a young boy," she explained. "I would tell people, 'I have a date with Scott.' " That reminded me of how Mary McGaffney, Women's World Aerobatic Champion once and U.S. Woman's Aerobatic Champion five times, said she thought of her Pitts Special: as "a little boy. We get along just fine," she remarked. "He doesn't seem to mind or even know the difference who's flying." I realized then that I didn't think of my plane as a boy *or* girl, although the Luscombe's lines are daintier than most, but rather as a pet, like a dog whose gender doesn't particularly matter, a friendly, reliable animal pal.

Carrot Top claimed to be the first woman in the U.S. to build her own biplane. She'd *heard* about a woman who built her own monoplane, but the evidence for that, she said, was "questionable." Meaning: Men probably helped. Men helping at airports was something a woman had to watch out for. "The biggest problem I have," she insisted, "is people thinking I got where I did because of men. I warn a lot of the other gals about the facts of life at an airport. 'You can easily get into trouble,' I say. 'Beware. Be on your guard. Men *expect* things.' You wouldn't *believe* some of the stuff I've gone through when I've asked men a simple question!"

Once she got her A & P (Airframe and Powerplant) license, Carrot Top took her father's advice: "Don't waste your life in one place." She left the museum and became a free-lance mechanic, going wherever she was needed to bring new life to old planes. She went to Denver to rebuild an American Eagle, somewhere else to restore a Laird Super Solution, another place in the country to reconstruct a Kinner. After fixing up Peterson's collection of planes, she planned to travel to the annual convention of the Experimental Aircraft Association in Oshkosh, Wisconsin, the largest gathering of lightplanes and lightplane pilots in the world, to teach a class in aluminum and steel welding. "For women only," she said, "to make their hubbies happy." After that she'd head for Lakeland, Florida, where she'd fix up a J-3 Cub that belonged to a Chicago restaurant owner. He wanted to hang the Cub from the ceiling of his steak house. However, he wanted it without its fabric covering. His customers, he thought, should know what a plane looked like inside: the tubular-steel skeleton, the control cables, the instrument panel. Carrot Top agreed to leave the fabric off but insisted on putting the rest of the plane in perfect working order, to the point where it could fly if only it had a skin. For her it had to be airworthy even though it would probably never leave the airspace above half-eaten T-bone steaks and baked potatoes with smears of sour cream. That was her sort of integrity. Men at airports might not understand that at first. They'd see the long, straight red hair, the skinny legs sticking out from under short shorts, the freckled face with no makeup, the T-shirt with nearly flat chest under it, and maybe they'd offer to help the little girl. Only later would they discover the steel underneath, the will, the integrity, and probably the anger that wouldn't go away.

I saw her again when I got back from Andersonville, the Civil War prison and cemetery not far from Plains. She was in Peterson's hangar holding a torch to the door hinge of a Cessna 172. Her hair was tucked under a railroad engineer's cap, where the flame couldn't get to it, and her mouth was set in concentration. She was so absorbed in her work that she hardly looked up when I said goodbye. The 172 she was working on, as it happened, was the very one that Jimmy Carter had ridden around in, back when it was all ahead of him.

Dawson

I don't know if generalizations can be made about female pilots, although people do make them. Those who say things to your face may say that women have a more delicate, or sensitive, touch, which helps. Maybe it does; any good instructor will tell you that gentleness and smoothness in handling controls are key, and maybe gentleness comes easier to women, who knows. Then there's the old one about women being better at detail (cross-stitching and all that), and flying well certainly involves attention to detail. In my own experience the one area where I believe that as a female I came *less* prepared to fly a plane than the average male, aside from not having all those years of automatic exposure to machinery that boys got when I was growing up, is in planning or thinking ahead while aloft. If I was up flying with my friend Ron, for instance, through some breathtakingly lovely sky and countryside, I'd be much more likely than he to be grooving on the whole scene, paying attention to the current moment and place, while he'd be figuring out the compass heading for a 45-degree entry into the expected pattern at an airport we were planning to land at 50 miles away. Women are supposed to respond in a more cosmic way sexually than men, so maybe I came by my Gestalt approach naturally, although who knows that either. What I do know is that I sometimes found it difficult to take my mind off the real and engrossing present when airborne and put it on the theoretical (and often sterile-seeming) future, unless of course there was an urgent need to do so.

Another woman pilot besides Carrot Top was at Peterson's when I was there. She came to the house while he and I were having iced tea and talking about Carter. She sat on the priority sofa next to me, her dark hair curled neat as a snood around her head. The straps of her kelly-green sandals, I noticed, were narrow as rose stems, and her stylish dress was unwrinkled. Her nails were manicured, her powder was dry, and her speech was soft and tuneful. As she sat thus beside me on the sofa, cool, poised, feminine, and intact, I became aware as I had not been before that my own hair, after the flight from Vidalia, had worked itself halfway out of the barrette and was sticking out from my head in straw-like clumps. That my face and arms were gummy with sweat and my ankles and sneakers coated with dust. That my blush-on had long ago sunk in. That I was dressed just right for a game of street baseball. The woman spoke almost exclusively to Peterson the whole time she was there, seeming hardly aware of me; therefore it came as a bit of a surprise when, as I stood up to go fetch the pickup truck, she turned, looked me full in the face, and said without hesitation, as if this was what she had come for all along, "Would you like to visit the largest peanut-butter factory in the world?"

Hmmmmmmmm. "They give tours," she went on, not rushing, self-possessed, sure I would say yes. "It's real interesting." She lived in Dawson, 20 miles from Plains, she said, and I could fly to the airport there and she'd pick me up and take me to the factory. Was this the essence of Southern hospitality, I wondered, you offered whatever it was you had to people who appeared in need of refreshment? I said I would like to see a peanut-butter factory, I had never seen one, and the next day when I got back from Andersonville I phoned her and said I was leaving Peterson's. What I didn't tell her was that I'd be making a detour on the way.

Someone at Peterson's, or maybe it was someone at Vidalia, had told me that Charles Lindbergh before he flew his first official solo spent three days sitting on a water tower overlooking the runway at the airport in Americus, Georgia, studying other people's takeoffs and landings. Since Americus was only ten miles from Peterson's I thought I'd drop in there before going to Dawson, to see the tower, if it was still standing (water towers tend to be long-lived), or its replacement if it wasn't, and get a sense of the occasion. There turned out to be *three* water towers at Americus, all about the same size and same indeterminate age, all on the same side of the runway and same distance from it, none better in any obvious way than the others as a place to sit and watch takeoffs and landings from. Not having the time to ask which was which, I taxied from the end of the runway around to the beginning of it and took off. I had just begun my climbout when a plaintive voice came over the radio. "Aren't you even going to stop

and *talk* to us?'' I came around and landed again, without really intending to, pulled down by some notion of etiquette left over from my
childhood, some rule about not offending a host, not eating and running, or a relict guilt about always flying off somewhere.

The voice came from a charter pilot, forced to stay in the office in
case somebody should call and order a charter. Restless, bored, he
promised me free potato chips and Coke if I would stay and talk to
him. I told him I couldn't stay but I would like to ask him something
before I left. Which of those water towers out there did Charles Lindbergh sit on for three days before flying his first official solo? Clearly
the man didn't know what I was talking about; he hadn't heard anything about Lindbergh and any water tower. I'd learned that he was
from Detroit, but he had been at Americus for two years, which would
seem long enough for him to have heard about the water tower if
anybody there cared about it. I left feeling a little let down. I hadn't
expected the tower to be an aviation shrine exactly, promoted by town
boosters and painted up in red, white, and blue stripes like the one in
Plains, but I had expected it to be a landmark of sorts, worth pointing
out to pilots passing through at least, worth acknowledging in some
way or other: a large and not undignified monument to the Lone
Eagle's first official flight alone.

I got to Dawson too late to see the peanut-butter factory, but Laura
didn't seem to mind. She appeared as unruffled as ever, and with the
same blend of graciousness and authority she had shown in asking me
to Dawson in the first place told me I could have dinner with her
family, stay overnight at their house, and we'd go to the factory tomorrow. Her house was as well-groomed and elegant as she, with
plenty of antique furniture and old china. I was to sleep in the ''former
slaves' quarters,'' a small wooden building at the back of the back
yard, where her 15-year-old daughter stayed. Another daughter, age
10, was away that day at the state prison, riding horseback with the
children of the warden (inmates serving as grooms), and a 9-year-old
son came home while we were having cocktails, his hair still damp
from a swim.

Laura's husband, Jim, was a handsome, cuddly-looking man who
had a degree in Russian literature from Emerson, she told me at dinner. He designed pig environments for a living, which meant he combined elements like slatted floors, automatic feeders, and heating units

so pigs could be raised from birth to death without ever having to go outdoors. Over dinner we talked about regional foods; they said people around there ate things like guinea, squirrel, and robin. *Robin!* I gasped. Well, they said, *they* never ate robin, but they knew people who *did*. Afterward we talked about flying. Laura was only the second woman in the history of the county to get a pilot's license. Jim had been the one taking lessons, with the intention of buying a plane so he could save time by flying instead of driving to his jobs, some of them in different states. On the day of his first solo Laura came to watch, and after he made it down his instructor offered her a ride in the same plane. She liked the ride so much she came back the next day for another one. The day after that she came back for a lesson. She kept coming back until she had her license. Meanwhile, Jim quit. "I decided she'd do the flying for both of us," he said gamely.

The next morning, before going to the peanut-butter factory, Laura showed me the sights of Dawson as she understood them: a yellow frame house with a picket fence where a famous nightclub performer with a dirty puppet act was reared. A thrift shop with a chihuahua sleeping on the cash-register ledge. The office of *The Dawson News*, whose editor said he would have our photo taken beside my plane and run it in the next edition. There was no testing of the waters in all this; she just showed me what she thought I'd find interesting, confident that she was right (she was).

As for the peanut-butter factory, it was essentially one high-ceilinged room with large machines chugging away around the edges. Some of the machines, said our guide, were grinding up peanuts to make "sprinkles" for ice-cream sundaes, and some of them were pressing peanuts into butter. We watched as a fat, excrement-like stream of yellow-brown butter oozed from a nozzle and fell as an obscene blob into a vat. Our guide also told us that it takes 140 days to grow a full-term peanut, and that peanut butter made for the Army has less oil in it than the civilian spread.

In the center of the room was a low wooden platform with three women on it, sitting on high wooden stools. Two of the women were old and white, one was young and black. All of them were wearing white gauze bonnets. A conveyor belt with shelled peanuts spread on it was moving from left to right in front of them, and as it did they passed their hands over it, picking up some of the peanuts and dropping them to the floor, leaving the rest of the peanuts to move on. They were removing the dark and spotted peanuts, which could spoil the whole batch, according to our guide. They were silent, not talking to each other to relieve the tedium, or even to themselves, not humming or sighing. Their faces looked blank, emptied out. Noticing that their hands were always arched, in the process of plucking a peanut off the belt or carrying it away or returning ready for the next plucking, and remembering the ache in my own hands the times I tried to knit, I worked up the nerve to ask, "Don't your hands get tired?" There was not a flicker of acknowledgment on their faces that somebody had spoken, and they didn't speak themselves. After a minute one of the older women said in a quiet, flat voice, still without changing expression, "No, but our eyes sure do."

My own eyes were fixed on the women; I couldn't help it. There they were, sitting high up off the floor, where employers and visitors could watch them, on seats with no backs, forced to listen to machines grinding away incessantly and to look at nothing but peanuts, peanuts, peanuts, about which they had to make decisions all day long. Watching them, I felt a vicarious sense of entrapment so overwhelming that I had a flash vision of my plane as something made of crystal, with rainbows glinting off the corners, and felt a flush of shame, in these women's weary presence, for owning a plane, such a frivolous, giddy thing, yet at that moment, it seemed to me, absolutely necessary for life and spirit.

Laura owned her own plane too. It was a Cessna 150, which she shared with her instructor. On our way to her house (she had decided that I should stay another day), we stopped at the airport to see it. To our astonishment the small airport was crowded with people, including several women holding babies, and a TV crew. All of them were standing around the ramp, waiting. We asked what they were waiting for. From the newspapers I already knew that Georgia was in the middle of a severe drought and that almost all of the corn within a 30-mile radius of Dawson, or 400,000 acres, was dead (the rustling corn husks). However, some of the peanuts and soybeans might be saved if rain came soon. So people had gotten together and formed a Rain Gain Committee for Southwest Georgia, to raise money to bring in a rainmaker from California. Someone showed Laura and me a letter the Committee had mailed to the most famous California rainmaker of all,

Burt Lancaster, who played the role in *The Rainmaker* opposite Katharine Hepburn, asking him for a contribution. Any donation he cared to make, the letter said, would be appreciated "by the farmers who grow these suffering crops as well as those who like to sit down to a dinner table filled with good things to eat." Lancaster never replied.

The real California rainmaker was at the airport, but he was waiting himself, for a cloud to seed. To make rain, or more precisely snow, he told a TV reporter, you needed a cloud with tops to 18,000 feet or so since the temperature inside the cloud had to be below freezing. You dropped a flare of silver iodide crystals into the updraft part of that cloud, where the crystals served as nuclei for vapor from supercooled droplets to form around. On their way to the top of the cloud the nuclei and vapor turned into snowflakes, then fell, and as they drew closer to earth melted, turned into rain, and drenched the fields.

We decided we'd like to see that, or what we could of it, so Laura and I waited too. How odd it seemed, a crowd of people standing around waiting for an ordinarily unobserved, slow-rolling natural event to occur, the formation of a cloud. We crossed the ramp and looked at her plane. It was a nice, clean swept-tail Cessna 150, white with blue stripes. I admired it publicly but privately had ungenerous thoughts, such as "no personality" and "boring." The Cessna 150 was the nosewheel version of the Cessna 140, which was itself an adaptation (ripoff, many would say) of the Luscombe. Poor Luscombe, it went extinct only a couple of decades after it was hailed as a major step forward in the lightplane field (easy to produce, sturdy, fast, affordable), while the Cessna 140 went on to become the Cessna 150, which became the second most popular airplane in the history of aviation, over 24,000 sold around the world.

Odds were with numbers like that that even on a field the size of Dawson's there would be other 150s besides Laura's. There were two, one a white with red stripes, next to which stood a gawky, bespectacled man in a jumpsuit. We ambled over to see him and his plane. It wasn't *his* 150, he informed us. A friend had taken him up for a ride in it recently, and he was paying the friend back by working on the engine. "If we hadn't-a been at two thousand feet," he said of the ride, "after the first 15 minutes I'd-a *walked* home!" He hadn't expected to be scared. He had had a few flying lessons himself, years ago, before the war. "Then I got married, had kids, built my house, built my garage, and couldn't afford to fly anymore," he said. "I figured someday when the kids were grown I'd have enough money to build myself an airplane. Now my daughter's through with school so I'm building myself a Pietenpol!"

He was building it from scratch, as all Pietenpols had to be. The Pietenpol had parasol wings which shaded the open cockpit and was designed in 1928 by a Minnesota farmer who gave it his name. Originally it was meant to be powered by a Ford Model A engine, but this man was going to put a 65-hp Continental engine in his. He was building it in his garage. "I thought it would take me two years," he said, "but so far it has taken me six. The family has started to get *nasty*."

The rainmaker took off in a Beechcraft Baron with someone else at the controls, and two airplanes took off behind him. The pilots of the other planes were to act as observers and confirm that the seeding actually took place and that the seeded cloud was the one that did the raining. Again we waited. Within a half hour one of the observer planes landed and the pilot got out. People gathered around him. He hadn't expected to be scared, either. "We flew through [the cloud] at 12,000 feet and it got real rough," he said breathlessly. "The cloud started boiling and tumbling. It went from white to almost pure black in 15 minutes. It more than doubled in size. We got ice on the cowling. There was a gunpowder smell. It became harder and harder to breathe. . . ."

We didn't get to see the rainmaker land because Laura had to get home to start dinner, but we did hear on evening TV that a quarter inch of rain fell on farms southeast of Dawson. Within the Rain Gain circle, we figured, and lifted our cocktail glasses to the rain and the rained-upon. The rest of the family was still out, so we had the house to ourselves. Laura sat on the sofa, her bare feet tucked under her, a pillow beside her she had needlepointed herself. I'D RATHER BE FLYING, it said. Without giving me any indication that she was going to do it, she started telling me a story, in such a way that I knew she had been thinking about telling it for some time. The story was about her flying. Not just about her flying. And not just her story, either, though she didn't know that, since she didn't read *Ms., Self,* or *Savvy.* She told the story fresh, as if she were the first woman to experience it, and struggled to find the right words.

"I was raised in the Black Belt in Alabama," she began. "It's even more Southern than Dawson. We would have big hunts along the river, with lots of food and lots of blacks to prepare the food. Families that had known each other for generations would come down to the river to socialize and shoot deer, dove, and quail. We spent a lot of nights down by the river. We fished a lot and always had blacks to row the boats. It was a casual type of living, but always with the old background families.

"We went to a lot of balls, like the Beaux Arts Ball in Montgomery. I came out in Birmingham. I dated a lot of boys but you might as well say I dated one boy. They were all programmed like I was. I went to a girls' college 18 miles from home but I didn't finish. Jim and I got married when we were both 19. After that I entertained a lot, played bridge, did lots of needlework, cooked, decorated my house, shopped with the girls. I never worked a day in my life. I was sheltered and had everything done for me. I never thought of not doing or not living that kind of life. It was the only thing I ever knew.

"Then I went up in that plane. The second time it just hit me. I went wild. I started going to the airport every day. It was like being let out of a glass bubble. Or out of jail. All of a sudden I realized that there was another world, that I could actually *do* something. Flying was the only thing I'd ever done that wasn't average, that the average girl wasn't doing. It thrilled me that I could do something a man does.

"I said to my mother, 'Mother, I can fly an airplane!' She never smiled. Flying wasn't *ladylike*. I went to bridge club and I was so excited. 'Guess what!' I said. 'I'm taking flying!' All I saw was thirteen faces of horror. I was excited and they were horrified. The reaction was, 'You are going to kill yourself and leave those kids by themselves.' I didn't say anything. They had let the air out of my balloon. 'Gosh, am I batty?' I thought. But I didn't quit flying. I quit bridge club.

"There was a lot of gossip about me. I was the only girl at the airport. The town was buzzing. Jim got flak from the men. He says they lost respect for him because of the talk about me. One night I was sitting here and suddenly I could see all the people around Dawson and I thought, 'I'm so tired of you. I'm so tired of Saturday-night dances at the country club and having new dresses for bridge club. You are all so *boring* to me.'

"For 15 years I did everything I was supposed to," she went on. "I had three children. I gave Jim a son. I did every social obligation I should have. I was voted 'Miss Greensboro.' I dressed right. I wrote every thank-you note. I was perfect all my life. Then when there was this abrupt change, I didn't know how to cope with it. When I finally did something on my own, it wrecked my life."

She was crying now and making no attempt to hide the tears or wipe them away. Her cheeks were wet, but her chin was held high. "I have this fantasy," she said. "It's horrible. I want to leave. Be by myself. Not even with the children. I want to live someplace else. I *yearn* for it. It's all I can think about. I tell myself, you're 35 and still young; is this the way it's going to be? Be the good wife, raise kids the rest of your life?" She was speaking more and more slowly, as if her voice itself were a burden to her. "I can't leave, though. When you've been sheltered all your life and have had everything done for you, you don't have the confidence. I wish I could be content with staying home and making a life for my husband and children. I truly wish I could be like I was before. But there's another part that has overpowered that and I can never go back. I can't leave and I can't stay. I'm so mixed up and so unhappy!"

So that was why she'd asked me to Dawson. I was a woman outside the glass bubble. My straggly hair and sticky arms advertised a life on the go. She'd figured out that I could take off when I wanted, head north, south, east, or west, get back in time for dinner or not, visit a peanut-butter factory or not. She had wanted to talk to another woman who was outside the jail, or the glass bubble, and her control was so perfect that I hadn't even guessed she was in one. Once she let me know, though, the control was gone. She was moody and distracted after the rest of the family came home; clearly they knew.

The next morning she drove me to the airport. Jim asked to come along, apparently fearing my influence on her, although I was feeling pretty powerless myself. I had commiserated with her but couldn't very well advise her to leave her family—or not to. "Jim's so apprehensive," she confided, but she told him no, he couldn't come with us, and they quarreled. While I did my preflight and packed up, she stood nearby looking tense and preoccupied. No longer the perfect hostess, the good little Miss Greensboro. A couple of times I glanced over at her Cessna 150 and thought how little good it was doing her. Not for her a giddy crystal thing. It had lifted her up, but only into limbo. It would not be what saved her. She didn't even fly it much anymore, she said, and declared, "If it hadn't been flying it would have been something else." She didn't stay to see me off. "Have fun," she said in a voice tight with pain, then walked, chin up, back to her car.

Luscombes · Fairhope

Once I decided a Luscombe was the kind of plane I wanted, I bought
the first one I saw that was for sale. Two weeks after I bought it I
bought a second Luscombe I liked better. Two weeks after I bought
the second one I went back to flying the first one. The first belonged
to a man in University Park, Pennsylvania, who lived with his wife in
a house in the midst of farms. He had flown his 8E only seven hours
in the last year and knew he had run his course with it. John and Ron,
another pilot friend, went to University Park with me to look at it.
The man sat us down in his kitchen and his wife brought cookies. It
hurt him to sell the Luscombe, we could see that. He was a Mr. Fixit
and had maintained it himself, even upgraded it from a model A to
an E. I wasn't dazzled but bought it anyway. It was the only Luscombe
in *Trade-a-Plane* in my part of the country at my price, around $2,500.
It had a fair bit of hangar rash, dents and lumps on leading edges,
which may have been the reason it stalled at 55 mph instead of the
usual 45. It had been painted several different shades of brown, in
stripes that didn't correspond to the lines of the plane; to me it had
the look of an army plane. I decided it was a man's plane.

So when, the day after I brought it to my airport, John reported
seeing a "cream puff" of a Luscombe at nearby Hanover airport with
a FOR SALE sign on it, I was ripe. The following night he, Ron, and
I went over there and had a talk with the owner. The man had had
the Luscombe only about a month but was already eager to sell. Not
everybody loved Luscombes. He claimed the nose dropped too fast in
a stall, but Ron and John decided—maybe because he had such a high
thin voice that between themselves they were calling him "Squeak"—
that he was afraid of it. The Luscombe was in fine condition, had
flaps, a square tail, and single instead of double wing struts, as the E
did. And, beauty added to beauty, it was painted pale yellow with
pale-blue letters.

So for a time I owned two planes; people joked that I had a fleet. Then, one day, as I was about to put Luscombe Number One up for sale, Ron took Number Two up to practice takeoffs and landings. He was wearing work boots and probably couldn't feel the brake pedals very well through the thick heels and got a little heavy on the brakes on rollout, because while I was sitting upright at my office the plane was doing a half-somersault on the airport runway, coming to rest on its back.

When I saw what was left of my cream puff, it was all I could do to be gracious to Ron; he hadn't been hurt but was repentant. He had heard about a mechanic in Pottstown who was supposed to be good at rebuilding planes, so one day we took mine down there, first removing the bent wings, during which process I was astonished to discover that the only things that held the wings on were small blocks of metal, one per wing, each about the size of half a Snickers bar. Ron, John, and I loaded the wings and the rest of the plane, including a twisted propeller and crinkled tail, on the back of a truck and headed for Pottstown. We got lost trying to find the mechanic's house, which is where he had told us to take the plane, and arrived late, toward dusk. As we rolled up the driveway a feeling of desolation such as I'd rarely known passed over me. In the yard where I was to put my precious plane were a doorless refrigerator, an old stove, several banged-up cars, and various pieces of airplanes. I never expected to see my plane whole again.

The rebuilding took a year. The Luscombe made its way out of the back yard and into a shop at Pottstown airport. Those were not unpleasant days. From time to time I'd fly Luscombe Number One down to Pottstown and check on how things were going with Number Two. The mechanic, Gene Day, ran a bizarre and lively show. Though only about 40, he was toothless, and he had a bawdy, cackling laugh, no reticence whatever about telling the lewdest of jokes and eyewitness accounts, an unquenchable energy, and a maintenance shop for which the kindest word would be "anarchic." Somehow John, Ron, and I trusted that he was a good mechanic. He had once worked for Wernher von Braun, testing oxygen pressure suits, and there was a photo on the wall of his office of him in Von Braun's lab wearing a white outfit and space helmet. He tested the suits by getting in them himself, and during one test, the word was, he was deprived of oxygen for too long and was never the same again.

When Gene Day finished rebuilding the plane, I had it painted pale yellow with pale-blue letters; I wanted my old plane back. As soon as I got it back, tied down at the airport, I put Luscombe Number One up for sale. Within weeks a couple of pilots from an airport in Pennsylvania bought it. They paid me what I had paid for it; Mr. Fixit had given me a solid airplane. That didn't win my heart, though. I sold it without a backward glance. A few months later I heard that one of the new owners had crashed it, on landing. He groundlooped it in a crosswind. He and his partner took it to Pottstown airport, so that Gene Day could rebuild it.

While Laura was still at Dawson airport, an ag plane took off from it. We watched (or I did, and she turned her sad face in that direction) as the plane rolled down the runway, lifted off, stayed low over the ground, then pulled up sharply into an almost straight-up climb, zooming up at first, then rising more and more slowly, finally hanging in the air, motionless, for a second or two, before dropping its nose and flowing down and out into level flight. It wasn't a difficult maneuver, the vertical climb, but it was the one I loved to see more than any other in an air show: an eager, unguarded embrace of the sky!

The ag plane landed after Laura left but before I did (it doesn't take long to spray a field). It pulled up at the pumps, and the pilot got out and walked by me. His appearance betrayed him completely, advertised his nature as surely as fangs, leer, and swollen belly do the essence of a medieval demon. Just by looking at the man you could tell, without a clue from his voice or police record, that moral shortcuts were his specialty, that he would never make an honest dollar if he could make a dishonest one. He propelled himself forward by kicking with his pointy-toed boots, his knees held obscenely wide apart. His butt was curled well under him, with the crotch of his jeans sagging below that, and his shoulders were rolled forward, making for an overall weasely, what's-it-to-you-buddy posture. His golf hat was set on his head at an insolent angle, and his hair was cut in a way surely not meant to please, disdainful of onlookers, chopped off and crooked, long in the wrong places. His mouth looked as if he were carrying something foul-tasting in it.

Laura had told me about an ag pilot who flew out of Dawson who'd been put on probation for stealing agricultural chemicals out of warehouses, and who'd been caught watering the chemicals farmers gave him to spray on their fields. Also, he'd been indicted for conspiring with the Mafia to fly dope up from Mexico, and the only reason the Mafia hadn't "bumped him off" for testifying against them, she'd heard, was that he was "too small potatoes" for them to bother with. This had to be the guy, I thought. Laura had also told me the man was a fantastic pilot. It bothered me now, watching him snake by, that a fantastic pilot, one who could perform so joyous a maneuver as the vertical climb, could be such a sleazeball.

For my own takeoff I did a sort of mini-pullup, a poor-girl's version of the vertical climb, more horizontal than vertical really, but still fun. After I was well up and away I celebrated my choice of the unfettered life, or at least the intermittently unfettered life (eager, unguarded embrace of the sky!). My next destination I had picked on the slimmest of leads (whenever and wherever!). One day in Dawson Jim had happened to mention the beaches along the Alabama coast. They were as lovely, he said, as any in the Caribbean, and the sea there as green. At the same time Laura mentioned that when they went down there they stayed at the Grand Hotel in Fairhope, and "it's really quite nice." Hearing "Grand Hotel," I made associations I had no right to: potted ferns, caviar, fox furs with little faces, champagne, waltz music, dachshunds, pearls. A bored voice: "People coming, going, nothing ever happens." An excited one: "How do you know there will be a Grand Hotel in Paris?" Another excited one: "Oh, there's a Grand Hotel everywhere in the world." The bored voice again: "Always the same." I couldn't afford to stay in a Grand Hotel, but I could at least visit one and see how much the same it was.

Landmarks were hard to come by on the Dawson-to-Fairhope leg. The chart showed only one town in the first hundred miles and no lakes or mountains. Most of the roads were crooked dirt ones not marked on the chart, and those that were marked on the chart appeared to be no bigger than the rest. Power lines were probably the best of the possible checkpoints, but they went zigzagging away from my plane at angles hard to match with those on the chart. As for rivers, they were as small, meandering, and unremarkable as the roads—and there were an awful lot of them. As I was tooling along somewhere over a jumble of trees and fields I heard a man say on Unicom, "I'm over a real windy [he pronounced it "wine-dy"] river. How far is that from Marianna?'' I didn't hear the operator answer but she must have had a time of it. On the chart I counted three rivers near Marianna—the Chattahoochee, the Apalachicola, and the Chipola—plus several creeks large enough to be drawn yet too small to be named, and all of them were ''wine-dy.''

The sky, though, was simplicity itself, a soft, baby-blanket blue, without a cloud in it. Another wretched day for farmers, I was thinking, feeling a touch of guilt. Every fine day for me came at the expense of some *crop*. Not far out of Dawson I saw several fields of dead corn, which looked from the air like old scrub brushes, pale, brown, and stiff. Farther on, though, I flew over fields that were quite green (not corn, some other crop), obviously getting water from some place besides the sky. The haves and have-nots could not have been more clearly revealed. In one of the fields, water was shooting out of irrigation pipes in several directions at once, making long, arching sprays, as translucent and delicate as insects' wings.

After a time the farms, living and dead, grew scarce, and forest took over almost completely. When there was nothing under me but trees I threw my chewing gum out the window. Probably I smiled as I let go. For that one small gesture gave me a big puff of pleasure, allowing me to feel the maverick, the rebel, a pilot above the rules, one of the rules being of course never to throw anything out an airplane window: You can imagine, the rain of litter, paper missiles, cold coffee . . . But a wad of gum onto a forest? I pictured this one hurtling down, down, picking up speed at 32 feet per second per second, plummeting toward the trees, smacking onto that first leaf, knocking it aside, ricocheting downward branch to twig to branch, whizzing past the scarred trunk, hitting a pile of dead leaves, bouncing up, settling, lying still, looking like a pebble.

Forty minutes out of Dawson I crossed the border from Georgia into Alabama. Five minutes later I crossed the border from Alabama into Florida. That was it for the state of Alabama; hello, goodbye, the plane just nicked off the southeastern tip of it. Fifteen minutes later I arrived at Marianna, the airport of the wine-dy rivers. I had planned to pass right by it, close enough to hear my name being broadcast on the VOR (radio station that puts out navigational signals), over and over in some soft Southern voice, ''Mar-i-*ah*-nna VOR . . . Mar-i-*ah*-nna VOR,'' but not stop. But Laura—feeling justifiably free to concentrate on her own problems once she had told me about them—hadn't offered me breakfast that morning, and I was starved. Marianna was listed as having a "snack bar." I had been there once before, to refuel, and someone told me then that the town wasn't named for anybody called Marianna but for the daughters of the founder, little Mary and little Anna, I presumed. He also said Marianna's business used to be making brassieres and now it was men's pants.

The snack bar was actually an unattended pile of plastic-wrapped hero sandwiches next to a microwave oven. I picked out a meatball hero and put it in the oven and was waiting for it to heat when a man came in and went through the pile himself. He had on a pair of those clip-on sunglasses that, when they aren't being used, stick out over regular glasses like awnings, or in his case more like a hand shading the eyes; for even as he stood in that back room next to the microwave, he appeared to be looking a long way off, gazing at distant clouds and mountains.

He had his first name stitched on his overalls pocket, so I figured he was local and decided to ask his advice. I was planning to fly under a couple of military areas on the Alabama coast and wondered if it wouldn't be a good idea to phone the Air Force ahead of time and let them know I'd be going through with a weak radio. I knew I didn't *have* to phone *or* radio since the floor of the restricted area was at 8,000 feet and there was no way I'd be going over 8,000. However, the coast had so many military areas I thought it might be a good idea. What did he think?

Good idea, he said. The Air Force could be pretty fussy. Once he was flying around over the forest looking for stumps when a couple of F-104s came up from behind him, flew by on either side, made a crossing pass in front of him, then turned around and dived at him. "I just got out of there," he said. "I was in a Cessna 172." Apparently he had strayed over the edge of some restricted area—not hard to do, I thought, in this lookalike landscape.

"What do you mean, stumps?" I asked. "Why were you out looking for stumps?" "The stumps of virgin pines," he answered. "If they're in the ground long enough, they'll turn mostly to fat. A few chips and a fire'll burn for days." Oh, I said, fatwood. *Fat* wood; I get it. "Once a year," he said, "in the spring, before the leaves start coming back on the trees, we go out looking for stumps." Which got me to thinking about how valuable a stump must be for it to be worth somebody's while to pay this pilot, and others like him, to fly around looking for stumps, to pay the owner of the land the stump was found on for the right to take it, to pay somebody else to go into the forest and, by following the pilot's directions, find the stump, dig it up, and cart it away to a lumber yard, to pay somebody else (or the same person) to chop it into sticks and pack them into bags or bundles, to pay somebody to transport the bags and bundles to stores, where somebody else would get paid for selling them to folk—not necessarily rich folk either—who wanted fires that would burn for days. *The Golden Fatted Stump.* A stump could also be used, the man said with a certain promotional fervor, for making cough syrup, gunpowder, detergent, and (of all things, considering what I threw out the window onto the self-same forest) chewing gum.

I did phone the Air Force, and a controller told me to radio in as I reached the coast, despite the fact that I had just told him I had a weak radio which was why I was phoning, and despite the fact that I would be going under, not through, the restricted area. But like a good soldier, as soon as the great gray plate of the gulf rose up, I lifted my microphone to my mouth.

"Eglin Approach," I said. "Luscombe Eight Zero Three Bravo. Over Miramar at 3,000 feet. Heading west. Okay?"

(Delay.) "Zero Three Bravo, we don't have you on . . . [crackle]."

"I'm small."

(Crackle, crackle.) "Say again, please."

"I'm *small.*"

(Delay.) "Zero Three Bravo, are you familiar with the inlet [crackle, crackle]. Panama City . . . west . . . There's a condominium."

(Panama City? That was *behind* me, by about 50 miles!) "I said, 'Over Mir-a-mar.' I'm over *Fort Walton* now."

(Delay.) "Stand by, please." (Pause.) "Zero Three Bravo, say type aircraft, please."

"Luscombe."

"Say again, please."

"Luscombe. El-yew-ess-see-oh-em-bee-ee."

(Delay.) "Zero Three Bravo, have you got Eglin VOR?"

Did he mean, was I *tuned* to Eglin VOR? Or did I know where Eglin VOR was and I should get it? It probably didn't occur to him that if

I tuned to VOR on my single-band radio I'd lose his voice. Quickly I went over the chart, not wanting to exasperate the man any more than I had already, but I couldn't find Eglin VOR; if it was there, it was extremely well disguised. It probably didn't occur to him either that I'd be using a sectional instead of a world chart. "Can you give me a clue?" I asked.

(Delay.) "Zero Three Bravo, report when opposite end of runway at Hurlburt."

"Roger."

Ten minutes later, just as I was lifting my microphone to report being opposite the end of the runway at Hurlburt, pleased at having found myself at last where the man wanted me, he got on the air first.

"Zero Three Bravo, are you at Hurlburt yet?"

"Affirmative."

"Zero Three Bravo, switch to"—he gave me a frequency. "Good day."

He didn't *have* to pass me off to anybody but probably thought he'd be more definitively getting rid of me if he did. I didn't have the frequency anyway and hadn't the heart to tell him. "Good day, Eglin."

Not a good idea. The controller, accustomed to brand-name air-planes, fuselages big enough to blip, multiple electronics, and world charts, had been frustrated and confused while I, the good soldier, had barely gotten a look at the beaches of Alabama I had come down that way to see. In any case, by the time I bade him good day, there was something else keeping me from enjoying to the fullest my view of the Alabama beaches. Thick, gray clouds had massed over the mainland to my right (where the floor of the restricted areas briefly reached the ground), as well as on my left, out to sea, which meant the air I was flying through was the only air with (1) land under it (another bony island), (2) no clouds in it, and (3) no military areas blocking it. Flying that stretch of air was like walking a tightrope. However, sunshine kept falling through that air, onto the beach, and the sand glowed creamy, as if it were blessed.

Shortly after I made the turn toward Fairhope, up the eastern shore of Mobile Bay, I saw somewhere over the middle of the bay a single blue-gray curtain of rain. There couldn't be much wind associated with it, I figured, since it slanted only a little off the vertical, and there couldn't be much rain, since it was thin enough to see through. Still,

I didn't like it being there. It represented a weakness in the system, a hole in the dike, a tear in the fabric that held up the clouds. Something more worrisome was sure to follow; God's finger raised in warning. And though I was only ten miles from Fairhope, and the warning was therefore not for me, seeing it made me uneasy.

An hour or so later, as I was unpacking my stuff at Bacon's Motel, down the road from the Grand Hotel but with rooms for $9 a night, I heard a stirring in the palm trees outside. Then a rumble and the splat of raindrops on the parking lot. I pulled back the curtain and watched rain bounce off the Airport Car I'd been given at Fairhope. Soon the palm trees were swaying and the rain was coming down harder and the whole scene blurred. Thunder grew louder and louder until it was exploding in some of the loudest claps I'd heard in my life. Then hail started falling.

The hail was the size of rice grains. It reminded me of another summer day when I had left my plane at an airport in North Carolina and rented a car so I could take a drive through the Smoky Mountains. On my way back, when I was about two miles from the airport, heading down a residential street, I became aware that the lawns on either side were no longer green. They were white—and steaming. Hail had evidently fallen just ahead of me, so much of it that it hid the grass. Stricken, I stomped on the accelerator, so I could get to my plane as soon as possible; hail can dent the soft aluminum skin of airplanes, or at least scratch the paint. But why are you hurrying? I asked myself. Your plane has already been peened and pocked beyond your power to help. When I got within a half mile of the airport, as abruptly as the lawns had turned white in the first place, they turned back to green. The next day I read in the *Charlotte News-Observer* that "hail an inch in diameter was reported. It broke neighborhood windows and piled an inch deep in yards . . . dented the chrome on Mrs. H. T. Alexander's station wagon [and] battered her garden into ruin."

I was also reminded of a summer day when I was sitting on a porch swing at the Sweetwater, Texas, airport, admiring a double rainbow that had formed over my plane out on the ramp. It was the only plane parked there and stood dramatically against the simple backdrop of plain and sky. The only things to be seen in that direction were the long, straight line of the horizon, the darkening sky, the two triumphal arches, and my Luscombe. The message was clear: This was an enchanted creature. As I was sitting there swinging, rapt in the epiphany, two men walked up and shyly suggested that I move my plane into a hangar. A storm was coming, they said. It was the first time anybody had made that suggestion to me, so I couldn't ignore it. During the night I heard some thunder but nothing spectacular, and in the morning the ramp was nearly dry. As I was doing my preflight, though, an old man whose job it seemed to be to occupy the office, act as a deterrent presence when the FBO was away (less lonely, I supposed, than staying home), approached me, his eyes bright with excitement. He started right in, with no greeting. "Hail big as golf balls fell last night," he said. "Then some big as marbles. Didn't fall anyplace else either. Just here at the airport. Hasn't done that in years."

Three hours after arriving at my motel in Fairhope, I drove to the Grand Hotel, as dressed up as I could get. The rain was still coming down hard, and I ran through it up the steps and into the lobby. The lobby: pine paneling on the walls, brick fireplace, Chinese-style furniture, patterned rugs. Men were wandering back and forth through it in navy-blue blazers with name tags on them saying "Jim Dandy." Even the wives' name tags said "Jim Dandy." An organization called Jim Dandy was holding a convention at the hotel, I was told. There were so many delegates that I had a hard time getting a seat for dinner. Well, I thought, hearing the burble of excited talk around the tables, the cocktail-fueled laughter, probably lots of stories here, too. People came, people went . . .

That night on TV a weatherman pointed to two "hot spots" on the national map, each the shape and color of a pickle. They were areas where severe storms were expected the next day, he said, and one of the pickles covered Fairhope. Yet at the lovely gulf beach I went to in the morning, sunshine coated everything, the snack bar built to look like a big potato-chip can, the inflatable rafts with bodies flung corpselike across them, the countless square feet of human skin darkening by the minute. As the day went on, though, clouds began gathering behind the dunes, small white buttons at first but after a while darker, larger clouds, and more of them, all oozing their way toward shore. At one point I heard thunder-cracks like shots from a gunnery range and immediately became isolated from all the other people on the beach, as if I had been flung up in the sky to deal with the coming storm alone while they could keep on playing. Would I confront something like this tomorrow, or the next time I flew? The worst they had to worry about was wet towels.

Back at Bacon's the desk clerk showed me a newspaper article she had saved (knowing I was a pilot). It concerned an airplane crash that had taken place the day before, during the storm, an hour or so after I landed. A student pilot and his instructor crashed in a Cessna 150 somewhere east of Foley, or about ten miles from Fairhope. Both of them were killed. In my room I got out the NEW ORLEANS chart and studied the area around Foley. Within ten miles of it I counted ten strips (including several named OLF—OLF Wolf, OLF Barin, OLF Magnolia, etc.—as if some prodigal Swede had once passed through and left behind, instead of illegitimate offspring, a batch of airstrips bearing his name—actually probably something military, like Off Landing Field). Apparently the student and instructor couldn't reach any of the strips, or else, not taking into account how little time can separate a button of a cloud from shots on a gunnery range, or a curtain of rain from a hailstorm, didn't try.

Tallulah

Again, God's finger was raised in warning, the message relayed through a briefer the next morning. From Fairhope I wanted to go to Cajun country near New Orleans, Thibodaux airport or maybe Houma-Terrebonne, but when I phoned Flight Service a briefer informed me otherwise. "You don't want to go down there," he said, "not now you don't. It's a mess down there now." (How, I asked myself, could the new automated computerized flight-service readouts, mandated to replace the majority of personal briefers across the country, improve on information like that?) I still wanted to go to Cajun country, though, so much so that I decided I'd do what I'd told myself I wouldn't on this trip: stop forward momentum. I'd pick some airport farther up the Mississippi, fly up and over to it, wait for the weather to clear around New Orleans, and fly back down.

But which airport? Spreading the chart across my bed, I traced the Mississippi north, watched it curl past False River airport, then Dipple & Enette airport, Angola, Rosewood Plantation, Concordia, K C Ranch (looking for a sign, something that would say this is the place), Red Beard, Scott, Reality, Priddy, Nicks, Love . . . Love? It was the obvious contender, but for some reason I looked back at Scott. That airport was sending out a signal. I wasn't sure what the signal was until I saw the name of the town next to it. Tallulah was a name you remembered. I had flown in there once, very briefly, planning to refuel, and the airport had registered strongly as Tallulah and only weakly as Scott.

It had been a Sunday, I remembered, the busiest day of the week at most little airports, but this one was eerily quiet. It wasn't so much that there weren't people at the airport but that people seemed to be missing. A couple of big, brawny biplanes (I might once have called them masculine) were sitting on the ramp, one of them dripping oil, as if it had recently flown, but they weren't tied down and they faced different directions, as if the pilots had jumped out of them and run off.

On one side of the ramp was a handsome, two-story, white stucco building with red tile roof and high, arched, red-trimmed windows, but the white paint was peeling and the glass in the windows was broken. I peered through one of the broken panes (the door was locked) into a large room with old wooden-bladed fans on the high ceilings and, on the opposite side of the room, more high, arched windows through which sunshine streamed onto the floor, or rather onto what covered the floor almost completely: dozens of oil-blackened radial engines and pieces of engines. I went back to the ramp but didn't get into my plane right away. I stood around, waiting for something to show up—a plane, a car, a dog even, a cat. But the only sounds I could hear were the buzzing of flies in the heat and now and then a drop of oil hitting the pavement. Still I stood, reluctant to go. There was something oddly compelling about the place. Inhabited but only sort of. A Flying Dutchman's airport, under sail yet manned by spirits.

So Scott it would be today; I'd see what had haunted it. From the northeast corner of Mobile Bay I drew a line on the chart straight to Scott, and in the 250 miles the line represented it passed one city and no more than half a dozen towns. Most of the rest of what I'd be flying over, judging by what I'd been flying over up until then, would be trees. Because of the trees I added a couple of thousand feet to my planned cruising altitude, so I'd have more choice of places to go into if I had to go down. As soon as I was up and away, though, I realized that a couple of thousand feet wouldn't make much difference. I'd be able to choose between landing on, say, oaks or hickories, that was all. Trees weren't the worst things you could land on, of course. Some could be like crunchable pillows. Davis, a friend of mine who learned to fly in college, once put his J-3 Cub on top of a poplar. After settling into the leaves, he just opened the door and climbed down, to live a quieter life. He had taken off from an airport that was observing its opening day with an air show, and in front of the celebratory crowd he had gotten caught in a downdraft at the end of the runway (which was essentially a carved-out hillside) and his underpowered Cub had wobbled up as high as the treetops and no higher. Two airplanes that took off after his crashed as well, one of them slamming into the hillside, bursting into flames, and killing all four people on board (a less-than-auspicious airport kickoff). So trees weren't the worst things, but if I had to go down, I'd still rather land on a field or road.

The scenery, after Mobile Bay, was unspectacular if pleasant, an unfocused jumble of light and dark shades of green. Boundaries between trees and fields were shaggy and imprecise, and there were no strong shapes anywhere. Houses were invariably simple, Monopoly pieces, four walls and a peaked roof, either white or gray. Yet now and then something would appear to lift the landscape out of the ordinary. In one section the trees grew in long, slightly undulating, parallel rows, so the countryside there looked raked, by the Maker's big rake. In other sections I could see patches of peach-colored soil through breaks in the foliage, and pieces of a wriggling brown river, with pale mudbanks highlighting the inside curves.

At one point I observed, off to my left, what looked like bubbles rising from a crescent-shaped field. They floated for a few seconds, then dropped back onto the field and shrank into tiny white dots. Shortly after that I saw a sprinkling of white dots burst from around a pond, each dot trembling like a pinpoint of light on the surface of moving water; then they too went down and nearly shrank from sight as the birds folded their wings. *Waterbirds!* Immediately I gave up my old heading and took up a new one, due west, so I could get to the Mississippi as soon as possible. There was no question of getting lost; all I had to do was sit and wait for the horizon to turn brown. On my new route even the occasional road that had been cutting through the trees vanished and so did the last of the fields and houses. I was flying over what looked like virgin territory, a vast, unexplored wilderness. With such a wide bulwark of trees leading up to it, the Mississippi seemed as remote as the Amazon.

After a while I came across a small tributary and dropped to the level of the treetops on either side and from there could see a flash of something ahead—sunlight on a mudbank?—but nothing of the river itself until I burst out upon it and everything cracked open, light, space, all around me an enormous watery brown meadow, a uniform bubbling coffee-colored smoothness, stretching away on my right to a curve as big as the base of a mountain, on my left to another curve as big as the base of the mountain, and ahead a line of etched trees, the distant bank. I kept on flying straight until I was halfway across the river, then turned and flew up the middle of it, going down steadily until the shadow of my plane on the water was almost the size of the plane itself, then rode the Mississippi like a boat, tilting the plane for curves, laughing out loud and singing "Up a Lazy River" while watching diamond patterns tremble on the undersides of my wings, from sunlight bouncing up off the moving water.

On either shore there was nothing except trees and grass and an occasional antierosion net of metal mesh holding up a stretch of bank, so the river still seemed surrounded by uninhabited wilderness. I did see a single cow, a black-and-white one standing in the water up to its knees, and a single middle-aged couple sitting on a grassy bank, with a rowboat drawn up beside them. They had on bathing suits, and she sat behind him with her arms around his torso, hands resting, crossed, upon his chest, in a pose of great serenity. Then I rounded a bend and suddenly it was all there, towers, power lines, office buildings, smokestacks, bridges. I pulled the stick back and left and the plane floated up and over a bridge, a levee, a railroad track, a highway, a power line, and into the pattern at Scott.

This time there was a dog. A German shepherd, lying belly-down beside the pumps. Its head was white but its body, legs, and tail were bright yellow, the color of pollen. There were planes, too, this time, in a double row along two sides of the ramp. I was sighting down one of the rows, trying to place the odd smell in the air, a sort of sour incense, when a woman stepped out from behind a Cessna: people this time too. The Flying Dutchman had flown the coop . . .

The woman's shoulder was twitching badly. She passed me without glancing over, seeming quite distracted. She continued on to the stucco building, which had a new coat of paint on it and glass in all the windows. I followed her inside. There were still fans on the ceiling, but the engines were gone from the floor, replaced by rug, bookcase, table, chairs, and sofa. On the wall at the far end of the room hung a large, framed Chinese embroidery of birds with real feathers for tails. On that same wall, as well as on the next one, was a row of ragged fabric squares tacked up like old washcloths on a line. All had writing on them, in black ink.

"Vonette Sharp," said one (aqua T-shirt). "First solo. Cessna 150. March 21." Another (brown-and-white-striped cotton) read, "Bob Buhts. First solo. BE 23. June 12." Another (white nylon with brown clouds) went, "Frank May. First solo. Cessna 150. July 7." These were products of a custom called "clipping the tailfeathers," whereby instructors cut pieces off the shirttails of students who've just soloed (a good reason to dress down when learning to fly). It's a custom not universally observed; some airports cut off shirttails and hang them up and some do not. Those that do tend to be the ones with a more lively airport spirit, or at least the ones where people are trying hard to make a go of things.

The woman's shoulder kept on twitching. I figured she was 19 or 20. She spoke to a man about her age who was lying on the sofa drinking a soda. "All those *trees* down there, I just wanted a place to land." He didn't say anything in response, just adjusted his body on the sofa, as if her talking made him physically uncomfortable. She kept talking, though, and I gathered from what she said that she was a student pilot who had just come back from her first solo cross-country flight, Scott to Jackson, Mississippi, to Natchez, Mississippi, back to Scott, but had gotten lost on the last leg. Listening to her now, I realized I had heard her voice on the radio as I was coming in. She had been asking a man to "keep on talking, please." He turned out to be the controller in Jackson, who had heard her cries for help and steered her home.

"It was so bumpy up there, I didn't think I'd *ever* make it back," she moaned. The kid on the sofa squirmed, but at that moment an older man walked in and she shifted her attention to him. "All those *trees* down there," she began. Soon it became clear that he was her flight instructor, the one who'd signed her off on the cross-country. He wore a worldly little smile, which seemed to say, "Things could be much, much worse and have been already." He sat at the table with her and together they figured out what had gone wrong. From Natchez to Scott, she was supposed to fly a compass heading of 004 degrees, but actually she'd flown a heading of 040 (not too dumb a mistake, since compass dials drop the final zeros and 040 would have read 04). So instead of going up the river she knew so well, she had struck out over the Amazonian wilderness and watched with alarm as the Mississippi slid away over her left shoulder, yet didn't dare ignore her instruments, or what she thought her instruments were telling her.

Kindly, the instructor told her about his own first cross-country solo, when he ran into rain. "It was the first time I'd seen rain in an airplane; it was light rain but it scared me," he said. "Nobody had told me about the windshield. I didn't know what would happen if you didn't have wipers. [The rain sheets and runs off to the sides.] I got stuck on top of clouds and a man at the Flight Service station helped me down.'' What a nice way to make a student feel less like a chump, I thought, then realized the young woman wasn't worried about being a chump but about dying. Her shoulder was still twitching when she left and her face bore a look of such distress I wondered if she'd ever fly again.

Her instructor was Benny May (father of Frank, I presumed, he of the brown-cloud nylon), and it was he who was responsible for all the changes at Tallulah, even the dog. When I mentioned my last visit there, he cleared up the mystery in a hurry. ''Scott was a cropdusters' field then,'' he said, ''and cropdusters don't fly on Sundays. The rest of the week they're up flying from before light to after dark, and their families don't get to see them much, so they save Sundays. Besides, most of them are religious.'' Probably a good thing, I thought. All those high-powered planes roaring along a few feet off the ground, passing up and down row after row, could drown out the sweeter sounds of Sundays: porch swings creaking, ice tinkling in glasses of lemonade, church clothes rustling.

Benny May cleared up another mystery. I asked about the odd smell outside. ''Treflan,'' he said, as if that explained it. I had to ask, ''What's Treflan?'' ''A liquid weedkiller,'' he answered. ''It drips out of nozzles when the guys are loading their tanks or taxiing around and it pools on the ground.'' I *had* noticed some opaque, yellowish puddles here and there on the ramp. ''When it's hot like this Fritz likes to roll in the puddles like a pig,'' said Benny May. Another mystery cleared up. Fritz was the German shepherd. ''Doesn't the Treflan hurt him?'' I asked, thinking of the soaked fur. ''Naw,'' said Benny May, ''doesn't even keep the flies off!''

Before coming to Scott, Benny May had been a truck driver for 18 years. He was hauling long-distance freight in 18-wheelers for Red Ball Motors when he quit. ''Driving makes you old,'' he pointed out. ''I started driving when I was 19 and was old by the time I was 21. Now I get half the pay for putting in twice the working hours, but flying makes me feel young. When you fly, every day is a different day.'' (How like a fishspotter he sounded!) Benny May not only did the flight instructing at Scott, flew the charters, and leased the airplanes, he built the office furniture himself, even brought the embroidery from home, yet he didn't own the airport. One of the cropdusters who still used the field did. The owner had his own hangar, and after I got fuel I went down to take a look at it. It had a ragged windsock on top and a sign on the front: GRAVES FLYING SERVICE. It occurred to me that Graves wasn't the greatest name for someone in a high-risk profession. He had managed to attain at least middle age, I could see. I found him sitting on a chair just inside the hangar door, leaning over and spinning a Dr. Pepper empty on the floor, around and around like a propeller. Behind him were almost a dozen planes, all the same type, Stearmans, the big biplanes I'd seen the last time. The ones toward the front seemed to be in decent enough shape, but those farther back would clearly never get off the ground. They had holes in the fabric, flaking paint, patches, missing tails, missing engines, missing props. Dust covered them, and their wings were striped with pigeon droppings.

Graves wasn't being sentimental keeping the old planes around, like horses put out to pasture after a long and useful life. Stearmans were WWII trainers which some people converted after the war into spray planes by attaching pipes to the trailing edges of the wings, but the company quit making them even before the war was over, and after a while people began to keep surplus planes on hand for parts. Over the years, many Stearman owners, like Graves, became packrats, and the planes they flew chimeras.

Graves wouldn't spray crops in anything but Stearmans. He'd flown 20,000 hours in them. "You can go in wide open upside down in a Stearman and not do anything more than bust your lip," he claimed. "We've lost only two pilots in them, one who hit a high line after dark and one who flew into a big pecan tree." He had been dusting crops for over 30 years, he said. "Few men stay in the business for more than five or ten years. By then they're either dead or gone. After three or four years they've usually had an accident, or two or three. One summer ten boys came out of Jackson, Mississippi, to work this area, and six of them got killed." Graves didn't have much the look of a risk-taker to me. He slumped in his chair, had a hesitant smile, pale skin, and rather colorless hair. Benny May said he had the kind of wife who drives men to solitary work.

Giving the Dr. Pepper another twirl, Graves said, "Most pilots sleep a lot the first three or four years, from tension. It's as nervous and fatiguing a job as you can get. It's all *physical*. You've got to have a one-track mind, you've got to stay awake, you can't let up till you're through. The big hazard used to be cotton houses—they stuck up in almost every field. They went out with mechanical picking, but now we've got power lines." Also new things to put on the crops. "DDT, you could eat it," Graves insisted. "It never *would* kill you. But some of the stuff we're carrying nowadays, one drop on your skin and half an hour later you're dead. Ten or 20 pilots a year die that way, just because DDT killed a mouse [he sneered on the word "mouse"] somewhere."

Graves had something to show me, he said, and led me across the ramp to a trailer, where he had his office. Jutting out from one tiny wall inside were three large, mounted animal heads, of a boar-hog, a javelina, and a white-tailed deer. He had shot all three but they weren't what he wanted to show me. He lifted a small framed picture off the wall, regarded it for a moment, reverentially, I thought, and passed it on to me. It was a photograph, already turned brown, of a small plane flying over some unprepossessing vegetation and trailing what looked like steam. The plane was a de Havilland 4b. The crop was cotton. The year was 1922. The field was the old Scott plantation, where the airport was now. And what looked like steam was the first insecticide ever to be dropped on crops from the air. "This was where it all began," Graves said. No wonder he was reverential. The photo was a genuine heirloom, a memento from his and his airport's professional past, as valid as bronzed baby shoes.

"Spray pilots," he bragged, putting the photo back on the wall, "do it all." They plant crops (soybeans, wheat, and oats) by air, spread fertilizer by air, and kill weeds, fungi, and insects (at different times) by air. One or two "good" pilots could spray 1,500 acres in less than two hours, including the time it took them to fly back to the airport and reload every 10 or 15 minutes. "On cool days it's a joy," he said, sounding even more like a fishspotter. "Somebody is paying you to fly!"

That evening I ate in the hotel restaurant ("dinning room," the entrance sign said). Fiddle music drifted in from the bar across the hall, and when I was finished eating ("fried Mississippi catfish" which the waitress told me was *not* from the Mississippi and a salad listed on the menu as "WOP"), I went over and found Benny May talking to two men. Both were lawyers, one up from Baton Rouge to help the other prosecute a murder case the next day. The lawyers refused to talk about the murder, but they would discuss another aspect of the legal life, what they had been discussing when I walked in—witnesses' memories and what jogs them. The one from Baton Rouge said he had had a client who testified that an event occurred exactly when he said it did because, the man swore in court, "that was the day I ordered pig lip at the bar and it was too fat to eat." The one from Tallulah said he had had a witness who offered as evidence that he could not possibly have been at home when something was supposed to have happened, the fact that "my wife had the first day of her period and there was nothing to go home *for.*"

The lawyer from Tallulah was also a pilot and until recently he had owned a Cessna 172, which he kept at Scott. One day a policeman called him to say his plane was in a swamp with two dead men in it. The night before, he learned, an acquaintance of his, a man he knew but not well, had borrowed the plane and flown off in it, with another man as passenger. There were no witnesses to the crash, no survivors, and no motives offered by family and friends of the dead men. No insurance money, either, since the man who took the plane was not checked out in it. I had to admire the gaiety with which he told the story.

"O Joli Blanc" was on the jukebox and the lawyers were tapping their feet to it. I mentioned that I was flying to Cajun country as soon as the weather got better, and they started talking about the wonderful boudin and crawfish *étouffée,* the streets of water, dance-fiddling, and cypress trees. I became so worked up about things Cajun that when Benny May said he was going to a breakfast meeting of the *Cajun* Wing of the Ghost Squadron of the Confederate Air Force in the morning I asked if I could come along. He said yes if I could get up early and told me it would take place at a resort on Lake Bruin, a snippet of the Mississippi left behind when the river changed course 200 years ago.

We flew there in a Cessna 150, with Benny May sitting in the left seat and I in the right. How odd it felt, being in the cockpit of another small plane, after having spent so much time in my own . . . like wearing a stranger's baggy, ill-fitting clothes. As we came alongside Davis Island, Benny May informed me that it wasn't named for Jefferson Davis, the father of the Confederacy, but for *his* father, who'd kept a cabin there. In the autumn Benny May flew hunters over the island so they could spot deer, then come back by boat and shoot them. A couple of years ago a flood drowned most of the deer or stranded them on high ground, where they starved, so there weren't many deer left to shoot.

As we approached Lake Bruin, I noticed a wrecked car beside the runway and asked Benny May about it. He said kids drag-raced the strip at night. Also (unwrecked) beside the runway were a Corsair, a Wildcat, and two T-6s. The Confederate Air Force was dedicated to restoring and flying planes from World War II and the Korean conflict, most of them owned by individual members but flown in air shows on behalf of the force. At this breakfast meeting there were more chicken wings than I had ever seen in one place, cooking inside a hot-water tank that had been cut in half lengthwise and set on hot coals. I was impressed; it seemed like thinking big. The get-together was good-natured and raucous, with many happy cries of "bullshit!" ringing out and, as far as I could tell, no business whatever conducted.

Goodhearted Benny May arranged a ride for me back to Tallulah in one of the two T-6s. It belonged to a cropduster who owned the Corsair as well and was flying that back while a friend was at the controls of the T-6. The friend flew with the canopy back so the hurricane-force airstream (200-plus mph) lashed our faces and yanked our hair around, augmenting the sensation of power and speed, which was already considerable, the 600-hp engine sending a roar into our skulls and vibrations through our backsides. I took photos of the Corsair flying beside us. It was painted the same deep blue that all Corsairs were during the war and had "Angel of Okinawa" written on the side, though it wasn't the original *Angel of Okinawa*. That was one of the benefits of being in an unofficial Air Force; you could play games with the past.

The owner and pilot of the Corsair, Merle Gustafson, owned one of the airports I passed up for Scott, called Marlin, and we stopped in there briefly for tea. The T-6's approach to landing included a steep dive followed by a pullup so sharp my innards seemed to be trying to exit through my knees, then a wingover. The Corsair's approach included several vertical rolls.

"I always wanted a fighter plane," declared Gustafson over tea. He had a deep wrinkle running down each of his cheeks, like a pair of dueling scars. "How I love that big horsepower!" When he talked he sometimes made pistols of his hands, pointing the barrels (index fingers) at each other. A wall of his den was covered with photos taken at air shows he'd been in, flying one of his warplanes or else a Waco in which he did aerobatics. One photo showed a little boy and little girl standing on the upper wing of a biplane, smiling. I was surprised, I told Gustafson, because I had read that wingwalking could be painful, even bruising to those who did it, but he insisted it wasn't so. They were his son and daughter, and they fought for the chance to wingwalk for him.

Later, at Tallulah, Benny May lent me his old car so I could drive across the Mississippi to a battlefield from another war, Vicksburg. There I took photos of all the Ohio monuments I could find, 16 in all, to send to my father, who had a deep, abiding interest in the Civil War. By the time I got back it was dusk, probably the finest hour at a little airport. The light was soft, the air still, the only sounds those that came to the field from far away. Planes on the ramp were silhouetted blue-gray against the faint rose of the sky and the gray-green sawtooth edge of the trees. Sitting there, they looked like nothing so much as big dogs, faithful family pets waiting for somebody to come along and undo their ropes and take them up for a spin. They were leaning a little against their ropes but weren't insistent, just sitting there, calm, like the rest of the world.

Suddenly loud noises broke through from the direction of the office. I glanced over and saw Fritz leaping out of the shadows, with two boys running flat out in front of him. One of the boys had a bicycle on his shoulder—probably too scared to stop and jump on it. Fritz barked the two of them off the field, then came back and joined Benny May. Benny May said he and Fritz had been doing their rounds when Fritz found the boys stealing money out of the office Coke machine. When they'd finished their rounds, Benny May offered me a ride to my hotel. He started the old Belvedere but didn't get very far. Fritz began running around it, counterclockwise, so fast that Benny May didn't dare go fast himself. Fritz stayed so close to the car as he ran that when he passed in front of the headlights only the top of his Treflan-yellow back lit up, and when he passed behind he bit the exhaust pipe. Or so Benny May said. "I don't know what he calls himself doing," Benny May

The author, dragging her feet before takeoff from Spring Valley. (Note goshawk painted on cowling, daisies blooming at tiedown.)

Reassuring factory ad: "Think Luscombes are strong?"

The Luscombe's sweet, comic face.

A Citabria picking up a banner and heading for the beach.

Marc Osmer and Hugh Mason with a tow plane: Boy-heroes.

The Wallins at their genuine lunch counter, Rehoboth Beach.

Orville Wright poses for a fan.

Pleasures of the
shoreline:
"Toy" boats . . .
on a sunlit sea.

Artie, with his sister,
offers a gullible
pilot a boat ride.

Carrot Top with Jimmy Carter's first campaign plane.

Navy vet and South Sea
island hospitality,
at Georgetown.

Cropduster's hangar in Tallulah: "Where it all began."

Nicole Lamotte: First civilian female to solo a Shooting Star?

Junior Burchinal
and Corsair:
"Oh to fly across
that old Texas
sky . . ."

grumbled, but he knew. Fritz had been doing the same thing for years, herding the old car, trying to keep it from moving off too fast, nipping its flanks so it wouldn't spread out too much, as his ancestors had their flocks of sheep on other fields in the calmness of dusk.

Harrell

There was nothing peculiar about a dog living at an airport. Other dogs (not to mention cats) did that. Named Flare, Skid, Spark Plug, Spinner, Carb Heat, and Chandelle, they lay splayed across cool hangar floors or padded across ramps behind the sturdy shoes of their owners, FBOs and mechanics who liked having them around as company during the long hours spent away from home. One dog at a field in Arizona, very much at home, sat immobile and apparently entranced the entire time I was there, watching a lizard scale the office curtain. A whole troop of dogs came on the field in Rome, Georgia, uninvited, at night, and seemed to belong. I was sleeping out and could hear them racing up and down the runway in the dark, howling. The dog that seemed to have the most complicated relationship with an airport, however, I never did see or hear. Ralph Broeske, the manager of a flying club at the Valdosta, Georgia, airport, told me about him when I came through.

The dog was young, nine or ten months old, and looked like Snoopy, "only a little leaner and taller at the shoulder," said Broeske. He was wild, although Broeske didn't know if he'd been born on the field or dumped there. "If you got within 50 feet of him he'd take off for his hiding place, wherever it was. That corner of the field is mostly swamp." Still, he was an airport pet of sorts. Broeske called him Airport and every evening would leave bowls of dog food and water outside the aeroclub office for him. Every morning the crew of a Southern Airways flight that terminated in Valdosta would set leftover galley food under the wing of their Martin 404 for him, too. Even controllers, those veteran observers of airport behavior, cared about the dog and would watch his movements through their binoculars. They called him "Nordog," for "No Operational Radio Dog," because, they said, "he never gets clearance before he crosses anything." Several times planes coming in to land had to take evasive action as he trotted, unperturbed and out of reach of regulation, across the active runway.

Not everybody liked Nordog. The airport's manager, who worried about lawsuits and insurance, hated him. One day he asked a dog-catcher to take him away. The dogcatcher spent a month trying. But "the vehicle didn't even get to the airport *boundary* before Airport made himself scarce," said Broeske proudly. "By the time it was on the airport proper, he was lo-o-ong gone." After a month, the manager ordered the dogcatcher to shoot the dog on sight. When he heard that, Broeske—who had never gotten over the death of his Labrador three years before from ulcers and couldn't talk about it without getting tears in his eyes—vowed to get to Airport first. He set out the usual food and water that evening at the usual time but not quite in the usual place, in the recess of the aeroclub entrance instead of simply near it. As Airport approached the food Broeske slammed a metal sign adver-tising aeroclub rates down behind him, blocking his exit. Or so Broeske thought. "That bugger jumped right over the sign and ran up the center taxiway!"

Broeske asked the controllers, "Where does Airport go when he runs up the center taxiway?" "Disappears," they said. "We don't know." Broeske borrowed their binoculars and spent the rest of the afternoon scanning the field from the control tower, looking for Airport. All he could see was two men walking around carrying rifles. But if he didn't find the dog that afternoon, neither did the dogcatcher or the manager. "That sign must really have spooked him." The next day Broeske went to the manager and made him an offer. He, Broeske, would take two days off from work and try to catch Airport *if* during those two days nobody would try to shoot him. The manager agreed but added, "If after two days you haven't caught him, it is *you* who will have to shoot him."

From his vet Broeske got some tranquilizers and mashed a couple up, hid them in a wad of hamburger ("not just hamburger but *ground round;* I wanted the best"), and set the wad in Airport's bowl. He watched from a distance as the dog ate the laced meat. Then he waited. Two hours later he was still waiting. "That bugger was still on his feet!" He took another tranquilizer, mashed it up, put it in more ground round, and laid that in the dish. Airport ate it too. Broeske waited. Half an hour later Airport lay down under the wing of a Lodestar, "his favorite napping place." Broeske thought he had him but every time he tried to move in, Airport would lift his head and look around. Broeske waited. A half hour later Airport stopped lifting his head. Broeske ran up and slipped a rope around his neck. That woke Airport up. "I was afraid he'd bite me," said Broeske, "but he just whined and cried."

Before leaving home that morning, Broeske had cleaned out an abandoned wildcat cage built around the base of a windmill in the trailer court where he lived, and when he came back with Airport in his arms he laid the dog in the cage, put food and water in with him, and shut the door. The next day he did the same, put food and water in and shut the door, and this time Airport "ran back and forth like a wild animal." The next day he did the same, but the day after that when he put the food and water in he stayed, briefly. Airport wagged his tail. The next day he stayed, briefly, and touched Airport. The next day he petted Airport and the next day picked ticks off his coat. The next day he let Airport out of the cage with a harness, and several weeks after that he let him out of the cage without one.

Airport didn't run away. In fact, he wouldn't leave Broeske's side if he didn't have to. "He'd follow my truck with more persistence than any dog I'd ever seen," said Broeske, who'd seen a lot of dogs. While Broeske was at work Airport would cruise the trailer park picking up gifts for him and laying them on the trailer step. Telling about it Broeske lowered his voice, as if someone might overhear and nab him. "Rugs, tennis shoes, tools, rubber mats, shorts, toys, once even a *potted plant*. He was a kleptomaniac! I'd have to throw the things in the garbage can as soon as I got home so people wouldn't see them."

The day I came through Valdosta it had been only two months since Airport left the airport. Despite the dedicated truck-chasing and gift-giving, Broeske wasn't sure what hold the field might still have on the dog. Would Airport take one look and head right for his hiding place? Broeske wasn't willing to risk finding out. Some day, though, Broeske vowed, his eyes watery, "I'm going to take Airport back and see what he remembers of his old home."

Cajun country was taking on the quality of a Shangri-La; it was near-perfection and could only be reached through some mystical slit in the sky. The morning I was ready to fly to it from Tallulah, having received a favorable forecast the night before, a briefer told me "a big high" was pulling "stuff" up from the Gulf with "big buildups" between Baton Rouge and New Orleans and "rain just about all over." *Sacré bleu!* would I never see the place? With every negative briefing it was becoming more desirable; a glossy ibis on every cypress knee, a zydeco fiddler in every pole boat. But the briefer also told me the front could stick around as long as a week, so in the end I had to give up on Cajun country, consoling myself that it was all there to look forward to, an experience not yet spent, a treasure I could claim some day, *O joli blanc!*

Deprived of a destination, I decided to ask Graves where else along the river I might go. I found him sitting at the edge of the ramp, giving instructions to two apprentice spray pilots. "You go up to this ditch," he told them, pointing to a line on a diagram he'd drawn. Touching a square, he said, "There'll be a red truck here." He looked over at me. "There's usually no map," he explained. Then, to them: "For future reference, it's a Z field." To me: "One guy sprayed the wrong field." To them: "The field is dark forest-green. There's no other field *that green.*"

Once the boys were gone, I asked Graves if he knew of any interesting spot about 50 miles up the river I could visit, briefly, before heading west. He sat a minute, then told me about a friend who had his own strip about that far up and his own hangar with some nice old planes in it; I might like to take a look at them. Since the strip was private and not on the chart he gave me directions, the way he'd given them to the apprentice pilots. "East of the river . . . five miles in . . . newly paved strip . . . not near a town . . . you'll see an east-west road . . ." He drew a circle on my chart, for his best guess where the airstrip was, then, considering it, drew a second circle, then a third, for his three best guesses. It surprised me, his having to guess. I would have thought that a veteran spray pilot would have a memory for land features the way, say, a barge pilot had for river bottoms: near-perfect recall. But the Mississippi, though gigantic for a river, was not all that big when you thought about it, a mere elephant's tail compared to the land around it.

My preflight inspection was carefully scrutinized, not by Graves or by Benny May. A young man stood nearby and stared in silence as I drained fuel from a sump under the engine into a small glass jar which once held artichoke hearts and, failing to find any grayish blobs in the pink of the 80-octane gas, poured it back into one of my tanks, good for another 20 seconds or so of flight. The man was tall, lean, with blond curly hair and angelic features, and couldn't have been more than 19. He seemed tense and uncertain, kept shifting his weight from one cowboy boot to another. His manner, I thought, was rather grave, for one so young, so fair, so curly-haired. As I was polishing the windscreen he came over, crouched by one of my tires, and said, "Needs air." Without my asking him to, he dragged an air bottle over, and together we filled the tire to the regulation 18 pounds of pressure. We gave a couple of shots of air to the other tire too; then he stood and said what he had probably come over to say in the first place but was too shy to come right out with. "Cropdusting is the third deadliest job in the world."

I looked up from the hubcap I was screwing back in place. "I saw it in the Alabama paper," he hurried on. "After astronaut and scuba diving." It turned out that his father was a cropduster and he was going to become one too, soon. I wondered if there was some ghastly history and asked, gently, had his father crashed? "No," he said, sounding sorry. Then he added, brightening, "*Except* he ran out of gas once. He landed on a highway and a couple of culvert markers tore the bottom of his wings off but nobody stopped to ask if he was hurt or anything. He just walked to a gas station and bought a couple dollars' worth of gas. It was their first day of business and were they surprised!"

I might not have been acting impressed enough because he seemed to be fishing around for something else to tell me. He came up with, "Lots of times we had to pull Johnson grass or coffee weeds or soybeans out of Daddy's gear when he got too low." After a pause he said hopefully, "Daddy always told me if you have to go down, don't go down in soybeans if you can help it. The vines'll wrap around your gear and pull your nose under." I told him I'd keep that in mind but wasn't sure I'd recognize soybeans from the air, be able to tell them in fact from cotton or even coffee weeds. I also said I'd read in a magazine that if you had a choice of landing in (1) an apple orchard, (2) an orange grove, or (3) a peach orchard, you should choose the peach orchard; peach branches had the most give to them.

He kept casting about, then announced, "I did see a guy crash once. His engine went right through the wing. I was surprised he got out alive." In a softer voice, he added, "All he got was a crushed chest and a broken foot." Before I took off he made sure I knew he wasn't going to be dusting crops for long. He'd only be doing it to build up some hours so he could get a job flying jets for an oil company. I climbed in my cockpit, waved goodbye, taxied to the runway, and took off, wondering, How scared *was* he?

Benny May had told me that some pilots when they flew over the Mississippi liked to dip their tires in the water, for fun. "Nose up, a little flare," he advised. I considered doing that; it could be like waterskiing, trailing a pair of little wakes. Or it could be like gymnastics—a forward flip, inverted sink. Another time, I thought, another river. Not today. Today the river had a glassy look, and it was hard to tell exactly how high above it I was flying. There was no obvious current pattern defining the surface, no driftwood or litter being carried along, like tracers, giving a sense of flow. Someone at Tallulah had told me that two or three people drowned in the river off Vicksburg every year, and not during floods or storms either, just on ordinary days, in the act of swimming. As I surveyed the placid brown mass it was difficult to appreciate that fact. In New York City once I had a taxi driver who told me that when he was growing up in Memphis his mother used to take him and his little sisters and brothers down to the river and throw them in, one by one, wait on shore as they splashed their way back to her, then dry them off with a big towel. Well, that's how the Mississippi looked today. Like a poor family's bathtub, a Ganges of the heartland.

When I got about 50 miles up the river I left it and flew over the area of Graves's first circle. I didn't see an airstrip so I flew to the area of the second circle, didn't see one there either so flew to the area of the third circle and did see a strip *and* a hangar, but there weren't any old planes in the hangar, any planes at all, I could tell without landing because the hangar doors were standing wide open and I was low enough to peer in. So I gave up on that place too, went back to the Mississippi, crossed it, and kept on going, west, into Arkansas.

By then the sky had started to fill up with clouds. They were those fluffy little fair-weather clouds which line up all on the same level as far as you can see, like an army on the march. Sweet little cotton-ball clouds. Lambsy ears. Angel butts. If you were on the ground looking up at them, you'd be charmed. But if you were flying underneath them, you'd know there was nothing sweet or angelic about them. Each cloud was visible proof that something invisible but real and unpleasant was going on below. A whipped-cream topping, you might say, on a dumpcake of air (convection currents, building and rising). As I flew underneath them I was being shaken, jerked, and thrown repeatedly against my seat belt, which I found not unlike being jostled on the subway and almost as annoying. I even said "Quit it!" out loud once. But the jostling didn't quit, and the farther I flew into Arkansas, and the more of the cute little bunnytails I saw, the worse the jostling got.

A former owner of my Luscombe—someone told me who saw it in the days before I bought it—had installed as cockpit seats a pair of genuine leather horseback-riding saddles, with matching tooled-leather upholstery on the door panels, and as I went bucking and bounding across the skies of Arkansas I thought of those saddles; how sensible they seemed, how *right*. And I began to wonder, in my rising and falling, were they Western or English saddles? Western seemed more likely, since a large proportion of male pilots these days have that image of themselves (one issue of the *Luscombe Club Newsletter* ran a letter from a Luscombe owner who compared "today's sport pilot" to the "cowboy of the 1800s—an individual," he wrote, "a free thinker, riding top speed on his steed across this great nation of ours at constant personal risk . . . his go-to-hell wrangler's hat [our] baseball cap, his six gun worn low on the hip [our] mike and headset . . . his boots, my Gawd, what's a man without boots!" and concluding with, "The cowboy of yesteryear and the pilot of today stand shoulder to shoulder. Sage brush to clouds. Lariat to Luscombe. We are a band of brothers [sic]. Stand Tall, Ya'All!"). But if Western, did the pommels ever get in the way of back stick? How about riding boots, chaps, cowboy hat— did the owner ever wear them as he sat astride his saddle and roamed the Eastern skies? And did he ever shout, as I've done a couple of times when ascending after a long absence and feeling thrilled about it, "Yahoo! Ya-*hoo! Ride 'em!*"?

Hoping for a smoother ride, I climbed to 6,500 feet, but the air at 6,500 was as rough as it had been at 2,500. Still, I stayed up, since there wasn't a whole lot to see from lower down. Arkansas seemed to be even more wooded than the last three states I'd been in and looked from above like one big, lumpy, green canopy, its edges frayed by haze. Except for two forest fires, which ran in ten-mile lines across my flight path. Or rather the *smoke* from two fires. The flames themselves were hidden by the trees and rising smoke. Flying somewhere in New York State once, I had seen a fire where the flames *were* visible: a large, trembling ring of orange, burning outward, devilishly beautiful from the air.

At the first airport I saw after the fires, I landed. I decided to let the clouds kick someone else around for a while, to eat lunch, cool off, and work on my hair. During the ride in the T-6 the wind had batted my hair about so much and tangled it so badly that I hadn't been able to get a comb all the way through it since. For days I had been picking at knots, pulling strands apart with my fingers, and forcing a comb along an inch at a time. No matter how careful I was, though, I always lost hair. I figured I had lost a tenth of my previous hair mass as a result of that one (hair-raising) ride.

My landing at Harrell was three-point, or nearly. What three-pointing a taildragger usually involves is trying in the final moments to keep the plane from touching the ground. It's as if you're playing the tease, lifting the nose a bit higher every time the plane starts to settle so the wings are at a slightly higher angle to the air it's passing through, thus providing a bit more lift, which keeps the plane flying a bit longer. When the angle gets so high the air over the wing ceases to be smooth—at the very instant when the wing loses all lift and quits flying—the wheels should be on the ground for the first time and you will have greased or kissed the runway. I will forever cherish and maybe pay the college tuition of a friend's child whom I took up for a short flight once and who asked as we rolled out after a pretty good three-pointer, "How do you know you're on the ground?"

The first thing I noticed after I kissed Harrell's runway, a bit slop-pily, was chains. There is an undulating line along the eastern edge of the Great Plains, which is comparable in its underlying reality yet geographic imprecision to the shortgrass line, the 20-inch rainfall line, and the line where Tertiary sediments from the Rocky Mountains stopped their eastward flow millions of years ago, and it might be called, if it were ever plotted, the Chain Line. Determined in part by average wind strength in the region, the Chain Line is the boundary past which tiedown ropes, used almost universally in the East to secure planes to the ground, are replaced by chains, favored all over the West except along the Pacific coast. If you are flying from the East Coast to the West Coast, it is inevitable that someday at some airport in mid-continent you will find chains lying coiled on the ramp or dangling from wings instead of ropes and you will know, without a glance at the chart, that the East is essentially behind you. Myself, I don't much like chains, not because they remind me that I'm getting far from home but because they can be a drag to use—seem awkward to attach, can scratch the paint, are noisy going through the strut rings (not to mention being psychologically unappealing, suggesting other, less benign forms of restraint, shackles, leg irons, etc.). I wasn't sure if Harrell was actually on the Chain Line—it seemed early—or if the chains were just an aberrant taste of the owner, a maverick display of Western mentality.

The next thing I noticed at Harrell was an awful lot of Cessnas. In the main hangar there was nothing *but* Cessnas, all high-wing, single-engine, swept-tail, nosewheel planes, Cessna 182s, 172s, a 210, and a Cardinal, all of them new or nearly new, and all of them white, with factory-painted stripes. Nice, reliable aircraft but so generic and undifferentiated as to be almost boring, or as boring as airplanes could get.

Out on the field, too, was a lopsided number of Cessnas, all of them new or nearly new, all white with factory-painted stripes. I didn't much like them, either, or rather so many of them. One of the glories of little airports, it seemed to me, was the variety of aircraft on most of them, testament to the freewheeling history of aviation in this country. Small, medium, and (rather) large planes, high-wing and low-wing, carrying lots of horsepower and not much power, with "no electric" and full panels, "clean" and scarred by the years, painted up with barracuda teeth and just numbers. Strolling down flight lines and rows of hangars you saw Champs, Comanches, Bonanzas, Pittses, and Cherokee 140s, Mooneys, Pietenpols, and Yankees, VariEzes, Skymasters, Swifts, MU2s, Stardusters, Cruisers, and Navajos, and if you were lucky a Tiger or Gypsy Moth, a Waco, or a Funk. Visiting a small airport was not unlike visiting a zoo, and finding yourself at one with almost nothing on it but Cessna lookalikes was like going to a zoo with nothing in it but, say, ungulates; you'd miss seeing the big cats, the seals, the capybaras.

The FBO told me what happened. He had a scheme whereby he bought Cessnas new from the factory, flew them for about 100 hours, on charter etc., and sold them to customers "with all the bugs worked out," at prices Cessna wouldn't allow him to if the planes were new. I didn't quite get the arithmetic but everybody supposedly benefited, except perhaps pilots passing through for whom ungulates were just not enough.

I decided to stay at Harrell anyway, not fly on that day. Coming in I'd been not only knocked about but overheated, and although the air on the ramp was as hot and close as it had been in the air—stepping out of my cockpit was like walking into a pillow—in the restaurant near the field where I went for lunch the air-conditioned air was so cold it almost stung my skin. As I slid my bare thighs (I was wearing shorts) over the chilled plastic seat of a booth, I felt my tense body beginning to let go. I spread my arms full length on the cool Formica tabletop, relaxed onto them, and thought, "O what solace there is in an icy room!"

That turned out to be a mistake, pampering myself with the comforts of cold. The following morning in my hotel, I woke to the sound of rain on my windows. I was shocked, unprepared for the sound. So sure had I been of the weather, that it would be more of what I had been flying through for weeks now, skies that offered no comfort to the farmers, were unrelentingly, unmercifully dry, that I hadn't even checked with Flight Service the night before. Why hadn't I flown *on?* I berated myself. Maxims formed in my head. "Don't let a good day die." "Always go on while you have the sky for it." If I had to be stuck somewhere, I could have been stuck in Paris, Texas, where I'd been planning to go, or at least Uncertain, Texas, where I knew there was a lake beside the runway a person could row a boat on, rain or no rain.

Heaving a sigh that would have sent a prop windmilling, I got out of bed and made my call—too late—to Flight Service, heard the briefer say the system could be around for *days.* Needing company more than food, I pulled on boots and a poncho and set out for the airport office, kicking at weeds on the way and thinking sourly about that motto of innumerable flight schools, "The Freedom of Flight." *Ha!*

Three pilots were in the office already, standing, drinking coffee. They had flown in that morning, on instruments, in a Learjet (now *there* was Freedom of Flight). They worked for a paper company in

Houston, they said, and had brought several executives to Harrell to meet with timber suppliers. They had to wait at the airport until the meeting was over, whenever that might be. (One of the principal qualifications for the job of corporate pilot, it seemed, was the capacity to put up with accordion-pleated time.) One executive hadn't made the flight so there was a spare breakfast and a pilot asked if I wanted it. I was curious to see what an executive of a paper company rich enough to be able to afford its own Learjet and three-man crew got to eat on the way to a business meeting in another state. The answer (in a cardboard box) was a scrambled egg (looked singular to me), a biscuit (no butter), a packet of grape jelly, a piece of hard candy, and a stick of chewing gum. I ate the egg and biscuit and saved the candy and gum for later; then when I heard the pilots talking about taxiing their plane to the other side of the field to get jet fuel I asked if I could go with them. I said I had never seen the inside of a Learjet.

Not only did they let me go along, they let me sit left seat. Despite all the instruments, the Learjet's cockpit didn't seem all that different from a Luscombe's: two side-by-side seats, pair of control columns, pair of foot pedals, all-black panel, narrow slice of sky ahead, etc. Not a whole lot more room than in a Luscombe either, all knobs and switches within easy reach, like in an efficiency kitchen. That was one thing about aviation that was democratic; cockpits couldn't grow much with the size of the airplane, turn palatial. The pilot in the right seat started the engines, then told me I could work the rudders while he handled the throttle. Excited, I set right to it but soon saw the nose of the Learjet swinging back and forth over the taxiway in a sort of mechanical slalom. "Boy," I said, embarrassed, "are these rudder pedals ever sensitive!" The Luscombe rudders worked by cable and had to be stomped on to produce much of an effect, but these were hydraulic, I had forgotten. When I let up on them, the Learjet went straight. Which gave me time to look over the dials and play a bit with the levers and knobs. Pulling knobs, I discovered, took only the lightest, fingertip touch, as if I were peeling a banana. It was odd how most people still thought of piloting jets as a man's job; strength was the least of it.

After that, I decided to fill my down time by having my brakes tightened. Not only the rudders but the brakes on the Luscombe worked by cable, and over time the cables tended to slacken so the pedals had to be depressed farther and farther before they engaged the brakes, which made the pedals harder and harder to reach. Even when the cables weren't slack the brake pedals were hard to reach, positioned as they were behind the rudder pedals and closer together so that in order to be ready to hit rudders or brakes or both during landing and taxiing (toes on rudders, heels on brakes), you had to keep your feet practically in the ballet first position, toes pointing way out and heels together—in addition to which the brake pedals were small, not much bigger than Oreo cookies (which in fact they resembled, being round and dark with raised crosshatching on top) and thus not much of a target, *besides* which they swung away when depressed, presenting more side than face to your heels: an even smaller target, the cookie's edge.

The person I asked to tighten my brakes was the mechanic in the all-Cessna hangar. He looked to me a lot like Rock Hudson, only more handsome, but he lacked something, star quality. In my experience mechanics were mostly hearty, outgoing types, downright gabby, some of them, guys who enjoyed having other people around giving them gossip, admiring their work, hanging on their advice, keeping them company while they tightened screws. Many were the kingpins of the airports they were in; they held court. Gene Day at Pottstown seemed happiest when his shop had a slew of pilots in it, doing their own things usually but wanting his direction or his tools or his wild, energizing presence.

This mechanic, though, was quiet almost to muteness, without expression, and alone. I tried to get a conversation going but he either didn't respond or just mumbled. I didn't think he was annoyed or even shy, just uninterested. After a while I gave up trying and worked in a silence matching his. While he adjusted the brakes, I changed the oil and listened through our mutual stillness to a drip in the ladies' room at the far end of the hangar. It produced a sort of tune as it hit the water in the toilet bowl, sounding like a far-off xylophone.

After pouring in new oil, I began waxing my plane, starting with the bugs. I had hit so many bugs in flight that all the leading edges of the plane—wings, struts, tail, cowling, and gear fairings—were covered with a tough, speckled-brown coating made up of the carcasses of countless winged creatures which had been moving along through the air nicely, doing their hunting, mating, migrating, molting, when suddenly the sky became hard and impenetrable. They were stuck so firmly to the metal skin they seemed welded on, whether from the impact or the drying of burst tissue or the roasting action of the sun, I didn't know. To get the bugs off without scratching the paint I had to soften them first with liquid wax, then scrape at them, one by one, with a thumbnail.

That accomplished, the waxing was a joy. A sensual pleasure, like spreading lotion on a baby's body after a bath. Using a wax-soaked cloth, I rubbed the swellings and hollows of the cowling, the slow curve of the fuselage, the parabolas of strut and fairing and fin. As I did so I felt proud of the Luscombe's fine lines, particularly its "shoulders." The shoulders were the part of the fuselage just back of and beside the wings where it widened to form the cabin and were so lovely, particularly when seen from behind, their shape accented by notches at the base of the wings, that they had done more than anything else to convince me when I was looking for an airplane to buy that this was the kind I should get.

Next, I rolled the newly waxed plane back into the rain and started walking to a complex of stores down the road, to get food for the time when I would be flying again. After I'd passed a couple of stores in the complex, I heard a man shout, "Come heah!" I looked around and saw a squat, bald man standing in the doorway of a liquor shop, looking my way and waving his arm like a baling hook. "Ovah *heah!*" he yelled in a loud, bossy drawl. Why was he ordering me around? I wondered. And so rudely? "HEAH!" he yelled and made more hooking motions. I kept on walking toward the grocery store, bought the usual—tuna fish, tomato juice, and crackers, plus something different this time, canned apricots—and when I came out saw him still standing in the doorway of the liquor shop, looking my way. As soon as he caught sight of me he began yelling again, in the same bullying tone, *"Come ovah heah!"* I turned away from him, to take a shortcut back to the airport someone in the store had told me about, and as I was slogging my way up the muddy road I heard a truck coming up behind me. It stopped when it came even with me; the man from the liquor store was at the wheel. He said something but I couldn't hear him. I motioned for him to roll his window down.

"What do you want?" I asked, suspicious.

He called down from his truck. "Have you got change for a fahve?"

"No." (More suspicious.) "Why?"

(Firm.) "I was going to give you a dollah."

(*Very* suspicious.) "What for?"

(Surprise.) "Whatever you're col*lect*ing for."

(Pause to consider.) "I'm not . . . collecting. I'm . . . *walking.*"

His turn to consider. A look remarkably like repugnance passed over his face. "Oh!" he said and rolled up his window, drove the truck up and around, and went back the way he had come, without looking at me again or saying another word. I stood in the mud feeling strangely diminished. What was *that* about? Did decent Southern women never go afoot except for charity?

Most of the afternoon I spent in the airport office, staring out at the rain with the FBO. It seemed to be doing him even less good than it was me. When it was dry he got paid for flying fire patrol two hours a day. "Forestry," he announced, "is Arkansas's number one business. If there's even a puff of smoke we've got to see it." All the rest of that day, that night, and the next day it rained, and the next evening when I watched the weather on TV I heard one man say the system would move east the following day and another say it would move west. By morning (paralyzed by indecision, perhaps), it appeared not to have moved at all. The rain was still coming down steadily, although in finer drops, and clouds still covered the sky completely, though they might have been slightly less dense. I sat in Harrell's office anyway, with my eye on the sky. From time to time it would seem to glow a brighter, more pearly gray and I'd put in a call to Flight Service; one time I got a briefer who said everything was the same and one time I got a briefer who said conditions had improved but not enough for a VFR (Visual Flight Rules, or non-instrument) flight. Both of the briefers delivered their pronouncements in deep, glum, Digger O'Dell voices, which probably did more than anything they actually said to keep me from going. In the middle of the afternoon, though, I got a briefer who said things seemed to be moving out and, well, why not try it?

I did a quick, wet preflight, then climbed into my cockpit and rather nervously went over my course. I had laid it out so it would take me over as many roads and near as many little airports as possible. Then, casting a final look at the sky, out of which rain was still falling, I taxied out to the runway and took off. At 1,000 feet I started seeing scud. Over Camden, the city closest to Harrell, it seemed to be mixed with smoke. Maybe, I thought, the afternoon briefer was just optimistic by nature, *toujours gai* and all that. (Why not try it, *chérie?*) I kept on going, though, and the situation became, if not good, at least interesting. The clouds were many different shades of gray, blue, and white and had bases riding at different altitudes, some with ragged edges, others rounded and better defined, others misty and almost transparent. It was like being loose at a street fair, there was so much to see. The scene was constantly shifting.

After a while I radioed Texarkana Flight Service for a weather update. "Buildups all quadrants," said the man who answered. Ahead on my left I could see a high white tower of cloud, on my right, over Lake Texarkana, an impressive expanse of darkness, yet directly ahead only blank, grayish air—a flying corridor. As I moved down the corridor it slowly widened until I reached the Arkansas-Texas border. Suddenly sunlight hit my windscreen. It was falling through open spaces between cottonball clouds. So this was Texas! *Hot, dry, sunny Texas!* Already the cockpit felt warmer. Fields on either side of the road I was following lay placidly in the warm glow of the sun. In one field a black bull stood motionless, as if stunned with contentment. In a back yard, a black-and-white dog frisked alone. I was lightheaded with relief, kept hearing somewhere in the back of my head, over and over, Piece of cake, Piece-of-cake, PIECEOFCAKE! It wasn't just a matter of weather being good or bad, then; there were passages in gray air; I could manage. Had I thus moved closer to Freedom of Flight?

In the next 75 miles I passed the cities of Boston, Texas, Detroit, Texas, and Reno, Texas, before putting down at Paris, Texas—the second-biggest Paris in the world, I was told soon after I landed.

Paris

In Paris, I couldn't figure out where to put my airplane. It wasn't just any old airport. As I pulled off the cracked, bumpy, tilted, pebble-strewn runway I saw parked ahead of me, across the field, a Martin Marauder (B-26). A few yards to my right was a Corsair, its wings, hinged for carrier parking, folded so their tips almost touched, moth-like, above the cockpit, and beyond it a Flying Fortress (B-17). Near that was a B-25, farther out a Navy Wildcat, elsewhere on the field a C-46, a Harvard (T-6), another B-25, and a Stearman. I was wondering where in this intimidating company I should put my plane when I heard a tapping at my left window and turned to see an oil-blackened face peering in, then an oil-blackened hand gesturing toward the back of a hangar. When I pulled in to a spot behind the hangar, I found myself next to a Grumman F9F Panther, a sleek, all-white jet fighter, first American jet to be flown in combat, in Korea. Its engine had apparently been removed because its nose was pointing up and its tail was touching the ground. Sitting there, it looked like a rocket ready for launch. Next to it my Luscombe resembled some early industrial gadget, a barley thresher.

I walked around the field. On the ground was some tourist spoor—paper french-fry trays, milkshake containers, soda cans—and on the fence separating the airport from the road a huge sign, "FLYING TIGERS AIRPORT—Visiting Hours Daylight to Dusk." This then was an aviation museum—but not just any old aviation museum. In this one the exhibits moved. Some of the visitors came there not just to look but to act. They came to learn how to do what most of them would probably never do again. To earn a line on their licenses that none of their buddies back home had. To make their dreams (or their nightmares) real. *I* came because, although I didn't have the money to do those things, I wanted to meet pilots who did. And to meet the man—the lone man—who owned the museum and every airplane in it.

I found him in the office, talking to a woman and man who kept calling him "Junior." He didn't look much like a Junior to me—too tall, too middle-aged, too deep-voiced, too commanding. He had gray-blond, thinning hair, pale eyes, and a face that had begun to sag, as if he were pulling an extra half-G all the time, yet somehow he gave the impression of being in his prime. He was wearing a bright red jumpsuit with matching red baseball cap, and when he stood he slouched, which someone told me later made him seem "more Army than Air Force." He had in fact played an Army general in the movie *MacArthur,* for which he landed his B-17 in front of the cameras, climbed out of the cockpit, and walked across the tarmac, presumably slouching.

He turned out to be a real junior, I found out when the woman and man left, Isaac Newton Burchinal, Jr. (named for the gravity he was to defy daily, or what?). He had a heavy Texas accent and used it tirelessly; how the man loved to talk! When I asked him to tell me about the warplanes, he tilted his chair back on two legs, stuck his boots up on the desk, and began at the beginning. "I always felt cheated because I couldn't go to the Second World War," he said. "My big brother got to go but I was too young. All those guys were heroes to me. There was an air base near our school and I'd sit in English class and hear those T-6 engines change pitch as they came in. They left that sound with me. Ever since, I've had a fascination with World War Two airplanes. Only American, though. None of the others turn me on, not even Germany!"

He wanted to fly "more than anything else in the world" after he left high school. "But I come from a long list of scared folks," he said. "I wouldn't stay at home at night without all the lights on, for fear of darkness. I'd look down from a tall building and . . ." He made descending, shrinking circles with a finger until it hit the desk. "My conscience was willing but my flesh was weak. So I drank to get my courage up. I wouldn't fly unless I had some whiskey or tequila or beer first. I'd grab a six-pack and a friend, a crippled boy I knew, and we'd go up and chase cotton-pickers. By the time I was 26 I had my license but I was an alcoholic. I shouldn't be alive today. Everybody else who had what happened to me is dead now. Three times something almost took my life, three totally unexplained events . . ."

He said "three times" ominously, like a preacher chanting, "Repent." I tried to count the three. "One day I was flying home from Dallas in a ragwing Luscombe [!] I'd cracked up the day before landing in a fog when I was half drunk and stepped on the brakes too hard. I put a cloth over the torn part of the windshield, had a couple swigs of tequila, and took off. I ran into fog and went on top but every time I tried to let down I had to go back up because there didn't seem to be any bottom to the fog. Finally I broke out over a highway with a sign saying so many miles to Ladonia. I knew where Ladonia was so I followed it home." Number One, I presumed.

"The next day I took a hammer and beat the dents out of the leading edges of the Luscombe, then traded it for a BT-13. That plane had more power, more noise, and more speed [oh shut up]. It started my 'military' career. I couldn't get anybody to check me out in it because nobody knew anything about BT-13s in those days so I used whiskey to overcome my fear and checked myself out. It was real dangerous. [Number Two?] Three weeks later the engine got a vapor lock and the BT-13 quit over a muddy field. The field had a great big ditch in it and when I landed the ditch opened up in front of me. I thought, 'Oh Lord, I'm fixing to die!' but at the last minute the engine cut in and the plane jumped the ditch. It ran into a terrace and that wiped out both gear. I had a strong feeling then that my life was coming to a close." Number Two? Three? Were the Luscombe-in-the-fog and BT-13-checkout incidents merely preliminary color, making *this* Number One?

"I traded the BT-13 for a Culver Cadet. That plane was sensitive beyond belief. One day a drinking crony and I took a pretty good lick before we went up in it, and when we tried to lower the gear we hit the top of an oak tree. [Four? Three? Two?] A couple of weeks later I flew the Cadet in an air show and was trying to cut the toilet paper [the pilot throws a full roll of toilet paper out the window of his airplane, then tries to slice the floating ribbon of the unfolding roll with his propeller as many times as possible—usually by descending in a tight spiral—before the paper touches the ground]. I decided to do a loop so I could cut the paper both top and bottom but I stalled out at the top of the loop and when I tried to roll out I got into a flat inverted spin. 'That's the end of life for me,' I said, 'and I'm not ready to go!' Those controls were slopping all over the place. People saw the plane go behind trees. To this day I can't say how I got out." (Number Five? No.) "Three times," Burchinal chanted, *"three times* something was fixing to take my life!

"I went to my doctor. 'Doc,' I told him, 'the next move I make I'm going to die.' The feeling was working on me daylight to dark. I was climbing poles for the phone company and something had to give. But I kept on drinking. 'It's your conscience working on you,' the doctor said. 'You don't need medicine, you need a *preacher.*' A few days before, a preacher had come by my house, but I run him off. I wasn't interested. Now I told my wife to get ahold of that preacher and ask him to lunch. He came to lunch but he said, 'You run me off.' Then he said Christ had died on the cross for me. For *me.* I had never taken it to heart before. I just hit them knees. That's all there was to it. When I got up off the floor I didn't want any more juice. From that instant on, it never crossed my mind, like it was totally wiped out. From that day on, I started building other people's lives."

Sanctimonious as that sounded, he was almost certainly sincere. "I wanted a church of my own. I asked the preacher, 'Can you get me some little-bitty church?' It took him a year. 'You'll like this,' he told me. 'It's 16 miles down the Red River, where you used to drink beer.' Well, my buddies and cronies were all hanging out down there, tough as nails. I never did get one of them into church."

He stopped talking and his face fell. Hounddog creases formed around his mouth. That happened whenever he stopped talking; his face fell. He started talking again and the creases went away. "I stayed at that church 16 years and got ordained a Baptist minister. When I bought the airport I started my own chapel." On my way in to the office I had seen a hangar with a P-51 Mustang in the front half and in the back half—separated from the plane by a curtain—a table covered by a white cloth with a metal chalice, wooden cross, and vase of artificial flowers on it and a few rows of folding chairs in front of it. Burchinal's congregation consisted of his family, his employees, and his flight students. His sermons were on the subject of flying. "Or safety and flying," he said. "Or drinking and flying. I use airplanes as a human lesson. I say, 'In the same way that God wrote a love story to man through the Bible, the Government wrote the Dash-One Manual for you. So you could have guidelines not to get killed. The Government thought enough of you to make aviation safe, so study! Prepare yourself for the mission!'"

So far the only warplane I'd heard about was the BT-13, which only *started* Burchinal's military career, so we got together over dinner (his wife and daughter were in Cincinnati picking up a jet engine) and talked some more. We went to a steakhouse down the road from the airport where carts with shelves full of raw beef slabs were rolled up to your table so you could choose the very ones you wanted cooked— the Texas equivalent of the French pastry cart, I presumed, or the New England lobster tank. I ordered wine with my steak but Burchinal not only didn't order any but *refused* to order any, an act of declining. I felt a little self-conscious sipping "the juice" in front of him and thought, watching him watch me, how deep the fear must have been, and at the same time how profound the love of flying, for one of them not to drive the other out. The two were locked together in such balance that they almost killed him. Hitting his knees had shifted the balance, and there was no fourth time, at least not one that he counted.

With his slickered-back hair, shiny, black patent-leather boots (he made sure I knew they were custom-made), and restless gaze, he didn't look like a teetotaler to me. When the dinner check arrived, he flashed a $500 bill and held it so his fingers blocked the portrait oval. "If you know whose face is on this, I'll give it to you," he said. I just thought he might, and mentally flipped through old school notes. "Jackson?" I said, my voice rising at the end so he knew it was a guess. He looked pleased and said I could have another try. "Adams?" Another try. "Wilson?" He lifted his fingers from the oval, revealing a clean-shaven face. "McKinley!" he crowed. Sometimes he carried several of these around at once, he told me, even, on occasion, a Cleveland ($1,000) or two. "I might see a plane I like," he said, unconvincingly casual, "and I'd rather pay for it than dicker around."

Most of his planes he didn't have to pay that much for. Surplus aircraft were plentiful after the war, he explained. "You could buy one in the 50s for a tenth or twentieth of what you can now. I got my Mustang from a guy who won it in a dice game; he just wanted someone to pay his gambling debts. My P-38 crashed in a jungle in Paraguay and they fished it out of a river and I had it shipped here. I got my B-26 out of a junkyard in Lexington, Kentucky, and my T-33 from an Air Force base where they were about to saw it in half and feed it to a furnace. I had to fight to save it."

As for his B-17, it had belonged to a man in California who flew it for the movies until the Vietnam war came along and people temporarily lost their taste for war movies. The man refused to check Burchinal out in it, and "there was nobody else to check me out in it either. They might have been the best there was 25 years ago but 25 years deteriorates a man's ability. Finally an old spray pilot agreed to go up with me but he'd never flown a B-17 either. Four days [same beat as "three times"] it took me to get up courage to risk not only that man's life but my whole fortune. *Four days!* Then I run out of excuses. 'Now you must fly,' I said. I dragged myself into that cockpit. I started the engines—*six thousand horses!* My heart was beating so fast I could hardly keep my feet still. I heard the tower say, 'You got it' and I pushed four throttles full forward. The plane started moving, slow at first, then the tail started to pick up, and at 90 miles an hour the tail *was* up and I felt for that sensation that differentiates pilots from all other people, when the weight of the plane is transferred into your hand and now you're a bird. At 130 it lifted off and I never had a feeling like that in my life. I was flying my *house.* The wings reached back clear from California to Texas. Once I got it up I had the feeling I couldn't get it down again, but the fear was overcome by the joy of accomplishment."

Later, to share not only the joy of accomplishment but the cost of it as well (for every hour the B-17 flew, it needed four hours of preparation and 400 gallons of fuel), Burchinal put an ad in *Trade-a-Plane* offering lessons in six of his planes, including the B-17, Mustang, and Corsair. The people who answered his ad over the years were mostly doctors, lawyers, and current Air Force pilots. Half of them had flown in World War II, said Burchinal, and "wanted to do it one more time before the curtain closed." All found flying the old warplanes "a release, an outlet, a safety valve," he swore. "They really have to reach for something here. I probably help more people than if I was a psychiatrist."

Women too came to Flying Tigers, but rarely as students. Men brought them along, to watch their takeoffs and landings and keep them company between lessons. Burchinal disapproved, not for the women's sake but for the men's. "When women are around, men lose their ability to think and react," he said with a straight face. "This DC-8 pilot for Air Canada brought a stewardess with him once, a nice German girl. With her around he couldn't even solo a T-6. It was a combination of guilt and distraction. 'Try laying off the German girl for five minutes,' I said, 'and see how it goes.' After that he did okay.

A doctor came one time with his nurse; he was 50 and she was 21. He tried to snaproll the T-6 on takeoff, and I caught it just before it would have gone on its back. 'Pops,' I told him, 'there are lots of things you did 20 years ago you can't do now.' The Army had the right idea during the war [World War II]. They confined men in flight training to base and declared women off-limits. They understood that women can affect men's flying beyond belief.''

The next day I met one of his students, a ''geoengineer'' from Kansas City. He wasn't the type to be called Pops but he was the age and struck me as having a similar problem with proving he still had what it took. In every situation in which I saw him he behaved in a cold, arrogant, tight, and humorless way, never relaxing into enthusiasm or even appreciation if he could help it. His hair was white, and maybe he was trying to keep all other manifestations of aging at bay by playing the part of an utterly superior, steel-hearted man. He stood under a wing of the Marauder before going up for his first lesson in the T-6, studying the specs, and the haughty expression on his face and pose of his body would lead any observer to conclude that he was the only reliable man in the squadron. I preferred Burchinal's brand of sloppy, extrovert macho.

After the two of them took off in the T-6, sending out a loud animal roar and a large cloud of dust, the field became exaggeratedly quiet. I looked for a place to wait for them to come back (like all those other women). I thought I was alone on the field but while passing the Corsair I saw four legs sticking out from under the stump of a wing. Two of the legs belonged to Burchinal's son, Bo. Burchinal had told me how he used to take Bo up flying when he was a baby, strapping ''the old jug'' (baby bottle) to an exhaust stack to warm it and landing in a farmer's field when Bo's diapers needed changing. By the time Bo was eight, he was flagging for his father, meaning he stood at the end of a row of cotton and held up a white cloth so Burchinal would know which row to spray next. The month when Bo turned 16 he soloed six of the warplanes on the field including the Mustang, and in the years that followed he learned how to spray crops himself, do aerobatics, and repair airplanes. Then he too got married, had a son, and took him flying.

Bo and another young mechanic were packing the Corsair's hydraulic flap-extension pump and chewing the fat. I sat nearby and listened to them. Bo was telling a story about a man who had crashed in a nearby swamp under mysterious circumstances. The weather had been fine, there was nothing wrong with the plane, but during the autopsy the doctors found spider venom in the man's blood. Which reminded Bo of the time a couple of yellowjackets got under his shirt while he was up spraying crops in the BT-13 and he went crazy at the controls trying to get them out. The second mechanic said he had been to an airport recently and seen a plane that was painted pink, bright pink, inside and out; even the throttle knob and cockpit dials were bright pink. Naturally, it belonged to a woman. Bo had a question: "Cats don't come in different sizes the way dogs do; why do you think that is?"

Meanwhile, a woman, man, and boy dressed in sunhats and pastel shorts emerged from the parking lot and started walking around the field. They seemed a little shy about it, reaching up now and then and gingerly touching a prop blade or insignia, tiptoeing up tiny staircases to peer through cockpit windows, speaking to each other in low voices. Burchinal had told me that visitors came from "all over the world" to see his planes. "Some of them sleep under a wing just to get a glimpse of a Mustang or a B-17." One Israeli made a beeline for the B-17 and started crying as soon as he sat in the pilot's seat. He told Burchinal why. During World War II his parents, who were Jewish, hid him and his little sister under the floor of their house in Holland and told them if they heard a noise in the night they should run away to a cave that had been prepared for them. One night they did hear a noise. "The Gestapo came to the house and slit his parents' throats," said Burchinal. "He and his sister ran away and hid in the cave. The cave was on a hillside and during the day they usually stayed there but at night they'd sneak down to the valley and take food from people's gardens. One day they were standing outside and saw Germans with bloodhounds climbing up the hill toward them. They stood hugging each other. They were sure this was the end of their lives. But instead of a few shots they heard thousands of rounds of ammunition. Then they saw a B-17 flying up the hillside, shooting at every German in sight. When it passed them the pilot waved. The Israeli said he'd never forget that as long as he lived."

How dangerous, I asked Bo, was flying the old warplanes? Burchinal had told me that more pilots died during World War II teaching in and being taught how to fly the planes than died flying them in combat, and of course they were decades older now. "Oh Dad's had a few close calls," said Bo, mentioning a few. "Once they asked him to do a vertical roll in his P-51 at an air show. It was a hazy day and after one and a half turns the P-51 tumbled and got into an inverted flat spin. The manual says it takes 12,000 feet to get out of an inverted flat spin in a P-51, and he was at 3,000 feet. The manual also says that you're supposed to blast out with power, but Dad did that three times [three times!] and nothing happened. We watched him go down below the trees. We were all shaking. We waited to hear the explosion. Before he hit the ground something must have happened. He had a passenger with him and the guy was tickled to death, said it was one of the best rides he ever had!''

Once during a takeoff in the P-38 the canopy's emergency latch came off and then the canopy itself, tearing loose the top of Burchinal's and a student's scalps. "By the time they landed, the student's scalp was flapping in the slipstream," said Bo. On another flight in the P-38 both engines froze at once and Burchinal bellylanded it in a corn-patch, claiming that as a first. Another time the engine on his PT-22 quit on climbout and he landed in the trees, which stopped the wings but not the fuselage. The fuselage kept on going, with Burchinal in it, into a yard where a woman was outside sweeping. When she saw him slide by, said Bo, "she threw her broom up straight away!"

Six, seven, eight, nine? Burchinal apparently didn't count these close calls, perhaps because drinking wasn't involved, or perhaps because he was now on the right side of the powers that regulate fate. No sooner had the T-6 landed than Burchinal stepped onto a wing and called out, like a director to a fieldful of eager campers, "Let's have coffee!" By "us" he meant the geoengineer and me, not Bo and the other mechanic, who kept on working. After telling us how to get to the coffee shop, he handed the keys to his bronze Cadillac Eldorado to the geoengineer and the keys to his red 1957 Chevy convertible to me, climbed on his gold Harley-Davidson motorcycle, and zoomed away. How clever of him to know we would like our own wheels. I was bowled over by that fire-engine-red convertible, with its red-and-white upholstery, white top, and huge tailfins, which went perfectly with the open country back of the highway.

Coffee, to Burchinal, meant iced tea—a man's drink down there.

He introduced a man sitting at the next table as someone whose wife had run away with a cropduster. The man appeared not to mind being pointed out as a cuckold. After saying "cropduster," Burchinal talked about his own cropdusting, how he'd sprayed over a million acres so far, and what he liked best was flying under power lines, near houses. He usually told people ahead of time when he'd be flying through their area so they'd know not to be out in their yards, but one time he forgot to call and "too late, I saw this back door open and a lady swing a pan—people used to throw their dishwater out the door," he said. "She screamed when she saw me, but the dishwater kept going and hit me in the face—it was full of potato peelings."

Still revved up, he said, "Let's go see the T-33!" Of all his planes, the T-33 was his favorite. "It's the *best,*" he said. "Flying it is like somebody grabbed you by the tail and threw you. You just *go.* You move with the same grace and ease you'd use walking out your front door. You head straight up at 400 knots and turn over and search for the nearest horizon, and when you get to 14,000 feet you're above the imperfections, looking down on a halo of blue fog . . ."

His own strip was too short for jets so Burchinal kept his T-33 at the Paris city airport. Parked on the ramp, it looked like a large silver cigar, its lines smooth and simple, engine intakes no more than swellings between tapered wings and fuselage, wingtip tanks like miniature silver cigars. It had no paint on it except for a black star on the side trailing red comet tails ("Shooting Star" was one of its nicknames) and, on the curved front, a pair of red lips, parted slightly, and the words, in case there was any doubt, "Hot Lips."

Burchinal offered the geoengineer a ride. Maybe he hoped to lure him into taking lessons in the T-33 once he'd soloed in the T-6, but probably he just wanted an excuse to fly the plane himself. The geoengineer didn't stoop to being impressed. Burchinal was clearly the more thrilled of the two when they taxied in after the ride. In his excitement, he offered *me* a ride, not a small gesture since the plane burned about 60 gallons of jet fuel every 15 minutes. I climbed in and hitched up my parachute harness and watched with puzzlement as steam and pieces of ice shot out over my legs (broken air-conditioner, I found out later). The T-33 did climb as Burchinal said it would, with grace and ease, and so fast that within a few minutes of takeoff I was looking down one slim wing at a garden of tiny clouds. The clouds moved above our heads and down the other side as Burchinal did a four-point roll. Then he signaled for me to take the stick. Shyly I took it and made a few shallow turns; what a light touch it had! I pulled the stick back and watched the T-33's nose rise a little. A little more, more . . . then I stopped, unable to bring myself to raise the nose higher. By the time I realized the reason I couldn't raise the nose higher was that the T-33 had reached the angle at which I would have stopped raising the *Luscombe*'s nose, to keep it from stalling, it was too late. Burchinal had taken back the stick. How disgusted he must have been! In a 4,600-pound-thrust jet, and she's still flying a 90-hp taildragger!

Perhaps to make up for any timidity on my part, Burchinal dragged his own strip on the way back to the other one, passing so low over the runway that drivers on the road next to the fence must have wondered if they had any time left, pulling up so sharply afterward my cheeks were pulled toward my chest. Even before we finished our roll-out at Paris, he shoved the canopy back, and the slipstream rushed in over our heads. I whooped; Burchinal turned around and beamed. He called out to a stranger as we pulled in to the ramp, laying his exuberance on me, "She hasn't had that much fun since *high* school!" Over iced tea he said to the waitress, "She hasn't had that much fun since *high* school!" To a man at the next table he might or might not have known he declared, "She hasn't had that much fun since *high* school!" I did have fun but it was tempered by the feeling that I had stood at a door to something special and had not gone through it.

Along with fun at Flying Tigers came duties, I soon found out. Hang around the field long enough and you risked becoming a draftee. Burchinal asked me to meet a student who was coming in that night on a commuter flight from Houston to take lessons in the T-33. He claimed she was the first female civilian to solo a T-33. At dusk I drove over in the convertible and waited as the sky grew dark and the stars came out. A glow appeared on the T-33's intake scoop and on its small, elegant tail. Burchinal hadn't told me what the student looked like so as passengers came through the gate I had to guess. One of the women was short and had on a dark, tailored, loose-fitting suit, brown walking shoes, and glasses. She was carrying a briefcase. Her brown hair was pulled back tight in a bun. A jet pilot—the perfect disguise!

Her name was Nicole Lamotte, and she was from Paris, France. On behalf of Flying Tigers, I welcomed her to our Paris. I started driving her to her motel but when she found out mine was $3 cheaper a night she switched—an economy I thought odd since she was about to blow $400 an hour on the T-33. Over a Chinese dinner I asked, Why the T-33? She told me she'd gotten a ride on the jump seat of an L-1011 during college, and she loved it so much she wanted another ride, only to be piloting the jet herself. She had gone on to become an aerospace engineer with a job in Boston making flight-control systems for lunar-landing simulators, and one day she saw Burchinal's ad in *Trade-a-Plane*. Though she had never piloted anything bigger than a 172, she came to Paris to fly the T-33. She knew that Burchinal was going to let her solo it when, as they were taxiing back to the ramp, she looked out and saw him sitting on the end of one wing, his legs wrapped around a tiptank, riding it like a cowboy.

Before he would let her solo this time, she had to be checked out again (the first solo had been months ago). The following morning I went to the airport to see her fly. While she and Burchinal were gone I waited on the ramp with Bo and the other mechanic, who were at Paris to look after the T-33. It was already hot out and they were spread-eagled on the asphalt under the wing of a Marauder, like a pair of farmers lying in the shade of a big oak tree. I sat against one of the Marauder tires, which was fat as a stump, and watched the T-33 take off, fly around the pattern, land, and do it all over again.

As the T-33 taxied in, Burchinal looked from the back seat toward us and made a gesture Lamotte couldn't see: thumbs down. How crummy, I thought, letting us know about her performance behind her back! Judging by her expression, however, she probably wouldn't have been surprised by the message; she looked tired and unhappy. Over coffee he told her she was squaring her turns as if she were in a 172 instead of rounding them as she should in a military plane. Also that her approach speeds were too fast and she was touching down too hard. "You have to speed up your thinking to jet reaction time," he said. That afternoon I watched her try again (it was easy to get picked up in Burchinal's orbit, like a stray electron), and as they taxied in he didn't do thumbs down *or* up, but her mouth was set tight. She hadn't made it this time either. During the debriefing over coffee the subject of women pilots in general came up. At first Burchinal suggested in a variety of ways that women pilots *might* not be as good as men, but as Lamotte kept at him he flared his nostrils and finally came out with it, just like that, bam! *"Women are inferior."*

Over our steak dinner and many iced teas I had heard Burchinal's views on New York City, welfare, extramarital sex, gun ownership, vigilantes, and atheists and had disagreed with them all, but I must have been dismissing them as natural if regrettable for a Texas male of a certain age who had grown up "tough as boots" (as in, "from the time I was five to fourteen I worked daylight to dark pulling cotton or chopping it with a long-neck hoe and I came out tough as boots") and who felt cheated because he couldn't go to World War II. I didn't even comment on "women affect men's flying beyond belief," let that pass. So why, when women *pilots* came in for it, did I flare my nostrils too, bang the table with my fist so hard the iced-tea glasses jumped, shove my chair back with a dramatic squeak, and stomp out of the restaurant to my Chevy without paying the check?

My Chevy? There it sat. Somehow under the circumstances it didn't seem good form . . . Oh, what the hell, I got in and drove off. Later I found out that not only had Lamotte not stormed out, she had taken her own sweet time, amiably drinking her coffee, and had scheduled another lesson for the morning. Her *sang-froid* seemed particularly thought-provoking since during dinner I discovered she had more ex-treme views on the question of women's rights than I. "Women should stage a coup at the national level," she said evenly, "and run the government for 20 years. It will take that long to change the system, and men's minds."

Still wanting to see her solo, I showed up for the morning lesson. Waiting for her and Burchinal to come back, I told Bo what his father had said. Bo's response was, "Women are made to love." I was grat-ified to see as the T-33 taxied in that Lamotte's face was all lit up— and Burchinal was riding a tiptank. While the T-33 was being refueled, she held herself apart from the rest of us, preparing herself for the solo, then climbed in, taxied to the runway, and took off in the great, gleam-ing silver cigar, alone.

Burchinal asked if I wanted a ride on his motorcycle, in what I took as a peace initiative. The place he had in mind for the ride was the runway. He barreled down the runway at 80 or 90 mph, much scarier on a Harley-Davidson than in a Luscombe. I felt like screaming but didn't want to give him the satisfaction of appearing girlish. The peace turned out to be a fragile one. After he'd ingratiated himself at the coffee shop, briefly, by telling a story that included the line, "He kissed my foot so hard my hat flew off," he marched, with full provocative intent, into another story, about the lynching of a black man in Paris, Texas, in the 1920s, making his feelings about it clear and insisting (nostrils flaring) that it was "time for another lesson."

As I hurtled away in the red car, without compunction this time, it occurred to me that aviation might have played a part in shaping Burchinal's major chauvinisms. Sitting high in an imperial seat, remote from the sweatings and strivings of ordinary citizens, exercising mastery over a powerful instrument in a broad, high sweep of space, moving more or less at will over a globe that was steadily shrinking, could make a man or woman feel disproportionately powerful and important. "You got to be a rebel to stand out," he had said in one of his coffee-shop monologues. "If you are just an ordinary John Q and want to find easier ways and not be rough and tough, our history will not recognize you. Ours is the football field, the battlefield. Anybody who can take a Wildcat or Corsair or P-38 and pit himself in hand-to-hand combat in the air is superior. We are taught that we are superior. And we *are* superior, to any race on this earth!" (By "we" and this "race" I wondered if he meant Americans, males, whites, or warplane pilots? Or only those who were all four?)

His voice ripened as he went on. "Oh for me to fly across that old Texas sky, to shoot high in the air, either by the sound of a jet or a Mustang or a Wildcat, to reminisce one more moment about a time when this country knew where it was going and why it was going there . . ."

On the other hand, it might just be that people who had that sense of themselves and their place in the world were more likely than others to want to fly. And Burchinal loved to fly, really loved to. I honored him for that.

Oklahoma City · Altus

A bus pulled into Flying Tigers as I was doing my preflight and a man got out. He stood by the door and looked around the field. He was in his 30s maybe and wearing a T-shirt and jeans. Nobody got out after him. He spotted me and walked over, then stood watching for a couple of minutes without speaking. Abruptly he announced that he had had a Luscombe too, once. "It crashed, though. Ran out of oil," he said. "I put it in the trees. Didn't even break the windshield!" It was amazing to me how many conversations at airports started that way, guys coming up and saying, "My friend had a honey of a Luscombe but he hit a powerline with it." Or, "My brother totaled his Luscombe as soon as his wife finished painting it." Or, "Joe had an 8A but he dropped it in a swamp." The accounts were usually told cheerfully enough, even when one of the participants had been hurt or even died—they weren't meant primarily to elicit sympathy, but as openers, a way to get things started, to make a connection. Myself, I thought it was an odd way to kick things off.

This man, I soon found out, definitely wanted to make a connection, somewhere, somehow. He had been driving through the country for a year, he said, "just talking to people." He had bought the bus from Greyhound and fixed it up so he could live in it while traveling around. He'd done the same thing in a Piper Cub several years ago, flown around the country, as I was doing, but that hadn't given him much satisfaction. "You don't get to know anybody up there," he complained. "You're missing eating the watermelons. I wanted to get back down to earth and talk to commoners."

So, now that he was back down to earth, in a bus, where did he choose to go but to little airports? And who were his commoners but other pilots? I did my bit, listening to what he had to say while checking out my plane, but it soon became clear that driving around the country wasn't giving him much satisfaction either. He spoke of his trip with a mix of resentment and longing that was painful to hear. Despite all his efforts at togetherness (he'd founded two communes in his life but both fell apart; "The things people *do,*" he said), he was as bitter and lonely a person as I'd met in a long time. After his year on the road he concluded, "Most people live in a world of darkness. They don't know who they are, why they are, or where they should go to find out. . . . You get Social Security and then you die. . . . The country is about to fall."

He wandered off to look at Burchinal's warplanes but five minutes later was back, gloomier than ever. "All my friends are dead," he said. "Killed, every one of them. Killed in P-51s . . ." I decided to let him share that particular sorrow with Burchinal, sat in my cockpit, fired up, taxied out past the Panther, B-17, and Wildcat, turned onto the battered old combat strip, went bouncing down it, and stayed low after liftoff to pull as much roar as possible out of the old 90-horse engine, feeling I owed that to the Luscombe, in the presence of these mighty stars of aviation, and to the doleful young man who was watching, and to the older man in the office I hoped was listening.

How great to be up and away, particularly away! The world had become round again, or rather both round *and* flat. From the altitude I was flying, it looked like one large, shallow plate, meticulously painted in the center with sylvan scenes (trees, towns, lakes), then gradually airbrushed toward the edges until the border of the plate was white. I took up a 310-degree heading after crossing the Red River, which turned out to be a seaweedy green. Magnetic heading, that was, since I was flying by compass. However, the heading on the line I'd drawn on my chart was the geographical, or true, heading, and it was 318 degrees. Around there, all geographical headings were eight degrees west of magnetic headings; back in New York, by contrast, they were all 12 degrees *east* of magnetic headings. You had to take into account the difference between the geographic and magnetic North Poles even when you were thousands of miles south of them, or you could end up 25, 50, even 100 miles left or right of your intended course. A phrase had been devised to help pilots remember whether to add or subtract the amount of variation: "East is least, West is best." I never used the phrase since I usually laid out my course on the chart in a more primitive way, by putting the side of my hand (like a fleshy ruler) parallel to my route across the nearest compass rose printed on the chart and seeing what heading (magnetic heading) it crossed. Besides, that phrase expressed all too well what people out there really seemed to think. "Ugh!" they'd say when I answered their question about where I was from. "New York! Why would *anybody* want to live *there?*"

As I got farther from Paris the land began to be divided up in a more regular way, roads ran straighter and more often to the four main points of the compass. I traced one of the roads visually, a red dirt one which shot out from under me and moved north into an *allée* of trees, emerged from the *allée* and kept on going until it reached a town, entered the town and turned into blacktop, left town and reverted to dirt, kept on going straight, straight, on past a field, a lake, farm buildings, another field, on, on, on, a straight line still, until it too became lost in the blankness at the edge of the plate. When north (geographic north) was so clearly drawn, a pilot hardly needed a chart to fly by.

Evelyn and Blanche were at Expressway Junction airport in the northeastern part of Oklahoma City, waiting for me. Loving sisters. Schoolteachers I'd known back East who'd retired to the West. They helped me unload my bags, but we had to move fast; red ants were all over the tiedown, crawling up our feet and legs. Blanche squealed; Evelyn laughed. In college, Evelyn had been known as a "fly girl," which meant, in her school at least, "flip" or "smart alec." I knew her as dignified, even stately, tending to courtly turns of phrase, but she had forced open some color bars in her time (before the 60's) and didn't suffer fools without at least remarking on them. For lunch at their house we had Blanche's own smothered chicken and cherry pie, but I later learned that they ate only two meals a day ordinarily, breakfast early in the morning and dinner at 4 in the afternoon. They acted surprised when I expressed surprise at their schedule, as if it were news to them that most Americans ate three meals a day.

Having two meals a day was typical of the gracious pace at which they lived, savoring everything, giving everything its due. The house was decorated rather formally, with items in it that if not luxurious themselves were full of the luxury of intent: velvet, silver, china. Every day we saw or did one deeply appreciated thing. One day we went to the National Cowboy Hall of Fame, which had photo exhibits of trick and "fancy" riders, who did things like rope other horses while doing headstands on the saddles of their own. One day we toured downtown

Oklahoma City with its oil-well skyline, and another day we watched a nightclub act by the latest Ink Spots. The only thing I had to complain about, and I whined mightily, was that although the house was equipped with air-conditioning, Evelyn and Blanche weren't inclined to use it. The temperature the first day I was in Oklahoma City was 105 degrees, and the second day it was 106. Like the night-blooming cereus they kept in the basement until its time came, they luxuriated in the heat. To shut me up Evelyn gave me a floor fan but made sure she stayed out of the breeze.

By the third day the heat had exploded into thunderstorms along my next flight leg, so I couldn't fly out on the fourth day. At that point, the peace of the house became threatening. I felt, irrationally of course, that I'd never get out of such a pleasant situation. While flying around I had developed a certain momentum, a propulsion even, a need to keep going, and not just because there was something at the next place. The thundershowers hung around into the fifth day so I couldn't fly out then either, and in midafternoon of that day I stood morosely looking out a back door at rain falling on the garden statuary (dwarves) when I heard the sound of an engine, different from other suburban engines—cars, mopeds, lawn mowers, chain saws—and I looked up to see, crossing the sky from my right to my left under loose, soft-edged clouds, a plane about the size of mine, which had to be on strictly local flight or else instruments, I figured, and felt a strong tug upward. What a siren song *that* was! the sound of that engine, humming. Evelyn's grand piano stood near the door, and I went over to it and hit keys until I found the one that matched the sound of that engine: high C.

As the two notes traveled along together, I thought how much of a place the sky was for me now, not just a nice viewing platform, or an opening to pass through on the way from one earthly point to another, but a distinct, inhabitable band above the earth, a shadow continent with its own walls, lights, trees, beasts, topography, laws, and company of travelers, and when I was away from it for long (on this trip, "long" was five days, bordering on four), I was seized with a fear that I might never get up again, never belong again. Ridiculously gloomy, I stood at the piano until both notes died.

.　　.　　.

The very next morning I flew out. The weather then was what pilots from the East would call "severe clear"; visibility was 50 or 60 miles. The earth was defined to its bluish edges, and roads ran across it like strings, straight and unbroken, all the way to the edges and over them, on to Juneau, Guadalajara, Montreal, Caracas . . .

Myself, I was going as far as Altus, Oklahoma. It was 120 miles away. It had two airports only five miles from each other, Altus Municipal and Altus Air Force Base. Both airports had a single runway and both runways ran north-south, but one runway was 13,400 feet long and the other was 4,000 feet, and side by side on the chart they looked like a tall pole and its foreshortened shadow, Big Mike and Little Moe. Coming up on Altus, I got an idea what it must have been like to be paired like that. Most of the way the scene below had been subdued: the terrain flat, the crops muted in color (pale greens and oranges with an occasional light-brown plow line running through them), ponds so still they held without trembling the reflection of tiny clouds. Little seemed to be moving; a car crept up a highway, a tick-size cow dropped its head to the grass, that was about it. The farms were rectangular with neat, well-defined borders. All in all, the countryside looked as storybooks often said it did: quilted.

Then something inappropriate appeared. It wasn't on the ground but in the air, below and to the left of my plane when I first saw it. It just seemed to be there, without actually arriving, and not to be moving, rather to be hanging—not hanging actually, to be *imbedded* in the air—then a wingtip rose and the rest of it rotated, and rose as well, in extreme slow motion, the motion not a plodding but a lightness, an exemption from the ordinary laws of physics, after which it vanished—didn't zoom off, just gradually lost substance in the afternoon light. I wasn't aware of a sound issuing from it until it was almost gone.

Not counting Howard Hughes's Spruce Goose, it was the largest airplane in existence then, the U.S. Air Force's C-5A, and when I saw it it had been taking off from Altus Air Force Base, and farther away than it seemed. Shortly after I landed at Altus Muni, I asked Erik, the friend from New York I'd come to visit, about the C-5A. He was a fellow Luscombe owner from my home airport and now a lieutenant in the Air Force. As I was taxiing in, I saw his Luscombe parked on the ramp, all black except for white registration letters and a white bunny head painted on the tail. The bunny was a Playboy bunny, or almost. The previous young male owner of the Luscombe had put it there, but one day he got a letter in the mail from the Playboy organization threatening to sue him for trademark infringement if he didn't get rid of it. He duly took half the head off, the back half, painted it black, which made what was left over look rather like a seahorse, but when Erik bought the plane he decided he preferred a Playboy bunny to a seahorse (he was 20 at the time) and put the head back on. He had a good laugh thinking about *Playboy* taking itself (or Hugh Hefner taking himself) so seriously it would sue and imagining the indignation some company loyalist must have felt seeing a small, old, low-powered taildragger carrying the same white-on-black paint scheme and same bunny head as his boss's 39-seat, 600-mph-plus bar-and-cinescope-equipped DC-9. Erik stopped laughing long enough to consult a lawyer, who told him that if he changed the head in any way it ceased to be *Playboy*'s trademark. So Erik painted one of the ears flopped forward, added a red button nose, began calling the plane "Rum Bunny," and never heard a peep out of *Playboy*.

He picked me up at Altus Muni, still dressed in his flight suit. It was made of some synthetic material and zippered to the neck, with long sleeves and legs which had pockets all up and down them ("we live in our pockets," said Erik, unzipping several and taking out checkbook, flashlight, wallet, and "survival" knife). The suit looked punishingly hot on that hot day, but being in it evidently bothered him less than seeing him in it bothered me because he didn't change out of it before taking me on a tour of the Air Force base. The highlight of the tour came when we parked near the Air Force runway, got out and sat on the grass by one end, and waited for planes to come in. Just as we might at any little airport on any hot afternoon in midsummer. I pointed this out. "I guess I'm just a kid at heart," Erik said, his eyes wide and guileless. "I never get tired of this."

Growing up, he had lived in a house under the downwind leg for Runway Two-Eight at our airport and spent much of his childhood looking at the bellies of Cessnas, Tri-Pacers, Champs, and Cherokees passing over. For his 11th birthday, his parents gave him a ride in a red-and-cream Tri-Pacer. "It was a perfect crystal-clear fall day," Erik recalled. "By the time we landed I was sold." From then on he hung around the airport whenever he could, mooching rides or earning them by packing people's wheel bearings with grease or washing their planes.

He got a job pumping fuel to pay for flying lessons when he was a teenager. The first day he could legally solo, on his 16th birthday, he soloed, and the first day he could legally earn his license, his 17th birthday, he earned it. By six months after his 18th birthday he had gotten his commercial and instructor's ratings, and by six months after his 20th birthday he had bought his Luscombe, "the plane I always wanted." Here he was now, six months after his 23rd birthday, zipped into a flight suit, waiting for planes of the U.S. Air Force to put down on a runway he would soon be landing on himself.

"C-5A," Erik announced, staring at a spot five miles out when it was still only a spot to me. "You know when one of them's coming in. It looks like a pterodactyl on final." So far, he had gotten two rides in C-5A's. "When you're rolling, it's like an apartment house is moving out," he reported. "The cockpit is three stories high." He thought a minute. "It's the World Trade Center with wings."

After the C-5A had boomed by and taxied off, ten minutes passed before another plane came in. It was a T-38, the jet Erik flew during flight training in Arizona. "My instructors always knew when I'd been in my Luscombe over the weekend because I couldn't keep my feet off the rudders," he said, grinning. "The rudders on that thing are so sensitive you can roll it just by touching them." The T-38 set down in front of us with its nose high and tail section tucked way under, looking not unlike a dog crouched to defecate.

Ten minutes later a C-141 appeared. It was the plane Erik was assigned to fly, once he'd learned how. "Backbone of the Air Force," he said, sounding like a voice-over. "The main strategic airlifter for the Air Force. It burns as much fuel taxiing to Number One as my whole plane weighs at gross, fourteen hundred pounds!" Before becoming a C-141 pilot he'd have to, among other things, memorize the entire 1,240-page flight manual, know by heart, for instance, which of the plane's four engine-driven generators powered each of its ten electrical busses and what the running-time limits for the engine were at 550 degrees F, 510 degrees, 488, etc.

"Everything's procedure in the military," he said. "Every move you make is so precalculated and regulated that it's hard to enjoy the flying." He looked dreamy. "There *was* one time, though . . ." In Arizona all the pilots got to make a solo cross-country flight in the T-38 when they'd finished flight training. "My solo was from Williams [AFB

in Arizona] to March [AFB in California] back to Williams at night, and I'll never forget that," said Erik. "It was mostly over desert, so everything was dark below, but above there were these thousands of lights—the stars! The stars didn't just shine, they sparkled. It was like a religious experience. I was at 29,000 feet and I could see L.A. behind me and Phoenix in front of me and I thought, They let me, a dull little kid, fly a million-dollar airplane. *I* wouldn't let me fly a million-dollar airplane. *I* wouldn't trust me!"

He wasn't indulging in the self-deprecation many pilots affect to seem cool; Erik was genuinely self-deprecating. "One of my terrible landings," he'd say after a squeaker with only the tiniest luff. I asked if he was sorry not to have been assigned the C-5A. Why not the biggest? "I like ice-cream sodas," he said, putting it in terms I could relate to, "but not one as big as this car. That's more than I can eat." At many airports the runways and taxiways couldn't support its weight, so it couldn't land and just refueled in the air. "The guys may take a 40-ton magnet to Russia or a fighter somewhere, but the mission isn't that diverse," he explained. "It isn't a popular assignment."

That night, in an Altus disco, we listened to a Texas rock group called "New York" and drank screwdrivers with Erik's buddies. I left the disco at midnight because Erik and I were planning to fly formation to Lubbock in the morning, but he stayed on. He was used to getting up early. Takeoff time in the Air Force was usually 5:30 A.M., with wake-up calls coming more than two hours before that, at 3:15. I wasn't used to getting up early and hated it. In addition to the physical struggle to rouse which seemed so bruising, the digging out from the murky pit I'd fallen into during the night, there was an emergency character to waking in the dark or near-dark: someone was sick, I had an exam to take, a friend was on the phone, crying.

From now on, I'd have to get used to getting up early. In the West pilots tended to fly early or late in the day since in the middle of it thermals were usually shooting up off deserts and mountainsides. When my wake-up call came at 6 A.M. in Altus, a narrow band of light was leaking through the motel window blind, the slimmest evidence that day might follow, and I let out a groan. The desk clerk said, "It's in the way of an obscene phone call, isn't it?" Agreeing, I lay for a few minutes, inert, then wrestled my body more or less upright and worked it over to the window, where I pried a couple of the slats apart and looked blearily out. Against a pinkish band of sky lay a violet triangle, a hill shaped like a mountain I didn't remember seeing on my way in. Above and to the left of the triangle hung a great full moon. The craters of the moon were pale blue and more distinct than I ever remembered seeing them, even at night. I managed a small intake of breath. Perhaps this early-rising stuff wasn't going to be so hideous after all.

At the airport I unchained my Luscombe and Erik untied his. His was the only plane at Altus Muni with ropes. He didn't like chains, he said, because they didn't have any give. "A lot of planes with chains get their wings bent bucking in the wind." His were marine ropes, tested to 4,000 pounds. "If you need anything stronger than that," he said, "the *airport* will blow away."

Before we took off for Lubbock, Erik phoned the Air Force tower and asked if we could fly down their runway on our way out. How cheeky! I thought. And he only a student! The tower must have said okay because a quarter of an hour later the Rum Bunny and the Goshawk were cruising along 500 feet above the wide concrete runway, their combined horsepower putting out a buzz like a pair of horseflies over acres of ramps, hangars, and parked planes, some of the planes as big as they get. I looked left and saw the flop-eared bunny head floating along beside me, red nose into the wind. *Very* cheeky! Inside the cockpit, I knew, was the wide-eyed, grinning boy, having fun bringing down the image not of *Playboy* this time but of the United States Air Force.

The formation we flew to Lubbock was casual, with Erik usually flying off my wing instead of me off his since he was (by far) the better pilot. At first we held pretty much the same altitude, but after a while I noticed that he was going up and down a lot, as if on an elevator. Meanwhile I had the sensation that my own flight path was level, absolutely bedrock. I knew, though, he had the impression that *I* was the elevator and *he* was the rock. Thermals were already revving up . . .

At one point we flew over an excellent example of indigenous Earth Art. A farmer had planted some green crop in an hourglass shape in a rectangle of mauve dirt. In one half of the hourglass was a pond, and in the pond were two mounds sprinkled, unevenly, with greenery. Using his tractor, the farmer had carved into the mauve dirt around the green hourglass a long, wavy line, ending it with a coquettish hook.

I took a photo of it, then caught up with Erik (my Luscombe had five more horsepower than his). After a while we saw in the distance, in an otherwise immaculate blue sky, a large gray-brown smear, and knew we were coming up on the city of Lubbock without actually seeing it. (Even out here the besmirchment went on!) "One of my terrible landings," Erik said when we met up in the office, and although I hadn't seen the landing I didn't believe him. The FBO gave us both fuel, then offered to lend us his truck so we could drive to a pizza joint down the road for lunch, *if* we took his dog along. The dog loved riding in the truck. It must have known what kind of deal was being struck because it ran to the truck and jumped on the back and hung its head over the side, waiting for us. It stayed back there, panting happily, while we went into the pizza joint. Erik's fresh face glowed as he wolfed down a pizza with pepperoni, mushrooms, and double cheese; it was the face of a satisfied man. After he finished, he leaned back against the seat of the booth and summed up his day. "Great," he said. "Flying formation in our Luscombes. The FBO being so friendly and all. Giving us his truck. The pizza was terrific. And that dog's a gas." Then he said something that thrilled me, considering it came from a pilot who'd had a religious experience in a T-38. "If I had to choose," he said, and it was a fine compliment to the kind of flying I loved, "I'd choose civilian."

Flight Plan · Carlsbad

Out of Lubbock, I filed a flight plan for the first time on the trip. What filing a flight plan meant was giving Flight Service by phone before takeoff, or by radio after takeoff, or in person if there was a Flight Service Station (FSS) on the field, information it could use later on to search for you if you didn't show up at the place and time you said you would. Information such as the cruise speed of your airplane, in knots; the altitude you expected to fly at (if heading west and above 3,000 feet above ground level (AGL), it would be odd thousands plus 500 feet, if heading east even thousands plus 500 feet, the thousand-foot levels themselves being reserved for instrument traffic); "alternate airports" in case of bad weather or vomiting passenger; fuel on board measured in time it would take to deplete it; home address (for letting your family or significant other know at the bottom of which gulch your remains were spotted); number of people on board including pilot; and color of airplane. Each item took only a few seconds for me to figure out and write down on my flight plan—except the color.

When my plane was painted after the crash, it was a light but unmistakable yellow; a man at an airport I flew into shortly after that called it a banana. However, after years of sitting outside in the sun and the chemical brine that is New York–New Jersey metropolitan air, it became paler and paler until some people started calling it white. I didn't like that. White planes in my opinion lacked individuality, oomph. New planes were overwhelmingly white. I had to admit, though, that my Luscombe no longer looked truly yellow, certainly wouldn't look yellow to a search party. So what should I put on the flight plan? Off-white? (No, that was still white.) Cream? Ivory? Eggshell perhaps? Flax, champagne? Ecru? After giving the problem considerable thought, I decided that what the color of my plane was most like, the thing that it most resembled, that caught its ambiguity best, was *human tooth*. That faint yellowishness of the white bone of a human tooth. How would Flight Service like that? "Estimated true airspeed: 90 knots. En route altitude: 3,500 feet. Fuel: 3½ hours. Plane color: Tooth." So in the end I passed it up, along with honeycomb, seafoam, and nougat, and told Flight Service, with only a small twinge of discomfort at the way it might mislead a search party, "pale yellow."

Another thing on the flight plan I had to give more than a few seconds' thought to was takeoff time. It was supposed to be the exact moment the airplane's wheels separated from the runway, *according not to local clocks but to those in Greenwich, England,* not to mention Uckfield, Sidcup, Whittlesea, and Biggleswade, also on the zero-degree longitudinal meridian. The clocks there kept "Zulu" time (Zulu standing for Z and Z for Zero), and pilots all over the world were expected to use it, the idea being that it eliminated confusion when crossing time zones in flight. Myself, I always found *using* Zulu confusing, *especially* when crossing time zones, being forced to compute the time anew on each leg, count ahead four, five, six, seven, or eight hours according to how far west I was and whether daylight saving time was in effect or not, then converting the number I got into military form, 1845 hours and all that. After I'd eaten a pizza lunch with Erik in Lubbock, Texas, for example, at precisely 1:35 P.M. local time, I took off, yet told Flight Service I was taking off at 1935 hours, the time when chaps in Uckfield, Sidcup, and Biggleswade were polishing off their dinners of mutton, two veg, and a pudding before settling down for an evening in front of the telly.

I was filing a flight plan now because I expected the terrain to get harsher southwest of Lubbock and fewer people to be on it to see me go down if I did. The terrain did indeed get harsher, as well as emptier, fast. Outside Lubbock the land was smooth and green and I got a satisfied feeling just flying over it, like having clean sheets to crawl into. Roads ran either north-south or east-west and had no curves except those forced on them by the bending of the earth's surface. This, I thought, must be how the globe looks under it all, the Basic Earth without all the extraneous stuff that had been exploded, leaked, or shoved onto its surface over the millennia, a neat polished ball, carefully inked for latitude and longitude. But as I kept on flying toward Carlsbad Caverns, the earth took on a worn, puckered look, in places seemed almost leathery, almost gray. Trees became uncommon, then rare. So did houses. By the time I got to a pumping station and spotted a white wooden house in one corner behind a fence with shade trees planted close about it, a lonely fortress against the sun, I was already thinking, "How brave!"

This would be my third visit to Carlsbad Caverns; I never seemed to get enough of the place. Natural history's Disneyland, with its suggestive stalagmite and stalactite formations, the Bashful Elephant, the Whale's Mouth, Gorilla's Shadow, Veiled Statue, Dinosaur, etc. On my last visit I had met Carlsbad's "cave specialist," Ronal Kerbo, who told me some things about caving that made me think of flying, though I couldn't remember now for the life of me what those things were. Or even what they *could be*. To me the impulse to go down in caves was the very opposite of the one that sent people up in planes (Carlsbad with its 80-foot vaulted entranceway and chambers of near-ballroom dimensions was an exception). Caves, as I understood them, were miserably short on the things that pilots value most: light, air, mobility, visual delight, spaces that give a sense of hope to the straitened spirit. Caves were airless, dark, slippery, treacherous, leech-and-beetle-infested pits, crevices, tunnels, sinuses, crawling tubes, and coffin-size holes where people got trapped, buried, crushed, lost, drowned, and suffocated. Instruments of torture for even petty claustrophobics.

Kerbo's job as cave specialist was to "inventory" the formations, creatures, and minerals in each of the 37 caves of the Carlsbad complex and make recommendations about how to take care of them. Also to rescue people who got trapped (suffocated, buried, lost, etc.) in them. Shortly after I landed I rang him up and asked if he remembered what it was that he had said about caving the last time I was there that might have reminded me of flying. He said he hadn't any idea but he did have a suggestion. He would take me to a part of the caverns not ordinarily open to the public and I could get a feeling for what they were like without all the labels, walkways, railings, trail lights, park rangers, and other tourists in them, and maybe I could figure it out for myself.

I hesitated. Would there be crawling? I asked. Tight fits? Oh no, Kerbo said, and although I wasn't convinced, the next day I followed him through a wood door that had been built into the rock wall of one of the lighted public chambers, into darkness. We were both wearing hard hats, headlamps, waist battery packs, and sneakers and carrying flashlights. He flashed his headlamp around and the beam picked out the rounded ceiling, rough gray walls, and lumpy floor of a tunnel. I was relieved; it had the proportions of a subway tunnel. We walked along the flat floor until we came to a wall with a ladder leaning against it, leading to a hole in the stone. Kerbo went up the ladder and through the hole and I climbed through after him, into another, narrower tunnel. It had a wet, slick, pale-yellow floor; "flowstone," Kerbo called it. (Hmm, not a bad choice for airplane color: "flowstone.") Where water pooled on the floor ladders had been laid across it and we walked on the rungs. In other places we stepped over deep cracks. As we thus made our way along, the tunnel gradually narrowed and became more convoluted, with the walls on either side increasingly broken up into hollows, ledges, cracks, and crannies.

After a while we came to a fork in the tunnel and Kerbo stopped, stood trying to decide which one to take. He finally picked the left one without telling me why, and headed down it. Slowly but surely the ceiling and walls closed in, in places producing a trail so narrow there wasn't room to put both of my feet side by side, only one in front of the other. In other places we had to use our hands to advance ourselves, pulling our legs along behind. It probably wasn't Kerbo's idea of a tight fit but it was fast becoming mine. Every time the tunnel shrank and I thought I wouldn't be able to keep going it opened up slightly and I could.

We climbed a short incline, using broken stalagmites as steps, onto another trail, a short way down which the way was nearly blocked by what looked like a stone pelvic bone. It had a slit in it just wide enough for a torso to squeeze through . . . sideways. The squeezing through wasn't the hard part; that came afterward, when I stood on the other side in full knowledge that I was encased in stone, in the middle of several worm-tubes of stone, with the way back to the living world no wider than a slit. Close to panic, I began grabbing for breath, then saw some crystals sticking out of a wall near my head—real and pretty things—concentrated on them, and slowly the fear let up.

As we carried on (*stooping* now and then), more crystals appeared on more walls until the cave seemed almost white with decoration. Kerbo named them: helictites (branching, twisted fingers of calcite), aragonite (fine, needle-like crystals clumped so they looked like the shredding around the heart of an artichoke, but shiny), cave popcorn (pale, coral-like knobs). "Don't touch them," he said of globules the size of pearls with a pearly luster but which had air inside them and were so fragile they could break at a touch (hydromagnesite balloons). In a pool beside the trail we found "moonmilk," a semiopaque liquid with white, pasty splinters protruding from it and elaborate yellow crystals lining the rim. Another pool had a "false floor," a layer of calcite scum hardened into a shell thin enough that water was visible through it.

These and other beauties kept me buckled together even as the ceiling and walls moved in. Kerbo put his foot on a rock in the middle of a pool resembling a frozen pond, stepped from the rock onto a ledge and from the ledge through an opening, and disappeared. Taking a deep breath, I crept after him into a tunnel, less a tunnel than a room since after 30 feet or so the tunnel ended in a rough, gray wall. There, at the back of the room, at the end of the series of tunnels, where a Mountain King would sit, was what had led Kerbo to choose the left fork. Rising about two feet off the floor, in a couple of crooked rows, were a dozen or so translucent, whitish, narrow, twisting, upright, tubular stone stalks branching on top into curlicues. They had the ghostly pallor of things that grew far from the light but not the creepiness; they were in fact delightful. Plants from Mars, I thought. A heligmite "vegetable garden," said Kerbo.

After we'd stood marveling at them for a while, Kerbo sat down and turned off his headlamp. So I did the same. The darkness was astounding, dark as I had rarely experienced it (above ground, light seemed always to be trickling into places, even closets). Silence too as I had rarely known it. The only things I could hear were sounds my body made. My neck creaked. My ears rang. I swallowed and the noise seemed thunderous. Embarrassed, I held my breath. What was Kerbo doing? What was he thinking, sitting there silent, sightless? What was *I* supposed to be thinking? My eyes were wide open with the effort of trying to perceive—something. Ten minutes passed, maybe five, then he said, softly, "This is how it is." I waited. "This is how it is," he said again. He meant the heligmite garden; it wasn't meant to be seen. Neither were the balloons, the false floor, the aragonite crystals, the cave popcorn, the moonmilk. He explained, "When you dive in water below a hundred feet everything becomes blue. If you send off a flash, all the colors are there—reds, purples, greens. But the beauty is there *only during the flash.* This [his voice swept the room] is all here whether we see it or not. A rock could squash us and it would still be here.''

Recently he had declared a single room in one of the Carlsbad caverns off-limits to everybody, including himself, he said, ''forever.'' Only nine people had seen it so far, ''all in their stocking feet'' (it was very fragile), and they'd be the last. The room was to go on and on, its beauty unobserved, its changes unrecorded, without human justification for its existence, forever (or as long as the U.S. National Park Service had it). ''We'll just let it fill up with whatever's natural.''

A minute later he stood, turned on his headlamp, and started back. Emboldened by the knowledge that the way could only get bigger, I began flashing my light around more, in case I'd missed something on the way in. At one point Kerbo stopped and brought his face close to a wall ahead. I caught up with him and saw it was covered with cave popcorn, no different from other cave popcorn as far as I could tell, yet he was clearly excited. He pointed to a ''soda straw,'' a stalagmite that didn't taper at the bottom as most of them did, and suspended from the bottom of the straw was a drop of water, with aragonite crystals on either side of it, each crystal no bigger than a pinhead, two crystals on one side and three on the other.

Usually, said Kerbo, explaining what seemed like a pretty specialized source of excitement, the crystals went all the way around the drop rather than just partway. He planned to come back with his 3-D camera and take a photo of them. How, I asked him, could he find them again among all the protuberances on all the cave walls? As a matter of fact, how did he find them in the first place? He said simply, ''I know the cave.'' Farther on, searching for marvels of my own, I shone my headlamp down a crevice to one side of the trail and thought I saw something. ''Hey, Ron,'' I yelled, ''looks like a Hershey-bar wrapper down there!'' He came back to where I was standing and peered down the crevice and thought he saw something too. That puzzled him, since the few people allowed in there weren't the littering kind. He decided to investigate. ''Oh no,'' I said, aghast, ''you'll fall.'' The crevice was about 50 feet deep, with walls that were rough and nearly vertical and had sharp projections of rock a person could hit his head against on the way to the bottom if he fell.

He ignored my cries of alarm and began "chimneying" down the crack, placing his feet against the walls and pressing outward with them while he moved his hands lower down, then pressing with his hands while he shifted his feet. Whenever he moved he dislodged flakes of limestone, which skittered down, hitting the rocky projections his head or body would hit if he himself were dislodged. Partway down he disappeared under an arch of rock but I could still hear the skittering sounds, then some footsteps. He had made it to the bottom. Rummaging sounds, more footsteps. A shout. "Chewing tobacco!" What? "It's an old Beechnut wrapper!" More sounds of rummaging. "There's a bread wrapper . . . and a newspaper . . . It's the funnies . . . February 10, 1929 . . ."

As he climbed over the lip of the crevice and stepped onto the path, he had scratches on his hands and stone flakes in his hair—and the newspaper under his shirt. It was a four-page spread of Sunday comics, the first and last pages in color, the center ones in black and white. For its age, it was in good shape, except for a few nicked spots, from falling rock presumably. We stood on the trail and read it. Skeezix, in *Gasoline Alley*, was about ten years old and brother Corky was a baby, playing in a crib with their mother's new blue flapper hat. Corky mashed the hat and their mother came in and bawled Skeezix out for giving it to him. That was it, the joke (or one of them). In *Barney Google*, Barney had a one-day guest pass to a "ritzy" men's club, the "Cosmopolitan," where gentlemen in cravats looked on in horror as he put his feet up on tables ("Oh, baby, if the gang could only see me now"), asked a member for a drink ("Got any hip oil in your locker?"), and bawled out a waiter for not bringing him a toothpick ("It ain't possible a club like this ain't got dining room lumber!"). Barney was kicked out (literally, onto his head) instead of being voted in. That was it, the joke. In an accompanying strip called *Parlor Bedroom & Sink*, a man told his wife that he'd send their baby boy (who he didn't believe was his) to reform school. The boy, scooting around the floor at his feet in snuggies and bonnet, cried and pleaded with him. That was it, no joke intended.

From Carlsbad bat-show lectures I had learned that Mexican freetail bats were roosting on the cave ceilings by the millions when the cave was discovered in the 1880s, and that the guano under them was piled as high as a five-story building then, and that during the 1920s somebody mined the guano and shipped it to California, where it was spread under orange and lemon trees as fertilizer (out of the blackest darkness and into the brightest of lights!). Maybe it was some miner who was here a half century ago, or some caver, or tourist, who ate lunch (bread anyway), partook of a postprandial chew, read all about the injustice of parents, class prejudices, and the heartlessness of husbands, then tossed what he no longer wanted, or needed, down the nearest, or maybe deepest, hole.

Back in the electric-lit, public part of the caverns, blinking, we fell in with a party of tourists moving single file along a narrow walkway. "Look at that!" Kerbo said after several minutes, pointing to the mouth of the cave, 50 feet or so above us. The mouth was nearly as wide as the cave itself but falling through it, in a near-plumb line to the floor, was a thin tube of sunlight, bluish, with motes swirling in it, so narrow and focused it looked like a beam that might accompany a Bible story, illuminating a saint at prayer or a miracle in progress.

Kerbo stepped to one side and let the others pass. "That happens only a few days each year," he whispered but with the force of enthusiasm, "and then only for a short time." The tourists kept filing by, looking down at their feet or ahead at other people's backs or, a few of them, up at the ceiling where cave swallows were circling. As for the miraculous beam, "Nobody's even looking at it," said Kerbo, sounding truly sad. We sat down on a stone bench and watched the beam widen bit by bit, a peaceful thing to do, like watching a cat sleep.

Before becoming a cave specialist, Kerbo had been a lot of things, including a doodlebugger, jughustler, roustabout, and roughneck on oil rigs. He had built ranch fences, laid sewer cables, and "hoed a lot of cotton." What got him to the point in his life where he considered narrow beams of sunlight and incomplete circles of pinhead crystals thrilling was a discovery he made one day in a western Oklahoma oil field. He'd been on his lunch break walking to a windmill tank for a swim ("anything to keep from hearing the same old stories from the other guys"), meanwhile keeping an eye open for arrowheads on the ground, when he spotted a hole in the dirt about eight inches across. He dug around the hole with his bare hands, then took off his shirt, set fire to it, and shoved it down the hole like a torch so he could look inside. He couldn't see any bottom to the hole so he dug around it some more until he could get his head and shoulders in. Still he couldn't see any bottom to it, and that evening after work he came back and dug around in the hole, came back on the weekend with his brother-in-law and did more digging, kept coming back and kept on digging until he had opened up a quarter mile of gypsum crawl tube and explored it all.

"That hole was muddy, dirty, and not pretty, but it helped me escape the drudgery of the oil fields," he said. "I'd stay up all night crawling through it looking for stalactites and stalagmites, and during the day when I was screwing pipes and digging ditches I'd look over, see the hole, and feel great." Soon he was digging around in other crawl tubes and going into caves, talking his family and friends into going into caves with him, driving to other states to see caves, spending vacations in caves, visiting underwater caves, famous caves, out-of-the-way caves. In time he became involved with caving in not just a physical and emotional but a spiritual way. "Going in caves is so much a part of me," he said, "that it's no longer a sport. It's not a hobby. It's not even a job."

By then we were sitting in the living room of his house, owned by the parks department and situated about 350 yards from the cavern mouth. The living-room shelves had a lot of explorer-seeker books on them: science-fiction books, nonfiction books on Indians, books by Halliburton, Cousteau, Tolkien, Heyerdahl, and Gibran. In the spirit of some of his favorite authors, Kerbo tried to explain what caves meant to him. "Once you grab the earth with both hands," he began, "there's no way to let go of it and be happy. . . . Caves are the darkness on the face of the deep, held over for us so we could enjoy it. . . . You can stand at the base of a mountain and look up and see the summit glittering and gleaming with snow, but if you're in an unexplored cave you don't know where you're going until you get there. And even then you don't know if you're there."

He showed me some of his 3-D photos, of the bottom halves of bodies caught in the light of camera flashes while protruding from holes in rock ceilings, and of tiny figures with legs dangling nonchalantly over the edges of abysses. When I shuddered he said, "Bravery has nothing to do with going in caves. You're so frightened sometimes your mouth is pure cotton. It's just wanting to see something so bad that you'll do what you have to do to see it." What he most wanted to see was cave decorations. "Some cavers," he said, showing me

3-D close-ups of decorations, "would rather take a walk through ten feet of undecorated virgin tunnel than go through the most beautiful cave. "It *is* fantastic to be the first, but to me it's just as great to see the Butterfly at Sonora or the Klansman at New Cave even if thousands of people have seen them before me. I'd wade through mud up to my knees to get another look at the Snake Dancers or the Christmas Tree or the Blood River flowstone even though they're all well known. I never tire of looking at those things." He summed it all up. "The justification of my existence," he said, "is just to let my legs carry my eyes."

There they were, then, the things Kerbo probably had said last time about caving that made me think of flying. The constant search for beauty; the physical self at the service of the visual (he quoted one man's simple motto: "I must go and see"); the seeking out of worlds usually hidden; the reminder of large, elemental earth forces; the aloneness; the testing ("no one knows when you're frightened; no one knows when you've made a particularly good move"). He told me Cousteau once wrote that he had wanted to fly until he invented the Aqua-Lung. "Afterward he didn't need to." Exploring the depths and the heights, then—was it so easy?—were in ways two sides of the same alluring coin.

FSS · Sunland · Santa Fe

In a perfectly timed, living demonstration of the ranger's evening lecture at Carlsbad, thousands of Mexican freetail bats spiraled out of the cavern mouth in a jittery cloud before heading off to eat their weight in moths and beetles that night. When all but a few had gone twitching off toward the sunset, I walked to the edge of the escarpment and sat down. Hundreds of feet below me lay the valley floor, which ran in a smooth, unbroken line more than halfway around the horizon. On the right-hand end of that line stood the rugged profile of El Capitan, a mountain I'd pass tomorrow. On the left-hand end, low in the sky and seeming to balance El Capitan's head, was a large, yellow full moon, made to seem even larger by the thin clouds that surrounded it and took on its color but did not hide its face. The sight of that moon on the bare desert stage was almost shocking, so aggressive in size and color, a gigantic lighted lamp thrust in our faces, as if to give Someone or Something a better look at us, right *there,* closer than it had ever been before, more obviously a companion body to us, belonging to Earth, not space.

A short while later, when the moon had climbed and lost its cushion of cloud, its swollen size and color and symmetry with the mountain, I drove down into the valley for a Tex-Mex dinner. One of the best things about flying west was getting to eat Tex-Mex as often as I felt like it, and the odd thing was that I felt like it often. In New York if I had eaten that kind of food within, say, the previous three or four days and someone suggested we go to a Tex-Mex restaurant some night, I'd say, Well, I had it Tuesday, and that would be that, he or she would understand and we'd go have Italian or Indian instead. But out West, where the Tex-Mex food (what I was getting, at least) didn't taste all that different, or better, I could eat it once or twice a day, as if availability and ambience changed my satiety setting.

Full of beans, etc., I drove to the Cavern City airport to sleep under
my plane. First I stopped in the Flight Service station for a weather
briefing. I liked having a Flight Service station right on the field, not
only for the face-to-face briefings but for all the great visual aids. Adi-
abatic flow charts with long, curved, Art Nouveau lines connecting
points of equal barometric pressure around the country, so that Billings, Montana, Kokomo, Indiana, and Montpelier, Vermont, for instance, could be united, briefly, by a common condition, a reading of
29.91 inches of mercury. Posters of cloud types, consisting of photos of
actual clouds, which like plants and birds were given mostly Latin names:
"Altocumulus translucidus undulatus," a striped cloud resembling the X ray
of the bony fish; *"Stratocumulus vesperalis,"* a rather nondescript cloud
behind a harbor scene at sunset with all boat sails hanging limp; *"Altocumulus* of a chaotic sky,*"* just as it sounded, a bunch of untidy clouds
strewn across the firmament; and *"Cumulonimbus capillatus"*—the great
white shark of aviation, the grizzly bear, the man-eating lion—a high,
dark cloud with its top pulled out into the wide anvil of a thunderhead.

For old times' sake I looked up the teletype printout for John F.
Kennedy Airport in New York. It went, "JFK 200350 6R-130 8269 2612
998 VR31 054." In part that meant that at the airport at 3:50 A.M.
Zulu time visibility was six miles in light rain, temperature 82 degrees,
dew point 69 degrees, wind from 260 degrees at 12 knots, and barometric pressure 29.98, a mere exhale higher than standard, which was
29.97. A symbols key was tacked up next to the teletype, and I realized
as I looked it over that I had never encountered, or even heard mentioned in a briefing (thank the Great Flying Boss), four of the conditions named thereon: BY (Blowing Spray), BD (Blowing Dust), IF (Ice
Fog), and BS (Blowing Sand). I did meet a couple of pilots once who
told me about running into BD. They had a job for the federal government sending up instrumented weather balloons and retrieving them
after they came down. The balloons fell just about anywhere, on farms
("Three heifers ate a balloon and died," one of the guys said, "and
we had to pay $300 a heifer"), on treetops ("A blackjack oak costs
$70"), on fenceposts ("One impaled a telescope"), and on mountains
("We take those out by horseback"). One day they were flying around
at 9,500 feet searching for a downed balloon when they became engulfed by blowing dust so thick that they had to go on instruments.
Dust clouds, they said, could go up as high as 40,000 feet.

When I walked in, two Flight Service briefers were on duty at Cavern City, drinking coffee and talking. They were discussing a retirement community near the Mexican border (where, as it happened, Pancho Villa chose to make a raid on the United States), which had its own airstrip and an unnatural concentration of aircraft. "The whole population of Columbus probably doesn't exceed 50 people, but it's sure got a mess of planes on that strip!" one of the briefers declared. That fact hadn't escaped the attention of federal narcotics agents, the other briefer added. "There's a game of cops and robbers going on but the cops don't catch more than one out of a hundred robbers. The dopers are so rich they can hire very good pilots and buy very sophisticated equipment. Besides, it's easy. All you have to do is land at night on some road or unlighted runway and throw the stuff over a fence, which takes about three minutes."

The weather briefing they gave me for the next day included the warning, "Don't fly near El Capitan." Winds around it, they said, were often strong and freaky and had been known to knock over trailers and vans on the highway running next to it. Also, pilots who followed the highway, particularly in winter when ceilings were low, sometimes turned by mistake onto a parks department road which was brighter than the highway and led into a box canyon. "That canyon is littered with wrecks." When I mentioned I was going to sleep by my plane that night, they gave me another warning: Don't. "There's scorpions out there!" one said in a shivery voice. They assured me I'd be safe in the lounge, not because there weren't scorpions in it but because at night the doors were locked. People had been coming after dark and carrying off the lounge furniture. I put my sleeping bag on the sofa in the lounge and from there could see out one window the pinpoint-blue of taxiway lights and out the other the green-and-white flashes of the airport's rotating beacon. From behind me the lighted face of a snack machine cast a gentle, diffused glow over my pillow. As I drifted off to sleep I could hear one of the briefers telling the other a story about how a couple of dogs caught a gopher. That's all there seemed to be to the story: A couple of dogs caught a gopher. They both laughed heartily.

The briefer who was still on duty in the morning gave me yet another piece of advice. When I started my preflight, I could see the profile of El Capitan behind the first row of hills, but when I finished it the profile was gone. BD? I wondered, then heard a couple of cracks and looked up to see the American flag in front of the station sticking out from the flagpole and snapping hard in the wind. At the same time the Luscombe began rocking and creaking at its tiedown, as if restless to be off; when I touched an aileron lightly it slammed the rest of the way down and I could hear the stick thud sideways in the cockpit. "Very unusual," the briefer said, "getting a morning wind like this." He suggested I wait for takeoff. "The wind may die, blow off." It was exactly what I wanted from a briefer: a familiarity with the quirks of local weather and terrain, and a willingness to offer advice based on that familiarity. The computers we pilots were increasingly being asked to use for weather information could never manage that. I waited by having breakfast in town with another pilot who got the same advice, and by the time we arrived back at the airport a layer of clouds had moved in over it at 1,000 feet. El Capitan's profile was in the clear again, though, so I took off for El Paso, and within minutes was climbing out past what I was sure was the mouth of Carlsbad Caverns. From the air it looked like nothing more than an old puncture wound. Deep inside, though, I knew there was a little stone garden, with unearthly, twisting, milky stalks. It's all there whether we see it or not.

Past El Capitan, I picked up a highway that ran west for 90 miles, all the way to El Paso. It had no light poles alongside it and few cars on it so it was one long emergency airstrip for me, a half-million-foot paved runway. On one protracted stretch it ran so straight and unwaveringly to the west that my compass needle never once budged off W. W being the theme, the soil on either side of the highway became increasingly pale and the vegetation increasingly sparse. In the middle of a particularly dry, barren area, I came across something unexpected: a street grid. Not the streets, just the grid, lines forming blocks and cul-de-sacs scraped in the dirt by some earth-moving machine. Apparently a blueprint for a town-to-be—or maybe a town *not*-to-be. For various reasons, some of the reasons not very honorable, a grid was as far as some new towns got. Here there wasn't a single elaboration of the grid—scrap of pavement, pole, structure, plant, hydrant, or even earth-moving machine—to suggest it might be more than that someday. Could it be one of those developments for which this would be the final development? I wondered. A ghost town from the start?

One time I was up flying and saw a different sort of "new" ghost town. Three houses had actually been built, but they had almost surely not been lived in, and might never be. Around them in all directions there was nothing but dirt, not even a grid. Wind had blown the dirt up against one side of all three houses, as high as the first-floor windows, in snow-like drifts. On the side away from the wind the drifts were hollowed out, like snow. Through the roar of the engine I had a sensation of silence. The scene suggested calamity—neutron-bomb attack, pestilence, drought—but more likely some mistake in financing.

As I drew closer to El Paso I passed a mountain with a large white A painted on the side. A, I wondered, for what? Not for El Paso, certainly. Not for Juarez, the city across the river. Not for Texas either, or for Jesus. For what, then? Elsewhere around the West I had seen letters like this one painted on hillsides, usually large white single letters not the same as the first letters of the towns they were nearest or the states they were in, and I imagined that if I flew high enough I'd be able to make sense of them, that together they might spell something, as the spaced-out letters on a map do, one every 30 miles or so: A M E R I C A.   S A L V A T I O N.   B E T A   S I G.   B E A T   I R A Q !   Or (last joke of the old speed pilot Howard Hughes) C A S H   I N   K L E E N E X   B O X.

El Paso, Texas, was the low spot in the U.S. for planes crossing the Rockies; to get to it I didn't have to fly much higher than 5,000 feet. El Paso was the low spot not only vertically but horizontally as well. While in the pattern for Sunland, an airport ten miles west of the city, I could have thrown a Frisbee into Mexico. Instead, I walked over a footbridge into Mexico, for lunch. Immediately on the other side of the bridge were shops and cafés painted the luscious colors of the Mexican palette—aqua, peach, and yellow. Men stood on street corners selling prickly pears from carts, little boys ran around hawking seeds and individual Chiclets, women sat in plazas selling votives and lottery tickets. A man holding a serape, sombrero, and camera waited stoically beside a lifelike wooden horse for the next American to come by who wanted his picture taken as a *caballero*. In the market there were whole barrels full of pinto beans and red, yellow, and green peppers and corn with windows cut out of the husks so customers could see the big, white kernels inside. Near the door in a church, women lifted children to kiss the smudged glass by the head of a full-size mannequin of Christ, lying in a glass coffin, under a lace coverlet, brown wig askew. Outside the church an armless man holding a brush in his teeth painted a picture of a yellow leopard as men in straw sombreros watched. On one wall there was a poster for a bullfight, and on another wall a scrawled slogan, REVOLUCIÓN PROLETARIA LATINAMERICANA. UNIDOS VENCEREMOS!

So many Latin clichés! As I crossed back over the footbridge, after another dose of enchiladas, rice, and beans, I realized I had expected Juarez to be more of a mixture, more of a hybrid of the U.S. and the Mexican, more influenced by El Paso than it seemed to be (on the surface at least, which is all I could see in a couple of hours). For, despite some English on menus (I was sorely tempted by something listed at my restaurant as "Tamales—pork, chicken, or sweat") and clothing on people that might or might not be American, Juarez appeared to be far closer to cities a thousand miles south of it than to the one a Frisbee-throw across the river.

My idea was to fly from Sunland to Santa Fe by way of the White Sands National Monument; a woman I met in North Carolina told me, "The sand looks like sugar or salt, it's so fine. I took my poodle and he began to lap it up." I would have liked to fly over the sands and see what they looked like from the air—sugar, salt, snow, sheets, or chalk perhaps—but, judging from the chart, every single blanched grain of them was locked inside two military restricted areas, the largest combined restricted areas in the continental U.S., one of them running from the ground to "unlimited," the other from the ground to 22,000 feet. So I gave up on the white sands, as I had on the bayous, put them aside to be seen some other day, and flew up the Rio Grande instead. Only later did I learn that, with the terrific visibility out that way, I could have gotten a look at the sands from outside the restricted area, at an angle, admittedly, and at a distance, but still a look.

When I arrived at Sunland for the flight to Santa Fe, it was early; the light was soft, the shadows misty, the only clouds thin sickles of cirrus—and the office locked. Always the last item on my personal preflight checklist was to go to the bathroom, but at Sunland I didn't see any place to take care of that gracefully. Like most small airports, Sunland was great on vista but lousy on cover. Roads ran around it, and cars and trucks were already out on them, giving drivers a clear shot of me wherever I chose to baptize the earth. I was about to crouch beside a stand of skinny reeds, of no more use to me as a screen than venetian blinds with the slats open, when a truck pulled into the parking lot and a man emerged, walked to the office, and unlocked the door. Fifteen minutes later, my checklist complete, I was airborne.

Airborne the problem takes on different dimensions, of course. I've found that when I'm flying I need to go to the bathroom more often, and sooner, and more urgently than at any other time when I am similarly seated and inactive. Men have it easy with their portable Little Johns and old milk bottles and (I've been told) little sliding vents on the pilot's side, but in the cramped quarters of a cockpit, sitting hip to hip with friends and family, sharing the same few cubic feet of air, there are times when even brave men hesitate. I overheard an instrument pilot about to set out on a cross-country flight with his wife and kids tell a briefer once that he really wanted a cup of coffee but he wasn't going to have one because it would be a *long* trip. Women have their "Jill's John," a contraption with its own flowered carrying case, but I've never been inclined to use one, being quite certain that, with shorts to wriggle out of and maneuver around and the stick to attend to in what was sure to be bumpy air while I was trying to manipulate a plastic gadget around my sitting parts, I'd end up in a soggy pool in my bucket seat for the rest of the flight.

On my way up the river, I passed Truth or Consequences, New Mexico, which set me to wondering: What did the inhabitants of a town that changed its name to that of a popular quiz show years ago in order to win some prize money call it among themselves now? Not the whole ball of marbles surely. Truth? Consee? T 'n' C? Whatever the old name was? Forty miles past it, near a bend in the river, I saw some large, white spots on the ground, all of them about the same size and same blunt shape. Were they sheep? I wondered. Or gravestones? From the altitude I was flying, 3,000 feet AGL, I couldn't tell. They were too fat to be gravestones yet too orderly to be sheep. Still, they had to be one or the other. I kept waiting for a spot to move to clinch it or turn into a cross as I passed, but none did. Sheep, gravestones, I never did decide.

Soon I was at 4,000 feet AGL instead of 3,000 without having climbed a foot; the ground just fell away. From that height the shadow of my plane on the ground was a grayish circle with a narrow band of light around it. I watched as it passed over a field, a road, and a parked car and wondered if anyone on the ground ever knew when my plane's shadow covered him, if there was a dimming of the air around him that he noticed in some way, a flicker to the light, or a chill he only sensed, as from some spectral, unhappy thought. Airplane shadows look quite different when the planes are at different altitudes, and not just because their sizes change either. Their shapes do too, and the amount of light they carry with them. When my plane is, for instance, a few feet to several hundred feet above the ground, with the sun directly overhead, its shadow is a recognizable copy of the original, a shaggy twin, as you might expect. When it is two or three thousand feet up, the shadow is mostly wing, with a stump of a fuselage and no tail, like a couple of war ribbons crossed to form a T, darker where they overlap. From 3,000 to 5,000 feet AGL, the shadow appears round and takes on a halo. Above 5,000 only the halo survives, filling the circle. The shadow is all light, a small moon riding the earth, sliding over grass and trees, shining up from fields and roads like a reflection on still water.

On approach to Santa Fe, I saw something sobering. On the steep slope that led up to the threshold of the active runway, scattered up and down the slope where they'd hit after being shoved over the airport edge, were a couple of dozen wrecked automobiles, lying every which way, some nose down, some on their sides, the glass in the windows broken, the dents turned to rust. From the grounds of the airport nobody could see them but from the air they were all too visible: smashed metal vehicles! There were enough *memento mori* in the aviation business without throwing in gratuitous ones like these, I thought, as the smooth and as-yet-unscarred belly of my Luscombe slid over them on final.

Santa Fe airport was controlled, but I made an exception of it because I was meeting a friend. She was in Santa Fe doing a master's thesis on shadows—not the pale, light-filled shadows cast by airplanes passing overhead but the darker, sharp-edged, anchored ones laid down by cacti, rocks, and churches. Sandy and I had agreed ahead of time to rent a car together, but since she got to Santa Fe first she had already picked out the car, a red one, her favorite color, and therefore thought of it as mostly hers and wanted to do almost all the driving. I discovered after she had driven me around for a couple of days that I didn't relish being a passenger, having been the driver for so long, the one making the decisions about how to carve up space, and realized it was rendering me a bit passive in other ways as well, less exploratory and participatory.

One afternoon as she was driving us back from a mountain meadow of wildflowers in the Pecos Wilderness, I glanced out the car window to see a flock of birds moving along beside us, rippling in flight very, very slowly, like a handkerchief being waved. Behind them was a sunset made up of yellow, rose, and blue stripes, with more blue stripes running across them to form a fan pattern. If I were in a plane, I couldn't help thinking, I could aim for that sunset, fly right at it, and if by chance the sun had set before I went up I could, by taking off and climbing a little, make it rise again, pull it red and fat from behind the horizon, then, by going down myself, make it set again. Staring out at the scene, empty-handed, I felt the terrible ache of desire, as I had the night before at the opera, under the open sky, watching the strobe of a distant plane wink among the stars.

I stayed on the ground in Santa Fe five days, and my only contact with the sky came through looking at it, a bright, new, almost turquoise blue. That blue was there every cloudless day, over Bandelier, an ancient pueblo 40 miles northwest of Santa Fe, and Santo Domingo, a modern pueblo 30 miles southwest of Santa Fe, as well as Santa Fe itself, the city that tried to *look* like a pueblo, with even funeral parlors and the stock exchange made of adobe. My last night in Santa Fe Sandy and I had a Tex-Mex dinner with all our favorites in it at once: sopapillas, posole, chalupas, chile rellenos, burritos, and natilla. In the morning my stomach felt as if it had a couple of rolls of pennies in it; I could barely take tea. She drove the red car clear up to my tiedown, where I saw, standing beside the Luscombe, fat with meaning, a large blackbird. "Nevermore!" I shouted (not up to being original), and it flapped off. I discovered while doing my preflight that five days earlier I had left the outside cabin-air vents turned upward instead of downward, so that their openings faced the sky (cupped, it occurred to me, like Hamlet's father's ear, to catch the poison dropped from Hamlet's uncle's hand)—a harmless mistake, at worst it would have meant rain on the rug, but to me in my queasy state somewhat disturbing.

I almost didn't have Zero Three Bravo. Not because of the crash; because of what happened after the crash, during the long months while it was being repaired. In those days I became easily seduced by thoughts of flying something else. Gene Day had a wreck of a plane, a worse wreck than mine, the mere skeleton of a Champ, and he went on and on one day about all the things he was going to do to that Champ when he restored it for himself, the features he was going to put on it that he'd always wanted on an airplane. It would be his dream plane. I think it was the mention of eyebrow lights that did it— eyebrow lights! When he saw how taken I was with the idea of a custom-built plane, he made me an offer. He would rebuild the Champ for *me,* put all the things that *I* wanted on it, turn it into *my* dream plane, a Super Champ, in exchange for my two Luscombes, the one that was still flying and the one that wasn't. I didn't give him an answer but I did some planning around it, drew up a list of the things I would want on a plane and even held a contest at the office for original paint schemes (one entry had dinner-plate-size polka dots). I also decided on the colors I wanted, burnt orange with apple-green stripes and black accents (now *that* could really be seen in the air!). Nowadays I couldn't imagine choosing to fly in such a Halloween getup, but the night that I decided on those colors for my new plane I was too excited to sleep.

I also picked out a new registration number. A plane's registration number usually comes with it from the factory, but the number can be changed for a fee of $10. Since the Super Champ would be almost a new plane, I thought it should have a new number. It would have to start with the letter N, since the plane would be based in the U.S., and have one to five numbers afterward plus no, one, or two letters. I tried out several combinations of letters and numbers, saying each aloud to see which sounded best over the radio. For radio communication, each letter has a word equivalent, to limit reception errors: Alfa for A, Bravo for B, Charlie for C, etc., and I decided the letters I liked the spoken sound of best were E–Echo, T–Tango, Q–Quebec, and S–Sierra, in that order. As for numbers, I had so enjoyed saying my first Luscombe's registration number, N71116, with the snappy "Triple One" in the middle, that I decided to use three 1's again. So I put them together with my favorite letter, E, and got my new number, N111E. "Triple One Echo, entering downwind." (The N—November—was unspoken since everybody in the United States had one.) Perfect!

Before formally requesting it, I had to check the national aviation registration directory to be sure nobody else had the number already. Nobody did, and I was about to send in my $10 when my friend John came back from an air show in Pennsylvania with hot news. In the middle of the show he had seen a twin-engine Jet Commader pull in and stop not far from where he was standing, and lo and behold written on the side of the plane was: N111E! He edged closer and waited for the pilot to emerge. The pilot was . . . Danny Kaye! *Danny Kaye had my number!* Probably made it up too, and recently, since it wasn't in the directory. I wasn't dismayed, instead saw losing my number as a meeting of creative minds. It became clear what I had to do. I wrote Oklahoma City asking for another number, N111E*E*. That sounded even better, "Triple One Echo *Echo.*" I couldn't wait to try it out on a controller.

I kept the number for a year. I never got to try it out on a controller because I never got the Champ. Something happened; I lost interest in the project or never could bring myself to give up two planes for one or Gene Day didn't follow through; at any rate the Champ never became a Super Champ and I kept Zero Three Bravo. But I did enjoy having my own handpicked registration number for a while, attached to a purely dream plane, only an echo away from Danny Kaye's real one.

Visibility when I left Santa Fe was over 60 miles; the briefer said "sixty" as casually, in as matter-of-fact a tone, as one in New York would have said "six." However, with all that visibility, there seemed to be less than usual to see. Landmarks away from the road became few and far between, and quite modest. "Windmill." "Tailings pond." "Ranch." "Tank." "School." In my part of the country whole suburbs and road systems were submerged in pools of urban yellow, but out here almost everything counted, was worth pointing out. "Corral." "Ruins." "Camp." "Hut." "Water." Maybe some day I'd see, next to little black dots on the chart, "Old fridge." "Pile of hubcaps." "Hank's boots."

Clarke airport at Gallup was named for a state senator, the father of an FBO who died in a plane crash a few months before I visited once. A briefer told me that in all the son's years of flying out of the field, he never once asked for a weather briefing. "He'd fly when the birds were grounded," the briefer said. "I'd see him about to take off in some lousy weather and I'd say, 'They'll pick D.B. up one day.' Well, they did pick him up, but it was on a CAVU [Ceiling And Visibility Unlimited] day, when there wasn't a cloud in the sky." While poking around the field I came across what was left of D.B.'s plane, a blue-and-white Cherokee 140 lying next to a hangar, in a twisted, mangled heap, out there in full view of everybody, long after the accident, apparently not causing anybody any distress, seeing the instrument of the FBO's death, his first tomb.

What people at Clarke *were* interested in looking at was parked on the ramp when I came in, next to a "Japanese rock garden" the new FBO had put in (driveway gravel and boulders). The object of their intense interest was the Marines' "Super Jolly Green Giant," largest helicopter in the U.S. military at the time, which according to its dapper little captain weighted 42,000 pounds empty and could carry up to 8,000 pounds in men and equipment. Its engines were so powerful, he told the crowd, the rotors could whip up winds to 105 miles an hour on a calm day or, if within 75 feet of the surface of a body of water, churn up spray so thick the crew had to throw flares out the window to figure out which way was down. Most of the power went into lifting, though; its cruise speed was 110 miles an hour, no more than my Luscombe's, I noted with satisfaction.

The "Super Jolly," as the captain called it, had been on its way to war games in Nevada when it "malfunctioned" and had to go down; Clarke happened to be the nearest field. What would they be doing at the war games when they got there? I asked. "There'll be a Red Force and a Blue Force fighting to take over a White Force," he said. "Our role will be to assist the White Force, a neutral nation. We'll get a call saying there's a downed pilot somewhere and we should go pick him up." When not at war games, what did they do? I asked. "We're a contingency squadron for worldwide conflict or disaster," he answered, as he had surely answered before. "We evacuated Mayaguez. We refueled B-52s in Vietnam. And we *almost* went to Guatemala after the earthquake." In the lounge, the crewmen were lying around, most of them very young men, stretched out on chairs and sofas, dozing in their flight suits. It was a Norman Rockwell scene: "A Long Way from Home." Word came that the Super Jolly was ready for a test flight, and they struggled up and out, climbing aboard the helicopter through a hole big enough to admit a small tank.

We stood back as the helicopter's engines started up. Its blades whipped around, blasting dust onto the rock garden and cigarette butts into the bushes. Then, with a combined beat and whine, it rose straight up about 25 feet and started swinging from side to side, in small arcs, as if on the end of a very short rope. After a few minutes of that, it turned and flew toward the runway, over it, and beyond it, kept on going until it was out of sight behind the hills. We waited but it didn't come back. Maybe, I thought, we weren't supposed to know this was more than a flight test. *They* had to know; everything's procedure in the military. The crowd drifted apart and I decided to go to the High Chaparral, a restaurant at the edge of the field, for lunch, even though a pilot standing next to me during the test flight told me, "It'll be a ptomaine lunch." The last time he ate there, he said, it cost him $800 in hospital fees.

Although the High Chaparral backed onto airport property, it didn't seem to have much interest in cultivating pilots' business. A sign on one wall inside said, WE HERE AT HIGH CHAPARRAL CATER TO THE TRUCKING TRADE. DRIVERS RUN ON SCHEDULE AND WILL BE SERVED FIRST. So aviators, forget about your ETA's! Stand quietly by and watch the kings of the road *eat*. I ordered "fried Icelandic cod," of all things, having decided against the "steak smothered in chili, choice of red or green," and as I consumed it watched the drivers being catered to. They were talking table to table, honey-ing the waitresses, playing loud and conspicuous pool, and blowing a lot of smoke around, all with such swagger and projection that they did make pilots, not ordinarily known for their diffidence, seem a humble lot.

When I went into the High Chaparral the weather was fair. When

I came out it looked like rain. The pilot who told me about the ptomaine lunch also told me about the weather. "Cells build up in half
an hour around here," he said. I ran for a hangar with the doors
standing wide open and made it inside just as the storm broke. At first
I thought I was alone in there, then something—a sound, movement,
shift of light—tipped me off that I was not. At the back of the hangar
I found a man in overalls standing in near-darkness beside the cowling
of . . . a Luscombe. He greeted me like kin. When I pointed to my
plane out on the ramp, being washed by the rain, he told me, with
great excitement, about his.

"I'd been wanting an airplane for 40 years," he said. "I was raised
on final approach to what's Los Angeles International Airport now and
used to crawl over 'Wrong Way' Corrigan's Robin. I even got my
pilot's license, but then got married and started having kids and had
to quit flying. I figured that someday when my four kids were grown
I'd start looking for an airplane. Any kind of airplane." The Luscombe sort of found its way to him. "Twelve years ago a man from
California bought a Luscombe in Texas and was flying it home when
he stopped for lunch at Santa Rosa [New Mexico]. A whirlwind picked
up the plane while he was eating and threw it on its back. He called a
cop to help him turn the plane over, then went home to California and
never came back. The Luscombe sat for ten years. A friend of mine
bought it at a sheriff's auction, but he never got around to fixing it up
because he already had a Parakeet. So I traded him my Harley-
Davidson for it."

He may not have chosen the Luscombe, but once he had it, he might
as well have, so great was his enthusiasm. He bragged about how
Luscombes were "designed for efficiency since they wouldn't have
much horsepower" and told me how he'd flown recently "all the way
to Michigan" to get new seats and a stabilizer. He kept a 1941 issue of
Air Progress on his tool shelf with a full-page ad in it for Luscombes.
He handed it to me. Seven Luscombes were pictured parked side by
side on a flight line, spinners pointing confidently skyward. Men in
military uniforms were standing in front of them. "Ready, Willing
and Able!" went one headline. "World's fastest, sturdiest and lowest
priced all-metal trainer," went another line. Well, the Luscombe may
have been ready and willing but it wasn't able, at least to impress the
men in uniform it aimed to. The Army bought Stearmans, Ryans,

and Fairchilds as primary trainers instead. (A note at the bottom of the ad announced that Luscombes were on display at 247 Park Avenue in New York City, something I would love to have seen—Luscombes on Park Avenue! There's a bank office there now.)

The man walked me all around his Luscombe, which he was fixing up, and showed me a "mysterious" hole in the fuselage. The hole was a little smaller than a dime. "I don't know how it got there," he said, sounding pleased about that. "It's like a very clean bullet hole." One reason he had taken so quickly to Luscombes, I concluded, was that he liked old things in general. "Might as well take a picture of an ice-cube tray," he said indignantly, "as have something new." He asked me to his house for tea so I could see his "antiques." They turned out to be an old banjo, a "banjo-uke," a pump organ, a player piano, and perhaps the cups we drank our tea out of, which had flowers painted on them. He put a roll of Scott Joplin's "Let's Walk To-gether" on the player piano, played he said by Joplin himself, and as we drank our tea we listened and watched the keys go up and down. If that wasn't immortality, what was? The impulse for what we saw and heard at that moment coming from Joplin's own fingers.

The rain had stopped by the time I left, and the air smelled to me of gardenias. "Probably sagebrush," the man said. Back at the airport I moved my plane to a tiedown with no puddles under it since I was going to sleep out, for an early start in the morning. Before settling in that evening, I took a stroll around the ramp, to have a look at the other planes. Floodlights along the edge sent an odd glow over them, and I became acutely aware of the planes' night personas, different from their identities by day. At night they were more flesh, less machine. A Cessna 170 was turned into a swimmer, with a long, lean, muscular body. A Skymaster became an old man, carrying his vigor in his chest, with no belly to speak of and scrawny thighs. A Tri-Pacer was a stripper, holding a vulgar pose in the spotlight, its tail cocked too high.

The briefer on duty in Gallup's Flight Service station when I went there to wash up was Bart Starr. That name was better suited to a rodeo king, football hero, or movie actor, I thought, than to the rather flaccid, gruff, sedentary man behind the desk, with a crew cut so extreme it had to be a statement. Starr too had once owned a Luscombe, a 1947 8A, but he'd gotten even less out of it than the man who stopped for lunch at Santa Rosa. He owned it with four other pilots, each kicking in $300, and one of the new owners went to pick the plane up from the airport where they bought it. As the man was taking off, a witness reported, he tried to "horse" the plane off the runway and "ballooned" (rose momentarily and then sank). He tried again and ballooned again, kept on trying until the Luscombe was over on its nose, tail up, "trailing fuel and fire." Said Starr, "I have six photos of the plane but I never did see it. My wife didn't even know I bought it until after it was busted. It was the only airplane I ever owned."

He was about to go off duty but seemed irritable. He was tired of shifts, he explained. He'd been with Flight Service for 30 years and had never gotten used to the shifts. They changed every single day. Then his replacement showed up, a man about his age, mid-50s, stocky, as Starr was, and a pilot too. The man had been in the FSS as long as Starr, yet it became obvious from the way Starr acted around him, with something more than irritation—distaste—that Starr didn't think the two had much in common. The new briefer seemed polite, bright, energetic, and manly in the football-rodeo mold, but he *did* have on a choker of peach-pink stones, a crescent-shaped gold earring, and soft, slipper-like moccasins.

His name was Al Guthrie. From my towel and cosmetic bag he must have deduced that I was going to sleep out because he offered to let me stay in a back room of the station (Starr had gone home by then). It was against regulations, he admitted, but he had lived in Alaska for a long time and people up there were in the habit of looking out for travelers. "Most places we worked didn't have a hotel, motel, restaurant, or even public toilet," he explained, "so if a pilot got stranded somebody in town would take him home or else we'd let him sleep in the back yard of the station. It was like the old frontier days down here. Everybody was friendly to everybody else; it was built into people's nature. If the guys were hunters, they might leave a hunk of game or jug of booze on the floor, for thanks."

Just then a man's voice broke in on the radio. "Five miles out, landing." Guthrie stepped to the console, picked up the mike, and gave the man wind direction, windspeed, altimeter setting, and known traffic (none). His voice was deep and resonating, and he delivered the numbers in a highly inflected manner, ending the call with an exaggerated *"Rah-ger!"* Bored, I thought. Forced to turn a standard transmission into a dramatic reading. As we stood looking out the station window, waiting for the man's plane to appear, Guthrie commented, "There's no wind, no traffic, and the pressure can't make any difference tonight." In other words, the pilot hadn't needed the information he was required to give him.

"But," I said, remembering some of my own long solos, "he might need your voice in the night." "Maybe," said Guthrie, sounding unconvinced. As the long, near-horizontal beam of the pilot's landing light moved from left to right across the picture window, Guthrie went on. "I suppose I serve a useful function but the feeling isn't there. These pilots have their navigational aids, their air-route traffic control, their cockpit electronics. We're just cogs in the wheel. In Alaska, they really needed us. They needed for us to locate them when they went down, they needed our communications, they needed our weather reports. Even pilots familiar with the area could get screwed up on tundra. On whiteout days we'd sit with maps in our laps and try to jog their memories. In Kotzebue we had six saves in one day—mostly polar-bear hunters, lost over the ice between Alaska and Siberia.

"*Everybody* came through the base at Kotzebue," Guthrie continued, after the pilot had closed his flight plan, gotten a weather briefing for the morning, and left. "We had such a feeling of people depending on us we'd make it to work in the worst weather. Sometimes snow drifted over the tops of buildings, and we'd crawl on our hands and knees to get to the station, which could take an hour or hour and a half, even though we lived only five houses away. We'd run smack into buildings and not be able to tell which was the front and which was the back or where the entrance was. Even the streetlights would be buried. We'd climb to the tops of drifts and fall off and climb up again. We couldn't rig up guide ropes since they'd drift over too. When we finally got to the station we'd dig a tunnel to the door and leave the shovel in a place the wind would keep clear so the next person could dig in again. There was hardly any insulation inside and it got so cold we sometimes sat around a smoky stove wearing mittens so our fingers could type."

Guthrie described all this with the warmth of feeling and romantic longing of someone recalling a vacation on a tropical isle. Back of the briefing room at Clarke was a kitchenette, and during a quiet moment Guthrie went in and put a can of soup on to heat, telling me I could have half. Not wanting to look shabby, I brought tuna fish, stoned-wheat crackers, and teabags in from my plane. While he was taking care of another radio call, I stayed in the kitchen, sipping my mug of soup, liking the Alaskan way. I only wished I had something more impressive than teabags and tuna cans to drop on the floor, for thanks.

After that radio call I asked Guthrie how he came to Alaska in the first place. After World War II he was living in New Jersey and got the word that the Flight Service was looking for recruits. He became one. "I wanted to travel and be a second Richard Halliburton," he said. The service sent him to Kotzebue, "a jumping-off place for bear hunters," and within a few months he had fallen in love with an Eskimo woman named Keenyawun, also Margaret, also Dee (Keenyawun for her grandmother, a medicine woman, and Dee for "Desire," what a whaling captain called her when she was a child). He left the Flight Service and moved with her to Tigara, also known as Point Hope, on the Pacific coast above the Arctic Circle. He was the only non-Eskimo there and lived as the other men did, hunting whales from an *umiak*, collecting murres' eggs from cliffs, fishing through holes in the ice for char, setting traps on knolls for snowy owls. He was given the name Ahkok. Part of the year he and Dee lived in a sod house with a frame made from whale ribs, whale jawbone, and "driftwood found floating on the Japanese current." (Igloos, he pointed out, were used only as windbreaks for whaling; "nobody lived in them.") Sometimes he and Dee heated their house with whale blubber, which burned "like a blowtorch, better than wood." For weeks at a time he'd go off caribou-hunting, accompanied only by his dogs and sleeping in a bag Dee made out of caribou-fawn skins. "A down bag collects moisture and ends up being covered with ice an inch thick," he explained, "but a caribou bag turns moisture into frost crystals and you just brush them off." Sometimes he and the dogs would be stuck in snowdrifts for days.

"They were the best years of my life," said Guthrie, again with warmth. "The Eskimos are beautiful, industrious, good-hearted people. Extremely clean, too, in their way. White hunters would start out being fastidious, bathing and shaving every day, then when they realized how hard it was to keep that up they'd go in the other direction and quit washing altogether. In a week or ten days they'd be real grubby. The Eskimos would get down to a certain level and not go below it. They'd at least splash water on themselves every day."

Guthrie learned a great deal from them in other ways. "They took their hardships in stride. If it rained or snowed, it was all the same to them. They wouldn't gripe. If a man got lost on the ice and didn't come home and everybody thought he was dead, the family showed nothing. They weren't panic-stricken. That was the way things were. If the man came back alive, they would still show nothing. If his finger had been cut off or frozen off, they didn't make a big deal out of it. They lived with nature and accepted life as it came. That helped me a lot."

Meanwhile, the FSS had other plans for Guthrie. One day he got a letter asking him to come back to work. He wrote back no. He got another letter. He said no again. He got a third letter and asked Dee, who by this time was his wife and the mother of a baby boy whose diapers she washed in water Guthrie hauled in as ice and melted over the blubber stove, "Would you like an iron and a washing machine?" "That was my downfall," he said ruefully.

The FSS sent him first to McGrath for two years, then to Kotzebue again, then to Iliamna, Anchorage, Grants, Tanana, and Iliamna again. Ten years went by, 20. He and Dee had eleven children. He began to think about retiring. It's hard to live on a government pension in Alaska, he realized. "If you're too old to chop wood you have to pay for the extra fuel, the extra clothes, the extra mukluks, and a heavy-duty battery." So, to begin a life he expected to be able to keep in retirement, he asked for an assignment outside Alaska. Two years ago he arrived in Gallup. Obviously, he still hadn't made the move emotionally. "Everywhere you go here," he said, "it's somebody's *yard.* We don't even know our next-door neighbors!" He missed the openness and the friendliness of Alaska, the freedom to wander around, preferably with your gun. He missed the music people made themselves, and the parties. "Twenty-four hours up there you wish were 48," he said. And he missed the food.

What food? Seal meat he missed the most. "It's my favorite meat. We ate it every damned day. Describe it? How do you describe an almond? How do you describe tequila? You can't compare seal to anything the way you can the other meats we ate. Caribou and moose and elk are all gamy, like deer. Polar bear is white but otherwise it's like beef, except it's tough, and occasionally fishy. Black bear's like pork. If I breaded a piece and fried it you couldn't tell it from a pork chop. But seal, it's like nothing else you ever ate. Once you taste it, you know what it is."

He didn't like seal meat at first. "When I got to Alaska I was practically a vegetarian," he said. "I couldn't stand a fatty pork chop. It was a bummer. I hardly ever ate butter or sugar and I didn't drink coffee. After a couple of months, though, I was putting butter a half- or three-quarters of an inch thick on my bread and drinking lots of coffee with heavy cream and several spoonfuls of sugar. In the cold I craved those things. I'd eat Arctic owls, which are very oily and rich but cooked in a pressure cooker are absolutely delicious, with a delicate flavor, except at Point Hope we boiled them in a pot and they were tough as . . . [he left me to fill in "boiled owls"]. We ate muktuk, the black skin of the whale above the blubber but with the blubber attached, either raw or raw-frozen, but aged a week or so. We ate fish that way, too. We'd chop up frozen fish with an ax and stick pieces in our mouths ·and let them melt. Grayling, tomcod, Arctic char—if it was fresh it was all good."

Guthrie felt out of place in Gallup, not just because it was a lot warmer than Alaska and hadn't any seal meat. "I got an entirely different feeling for life in Alaska," he said, trying to explain. "Before I went up there I experienced things through my eyes, my nose, and my mouth, but when I was by myself in the boondocks and there was no way to get out or back and I was *committed* to something—once I convinced myself that I was the only one able to do a particular thing and there was no chaplain or doctor around, and I went through it all and got past the bottom and came through to the other side, I could appreciate the whole damned picture. I saw the universe, the animals, how people used to live with things, the birds, the mountains, the flowers, how they're inside of us. I knew my capabilities and I belonged to things. I'd look at the scenery in the woods, but what I got was not coming through my senses. It was coming through someplace else. I'd breathe the air, look up at the night stars, and feel a part of it all."

He stared into the briefing room and out of it. "Up there you find out what's really important. There's a spot on the kitchen wall? *We just wanted a wall to keep the wind out!* Who spilt tea on the doily? *You've got to be kidding!* Whenever I find myself getting uptight about a broken light switch or something, I think about the times we had the bare necessities and went out past the bottom and came through to the other side . . .''

I laid my bag on the floor of the back room, between a desk and a file cabinet, and climbed in. My body was warm, with soup and tea, but I almost wished it weren't. I was feeling the contrast too keenly. With the federal government's pile rug under me and a three-drawer metal file cabinet blocking the hall light, I was feeling flabby, of body and spirit. Far, far from the bare necessities, the howl of wind over snowdrift, the demands of muktuk and boiled owl, the mind-set that would allow me to accept graciously the cutting off of a finger. Lying in the soft grip of my sleeping bag, I wished fervently for a tougher spirit, a deeper, companion relationship with the natural world—to quit griping, and overeating. But I wasn't optimistic. I didn't think I was capable of going as far down as it would take, all the way, to the bottom and out, in order to get to the other side . . .

Oljato · Lake Powell

Past Clarke lay all sorts of Western wonders: craters, canyons, hot springs, stone arches, painted deserts, lakes that had once been canyons, salt flats that were sometimes lakes. I couldn't make up my mind where to go next. Three briefers had been on duty at once when I got to Gallup, and I asked them for ideas. One said Monument Valley. Another said Canyon de Chelly. The third insisted on the Grand Canyon. After Guthrie got there I asked his advice too. Almost in anger, he said he couldn't think of any place worth seeing in the lower 48, then relented. Lake Powell, he admitted, was "spectacular." So in the morning I decided to try all four places, fly a large inverted U starting with Canyon de Chelly and ending with the Grand Canyon. Starting, however, involved figuring out where Canyon de Chelly was. The chart showed only a series of broken blue lines ("intermittent streams") about where I thought it should be. Guthrie was gone by the time I got up (having left some grapefruit juice in the refrigerator for me—still looking out for travelers) so I asked the briefer who came on duty after him. "You see that chimney?" he asked, leading me outside and pointing toward a range of mountains, one of which was higher than the others. "Well, aim to the left of it and you'll be here"—he touched one of the blue lines, no different from the other blue lines so far as I could see and miles on the chart from the words "prominent canyon." *"That's* Canyon de Chelly."

I did indeed find a crevice to the left of the chimney and followed it westward, hoping the briefer was right (there were times when you'd like confirming signboards aloft). Narrow and high-walled at first, it gradually opened up, as if reluctantly yielding its ancient secrets, the walls growing lower, moving apart, until the whole thing emptied out into the valley of Chinle. However, it didn't yield many of its secrets to me. Even throttled back I flew down it so fast I couldn't spot as I'd wanted to any of the apartment-style pueblos carved into the rock walls by the old cliff dwellers. Out of consideration for the sightseers below, I didn't allow myself a second run, but I felt unfulfilled by the first. By Jeep, I figured, the run beginning to end would have taken a day, on foot as much as three days. By plane it took under 20 minutes. When I found myself at the end of the canyon, I felt as if I'd gobbled a gourmet meal in the time it took to shake out the napkin.

In compensation, Chinle was a lovely valley, of wide, green meadows with cascading pale-orange cliffs on the side away from Chelly and a dry wash running up the middle. I turned and flew north over the wash, toward Monument Valley. A few cows were standing here and there on the grass, as well as in the wash, and a few abandoned cars were standing on the grass too, like cows, except being metal they caught the sun as I passed and gave off tiny bursts of light. Where I first started following the wash, it was almost flush with the fields around it, but gradually it sank in relation to them until it had walls on either side maybe 25 feet high. In places niches had been gouged out of the walls by erosion, and in several of the niches I could see something green—sagebrush?—growing part of the way up, which gave them the look from the air of little outdoor amphitheaters, with stage scenery already in place for sylvan dramas.

After 60 miles, a highway slashed across the wash, and on the other side of it was, I believed (again I wouldn't have minded a floating signboard), the southernmost section of Monument Valley. From there I flew pretty much free-form, to a monument I liked the shape of, then around and around and sometimes over it, watching the rock contours bend and bulge and contract as I flew by, peering out at spires and into the recesses between spires, then picking another monument and flying the miles of empty scrubland to it, circling it. On one long passage between monuments I flew over a Navajo hogan, a six-sided, metal-roofed dwelling with two white geese attacking the dirt beside it, and tried to imagine what it would be like to live daily with these monuments, as if they were ordinary. Some of those I'd been circum-navigating were charming, gay even—crooked chimneypots, cone-heads in capes too long for them, chubby thumbs—but most were dignified, imposing, keepers of secrets too. I imagined they could serve a local resident as mountains, icons, sculpture, and the architecture of the neighborhood all at once. What a skyline they produced! Years ago I got a postcard from young friends who visited Monument Valley shortly before one of them died, and on the back of the card they had copied lines from the well-known White Corn Boy Navajo creation-myth poem: "Beauty before us, with it we wander/Beauty above us, with it we wander/Beauty all around us, with it we wander/On the beautiful trail are we, with it we wander." Beauty was the ordinary, everyday thing here, and when it came time for me to go down I wasn't ready to forget it. I landed at Oljato, an airport on the western side of the valley, just over the state line in Utah, with the idea of canceling my flight plan, getting more fuel, and taking off again, wandering again in the valley, Beauty below me.

Oljato was a Navajo trading post with a "composition" airstrip beside it (whatever the composition was was a pale, sickly green color). Between the strip and the post ran a fence of thin wire strung between small wooden poles, too low and too weak, it seemed to me, to stop anything from wandering onto the runway except maybe an exhausted sheep. I stepped over the fence—there was no gate—and walked up a path to the front door of the post, a one-story, mud-brown building. Inside was a modest-sized room painted a slightly darker green than the runway. It had shelves running from the floor to the ceiling on two sides, and on the shelves, arranged neatly but according to no scheme I could figure out, were among other things, bolts of electric-blue and electric-pink cloth, horse saddles, plastic bracelets, metal lunch boxes, a bed pillow, cowboy boots, umbrellas, potholders, Jockey shorts, paste-on tattoos, hand saws, aprons, Frisbees, sequins, nylon blankets, tweezers, suede shirts, penny candy, chiffon scarves, and canned and packaged food.

At the back a Navajo woman was standing behind a counter. There was nobody else in the room. I noticed a radio on a shelf near the counter and assumed it was the Unicom; I also assumed it was turned off because I didn't hear any of the faint static fuzz, like breathing, a radio of that type puts out when it's set to receive. Why have a Unicom, I thought grumpily, if you kept it turned off? I told the woman I needed fuel for my plane. "Mr. Smith isn't here," she said, as if that settled it. Mr. Smith? "He's got the key to the pumps." Uh-oh. Before I left Clarke, a briefer had told me, "If you go to Monument Valley it'll be a one-way trip, since you can't go anywhere else on your tanks, not without refueling. There's only one place to refuel up there

and that's Oljato, but don't worry, Oljato's always got fuel.'' Uh-huh.
I pictured Mr. Smith splayed under some beach umbrella, or hunched
beside the bed of an ailing mother, the key to the pumps deep in his
pocket, and I ran through my options. Taking off with the little fuel
remaining in my tanks and hoping for a 60-mph tailwind all the way
to Lake Powell; draining fuel from somebody else's tanks to fill mine
(the Luscombe was the only plane on the strip); using automobile gas
and risking a fouled plug or vapor lock over rocky terrain; kicking
myself for not phoning ahead. Then I heard the woman say, in answer
to a question I must have asked, ''Tonight. Mr. Smith will be back
tonight.''

So I waited on fuel, instead of weather this time, but I didn't much
mind because I had never been to a trading post and was curious.
When I went out to tie down my plane I noticed a handwritten sign
on one of the (locked) fuel pumps. ''OLJATO HAS AN IDEAL CLIMATE,''
it went. ''NEVER TOO HOT AND NEVER TOO COLD. NEVER TOO
HOT IN WINTER, NEVER TOO COLD IN SUMMER.'' Oh that Mr.
Smith must be a sketch!

It was too hot to wait by the strip, so I went back to the post, and
by then several customers had come in, a Navajo woman with a baby
and two young Navajo men. She sat on one end of a short bench, a
bit tentatively, as if she might be chased off at any minute, although
it was the only place in the room to sit. I soon caught on that the post
didn't exactly encourage hanging out, in the tradition of general stores,
which trading posts certainly were. I bought things for lunch—
baloney, potato chips, and a large, round, soft, prepackaged loaf of
unsliced white bread, rather like a communal hamburger bun—then
sat at the other end of the bench from the woman with the baby and
made sandwiches for myself by tearing off chunks of the bread, pulling
the chunks apart, and stuffing the openings with baloney and potato
chips. As more people came in I began to feel self-conscious, eating in
front of them all, the potato chips snapping. The mood in the room
was constrained, almost formal; the talk—what talk there was, all of it
in Navajo—brief and carried on in low tones. There weren't any hearty
greetings or long-winded exchanges, in the tradition of general stores,
although I guessed most of the customers had driven a fair distance to
get there. The post was quiet even with people in it, *awkwardly* quiet
from my perspective. There I sat, right in the middle of traffic, almost

underfoot, sometimes making the only sound in the room, smashing the potato chips with my teeth, masticating publicly.

Lunch over, I leaned back against a display case and watched customers come and go. A bell above the door would ring and the screen door would open and somebody would enter (twice it was a woman with silver-and-turquoise jewelry in her dark hair pulled back in a bun, a gathered three-tiered ankle-length skirt—in one case the skirt was purple, the other aqua—and white sneakers), approach the counter, say something softly to the woman behind it, then wait, usually without saying anything more. Even teenagers in jeans and T-shirts didn't do anything more rambunctious than that. One white family came in, looking like Appalachian poor, the girls pale and skinny with peaked faces and patched clothes, the father picking up his mail and buying antifreeze (for which climate? I wondered). They didn't say much either.

One Navajo man particularly intrigued me. He was about 40 and powerfully built. His cheeks, forehead, and chin had the strong, sharp planes of the old Indian portraits. His hair was pulled back into a ponytail bound top to bottom with strands of white string and pulled up to form a loop on the back of his head. The same white string had been wound around his high-crowned black hat, as a hatband. He spoke to the clerk in Navajo, and I stood up, feigning a stretch, so I could see what it was that he had ordered, what an obviously authentic Native American would choose to buy, probably for lunch. She took one thing out of a refrigerator, one thing out of a case, one thing off a shelf, and set them on the counter. There for me to see and marvel at were a six-pack of 7-UP, a can of Spam, and a loaf of Tip Top bread. I sat down. What had I expected? Wolf jerky? Dehydrated bear paw?

I was suffering from a case of Indian awe. It had started probably when I was a kid back in Ohio and read about the special powers of Indians, how they could smell weather on the wind, talk to muskrats, take the pain of sharp sticks through the collarbone, etc., etc.; amplified by adult guilt about what my kind had done to theirs; and complicated by my current tendency to interpret solemnity as spiritual strength. The gravity of these Navajos made me shy, as if they could see through me, knew I was flying around just for fun, or for some vague enlightenment that they had already attained. I realized I wanted to impress them, or at least not look stupid to them. At one point I got up and looked into a miniature display case on top of the larger case I'd been leaning against, to take an unfeigned stretch and pass the time, and I found several pieces of "Indian" jewelry inside with machine-stamped designs and plastic "turquoise." Who bought it? I wondered. Was it the jewelry equivalent of Spam and did the Navajos buy it? One item was clearly handmade, though, and looked old. I lifted it out so I could get a better look at it. It consisted of a dozen or so embossed silver rectangles, each rectangle about the size of a large postage stamp, with a leather cord strung through them, to form a belt. I wrapped the belt around my waist and maneuvered myself in front of a mirror on the countertop so I could see how I looked in it. I heard a strange sound: laughter! A soft giggling from all the women in the room—an older woman, two teenage girls, and the clerk—all trying not to giggle but unable to stop. What, I wondered, was so funny about a belt? About *me* in a belt? Was this a *man's* belt? A belt for brides? Babies? The *dead?*

One of the girls looked at me shyly and tapped her temple. I didn't understand. "For the head," she whispered. Ohh, I said, "a *head*-band!" More giggling. She pointed higher on her head. Oh, "a *hat*band!" I said and laughed too. Then, although I had been thinking of buying the belt, when it was a belt, I laid it back in the case and closed the door on it, not wanting to appear any more stupid to them than I already had, stupid tourist.

Shortly after that an old woman came into the post and walked straight up to the bench instead of the counter and gestured for me to come outside with her. She climbed into a truck where another woman was already sitting and began pulling from a large plastic bag pairs of crossed sticks with yarns of different colors wound around them in a diamond pattern: Ojos de Dios. The things were all about two feet long, and one by one she held them up for me to see, her movements saying what she evidently couldn't in English, "This one?" "Do you want to buy this one?" In my turn I told her, using my hands a lot, that I had flown an airplane in—see, that one over there, the only one—and I didn't have room for anything so large—crowded cockpit, no room, sorry, sorry, sorry. I *was* sorry. As I watched her put the Ojos de Dios back in the plastic bag, one by one, I felt, again, unable to do the right thing.

Sometime in mid-afternoon I discovered another room in the post, one behind the store, a combination "museum" of old Navajo artifacts (tomahawks, squaw dresses, medicine-man kits) and display area for new Navajo crafts, rugs and baskets mostly, for sale. A sofa in the middle had a tall stack of rugs on one half so someone could sit on the other half and go through the stack and pick out a rug to buy. I headed right for that other half, made myself as inconspicuous as possible behind the stack of rugs, and dozed off. Now and then I would wake up to see, tacked up along the dark, wooden beams of the ceiling and walls, dozens of old Indian baskets, all of them round and shallow like plates, with red, brown, and black fibers forming designs, of birds, swastikas, and mazes, against pale grounds. Some of the designs were complicated and some were simple, but all had one thing in common: a break, sometimes no more than a single strand of grass, in the finished pattern. No border on the plates was ever closed, no silhouette remained intact. Beaks were always open, circles broken. "So the spirit can get out," the woman behind the counter said when I asked her on her way through to the bathroom. For a couple of hours I half-sat, half-lay on half of the sofa, content knowing there was always a ray of light coming through somewhere, a door left ajar, a straw to breathe through . . .

Thus the afternoon ticked away, punctuated with sounds from other parts of the post: soft voices in the main store, the doorbell tinkling, muffled noises from trucks pulling up in front. At one point the sounds grew louder and went on longer and I deduced that Mr. Smith had something to do with it. I went into the main room and saw a lanky, round-shouldered man of a certain age wearing a bemused expression, as you'd expect of someone who'd put up a sign like the one at the pumps. I told him I'd been waiting for fuel and he went right out and gave me some, but when I mentioned that I was getting it so I could go flying around the valley as soon as he finished giving it to me, he didn't encourage me. "I'd think about it," he said. "The air's pretty choppy." I decided he should know, but not flying around the valley left me with a lot of time to fill before bedtime, and no place to fill it except around the empty strip. The trading post closed at 5 o'clock, and it was almost 5 by then. I began bombarding Mr. Smith with questions about flying in Monument Valley, so after a while, unable to get away from me but wanting to get out of the sun, he asked me inside to answer them. He lived with his wife in rooms back of the store, and while she busied herself across the living room he and I sat on rocking chairs near the door and talked about flying. He didn't introduce her but he did mention her; it was really *her* trading post, he said.

Years ago, he recounted, he had been a cowboy, helping the federal government reduce stock on public lands. One day he stopped by the trading post; it was the same day that the owner's second daughter was home from school. Three weeks later he and she were married and he became what he said he was now, "the husband of an Indian trader." (Bemused look.) "We really were *traders* back then," he said. "The Indians would give us wool, sheep, blankets, and cattle, and we'd give those to the wholesale house, then the wholesale house would give us groceries and we'd give those to the Indians. It was uranium that started the cash flow. Now we don't buy lambs or wool anymore, we don't build or repair wagons the way we used to, and the Indians usually pay by check, from welfare or the new coal mine on Black Mesa, but otherwise, outside of a few tourists, things aren't much different than they were at the beginning. If an Indian wants something notarized or a check cashed or car parts or somebody to write a letter for him, he still comes here."

The flying got started during World War II, and largely because of it. The reservation didn't have any paved roads then, and the Navajos used horses and wagons to get around. "We used horses and wagons too," said Mr. Smith, "except we had a bobtail truck for picking up groceries in the city once a month. Even in the truck we had to drive daylight-to-dark to go 150 miles; the road was mud and wagon ruts all the way. During the war there wasn't much fuel even for trucks, so a guy over in Farmingdale got the bright idea of flying around the reservation. He figured a small plane could do on ten gallons of gas what a car could do on 200. He bought a T-craft [Taylorcraft] and flew it around to different trading posts to pick up food orders [there weren't any phones then]. If he couldn't land near a post, the Indians would clear a space for him with mules. *That* started the flying in the valley."

As for Mr. Smith, he started flying after the war, in a Tri-Pacer. "Even the big airports didn't have paved runways in those days and *nobody* had towers, so we pilots would look out for each other," he said. "We'd call Unicom and say, 'Has the dust settled from the DC-3s yet?' and if somebody said no we'd circle ten miles out and then come in. Those days were heaven, just horses and airplanes, hardly any trucks.

"Then came the uranium, and there were Supercubs all over the valley, prospecting. Fighter pilots with thousands of hours were up in little bitty Cubs using scintillators. Every trading post had its own strip then. Ten or 12 planes were based here all the time, and we had a trailer park beside our runway with thirteen trailers in it. Five years later the uranium market fell flat and all the planes left. Then the government paved the roads in the reservation and that cut out the excuse for flying. A car needed as much fuel as an airplane but a car could carry a ton. Instead of it taking ten hours to get to town by truck, it took about three. By then some of the posts had already moved out to the highways to take care of the suckers from the city, and they didn't build any new strips. They didn't need to; it didn't pay to fly anymore. Even I went everywhere by car, except for emergencies, like hospital runs. I never flew for fun; I still don't. When you get over 150 horsepower [he owned a 230-hp Cessna 182], you don't fly for fun." I must have had an expression of pity on my face because he added quickly, "Well, I *could* go back to flying putt-putts, but when you've been married to someone that long [he'd had the 182 for ten years] you don't get divorced easily!"

Speaking of marriage, I asked Mr. Smith if he and his wife got the articles in the museum by trade (medicine-man kits for bread or baloney?). "I don't know," he said. "My wife collected those things. I didn't pay much attention. As far as I'm concerned, if you can't eat it, shoot it, fly it, or ride it, it has no purpose in life. What good is it?" There was, however, one item he did get himself, and he couldn't eat, shoot, fly, or ride it. He could, but didn't, wear it. It was the wristwatch that Paul Mantz, one of the greatest stunt pilots in the history of filmmaking, was wearing when he died. Mantz had been in Arizona working on *Flight of the Phoenix,* a movie about a group of men who crash in the Sahara and save themselves by rebuilding, under the direction of a German "engineer" who turns out to be a toymaker, their wrecked twin-engine plane as a single-engine one. The single-engine "Phoenix" was jerrybuilt in fact as well as fiction, and at the time Mantz was to fly the contraption over the desert the temperature was 85 degrees. The director insisted on a third take, and during it the Phoenix split in half and Mantz went down with one half. He died instantly. His son sold the wristwatch, one of three Mantz always wore simultaneously whenever he flew cross-country air races, to Mr. Smith. It wasn't damaged in the crash and worked perfectly but Mr. Smith wouldn't even put it on. "I'm too Navajo," he said, "to wear a dead man's watch."

Yes, I thought, too Navajo. For despite the droll sign at the pumps and his look of bemusement and the fact that he invited me in to talk when I made it hard for him not to, there was a reserve about him, a social distance unusual at little airports. Nothing about the trading post or the airport got too friendly. Even with Mr. Smith I felt like an outsider, a bit *de trop,* also unusual at little airports. But then Oljato wasn't primarily an airport; it was a trading post with an airstrip next to it.

It was still light out when I started making up my bed by the runway, and I found another hand-lettered sign taped to the pumps. BEWARE OF RATTLESNAKES, it said. This one probably wasn't a joke. All I could do to beware, though, was drag my sleeping bag closer to the runway and farther from the bushes. I sat on top of the bag and ate the last of the baloney, then lay down and looked at the sky. From a passing truck somewhere I heard a sheep bleating; probably on its way to market, dead soon. The sky darkened and the stars came out. Some of them were shooting stars; it was the season of the Perseid shower. I lay awake and watched the stars for a while. The tip of one wing intruded on my view of them but I didn't mind. I liked having the wingtip there, a dense black tongue against the more watery black of the sky, an anchor among the heaving stars.

After the sheep's cry I didn't hear anything for a long time. Lightning flashed somewhere to the east but so far off the sky just shook around the edges, without sound. Then a dog barked. Before long another dog barked. Then a third dog, and a fourth. Soon the sound of dogs barking came from many directions and distances, in many keys and states of arousal, so many dogs that I thought they might be in packs. One dog was so keyed up that he responded to the smallest grunt, the faintest moan of any other dog with a bark of his own. Then followed a long period of quiet, and sometime in the middle of the night the barking began again. I opened my eyes and looked up. The Milky Way was lined up perfectly with my plane, and my body. We were all on the same axis. Finally I felt right with the world in Oljato.

Before dawn I woke again and washed with water from my Thermos, then did a line check, repacked my baggage, and sat on the strip and ate the last of the big bun. As I settled into the cockpit and was about to taxi out of my spot—at the very instant that I pushed the throttle forward—the sun broke over the hill in front of me and white light shattered, exploded on the sharp point of the stone. It was now day and I took off.

Mr. Smith's phone had been out of order—okay by him, he'd had it only two years anyway—so I couldn't file a flight plan before taking off. Nobody else knew where I was, even what state I was in, and nobody back home would think to go looking for me until at least a week had passed without their getting a phone call. So I'd be going solo on this leg, truly solo. Quickly I became all too aware of my solo status. I planned to fly back through the valley again, aiming north so I could intercept the San Juan River well upstream, then turn and follow the river west all the way to Lake Powell, then follow the lake (really a flooded canyon, long, thin and vine-like) to the airstrip at the far end, where I'd land, I sincerely hoped.

At the point where I picked the San Juan up, near the town of Mexican Hat, it flowed through a very deep, steep, and narrow gorge, yet it was the rock the gorge was cut from that made my breath come faster when I saw it. The surface of the rock all around was never flat, never smooth. Always it was either scored, pitted, chiseled, corrugated, or spiked. In places it had been cut into rectangles as regular as sidewalk squares but containing surfaces that were insanely irregular. Rocks lay on top of rocks down there, stuck up through other rocks, split from rocks to form steps of rock. What bushes there were looked small, round, and hard as rocks. I didn't see any place within gliding distance of my plane where I could put it down and survive, period. I might as well have been on Saturn, I figured, for all the good Earth would do me in case of trouble.

As I flew along I became preternaturally conscious of my bones— hollow and crushable! My brain—squash on the rock! My insignificant size—I was like prey, my only chance in life to be as alert as prey. I opened my eyes wide. I took out my earplugs. I made no sudden moves. Slowly, not calling any attention, I picked up my camera, focused it—wanting a photo of this cold, Saturnian landscape—and pressed the shutter. The lens went black! I stiffened; if the camera failed, why not the airplane? Without realizing I was doing it at first, I ran my fingertips back and forth over the fabric on the ledge above my panel (black, to soften sun glare). In appeasement: "Nice plane, nice plane."

Weeks, hours went by as I kept on going down the river, scared but not expecting any favors. Then I became aware that something below was changing. At one point the waters of the river clearly ended and those of the lake began. The river had been a brownish color but the lake was a deep forest-green, with a band of white mineral-stained rock just above water level on either side, separating the green of the water from the rose of the canyon walls. Although the lake didn't appear to be much wider than the river had been, and the rocks on either side of it weren't much flatter, somehow with the change in colors everything seemed more . . . sympathetic. Inlets began appearing in the steep canyon walls, and there was a modest, almost cozy look to them. Halfway down one of the inlets I caught sight of a couple of small white boats, bobbing at anchor, and felt immediate relief at seeing this unexpected sign of humanity—lighthearted, carefree, frivolous humanity!

But as I kept on going down the lake, and as more small white boats made their appearances in more cozy inlets, and as the surface of the rock on either side developed an occasional smooth patch, I wasn't so sure. Then I saw, worming its way down the middle of Lake Powell, coming from out of nowhere it seemed, trailing a tiny white rickrack of spray . . . a water-skier. A *water-skier?* I was appalled. Too frivolous! I felt like some hermit who had just emerged from months of meditation and been forced to sit and watch a sitcom. There I'd been, suspended in ether by the thread of a single functioning camshaft, alone over one of the harshest, most unconsoling landscapes in the world, my thoughts reduced to core subjects, living, dying, luck, the unforgiving quality of stone, the perishability of the human frame, the lie of my personal mastery, what would my family think?, etc., etc., while all the while on the water only a few miles away there was this wriggling water-skier!

Soon another water-skier swished into view, then another. Peeved at the sight of them, I began to curse the confusion in me, the way I sought isolation (had in fact delighted in the condition of being out of reach, without a flight plan), the invigorating effects of (reasonable amounts of) danger, the perspective that being in austere circumstances provides, the opportunity to forget so completely the daily gerbil wheel, etc., yet the nervousness I felt sometimes if I got these things; the need when I was at risk to be reminded of other's people's existence, then when signs of their existence presented themselves the resentment at the intrusion and the yearning all over again for the separateness, the uncertainty, even the fear I left behind. "I can't take total freedom," I said to myself when frightened. "I must have it," I said when reassured. There they were again, those two old birds, just in a different set of feathers: dread and desire.

Wahweap · Cottonwood · Stellar · Three Point

The water-skier turned out to be a true herald. Shortly after I landed at Wahweap (Navajo for "bad water," I was told, in this case a stream with laxative powers which ran between the airstrip and the lake), I signed up for a group boat tour of Lake Powell. From the air the cliffs had looked rather like bas-relief, the perspective flattening them, and I wanted to see them in the round. Halfway through our tour the guide let us off at Rainbow Arch so we could climb around on the rocks and get a feeling for the cliffs close up, but touching land seemed to trigger something in the passengers, an orgy of self-display, they began shouting and calling to each other over the rocks—jokes, orders, greetings— very very loudly, even when the people they were calling to were on the next rock—see me see me *see me*—so loudly and unceasingly that it became difficult to perceive the rocks as products of nature, without the human voice attached. Elsewhere at Lake Powell too, all that day and all the next, I had a sense of nature being reduced to backdrop, of a pouring out by visitors instead of a taking in of the (Guthrie was right) spectacular sights. Glen Canyon had, I knew, been flooded in part for "recreation," so I shouldn't have been surprised that that was the spirit in which so many people had come, but the ones I ran into seemed so thoroughly self-absorbed that I felt lonely, truly lonely, for the first time on my trip.

There weren't even any pilots to talk to. My plane was the only one at the airstrip. The hapless grocery-store clerk in the trailer court next to the strip got the brunt of my need for society. When I mentioned, quite unnecessarily considering I was buying soap and fruit juice, that I was going to sleep out at Wahweap that night, she kindly advised me not to; people had been seeing rattlesnakes around there lately, she said. The day before, a man had found a sidewinder beside his trailer. I thought about that, then remembered something I had heard about cowboys. When they were out on the range, cowboys laid their lassos on the ground in a circle around their bedrolls, and that kept the snakes off. Snakes didn't like ropes. Since Wahweap had two parallel metal cables running along one side of the runway for pilots to tie their wings and tails to (cheaper than sinking tiedown rings), I figured they might do for me what the lassos did for the cowboys. I laid my bag between the cables that night, to discourage snakes both coming and going, and went happily off to sleep. The next morning, pleased with myself, I told the grocery-store clerk about the terrific, built-in, automatic snake deterrent I'd discovered at the airport. She shook her head. "Oh no," she said. "It's those stiff little hairs on the ropes the snakes don't like. The hairs scratch their bellies. The snakes wouldn't mind a bit crawling over a metal cable."

The following morning I was taking off from Page, an airport five miles south of Wahweap where I had stopped to refuel, when I heard myself say "Wilco" on the radio. The word just slipped out, and I was embarrassed. For a pilot in a two-seat airplane leaving an uncontrolled airport on a clear day with no traffic in sight and no weather building and no passenger on board and a short flight ahead to say "Wilco," or for that matter "Roger" or "Over" or "Out" or (heaven forbid) "Tally ho," was putting on airs, playing the flight commander, Spencer Tracy in *Thirty Seconds Over Tokyo*. Well, I was probably *feeling* melodramatic that morning. I was on my way to the Grand Canyon, and everything about that seemed a big deal. On the chart the canyon looked like an enormous brown dragon writhing across northwestern Arizona, with many flamelike projections (the side canyons) protruding from its body—an impressive sight even on paper. At the eastern end of the dragon was a long, narrow "tail," Marble Canyon on the chart, which I'd be going down first since Page was at the tip of it. Where the Colorado River flowed through Marble Canyon it was olive-green, with strings of white foam running through it, but after about 40 miles the water abruptly turned all white, boiled into rapids, and the slit opened wide, like a hallway into a ballroom, and Marble Canyon became Grand Canyon, a slower, bigger, in a way less extreme landscape, with mesas lined up behind mesas, like wave after wave in surf, a long, articulated line of rock.

The first time I ever saw the Grand Canyon I saw it from the ground, although I had come in my plane. I left the plane at the Grand Canyon airport, seven miles south of the canyon, and hitchhiked from there. An Air Force pilot on vacation who was also seeing the canyon for the first time gave me a ride. He parked a short distance from the rim and we walked over and looked out. After the first mindless sensual stammering and emotional catapulting my thoughts were: Oh what a poor vehicle a plane is for flying after all! Shutting out sensations, distorting space . . . A person's own *body* needed to be out there in the open air over the canyon, as she made a long swan dive, arms held out, throat arched, skin feeling the slipstream, eyes seeing cliffs rise as she gently, safely fell . . .

The Air Force pilot had decided to take a drive along the canyon's Scenic East Road and asked me along. At the first turnoff he pulled the car in, got out, strode briskly to the canyon edge, raised his camera to his face, took a snapshot straight ahead, to the right, and to the left, mumbled something like "pretty" or "nice," then turned and walked back to the car, waited for me, and drove off. It was the same at the next turnoff and all the turnoffs after that; he'd march to the rim, look around for milliseconds, take a photo, say something complimentary to the canyon, and turn away, all as automatically as if he were ringing a series of doorbells. It wasn't I who was making him impatient, I realized; it was the canyon. He wasn't seeing it.

I also realized, watching him, that I had been taking something for granted all along. I had been assuming that pilots were by their nature—by the very fact of their having chosen to fly, to spread the ground out beneath them like a rich canvas every time they took off—*visual romantics*. I had assumed that flying was for them, as walking in caves was for Kerbo, justification for carrying their eyes. In all the years I'd been flying I didn't remember meeting any pilot, no matter how cynical or gruff or obsessed with the mechanical side of flying, who wouldn't at some time or other get soft in his talk about the beauties of earth and sky as he saw them from the air.

When the pilot had driven off, I hiked down a trail into the canyon. After a while I stopped and sat on a rock facing a cliff that looked like a side of dark, aged beef and from there watched other people walking down. The temperature at the top was 95 degrees and at the bottom it was reported to be 110. It was still morning so most of the hikers were on their way down. The ones with backpacks would probably be spending the night on the canyon floor and hiking up the next day. A couple of the women, though, were carrying white handbags. Everybody seemed jaunty, quick of step. There was lots of talk:

"It's hard to say what a mule thinks."

"I'd like to know what is so great about champagne."

"Armadinkerwinkerdinker" (from a Boy Scout).

"Maybe dogs could build cities if they had hands. Maybe dogs are more intelligent than we are and just keep quiet so they'll be taken care of, and can live the simple life."

"All teeth brushing is, is friction."

The happy chatter lifted up to me on my rock as they headed down the path, chipmunks frisking at their feet.

In the afternoon I sat on the same rock and watched hikers coming up. This time there was no chatter. Breathing was audible, labored. Feet moved slowly, ponderously. Eyes were wide open, in blank stares. A man and woman were limping. One man vomited beside the path. Two women sat on the backs of mules, slumped forward as if dead (they'd collapsed farther down, I learned, and the mules were sent for). All looked like survivors of some mass disaster—a mine collapse, the sinking of a cruise ship—who had been through horrors too awful to speak of but had still more horrors to endure before rescue, couldn't quit yet.

That time at the Grand Canyon I slept at the airport my last night, not the campgrounds, so I could get an early morning start. Most airports are fine places to sleep in, or at least okay, but some are neither. Weirdly lit, remotely set, deserted except for who-knows-who wandering in off a back road (plenty of back roads around little airports), they can be downright sinister. One summer my sister and I and her three kids were driving around Cape Cod looking for a place to camp when, toward dark, having found all the campgrounds full, with long waiting lists, we spotted an airport, and I suggested—right of the fraternity—that we camp there on the field, just as if we had flown in. Everybody agreed it was an excellent idea: The site was free and there was nobody around to object, if anybody even would. We already had several of the tent stakes in when—I don't know what it was but all of us felt it, something that made our flesh creep—with no argument whatever we pulled out the stakes, folded up the tents, stuffed everything back in the car, drove off, and uncomplainingly spent another hour and a half looking for a place to stay before ending up in a pricey motel room.

Grand Canyon was one of the sinister airports, at least then, and to me. The last man on the field to go home told me to sleep where the manager wouldn't see me; the manager didn't like people hanging around at night. "Airplanes get stolen at night," he explained. "It's easy. Just cut the p-leads [wires to the magnetos]. Takes only 15 minutes. Mexicans especially like little planes like yours. They're good for working out of small fields." I laid my bag way out on the field, in high grass, near a woods. Out there I was beyond reach of the ghoulish light of the ramp but wasn't sure I liked the darkness either. I scrunched down into my sleeping bag so nobody would be tipped off by the sight of a head. I heard the whisper of cars passing and figured a highway was somewhere back of the woods. One of the sinister ones all right. I was thinking not so much about guys coming to steal airplanes— after all, they'd be pilots—as about crazy Manson drug types lurching off the highway or out of the woods, looking for sacrificial flesh. And there I'd be laid out, supine, solo. It took me a long time to get to sleep, and several times during the night I woke up, expecting to hear a swishing in the grass (filthy jeans) and a man's voice saying *"Over there."*

At the first hint of light, I hurried to the office and was delighted to find it open already and a man inside who was the opposite of sinister. He didn't work at the airport but flew his Cub every day for fun and liked to start early. He and the Cub had become quite a team over the years, they'd done so much flying together. "The gear are my feet," he said, looking downward. "The wings"—he held his arms up and out to the sides, waggling his fingers—"are my fingertips. The nose"— he extended a hand, palm first—"is my nose." Then he gave me some free advice. "You see those mountains?" he said of two peaks sticking up pretty much by themselves. "Well, don't lose sight of 'em. Keep 'em on your right."

I asked myself, Did I look that dumb? Like that much of a novice? I thanked him but wondered if he would have given the same advice to a man. After all, I would be following the canyon almost all the way to Las Vegas, and how could anyone get lost over a trench ten miles wide? Besides, I had the chart. A short time later, as I was cruising along over an unremarkable stretch of canyon, I happened to notice that the two mountains, which up to that time had been more or less within the frame of my right window, were no longer there. I looked around and saw that they were *behind* me. Quickly checking the chart, I retraced my flight path and figured out that I had flown up one of the side canyons, wider at the turnoff than the main one (with all the twists and turns the canyon was taking, a heading change hadn't alerted me). If I had kept following that side canyon much longer, I could have been up a figurative, as well as a literal, creek.

This time I saw Grand Canyon only from the air. Coming out of Marble Canyon I flew up the middle of it, staying just above the level of the rims (regulations forbade going below them), from which altitude I couldn't reach either side on a glide in case of trouble. While admiring the scenery I was also assessing it for places I *could* reach. The only ones I saw were a few short, sort of flat ledges on the slopes of the canyon and some mud bars in the river. Mentally I tried landing on several of the ledges, watched in my mind's eye as my plane descended toward one in a slow, unwavering glide, slipped the last few hundred feet, pulled straight at the last instant, touched main gear down on the first few inches of even ground, and rolled to a stop just short of a thousand-foot dropoff. From my cockpit I could hear the shouts of onlookers on the rim overhead, "In-*cred*-ible!" "Not a scratch on her!" (meaning the plane), then (time telescoping) the exclamations of an amazed rescue team (sounds amplified by the mightiness of the feat), "What a cool nerve!" "What a great eye!" Every time I flew thus to a perfect landing, in places that in reality would have creamed both the plane and me, I felt better, more relaxed, and enjoyed the scenery more.

After 40 miles I turned south and flew past Grand Canyon airport toward another airport almost 100 miles farther on, which I had picked partly because of its location, halfway to Phoenix, and partly because I liked the name, Cottonwood. Or rather I liked the tree. Cottonwoods were about the only good-sized hardwoods in the area that grew in large numbers on riverbanks, such large numbers in fact that the rivers often had the look of oases when seen from the air, even when there was hardly any water in them. The stems of cottonwood leaves are flat and flexible, like ribbons, and in almost any breeze the leaves twist and swing on their soft stems and catch the light so that, moving all together on a windy day, they look like many coins being tossed or, if seen from the corner of the eye, like the ripple of hands speaking sign language.

Finding Cottonwood airport was like finding a house using the hostess's directions—left turn at the gas station, two blocks to the blinking yellow light, right turn past the Church of the Most Holy Lamb—making a lot of small, precise directional changes when you got in close. About 40 miles below Grand Canyon airport I angled right until I picked up a highway, followed that for eight miles, then got to the more refined stuff: left turn at a road with a railroad beside it, stick with the left fork of the railroad even after the road leaves it and a river joins it, take the left of two roads where the railroad dead-ends, and three or four miles down that road the airport should be—and was. A pretty little airport it turned out to be too, one of those where even the light seems right. It was situated on the slope of a mountain overlooking a valley of pea-green farms and river dark with cottonwoods around the edges. It had a hangar on it that was painted the rich shade of blue seen in photos of the earth taken from outer space; as soon as I cleared the runway I headed for that hangar, or rather the fuel pumps beside it. As soon as I shut down, a lean, young man with a brown mustache came out of the hangar and ambled over. He stood looking at my plane for a minute, then asked, "Where you all from?" "New York," I said. He made a face. "In that thing?" Then *I* made a face. I'd been hearing that, or things like it, at other airports lately. "In that thing?" or—once—"In *that?*" As if I'd *walked* all the way, for heaven's sake, or come by buffalo.

Soon another lean, young man with a brown mustache came out of the hangar and ambled over to my plane, then *another* lean, young man with a brown mustache, another, and another. Soon five lean, young men with brown mustaches were standing in the vicinity of my plane, examining it from various angles. It's something that happens often at little airports; people you never saw before come up to your aircraft and, unsolicited, begin inspecting it, sometimes quite thoroughly, sighting along the oil-filmed belly, running their fingers over the slightly rusted brake disc, crouching by the tail assembly and peering at the leaf springs, pinching a couple of spark-plug leads if the cowling happens to be up, leaning across the seats and studying the panel if the door happens to be open, then saying such things as, "Oh what a small engine mount you have!" or "Your oil-temperature-tube covering sure looks like it's going to snap!"

The guys at Cottonwood, though, were in it for a living; they couldn't help themselves. All of them were mechanics in the blue hangar, although they seemed to be looking at my plane not so much to get business as to get the goat of somebody from New York. Laughing amiably, they told me they'd found a crack in the trailing edge of one flap (it was tiny), a crack in the cowling (I'd been keeping my eye on that), gas caps too tight to turn without pressure on the vent tubes (the linemen had been complaining), and an air-intake screen too coarse for the air I was passing through (full of BD, presumably). Since I planned to stay overnight anyway I asked them if they wanted to fix the things that seemed to amuse them so. Immediately they rolled the Luscombe into the blue hangar and two of them set to work on it.

They seemed gentle men, good to each other. As they worked, they chatted and joked and listened to rock music on the radio. One was a vegetarian, which tickled the others. One knew my second cousin in Kansas City and was able to tell me she had a job scouring toilets in a tennis camp that summer. One planned to take another job soon making remote-controlled, winged submarines, which apparently paid better than working on winged aircraft. One had decided, seeing as how I'd come all the way from New York, that he would take the afternoon off and show me the sights of Cottonwood. For that he put on his "colors," a short denim jacket he said hadn't been washed in eight years. The patches on it were so dark with gunk I needed him to name them: a butterfly, a Union Jack, a Canadian flag, and a Harley-Davidson insignia. Ordinarily he wore his colors when he rode his Harley-Davidson, to keep "creeps and cops" from harassing him (the idea being that if he looked filthy what else mightn't he be?). For the same reason, as well as to "bring down an occasional dinner," he carried a rifle in his truck. I thought he might be bluffing; he struck me as a softie. I saw an Easy Rider Rack over a window in the truck but not a rifle.

The sights of Cottonwood included an old mining town on the hillside above the airport which was a ghost town except for stores selling ghost-town souvenirs, a café in a cottonwood grove with a good country-music jukebox, the mechanic's own cinderblock house, which he shared with another mechanic and a parrot named Lindbergh; and the sunset as it unfurled behind the red hills of Sedona. We sat on a curve at the side of a road with a six-pack of Coors and watched as clouds drifted over the sunset, breaking the light into apocalyptic shafts. The Sedonas were famous for their redness, he told me proudly; some people preferred them to the Grand Canyon. The finale of the tour involved those hills, peripherally. It was, according to the sign, a "Roadside Attraction." Under a plastic shelter, floodlit so that people could see it from the road at any hour of day or night, were four life-size statues, one of Christ and three of his disciples. They represented figures in da Vinci's *Last Supper* and had been made from wet sand. The sand was a reddish color, had apparently washed down over the years from the beautiful red hills of Sedona.

In the morning I flew over the hills so I could see them without the red glow of sunset on them, making them seem redder than they actually were. Still, they were pretty red, a hot brick color. Some were rounded in character and had folds in them like those on the limbs of big, healthy babies, others were broken up into intricate layers, like the temples of Angkor Wat. I kept my radio tuned to Unicom after takeoff, and for a while the frequency was quiet; then I heard, with no mention of who was radioing whom, a man's voice. "Cattle rustling," he said. Just like that. Then he, or another man, said something I couldn't make out. Then, from at least two men, "Heist . . . [indistinct] . . . Cottonwood . . . [crackle crackle] . . . Less congested . . . [crackle] . . . Want us to call . . . [garbled] . . . sheriff?" After "sheriff," I didn't hear anything, not even something garbled. Not one sound. I turned up the volume, pulled back on power, fiddled with the dial, but couldn't get another word out of that radio.

What was going on? I wondered. Had a pilot discovered cattle rustlers from the air? Or was he taking rustlers to *jail* by air? *Who* would be taking rustlers to jail, or arresting them, if not the sheriff, who had yet to be called? "Heist," indeed! I hadn't ever heard the word used in real life. "Rustling" either, for that matter. Was a pilot thinking of flying the rustlers to Cottonwood airport, and if so was that because it was smaller than most ("less congested") and therefore contained fewer human targets? Or was a pilot flying to Cottonwood because its *jail* was less congested than most? "Rustlers" plural, he had said. How many rustlers could a pilot carry and still retain control of his plane? I felt a bit frustrated, weaving around the Sedonas, as if I'd been watching a Western in which all the action took place out of sight of the camera, behind a large cactus, down in an arroyo, on the far side of a butte.

(Later I found out that when official planes are busy, private pilots sometimes transport prisoners to jail in their own planes. The pilots are not allowed to handcuff the prisoners to parts of the plane, in case the plane crashes, but if there's trouble aloft they are allowed to shoot them. Also, cattle rustling still goes on, sometimes in a big way, with semis pulling up beside cut fences at night.)

Coming out of the Sedonas I picked up a highway that ran southwest through low, smooth, dun-colored hills—mousy-looking after the showy reds. Ten miles down it a notch was cut from a ridge so that the road could go through, and as I passed over the notch the air in my cockpit chilled noticeably. Then I saw to my left an enormous valley, with low hills running like waves across the floor of it far into the distance. Entering the space above that valley I felt a sense of empire, actually lifted my chin, could almost hear the trumpets announcing my arrival. However, the real topographical change came 30 miles farther south. "Below Black Canyon," one of the mustachioed mechanics had told me, "it's a different state." Below Black Canyon ground level fell nearly 2,000 feet in under 20 miles, hills flattened out into fields, and roads that had been winding around hills straightened out to form grids. Phoenix was one big, flat grid, and I skirted it, to get to an airport on the other side, which was like no airport I had yet seen.

The airport was named "Stellar Airpark." After a landing that Erik would have called three since I bounced twice, I turned off onto a taxiway that led toward the ramp. But before I got to the ramp I turned onto another taxiway, then before I got far on it I turned off onto another taxiway, which had lawns on either side, and decorative boulders, flowering shrubs, trees, pools, patios, and houses. Not the usual kind of houses you find at airports, trailers and old farmhouses the owner or FBO lives in with his family, but substantial, expensive, multilevel, modern, suburban-style houses. Which made the taxiway a street, except that it hadn't any curbs, sidewalks, or cars. Taxiing down that "street" with my wings taking up the full width of it and my engine putting out an alarming amount of noise considering that there were houses around, I felt vaguely naughty, like in those dreams where you go to school in your underwear.

After a couple of blocks, I parallel-parked my plane on one side of the street as I would a car, except one wing cast shade on a patch of grass and I chocked the wheels. I walked up a path to the recessed entranceway of a house. The house was new. A man answered the door; I had phoned ahead so he wasn't surprised to see me. He led me through a living room, apologizing that it didn't have a carpet yet, into a kitchen, apologizing that it didn't have counter tiles. He introduced his wife, Linda, standing at the sink fixing lunch, their kids Julie, Brent, Fred, and Carl, sitting at the kitchen table waiting for lunch to be served, and son Scott, on the floor, in a baby seat, asleep. The man himself was Stratton T. Herman, founder and president of Stellar Airpark, described in the promotional brochure I picked up at Cottonwood as "the ultimate in aircraft ownership . . . a flying residential community."

They had just moved in. When Herman had first thought of living in this house, he had no children and was just dating Linda. It had taken him 14 years to realize his dream; his dream was of living with his airplane. "I thought, if people in Florida can keep boats in their houses, why can't we keep planes in ours?" So with another pilot who felt the same way he bought part of a 320-acre farm, paved the farmer's dirt strip, and started designing the community. There would be 80 lots, they decided, some of them half an acre and some two-thirds, most of the lots to have driveways both front and back, with the driveways in front leading to streets reserved for cars and the driveways in back leading to streets reserved for planes. Cars and planes would thus never meet except in "planeports" (garages), where they'd be parked facing each other, nose-to-nose, hood ornament-to-spinner.

So far 49 of the 80 lots had been sold, and most of the lots had houses on them already, built in Mediterranean, Pueblo, and ranch styles, with bougainvillea, cacti, bottlebrush, and Indian paintbrush growing in their landscaped yards, some with observation decks looking out over the runway. Herman had expected that people who'd buy the lots would be mostly retired pilots, "like retired Air Force," but they turned out to be "young people with families, engineers and guys in business for themselves, plus airline pilots." One man was a flight controller at an airport on the north side of Phoenix who flew his Skyhawk to work every day, taxiing right up to the tower. Another went hunting in his Maule. He'd take off and fly over the desert, spot javelina or deer, then land on a road or flat stretch of dirt and go after the animals on foot.

As for Herman, he flew a V-tail Bonanza to Mexican beaches for weekends (Linda acting as "stewardess," she said), to the mountains of Colorado for skiing, to the Canadian Rockies for fishing, and to the

White Mountains of Arizona, where the family had its own cabin. It was all so convenient! said Herman. "If you want to leave early in the morning, you put everything in the plane the night before and just get up the next day and go. When you come back, if you're tired you can taxi in and not bother unloading the plane, just leave it for the next day." That didn't sound too bad to someone who usually spent five hours getting to and from her airplane by subway, bus, and foot every time she wanted to fly, but how about the noise? I asked. All those aircraft taxiing up and down the streets, doing runups nearby, taking off and landing at all hours? The question seemed to surprise Herman; noise must not have been a common complaint. "I suppose," he said after a moment to think about it, "it's like living next door to a railroad track." Then, after another moment, "Actually, we get more noise from diesel trucks on the highway than from airplanes."

Nowadays he was busy designing a house for a friend, one that he almost wished he'd designed for himself. The front door would be higher than his and be made mostly of glass so people passing in and out could stand on the steps, look toward the planeport, and see the airplane. Once inside, sipping cocktails in the living room perhaps, they would get another chance. Herman was putting a glass panel in one wall so they could view the plane from yet another angle. "Some people, and I'm one of them," he said, not apologizing this time, "just can't get enough of looking at their airplanes!"

On my way out of Stellar, I passed over a fair number of swimming pools, mostly in people's backyards. Swimming pools weren't, of course, special to the scorched Southwest; I had seen them almost everywhere I'd flown, shining up at my plane with a tart, unnatural blue. They were the most brilliant things to be seen from the air: America's jewels. There were, in fact, so many swimming pools scattered around the country that you could imagine someone coming upon them fresh (from, say, Alpha Centauri) and concluding that they were part of some pervasive religion (hollows in the shape of the human kidney, circular kivas, kinship pits), the smaller ones dedicated to family worship, the larger ones (T's, L's, and crosses) places where rites of the group were performed.

When I was growing up, rites of the group did indeed take place at swimming pools. Nearly every day of the summer we teenagers would converge on the public pool, there to be initiated into the mysteries of human flesh (anointed with baby oil), the sensuality of languor, grace under water, the courage of the high board, the specter of polio, the social complexities of playing kid-bridge barelegged with straps down. Nearly every evening after dinner, as our mothers saw us heading out the door dressed in shorts and shirts (rarely bathing suits, at night), they'd ask, "Where are you going?" and we'd say, "To the pool." "What are you going to do?" they'd ask. "Mess around," we'd say. "Who's going to be there?" they'd ask. "Everybody," we'd say.

And everybody was, almost. Years later while watching scenes from MGM's *That's Entertainment!* in which Esther Williams did stylish crawls and backstrokes as Van Johnson, Peter Lawford, and Fernando Lamas (in different movies) struggled to keep up and the audience laughed at the ridiculousness of it all, I realized it had seemed only natural to me growing up—I had never questioned the fact of it—that relationships began at swimming pools, blossomed over dripping hair and beaded skin and good form in a racing dive, depended on regular joint immersions. For hanging around a swimming pool was what young people did in the summer, when they weren't eating or sleeping. A pool was the center—the emotional, tribal center—of our young lives.

Thus it was that I never understood the phenomenon of the backyard swimming pool. Too small, and too private. Yet as I was flying south out of Stellar, at midday in midsummer, and saw from my overheated cockpit the dazzling blue of those little home pools, I found myself wishing I could jump, or lower myself on a rope, into the icy heart of one of them.

At the next airport, another sort of liquid refreshment was available, although I didn't know about it beforehand and wouldn't have been able to take advantage of it if I had. The directory listed it as having a "snack bar," but what Three Point (Casa Grande) really had was a tavern. A tavern is an odd thing to have at an airport since it offers for sale the very thing that pilots are most urged to avoid, yet there it was, a small white wooden building with two signs on it, the straightforward AIRPORT TAVERN beside the front door and the more circumspect DO SPIN IN above it.

After getting fuel, I spun in to a cool, dark, quiet room with a billiard table in the middle, booths along one wall, and a bar at the end backed by mirror, neon signs, and glass bottles—the real thing. The windows were covered with dark-red burlap, which allowed so little light to penetrate that the place had a sickroom feeling, as if customers were expected to have ailing eyes, or nerves. A woman was sitting alone in a booth and two men on stools at the bar. I sat at the bar and ordered a hamburger and iced tea from the bartender. She was about 60, thin, with her hair in ringlets. The ringlets trembled when she moved, even when she didn't move. Her hands too trembled. Her eyes were pale and sad, and her voice, when she repeated my order, was soft and sad.

While I ate the burger she cooked in some room behind the bar, she told me how she had once owned the airport with her husband, who did the flight instructing and flew all the charters. One day he was coming back from a charter, letting down from altitude, bringing some people in to Three Point, when another plane collided with his. "They never knew what happened," she said, her eyes focused somewhere outside the room. "A couple of newlyweds from New York were in the other plane, on autopilot. Maybe he was showing her how beautiful the scenery was . . ." Her voice trailed off to a thread. She was trying not to lay the blame but laying it nevertheless.

Two years later, their only son, who was flying the charters as well as dusting crops, took off from Three Point early one morning to spray a nearby field. "The light was still weak so he had his lights on but the other man didn't," said the woman. The planes collided and his crashed on a road. "He was okay at first," she related, "but when he walked out on the wing to jump the plane exploded. He lived for eight days, but . . ."

She gave off melancholy like scent. "Now," she said, "I do the best I can, alone." How could she, I wondered, from behind the bar? In the Airport Tavern, aviation seemed a long way off, to belong to a more energetic, more hopeful world. How could she carry on the clear-headed business of fuel delivery, flight instruction, engine mainte-nance, and aircraft sales while standing in the seductive dark, pouring drinks and cooking hamburgers and reliving her hours of sorrow?

El Mirage · Santa Paula · Los Angeles

One thing pilots often do when they make cross-country air trips, as people who travel by other means often do, is be on the lookout for a place they might move to someday. A place where the terrain or climate or vegetation or architecture or life-style of people already there sets something going in them, a place they can see themselves living in for good, in a dream valley, by a dream shore, in a dream town. When flying around I kept my eyes open for such a place, but I had to bear in mind an image that popped into my head from time to time over the years, unbidden, suggesting what I might need and not know it.

In this image there's a pair of French doors. The doors are partway open. A breeze is passing through the opening, stirring the gauzy, white curtains that hang over the doors. Through the opening there is a view of a lawn, which rolls, in the suggestion of a dome, down to the edge of a woods. The trees in the woods are in leaf but the only thing that can be seen is the tops of them, above the lawn. We know there are streams in the woods, but they cannot be seen either. From somewhere comes the sound of pipes being played (influence of French cinema), drawing out of the house behind the French doors friends visiting for the weekend, who dance on the lawn, chase each other into the woods, otherwise go sweetly, merrily daft. They cannot be seen either, however. Only the grass (stirring in the breeze), the trees (also stirring), the curtains (stirring), and the French doors, open.

There are elements more splendid than these and definitely more rousing—mountains, rivers, cliffs, oceans, plains, islands, beaches, forests, lakes—but they are not in my picture. Only the grass, streams, leaves, and sometimes sunlight falling between leaves (dappling). When I realized what my dream setting consisted of, I was surprised, and not a little chagrined, to find it so tame. Was it a question of imprinting? I wondered. The house I grew up in had two sets of French doors that led outside, although the lawns they led to didn't roll and one lawn could be seen only through a porch. Our place of adventure as kids was a tiny park near the house with trees and a stream, and our lawns were places of play (no pipes), and peace.

Imprinting couldn't explain Tucson, however, unless negative imprinting counted. Half the people there, it seemed, had come recently from some other place, mostly because they liked what was different about Tucson. The woman who waited on me at the rental-car agency came from Wisconsin on vacation and went back only to fetch her clothes. The managers of the motel I stayed at were from Georgia and never wanted to go back at all. To me, Tucson was a nice place to visit *but*, as they say of New York, over and over and over. One day I wandered through the outdoor exhibits at the Arizona-Sonora Desert Museum near Tucson, where nothing cast a shadow wider than my waist and the air was so clear and revealing and the sunlight so steady that I found myself yearning for some obfuscation, not to mention covering: a tree with a flexible crown, a gloomy cloud, drizzle even.

So the naked, overheated, desiccated Southwest wouldn't be my dream place, but while flying around I had seen some places I might consider: parts of North Carolina where the soil was red and boundary lines were often curved because they were drawn by nature (waterways, hillsides); southern Vermont (lots of dappling); northern New Mexico (where the proximity of cool highland forests to the desert made it tolerable). But these beauty spots were well known; other people had found and loved them as well. One time when I was flying around mid-country and putting down every night at a different place, most of the places pretty out of the way, not very special, I was floating in a motel swimming pool next to a beltway across from a used-car lot with oil rigs and drilling towers in the distance and was watching clouds blow over and listening to people who lived around there talk to each other as they sat around the pool, and it was the same round of life—friends and eating and rain to come and money and kids—and I thought, felt at least: Well, there are lots of places to make a life. At some level, it's all the same.

At my motel in Tucson I was awakened by the sound of breaking glass and shouting men. I saw policemen running by the window, then the motel manager. I called out to her and asked what happened. Oh, a man in the next cabin was on an all-night drunk, she said, started breaking up the place. Well, at least he got me off to an early start. The sky I could see out my window was covered with thick, gray, morose-looking clouds—not what I wanted after all. When I got to the airport there was a tassel of rain in the middle distance, hanging over what was probably a single farmer's field. As chance would have it, the darkest, most ominous-looking clouds in the sky were in the very part I was flying toward. I kept a close watch on them as I took off, climbed out, and settled down to cruise, in case they should grow any darker or more ominous—concentrated on them the way operating-room attendants in old movies used to concentrate on the gas bag, that dark rubbery thing swelling and collapsing with each breath the heroine or hero took—life, death, success, failure, love, the plot hung on that gas bag. Except I hoped this one would collapse . . .

In the museum's outdoor exhibits I had seen live specimens of, and read labels about, creatures that lived in the Sonora Desert, over which I was now flying and the dark clouds hung: prairie dogs, coatimundis, lizards, bobcats, snakes, Gila woodpeckers, and collared peccaries (javelinas). From the air the ground looked devoid of zoological life: Nothing seemed to be moving below, even *not* moving, yet knowing animals *could* be down there gave the landscape a richness, a personality it wouldn't otherwise have had. After all, they could be inside burrows, or under rocks or brush, breathing, gnawing, flicking, voiding. Thus was the countryside rendered more animate, vibrant, complex. The only live things I actually saw, though, didn't happen to look it. Tall, dark, straight saguaro cactuses, sticking up off hillsides like rigid poles, so many of them so nearly identical to each other that they could have been part of some rural electrification project.

As I flew along on a westward heading, the clouds didn't exactly collapse, but they did show signs of wear. Slits developed in some of them and sunlight fell through the slits to form oddly shaped yellowish stains on the ground. By the time I reached Blythe airport, two and a half hours out of Tucson, the clouds were almost gone. Blythe was yet another of the World War II air bases deeded to civilians, but a particularly large one, with runways so long that 727 pilots sometimes practiced landings there (what fun it is to see a 727 bounce like a Cub!). I learned in my bones just how large Blythe was when I followed the FBO's directions to a truck stop at the edge of the field where he said

I could get lunch. Taxi down the inactive, he told me, turn right across the ramp, pull in behind the truck stop, and leave your plane there. The inactive runway did indeed look inactive, with weeds sticking up through long cracks in the concrete, and my Luscombe seemed to take forever to taxi the length of it. When I turned onto the ramp, I found it larger than any I'd remembered seeing at a general-aviation field, where B-24s once sat, a vast stone veldt, another desert to cross in the heat, and only whiffs of air being forced through the windows and cabin air vents since I was traveling at no more than six miles an hour; cockpit cooling was zilch and engine cooling must have been zilch too, chug, chug, chug, chug, this part also seemed endless, *was* endless, at times the restaurant appeared to be receding in the heat, chug, chug, chug, chug, a car would have been there long ago (lickety-split!) but a plane, out of its element, or nearly out of it, could only struggle along, like a pigeon in its distribution of capabilities, graceful in the air but a waddler on the ground. When I finally reached the truck stop and pulled in back of it and shut down, mine was the only plane there. The restaurant was full of people; I was just the only one who'd come in a three-wheeler.

From Blythe I pressed on, past the great Salton Sea, which looked dreamy (almost the same, faintly greenish color as the sky), then Thermal, the lowest airport in the United States, 117 feet below sea level. Passing Thermal, I pictured how my altimeter would look if the plane were sitting on the ramp: both hands pointing back of zero on the dial, digging into the 9s. If I didn't glance out my windows, would I think I was 9,883 feet in the air? Minutes later, as I was headed toward Palm Springs, my windscreen darkened, then lightened again so fast I knew there had to be something overhead besides a high cloud. Soon I was looking at the rear end of a four-engine airplane in front of me on extremely fast descent. Hotrod! Probably showing off for Frank Sinatra or Jerry Ford. The plane kept going down like a ton of (gold) bricks and I kept going toward another desert, a high one this time, the Mojave. That took me north, then northwest, near airports with names like Hi Desert, Soggy Dry Lake, and Giant Rock, where, someone told me, there was nothing but a runway and a big rock. UFO "freaks" held conventions and barbecues there, the man said, and discussed sightings in the desert. They invited guest speakers, including "the kid from Arizona who was abducted by aliens," and sold UFO T-shirts. "But when they're gone, there's nothing there but a big rock."

The Mojave could make a UFO believer out of anyone. The heat there was enough to boil the brain, the shimmering air could play tricks on the eyes, and the thermals could quickly transform a strip of siding, a bush, a chihuahua, anything maybe except a giant rock, into a flying object. Although I pulled back on power and pointed the nose of the plane down I kept being carried up instead. "Stop it!" I said at one point, "I don't want to go to the *moon,* you know" (it helps to talk to your plane like a horse). When I finally wrestled the plane to the ground, I found plenty of pilots whose idea of fun *was* going to the moon, or at least as far in that direction as they could go.

They were glider (or sailplane or soaring) pilots, for whom thermals were engines, and El Mirage (named for the tricks a dry lake nearby played on the eyes) was an airport by, for, and of glider pilots. There were gliders all over the place, lying on their little belly wheels in the dirt waiting for a tow, sticking half out of tiny hangars that looked like goat sheds, circling overhead like predatory birds. The man sitting on the stool next to mine in the coffee shop flew gliders too—model gliders. Models were "infinitely harder" to fly than full-sized, manned gliders, he told me. That spring he'd broken the world distance record for models using a quarter-scale, radio-controlled sailplane with 12-foot wingspan that he had built himself. He "hand-towed" the model out his car window and "threw it into a thermal," then followed it in his car, guiding it with radio signals. After 33½ miles, it got caught in "the lee of a wet alfalfa field" and went down in a field of yellow lupine.

The owner of El Mirage came in and ordered the house drink, a Sunshine Special, an overly sweet combination of orange sherbet and orange juice I'd have thought he'd be sick of by then. His name was Gus Brieglieb, and he designed his own gliders. The first one he'd designed when he was too young to fly it, 13. That was only a few weeks after he took his first flight in an airplane. "My dad knew Herbert Hoover and Hoover arranged it," he said. Brieglieb sold his gliders as kits, his favorite being the Cx-50, which "an early astronaut flew." After World War II he bought El Mirage from the Air Force, which trained glider pilots there so they could land troops quietly behind enemy lines.

"Everybody thought I was nuts for opening so far out," he said.

"One winter snow was three feet deep here and we had to tow our car with an airplane to get it started. Sometimes we'd fly the kids to school in a BT-13. We didn't make money so I had to work in a tungsten mill to pay the bills." The coffee-shop furniture he built himself, from spruce the Air Force bought to make wooden airplanes with; spruce, he explained, was the best wood for making airplanes since it was strong, lightweight, flexible, and capable of being sanded to a smooth finish. His hangar he got from Pancho Barnes, famous woman speed pilot of the 1920s and 1930s and raunchy proprietor of the Happy Bottom Riding Club, where Chuck Yeager and other test pilots from nearby Edwards Air Force Base hung out, making her more famous. She owned the ranch next door, and "stick by stick we moved her hangar over."

In time, Nature in the form of dependable thermals allowed Brieglieb to quit his job at the tungsten mill. Gliding clubs got going on the field, pilots from Edwards came over to earn their civilian soaring licenses, Japanese pilots dropped in to work on their high-altitude medals, since back in Japan there was no place with world-class thermals except Mount Fuji. El Mirage played host to the national soaring championships and furnished gliders for movies, including *One Step Beyond,* in which the pilot had to duck below the instrument panel whenever the glider came within range of the cameras because in the story the pilot was supposed to be a skeleton.

At the counter, Brieglieb noticed a cat rubbing against the leg of my spruce stool, which reminded him of a story. "A Navy doctor who flew out of here had an idea about cats. Everyone knows cats are quick on their feet and if you blindfold them and hold them upside down and drop them they'll land on their feet. Well, this doctor thought that if you flew into bad weather and your gyros tumbled and you didn't know which way was up or down, all you had to do was drop a cat. So I got a cat and set it in a bucket and hung the bucket by a rope and twisted the rope around and around, then let the bucket go and kept pushing so it would unwind faster and when it stopped I took the cat out and held it upside down and let it go. That shot the theory of using a pussycat for a gyro!"

By the time I left El Mirage it was so late the sun was almost at eye level, hanging low over the mountaintops. The entire scene before me was a Japanese print come to life, with the standard golden ball of sun; the wavy mountain ridges lined up one behind the other, each a lighter, more delicate blue than the one before; sunbeams shooting into dust clouds over the mountains and turning them misty, also brightening the surface of a small lake so that, for a moment, it became a dog's head in profile, holding a fish in its mouth. All that was missing was a long-legged bird winging its way across the sky.

The airport I was headed for was a couple of degrees to the left of the sun (what a navigation beacon *that* was!). It was a special airport even for pilots not based there, a model for what a great airport could be. Twenty men founded it during the Depression, with the goal of enabling "the common man [no such thing as a common woman in aviation then] to fly without excessive costs." Ever since then, Santa Paula had kept the creed. Tiedowns were still only $5 a month, ground rent under hangars $10. Pilots could put anything they wanted to in their own hangars—kitchens, bathrooms, gas pumps. The working philosophy, I was told, was, "The private flyer has all the rights." The private flyer had lots of privileges too. There was an aviation bookstore on the field and a white-tablecloth restaurant with windows looking out over the runway. All of this attracted a disproportionate number of pilots who owned fine old airplanes—Messerschmitt, Davis, C-2 Champ, Ryan, Spartan, Travel Air, Gypsy Moth (Cliff Robertson kept five Moths at Santa Paula)—which they tended to keep in immaculate condition and fly, really *fly*, as if the planes were new.

It was nearly dark when I landed, so I didn't get a look at any old planes that evening, and the following day I didn't get a look at many because the runway was being repaved and most pilots had locked their hangars and stayed home. Nevertheless, a courtly, gray-haired local citrus farmer who came to supervise the repaving volunteered to show me what there was to see. We walked up and down the rows of hangars and found one open and a man inside dressed in a white jumpsuit and orange socks. He was a TWA pilot, according to my guide, and the plane he was working on was a Bücker Jungmann. The Jungmann was painted dark green with "Perry ('Orville') Schreffler" written in gold antique German script under the open cockpit, and next to that, in ordinary black letters, were the words CAN DO, and above them was a crumbling swastika, and above it was a black bomb held in a silver fist, and next to it was a family crest.

It was the Schreffler family crest, the pilot said. He could trace his name back to A.D. 750, "when Germans were all shepherds, herders, farmers, or barrelmakers. We were the barrelmakers." He had bought his Jungmann when he was stationed with the U.S. Air Force in Europe after World War II, he told us. He had gone all over Germany looking for one and finally found this, "the last Bücker Jungmann left in Germany," in a town at the end of the Ruhr Valley. He shipped it to Santa Paula and spent a year and $8,500 restoring it.

I asked him about a sign taped to his fuel pumps: "MUT STARKE EHRE." He translated, "Courage Strength Honor." I was confused. Clearly Schreffler wanted to express a winning, even crushing spirit, but for which side? "CAN DO"? "MUT STARKE EHRE"? Crumbling swastika *and* German family crest? Who held the bomb in a silver fist, American knight in armor or German iron dictator? And why a Bücker Jungmann, which bore a swastika on the tail and trained pilots for the Luftwaffe, instead of a T-6, which bore a star and trained American pilots? Schreffler must have been confused too. "During the war," he mused, "people in my outfit were dropping bombs on my cousins."

One other hangar was open, and inside was a Staggerwing Beech, the plane I'd buy if I had Cliff Robertson's money. The owner was in the hangar, too, another citrus rancher and one of Santa Paula's founders. He was in his early eighties, confided my guide—who was near 70 himself and apparently proud of this member of his age cohort—and still flew the Staggerwing "beautifully." I wasn't surprised at that. Turfing professional airline pilots out at age 60 may be good business policy, but in the field of general aviation age doesn't seem to be linked in people's minds so closely with ineptitude. I took it as the highest compliment once when I landed on a short runway and one of the people who'd been watching said as I climbed out of the cockpit, "We thought it was an *old man* flying." Also the time two elderly pilots who flew a Cub together every weekend approached me after I'd finished a practice round of takeoffs and landings and was feeling pretty rusty and unsure of myself, "We saw those greaser landings you were doing"—well, it was better than being elected President.

My guide took me along the flight line, where we saw a plane that was home-designed and home-built. It had a narrow, black, coffin-like fuselage and wings about the size of teeter-totter boards. It looked to me like a Soap Box Derby entrant, small and eminently crashable. I told him I'd be scared to go up in it, and he said the designer-builder-pilot had in fact died recently in a crash. It wasn't an airplane crash, though. The man had been riding his bicycle near his home, fell off, hit his head on the ground, and died.

At one end of the flight line was a Piper Cub whose owner had died recently too. He had been deaf, mute, and "very kindhearted," said my guide. One day he came to the airport intending to fly his Cub and found a bird's nest on top of the engine with eggs already in it. Instead of throwing out the nest and putting up with his guilt as the rest of us would have done, he grounded himself until the eggs had hatched and the chicks fledged. Then he too flew. A couple of weeks later he went up in another plane on a fair day and hit the slope of a mountain. "Nice guy," said my guide. "Nobody ever knew what happened."

In Santa Paula's bookstore, I bought a postcard with a picture on it of the first airplane (rather a picture of a *replica* of the first airplane) ever to cross the U.S. by air. Crossing the U.S. by air was very much on my mind at the time. In an hour or so I would be taking off on the last flea-hop (I could smell the sea from Santa Paula, although I couldn't see it) of my New York-to-California leg. That first plane to go across was a Wright EX biplane, the pilot was a six-foot-four-inch unemployed New Yorker named Calbraith P. Rodgers, and the year was 1911. Rodgers was trying to win a $50,000 prize offered by newspaper publisher William Randolph Hearst to the first person who could fly from one coast of the United States to the other in 30 days or less. He took off from Sheepshead Bay in New York City on September 17 and landed in Pasadena, California, on November 5, having covered over 4,200 miles at an average speed of 52 miles an hour. He crash-landed the plane so often and it had to be repaired so often on the way that by the time he got to the coast all that was left of the original was the rudder and the oil drip pan.

The plane was called the Vin Fiz, after a carbonated drink whose manufacturer paid for a private train to follow Rodgers wherever he went, carrying his wife, mother, several mechanics, and a carload of airplane parts. In return, he bore on the underside of his wings the slogan VIN FIZ—THE IDEAL GRAPE DRINK, so that people below could read it as they threw horseshoes, twirled parasols, and cranked the starters on their Model T's. The flight to Pasadena took 49 days so Rodgers didn't win the prize, but he did show how he felt about having made the first aerial crossing when, about five weeks later, he flew the remaining few miles to the oceanside and set the plane down on the beach: First he flew over the surf and let the spray get his wheels wet.

After taking off from Santa Paula, I put off the moment a bit, circling a flower farm I spotted on climbout and snapping a photo of it. Poppies, or some other flowers equally red, grew together in a block that ran clear across the plot, and blooming next to them, forming a band of solid yellow, were what looked like daffodils. Next came a band of purple (irises?) followed by stripes of orange and brown (chrysanthemums?). The farm was a cheery sight, and I lingered over it; I needed cheering. As I was taxiing out for takeoff, several men had lined up along the runway to watch. Some of them were, I presumed, construction workers who'd been paving the runway, but others had to be pilots. (Pilots based at Santa Paula weren't being allowed out because of the repaving, but being a visitor, I was.) Half the width of the runway had already been paved and was still soft so I was to take off on the other half. Seeing all the men turned so expectantly in my direction made me a little nervous. Santa Paula pilots were, I was sure, as finicky about flying technique as they were about everything else, the upkeep of their fine old planes, the exercise of their individual rights, the operation of their ideal airport. All were able to land on a ten-dollar bill, I was certain, and take off on a 20.

So, turning onto the threshold and seeing them lined up out there, I felt the pressure—fretted as I advanced the throttle and picked up speed, went rolling down the runway—keeping straight nicely in my half, then pulling up, and, in too much of a hurry for the weight I was carrying, *skipped* on takeoff, gave a last glancing blow—pair of blows— to the old asphalt, then rose weakly and headed off, in full sight of all those guys, yet wishing that I were quite out of sight beyond the hills, *knew* what they were saying down there, what men have always said about women drivers . . .

In this I wasn't thinking only of myself. These days, over three-quarters of a century after the first American woman got her license, there are still 16 times more men than women pilots in the country, so we are conspicuous if we flub. Whenever I don't do as well as I think I ought to at flying, I feel I've let down the sisters, made things harder on the others. There are still a lot of men eager to blame all female pilots for the mistakes of one, to lump us all together, assume shared deficiencies.

On the other hand, the guys at Santa Paula might not have given a hoot who was flying the plane, just couldn't resist the sight of a moving object on a runway. I took the photo of the flower farm, then continued down the valley, over citrus groves mostly, made a detour around a civilian airport zone, then a Navy zone, passed to the left of a 3,111-foot peak, then there it was. So simply *there it was*. The other shore. The second shining sea. The end of the land I had been laboring over. In front of me lay a neat white collar of beach holding in place a voluminous cloak of blue-gray water. The continent stopped *here!*

Like Rodgers, I flew toward the sea but stayed a couple of hundred feet above the surface and stared out at my left tire, that touchstone of my feelings about flying. It was surrounded now entirely by water—not once on the crossing had it skidded or gone flat! The cowling caught a flash of light—it had needed only one small patch on the trip. My propeller, turning now in a blur of gnats, hadn't picked up a single nick on the way. My engine, humming its theme song at cruise, hadn't coughed once. The surge of affection I felt for my plane was so powerful that an image came to me of it taxiing into the sea, attacking the surf, plowing its way through waves, half-submerged, a powerhouse, then rising from the water, graceful, with foam streaming from its wings (white heron feathers!), and ascending effortlessly toward a bud of a cloud, ready to carry me, and my folding saw, portable still, signaling mirror, and wheel chocks anywhere I wanted to go. Looking ahead, I thought of Hawaii . . .

After a few celebratory Dutch rolls (the dipping of one wing after another while keeping the nose pointed straight ahead, which produces in the pilot the pleasant sensation of sitting sideways on a swing), I turned and tacked my way back to shore. Following the shoreline south, I kept a sharp eye out for other planes; by Los Angeles standards the day was severe-clear, visibility eight miles, and I figured a lot of pilots would be up taking advantage of it. I didn't see many pilots but I heard them on the radio. Three tries it took me to get through to the controller at Santa Monica, and once I did I couldn't get through again to tell her that I'd have trouble doing what she asked me to: "Report base over the San Diego freeway."

Freeway? Below was a mess of roads, streets, highways, byways, who knows; which one went to San Diego? Flight controllers had a way of doing that, asking pilots to report over local landmarks, the nursing home, the greenhouse, the intersection of Such and Such, the mall, the accelerator, the toll plaza. At that very moment a man was announcing his arrival over "the brewery." How could an out-of-towner tell a brewery from a bomb factory if he wasn't low enough to read the sign or smell the barley malt?

I found base leg at Santa Monica without ever finding the freeway, but there were three of us on it when I got there, two on left base and one on right. The pattern was so crowded that when the controller told me to be ready to go around I assumed I *would* be going around and got ready, too ready, had already started adding power when she cleared me to land and there I was, hanging over the runway like an apple on a high limb, wishing I could drop like an apple, but I did the best I could, a steep slip, and made it onto the second half of the runway.

It didn't matter how I arrived. Friends were waving and smiling at me from the ramp. When I stepped out they took a picture. Together we rolled the Luscombe to a tiedown next to a hedge with purple blossoms beyond which we could see the red tile roofs of Santa Monica. It was something, then, to have crossed. Although it took me as long as it did Rodgers, exactly 49 days.

One of the friends was Melinda, from New York City. Among all the voices on the busy tower frequency I had heard while coming in, I had recognized hers. She had been asking for permission to do a touch-and-go, one of the last things I ever thought I'd hear her ask for. Back in New York she not only didn't fly planes herself, she didn't like going up with anybody else. Her boyfriend John (he who helped me buy my Luscombes and saw Danny Kaye's plane) owned a Skyhawk, but when he flew it she preferred to stay behind at the airport. "I'll just wait," she'd say, and open a book. The times she did go up in his plane she'd complain afterward, saying the flight was too long, or too bumpy, or that flying always made her want to pee. As she drove me into L.A. I asked what had changed her mind. Why did she decide to take flying lessons? She didn't know, she said; even she was surprised. One day she just wanted to fly, that was all. Something that might have kept her from wanting to fly until then, I conjectured, was what happened to John's plane.

When he bought the Skyhawk, it had six coats of paint on it, one for each of the previous owners, the penultimate layer being a particularly tough coat of turquoise vinyl. Before adding a new layer, he decided to strip off all the old ones. Around that time he started getting serious about Melinda, and his idea of courting was to drive her to the airport in eastern Pennsylvania where he had moved the plane for stripping since its ramp was larger than ours in New York, and they'd spend the weekend stripping paint—although as time went on, John admitted, "she took more to watching."

Now stripping the paint off of airplanes, like stripping the paint off of anything, is lousy, stinking work—blobs of soggy, gummy paint flipped onto John's shoes and into his hair ("I started out Warren Beatty and ended up Kojak")—only worse since airplanes have countless rivets to pick at, each one providing the nucleus for a deviant flake of new paint to form around if not rendered absolutely clean, plus enormous surface areas, 50,000 square inches on the Skyhawk's wings alone. Also, aluminum is soft as metals go and scratches easily, so a stripper can't be too vigorous, making a slow, tedious job even slower and more tedious. John spent 200 hours stripping the Skyhawk. Somehow his relationship with Melinda survived the long days spent in the heat of the unshaded ramp, the splinters of aluminum wool stuck under blackened fingernails, the acid fumes, the fingertip burns, the sore arms. When, near summer's end, the Skyhawk stood in its primal silver skin, John bought a dozen gallons of the most expensive paint in the store (vermilion and yellow, to match author Richard Bach's biplane), installed a new engine with higher horsepower, added drooping tips to the wings (for lowering stall speed), and flew the plane back to our airport, where the painting was to be done. In place of the airport ropes he bought heavy ones and used double half-hitches when tying the plane down. "No breeze going to send *that* baby," he declared.

On a Saturday afternoon shortly afterward, he was in his Greenwich Village apartment reading (it was a drizzly day). Meanwhile at the airport another Skyhawk was taking off, on Two-Six. It rolled about a third of the way down the runway, lifted off, then made an immediate right turn, so sharp that while still only a few feet off the ground the plane was heading 90 degrees away from the runway, toward a row of parked planes. In the middle of the first row sat John's Skyhawk. The right wheel of the airborne Skyhawk connected with the left wing of the parked Skyhawk and was in the process torn off and left sticking to the (now badly bent) wing, while the rest of the plane carried on, leapfrogging the next row of planes only to sink onto the third, where it ripped off the wing of a Tri-Pacer and carried it 25 feet before dropping it to the ground.

Meanwhile, up in the coffee shop, hangar bums on their third cups of coffee who'd been watching the events through the picture window began to catch on that it was their turn, and one shouted "Hit the deck!" ("Probably been waiting all his life to say that," John later noted), which they did, diving under tables and covering their heads with their hands, as the plane grew larger and larger in the window. At the last minute, in a "prestall buffet," according to an observer, the plane wobbled up and over the roof, then went for trees next to the Russian church across the road and, "continuing to elevate in a manner amazing to those who watched," skimmed over the tops and kept on going, south, until it was out of sight.

The next day someone took John's photo standing in front of his plane, wearing a license plate on a cord around his neck with the same words on it that Laura had needlepointed on her pillow: I'D RATHER BE FLYING. The wing over his head was drooping from midpoint, straight toward the ground, like a chow's tongue on a hot day. Things that *couldn't* be seen in the photo but that John discovered on close inspection were wrinkles in the skin of the fuselage and popped rivets on the cabin roof. Not wishing to fly a plane that had suffered such a structural wrench, he sold the Skyhawk at a considerable loss to a man in Maine who liked to rebuild wrecks. Within a year he had bought another plane, this time one with good paint, married Melinda, and moved out West to Los Angeles.

Shafter

By this time millions of people had crossed the country by air, in seaplanes, dirigibles, turboprops, balloons, helicopters, gliders, auto-gyros, jets. They had flown across high and low, slow and fast, in a single long line and 50 flea-hops, yet nobody had gone even a few miles in what was probably the first way a human being ever thought of passing through space: under his own power. That is, on the strength of his arms, legs, back, and shoulders plus the power of his mind—his will, his inventiveness, his capacity for prayer. Probably ever since they'd been watching them, people had been trying to fly like the birds, attaching something to their bodies (feathers, hide, stiffened cloth) or rigging themselves up to some device (wing paddles, boat-and-oars), then,, while looking heavenward, jumping off something high, flapping, kicking, cranking, or just believing. John had always been interested in attempts at human-powered flight—he kept an elegant drawing of an ornithopter on his closet door—and from his interest I had picked up a somewhat milder one.

There was the twelfth-century Turk who, attired in pleated robes strengthened by willow branches, leapt from a tower while a throng below shouted, "Fly, Turk, Fly" but did not fly, fell to earth and broke his neck. The British monk who, in the same century, flung himself into a violent wind with wings strapped to both feet and hands and hit the ground with such force that he was lame ever after, attributing his failure to fly to not having attached a tail to his "hinder" part as well. The "Daedalus of Perugia," who was said to have fallen onto a church roof when an iron bar supporting one of his feathered wings snapped; an abbot under King James IV of Scotland who tried to ascend on wings of chicken feathers but descended instead, later regretting the choice of chicken because "fowl," being earthbound in its original state, the feathers "coveted the midden and not the skies."

The tenth-century Islamic calligrapher and scholar who cleaved the air with wooden "doors"; the newly knighted 19th-century English gentleman who paddled an eagle-prowed "boat" to a height of six inches; the 16th-century Italian who vowed to fly "like a turtledove" but sank like a pig instead.

Always, so far as is known, the bodies of the would-be aeronauts proved too weak for the task; those who leaped died, broke limbs, or simply sank, those who labored on the ground grew exhausted and never (or only barely) left it. Modern scientists now know how ill-suited man is for the role of bird. Studies have shown that the most power even a good athlete can put out in a sustained way, after an initial one-minute burst of energy, is little more than half a horse-power, not enough apparently to have propelled more than a few feet any of the contrivances used in all the centuries before this one by people trying to fly under their own power.

People kept on trying anyhow, even when the Wright brothers showed an easier way to do it. In the years before and after World War I prizes were offered in Europe for successful human-powered flight (the best way to accomplish something in aviation, it seems, besides starting a war, is to offer a prize). Strong, determined Frenchmen, Germans, and Italians pedaled winged craft through the air for 40 feet (in 1921), 66, 771, 1,401, and (by 1938) over 3,000 feet, winning acclaim and in some cases prizes (and in one case the congratulations of Hermann Göring), but the longest flights were launched with rubber cords, and none of the contraptions was able to make much of a turn, so in most people's minds the goal of true man-powered flight had not yet been attained.

People kept trying, even after World War II, when planes were flying at Mach 1. In England in particular, there was a surge of interest in the problems of flight at the slow end of the envelope on the part of serious professionals, including the developer of the Spitfire and chief engineer at British European Airways. In 1959 Henry Kremer, a British glass-yarn manufacturer and aviation enthusiast, offered another prize, £5,000, for the first successful flight of a "British designed, built, and flown Man-Powered Aircraft, such flight to take place within the British Commonwealth." In announcing the prize, he said he wanted to "help mankind cross this last frontier. We can run [meaning fly jets] but not walk." The rules, set up by the Royal Aeronautical Society, would be: A craft had to leave the ground without aid of incline or launchers, pass over a ten-foot hurdle, make two 180-degree turns around pylons set a half mile apart, one clockwise turn and one counterclockwise, thus describing a figure eight, and at the end pass over another ten-foot hurdle, all in winds not exceeding 11.5 miles an hour and over ground varying in height no more than 1 in 200. Prohibited were the use of stored energy, like wound-up rubber bands, the jettisoning of anything including a crew member, and the employment of lighter-than-air gases. Once the rules were agreed upon, they became the generally accepted way of deciding—officially and worldwide—what a man-powered aircraft really was and when it had really flown. Anything that won the Kremer Prize would have proved itself capable of "authentic sustained controlled flight," as no craft before had done.

"Every man his own aeroengine!" *The Times* of London challenged its readers, but as things turned out it wasn't Everyman working in his basement or garage who took up the challenge most keenly but engineers, pilots, and physiologists at the Royal Air Force, the De Havilland Aircraft Company, the British Aircraft Corporation, and Southampton and Liverpool universities. Working in competing teams each of which pooled its considerable expertise, they designed and built a variety of aircraft, mostly on clean, low-drag, glider and airplane models, out of lightweight materials such as balsa, pine, wire, polyester film, and parachute nylon. Two years after the prize was announced, the first of them, "SUMPAC" (for *S*outhampton *U*niversity *M*an-*P*owered *A*ir*C*raft), took off and flew 50 feet through the air, and the following year a revised SUMPAC flew 2,000 feet powered by a man dressed in pajamas (to cut down on weight), and De Havilland's entry, the "Puffin" (puffin', get it?), traveled more than 3,000.

"Terrific excitement!" as one participant put it, but, as time went on and these and other planes failed to better Puffin's performance, disappointment as well. By 1967, eight years after the prize was announced, no craft could fly anywhere near the required distance or, more important, make even half a turn. People started saying it couldn't be done; the rules were too tough, the goal aerodynamically unreachable. It appeared that anything a human being could drag or push through the air with his legs (most man-powered enthusiasts had long ago given up on those weak sisters, the arms) had to be so lightweight that it was vulnerable to even small shifts in air current and instabilities of design (minor gusts were a major hazard). Kremer upped the prize that year to £10,000 and threw the competition open to non-Britons living outside the British Commonwealth. Before long other British craft had made their way into the skies, including "Jupiter," on which members of the Royal Air Force expended 4,000 working hours and which set an unofficial distance record of over 3,500 feet, but even that was not nearly enough. The following year Kremer raised the prize to £50,000, the largest in aviation history.

One non-Briton who had been working on a man-powered aircraft all along, even before his change in eligibility status, was Professor Hidemasa Kimura of Nihon University in Japan, designer of several long-distance, high-altitude transport planes. As a class project, Kimura had 15 of his engineering students at a time design and build a man-powered aircraft. In 1966 the first group of students produced a Linnet, named for an Asian finch that is no great shakes as a flyer (the professor not wanting them to make too great a claim); other groups built other Linnets, then several Egrets and (confidence rising) two Storks. One Egret flew 666 feet, and the first Stork, which featured a boom fuselage and low wings with high dihedrals, went 1,952 feet in a straight line one day and turned 180 degrees the next. Terrific excitement! Soon a rebuilt Stork had flown 6,869 feet, and although the craft didn't make any turns, it appeared as if some day it—or yet another Stork—would. People were saying it could be done after all, and this was the group (or groups) to do it.

Meanwhile, in the United States the best anybody had done was the Olympian ZB-1, a spruce-and-balsa tail-boom cyclecraft which retired Air Force lieutenant Joseph Zinno reported pedaling 77 feet down a Rhode Island runway in 1976 at an altitude of one foot. While I was out in Los Angeles with John and Melinda, I read about another American effort, one that had been carried on in near-secrecy until recently because its creators didn't want the Japanese students to hurry their rebuilding of Stork B—an indication of how dead seriously these Americans took themselves. They had been at it less than a year but had already made many test flights, including one in a parking field beside the Rose Bowl, managed some turns, and gotten some good distances. They were working now out of an airport in the San Joaquin Valley north of Los Angeles, called Shafter, which I'd be passing on my way to San Francisco, so I thought I'd stop in there and see for myself what a human-powered aircraft looked like—and what kind of people would spend nearly a year of their lives putting one together and trying to make it do a mile-long figure eight.

As I exited the mountains north of Los Angeles to face the broad San Joaquin valley beneath a cloudless sky, the possibilities seemed limitless: Why *not* a manpowered airplane? At Shafter, though, I had difficulty finding evidence of one. I could see no activity whatever on the ramp, and the biggest hangar, which I assumed the team would be using, was locked, with the lights out. Maybe, I was thinking, I had come on the wrong day, or at the wrong time (Monday, 5 P.M.). Finally I found a mechanic in a smaller hangar installing a radio, and he told me that the man-powered team had been around that day, and they might just be off having an early dinner. Maybe they'd be back that evening, or maybe not. They came, they went, you never knew.

In case they were having an early dinner, I walked to the nearest restaurant, El Rancho Grande, and found two old men in the bar drinking Salty Dogs, clearly not in shape to organize a flight of anything except maybe a good belch. Two people were in the dining room, a man and woman sitting together, looking long married, all dressed up but not talking. I had a Salty Dog in the bar myself, then went back to the dining room to eat and found another person had come in, a rugged-looking man sitting alone. As soon as I got a table he came over and asked if I'd join him at his; I suggested he join me at mine. He turned out to have a connection with Shafter, although not the one I was looking for.

He said he was a "custom miller," which meant he took the waste (skins, culls, pulp, linter, and pomace) from the produce grown in the San Joaquin Valley (grapes, potatoes, beets, cotton, and tomatoes—in the case of tomatoes "what's left after catsup"), dried it, and sold it as cow and chicken feed. Dried feed, he explained, was better than wet feed because it made the animals' droppings drier and easier to pick up. Other millers relied on a complicated system of gas dehydrators and blowers, scoops, and whips, but he used a technique he said was just catching on in California, called "solar drying" (sounded older than *Beowulf* to me). Essentially, it meant dumping the waste in piles where the sun could shine upon it.

Solar drying did require space, however, which was where Shafter came in. The miller leased land around the runways to dump his piles on. As a result, he claimed, Shafter was the only one of the county's five airports earning money. Which made the criticisms rankle all the more. People said that the piles smelled bad and attracted flies. The miller was indignant. "It takes four days to incubate a fly," he said, "and it takes the sun four days to dry the feed, so by the time the flies are ready to hatch the feed is too dry for them to live in and there *couldn't* be any flies." Recently the pilot of a Cherokee had caught one of his wingtips on a pile of potato skins while taxiing around and lodged a complaint. The miller was uncowed. " 'Those potatoes,' " he told the pilot, " 'are worth more than your whole damned airplane!' "

After dinner, he gave me a ride back to the airport. A full moon was out, one of those unromantic full moons that light the sky harshly, like a searchlight. The miller kept on driving past my plane, out onto the field, until his headlight beams were trained on a pyramid-shaped mound. "Cotton," he said, although the mound was brown. We saw something dart out of the light into the darkness back of the pile. "Jackrabbit," he said. "I let 'em eat the profits." He sat in the car for a while, staring at the mound. Then he spoke. "I'd be very happy if all this made me rich." He said that he wanted to be rich for his daughters, four-year-old "Misty" (real name Jerry Jeanette) and five-year-old "Tinker" (real name Laurie Ronette). "Already," he said in a tone uncharacteristically hushed, "they have their own little brains, their own little hearts, their own little hands . . ."

Except for the two of us, the field was dead still. The man-powered team hadn't come back after dinner. I wasn't dismayed, however, since during dinner the miller had told me they had had a very good flight that day; in fact the plane had almost made it all the way around the course, failing only to clear the ten-foot pole at the end. (That close?!) They were talking about trying again in the morning. (So soon!) I didn't want to miss that, so I decided to sleep right on the spot, and when the miller had had his fill of admiring his cotton pile he helped me roll my plane closer to the ladies' room, which was a freestanding cinderblock building off to one side of the hangar. Then he showed me something he thought I could use in the men's room, another freestanding cinderblock building. It was a ring about six inches across which reminded me (but probably not him) of an embroidery hoop, hanging from the ceiling, higher up than I could reach.

When I brought the tiedown rope he asked for, he threw one end through the ring, made a half-hitch, and let the other end dangle, where I could reach it. The ring was a shower pull, so that (tall, long-armed) cropdusters who'd spilled chemical poisons on their skin could rinse them off in a hurry. There was no such ring in the ladies' room— probably no women cropdusters at Shafter. In all the time I'd been flying I'd met only one female ag pilot.

After the miller had gone off to his little Misty and Tinker, I laid my clothes, flashlight, handbag, towel, sneakers, etc., on the floor of the men's room just inside the door, stepped under the ring, and gave the tiedown rope a yank. A dead weight of water fell on my head, almost staggering me, as if a river had been on the roof and the ring had let it in. Within seconds water was running across the floor and out the door and down the steps, carrying my purse, shoes, towel, etc., with it. I ran out and grabbed them and laid them further out on dry ground in the moonlight, then went in and finished my shower. Rinsing was instantaneous, the way you'd want it to be if you had chemicals eating your skin.

During the night I woke up repeatedly as strands of my hair moved across my face, tickling it. The fact that the strands were moving meant a breeze was blowing, and if a breeze was blowing at night, I reasoned, it would almost certainly be blowing, and probably harder, in the morning, in which case there'd be no human-powered flight. Whenever the tickling woke me up, I stared at the glaring moon and fretted for a while. It was still dark out when something else woke me, a noise, coming from the ladies' room. I hurried over to see what was going on. A woman was standing at the sink combing her hair and humming. She was "the mother of the engine," she told me, the engine being the man who powered the aircraft, Bryan Allen. Bryan had been depressed this morning, she said—not seeming at all depressed herself—because of missing the final pole yesterday. Light had hit the plastic cockpit in such a way that he couldn't see the pole and didn't know when to start sprinting. She had driven over from Tulare, 60 miles away, to watch him try again, even though she knew her boss would be furious; he didn't appreciate all these goings-on.

I went out, grabbed my camera, and ran around to the front of the hangar, where to my amazement, since I hadn't heard anybody come in, a dozen or so people were standing, in small groups, chatting quietly, without a central focus, as at a cocktail party. The hangar doors were still shut but I could see lights on inside. I asked around but nobody knew quite what was going on, or whether anything would. There was a strong sausage smell on the ramp; Maude Oldershaw was making breakfast in the motor home over there, someone said. Her husband, Vern, was the project's structural engineer, and for months they had been coming back and forth in the motor home so he could be on hand to work on the plane whenever he was needed.

The sky had lightened a little although the sun was still not up, and I took a look around the airport. It seemed a good place for a human-powered flight. There were three runways, so while a pedalcraft wobbled around on one of them, ordinary planes could take off and land on the other two. The area was flat for miles in every direction (except for the miller's piles, which gave a hint of contour), the mountains so far off they probably didn't dump too many winds. More people showed up, including the father of the engine, a fifth-grade teacher wearing a straw hat and smoking a pipe. A TV crew appeared; it had been there yesterday but would leave if there wasn't a flight today or the flight was unsuccessful. We all stood on the ramp, talking, waiting, a breeze washing over us. Then without any fuss or warning the hangar doors slid open and the object of our speculation was rolled out, four men holding onto ropes attached to the underside of its wings.

Even in the weak, early-morning light, the whole thing shimmered. I had read that it resembled a dragonfly in looks but that what inspired its design were soaring birds—hawks, vultures—and hang gliders. It was covered in clear plastic, which wrinkled and luffed in the breeze so that light was reflected in patches on it, rendering it at once transparent, opaque, and translucent. Its swept wings were very long, almost three times as long as the Luscombe's and more than twice as wide, and as light passed through them it picked up the amber of the wooden struts inside and carried the color down through the bottom layer of plastic onto the ramp, casting golden shadows, against which were traced the delicate lines of the aluminum frame.

Lovely, in its way, but not sleek, or powerful, or professional-looking, as you might expect of something competing for a prize worth (by then) $87,000. There was an ephemeral, nonserious, mussed-up, *Midsummer Night's Dream* quality to it. It had been given the name "Gossamer Condor" (gossamer being by dictionary definition a "film of cobwebs floating in the air in calm clear weather'' and condor being of course a bird, an endangered Californian, as well as probably the world's slowest soarer). The cockpit was a two-foot-wide pod under the wings, with three toy plastic wheels under it, each protected by a dainty, pea-green fairing. Protruding in front of the cockpit like a fishing pole was a rod with a horizontal bar at the end, and back of the cockpit was a large propeller with plastic blades, one red and one yellow, so the crew could count revolutions. The blades were beating on their own now, I was sorry to see, pushed around by the wind.

I edged over and peered into the cockpit; nobody seemed to mind. Inside were a red plastic toy seat, two bicycle pedals, and what looked like a bicycle chain, plus a metal rod curved on top like a cane which stuck up vertically from the floor and another rod which stuck out sideways from under the seat (controls, obviously, but for what?). I peered too at the engine, which stood nearby. From his mother I knew Allen was an unemployed biologist, hanglider pilot, and racing cyclist, who for bike races usually got down to 140 pounds but for this stren-uous event was down to 135. All he had this morning was a little lem-onade and a banana, she said (''He's nervous''). He was thin all over, chest, shoulders, face, nose, mouth, arms, legs, even mustache. He had on his ''patriotic shirt,'' as his mother called it, ''since he's rep-resenting America,'' a red-white-and-blue-striped jersey, with the white actually half-pink since the red had bled in the wash. I noticed pale lines on his tanned arm and hand where a watch and ring would or-dinarily be: more weight control . . .

The official observer arrived carrying a stopwatch, Polaroid camera, and several elevation charts. Although American, he was representing the Royal Aeronautical Society, making sure the aircraft and the course met the Society's rules. He was chief of maintenance for the five county airports and wearing his uniform for the occasion. He confided that he didn't think there'd be a flight that day because of the wind; while it was legal under the rules to fly in winds up to 11 miles an hour, he said, the plane hadn't yet been able to fly in winds over three or four.

He waited anyhow, and so did the rest of us. Preparations for a flight, if there was to be one, seemed casual, even minimal. An un-obtrusive man stood in front of a wing, taping a hole in the leading edge. He looked the part of a rumpled professor, with uncombed gray-brown hair, baggy corduroy pants, five o'clock shadow, scuffed shoes, sunburned nose, glasses. I was told that he was the head of the project, Paul MacCready, Jr., president of his own environmental research firm in Pasadena and three times national soaring champion. "Vern," he was saying to a man in a silly golf hat, "we've got to put a small air vent in the front and a little bit more of a hole in the back." They sat cross-legged on the asphalt together and dug at the pod's Styrofoam hull with razor blades. The temperature in the cockpit, I was told, could reach 109 degrees.

Allen's mother left to go back to Tulare. Like the official observer, she didn't think there'd be a flight that day because of the wind. At least his father was staying, and looking serene, I noted. By then more than 40 of us were on the ramp, talking in little groups as before, standing, waiting. MacCready hit his head on a piano wire while walking around the plane; the wire was one of dozens holding the wings to a central vertical post. Then, with very little ado, a barefoot boy of about 12, MacCready's son Tyler (an early test pilot who wasn't considered strong enough to be the ultimate engine), climbed into the pod and sat on the seat; the word was he was going to make a test run. "Don't steam up the cockpit," MacCready told him, sounding like a father. "I imagine for the landing you'll do a little left turn." "Yeow!" Tyler responded, making roaring sounds, like an engine revving. "Remember, you have to be pointing up six degrees more than you are pointing now so that things have to be . . ." his father went on, and Tyler started pedaling, the plane lifted off, floated several feet, touched down, and was wheeled back. What MacCready learned from the test it was hard to guess because he gave no indication.

We waited. Someone complained about the flies. There *were* an awful lot of them. The smell of sausage still hung heavy on the air. The air was already hot. The prop still turned on its own. By then it was 7:30, already a half hour later than any other flight had taken place. Go? No go? Then, with no discernible excitement shown by any of the participants, and no announcement about what was to take place, Allen approached the cockpit, slid through the flap, sat on the red seat, and strapped his feet to the pedals. MacCready taped the flap shut, encasing Allen entirely in plastic except for the hole that had just been cut out by his feet, another hole higher up with a tube running toward his face (also for ventilation), and a small hole about eye level, for emergency visibility, in case the plastic filmed over. Allen's legs were extended well in front of him and his torso was angled back so that he looked almost languid in there, as if he were half-reclining in a deck chair.

The official observer climbed into the cab of a truck; then a man holding a camera jumped onto the back of the truck, so I ran over and jumped on the back too, brandishing my camera so I'd look as if I belonged there. Nobody paid any attention. The other stowaway was a free-lance writer, and it wasn't clear to him what he'd do with this, but we stood together, excited as kids, telling each other this might be History. By comparison, the people around us were quite calm, maybe because the plane had made 430 other flights so far, nine of which were official attempts on the Kremer Prize, and they were probably wary of expecting History. A man stood beside the Gossamer Condor holding onto a wingtip, and Allen began pedaling. The plane rolled forward and the man ran alongside it until he could no longer keep up so let the wingtip go, and the plane rose an inch, a foot, two feet, four feet—flying!

The truck followed, off to the side, and so did several bicycles, with guys on them, their feet pumping along with Allen's feet as the plane kept climbing—six feet, eight feet. Then sunlight caught a bulge in the plastic and we could no longer see Allen's head and legs in the cockpit, only the red seat—ten feet, twelve. His body came into view again, reclining, seeming not to strain. Tyler, barefoot still, was standing up ahead, holding upright a pole with a horizontal bar on top, and the Gossamer Condor floated toward and over it easily, two feet to spare. Could this be *it?*

Once over the pole, the Gossamer Condor sank, to about five feet off the ground. It was moving smoothly, with none of the wobbles or jerks I had expected, no sudden saves or dips. My hopes rose— although the plane did not. It dropped to within a couple of feet of the runway. Why? I wondered. Was something going wrong? (One touch to the ground, however gentle, and it was all over.) I noticed people standing scattered along the edge of the runway, some holding cameras, and past them, on the far side of the airport fence, a couple of cars were pulled off the road, with men standing beside the cars, looking our way. I wondered what they thought they were seeing . . .

The guys on bicycles were shouting now, which they were supposed to do, letting Allen know when to pour on power, start turning, that sort of thing. He entered a right turn around a pylon. The pylon was a thin, stiff pole which stuck up about three feet off the runway with a couple of strips of silver plastic tied to the top, refreshingly primitive. The turn was wide and without bank, so flat that the plane looked as if it were driving rather than flying around the pylon. During the turn, sunlight shot through the cockpit in a way that gave the pod a watery look, and we could see just the outline of Allen's body, head and shoulders rolled forward, back rounded, one knee up, then the other knee up, like a fetus curled inside a giant fluid-filled sac, kicking.

The plane went up and down after the turn more than it had before it—three feet, four feet, two feet—up, down, *down*. Was this strategy, I wondered nervously, or instability? Good news, or bad? Probably not good news. Allen was pedaling hard now, looking anything but languid, a creature treading water, working to stay afloat. The craft entered a left turn, as flat as the first turn but even wider. Bad? Coming out of the turn it dipped to within a foot of the runway. Yesterday this was where the flight had started to come apart.

More shouts, from what appeared to be more bicycles. "Go, Bryan." "*Go!*" Ahead was the ten-foot pole, held this time by a man with shoes on, who was standing not at the edge of the runway but out past it, on dirt. "Get some altitude, Bryan!" the bike brigade was yelling, and the plane nosed up. "You can do it, Bryan!" A TV crewman stood beside the pole, camera pointed upward. "Go, go, Bryan!" Allen bent to it, head and shoulders heaving, hair whipping around, legs churning. The plane climbed as steadily as if it were being pedaled up a dirt slope. *"Go Bryan!"* People were running and pedaling and driving alongside, yelling and taking photos as the man with the pole took a step backward and the Gossamer Condor kept climbing, climbing, reached the pole, and floated over it, just as it had at the beginning, with two feet to spare.

"Yea!" *"Yea!"* *"Whoopee!"* People jumped up and down, whooped, raised their arms over their heads, and ran, as the plane kept on flying, made a right turn until it was back over the runway, then straightened out and touched its toy wheels down. Allen tumbled out through the flap and sat on the runway, laughing and shouting, while we caught up. "We did it! We did it!" he shouted, laughing, and we gathered about him, staring in astonishment, as the shades of Turks in stiff cloaks and Italians in feathered wings and Arabs with doors on their arms and Englishmen covered in chicken feathers hovered in the air around us, and he sat, laughing and shouting, on the asphalt on a hot

day in Southern California, he who had at last flown truly under his own power, with the strength of his own gaunt, birdlike body.*

Everyone was smiling. Allen was smiling so hard his teeth stuck out. He stood, his shoes under his arm, and took a swig from a jug of water someone handed him. We compared notes— *"this* far over the bar"— gestured to each other, stared at him, smiled. At the edge of the crowd around him, unnoticed at first, adjusting ropes, moving poles, tidying up, something, was MacCready, not smiling—yet. Someone drew him into the crowd and said "Congratulations!", which produced a small smile, significant to those who knew him. Quickly, though, he got back down to business. He took Allen's wrist in one hand and consulted his watch: 120 beats a minute. Allen, trying for the moment to look serious himself, said, "I worked up a sweat but my eyeballs weren't bulging. It was pretty easy."

Champagne appeared in plastic glasses. It was champagne the Oldershaws had been keeping on ice for seven months, I heard, ever since the first attempt on the Kremer Prize. Vern Oldershaw's face was more radiant than anybody else's. "You have this feeling of happiness right *here,"* he said, tapping his heart. "I don't know which was more exciting: getting married, test-flying my first sailplane, becoming a grandfather ten times, or this." The observer announced the official times: seven minutes 27.5 seconds takeoff to touchdown, six minutes 22.5 seconds pole to pole, average speed ten miles an hour. He hadn't expected the plane to make it, he admitted, because the wind was so variable. But as far as he, the Society's representative, was concerned, it had won the prize. "We have all the bases covered," he pronounced. "I can't picture any problems." He added, as if he'd rehearsed it, as he probably had, "This goes back to Greek mythology when they flew so close to the sun the wax melted on their wings."

"Aren't you happy?" people kept asking MacCready, who after the first smile had reverted to an inert expression. "Don't you feel great?" He was heard muttering, "Everybody wants me to jump up and down." He had been worried about "conditions," he admitted. "The wind itself doesn't hurt; it's the up-and-down variations. When you get a one-foot-per-second downdraft and you're three feet off the

*The Gossamer Condor now hangs on exhibit in the National Air and Space Museum in Washington, D.C.

ground, it can kill you." Allen reported some variations. "On the way back, I had a tail wind of three or four miles an hour," he said, "which is like 22 or 25 miles an hour on a bicycle. It was hard to maintain altitude . . . so I really poured it on."

Had MacCready expected to succeed today? "Yes," he said, "but I had that feeling 80 times before." How was he able to manage when all the others through all the eons had not? What part did modern materials and scientific advances play in his success? "They could have done this 50 years ago," he said, to my surprise, "with what was known then. The technology is not particularly advanced. Silk could have been used instead of Mylar. They certainly had bicycle parts and gears. A lot of the dreamers," he continued, "had the right dreams but didn't know how to pursue them. [Was I mistaken, or was that less than gracious?] Leonardo sketched and talked but he didn't do anything about it. We've gone a bit further. We were aware of the very complex [machines] built by very capable builders in England and the huge amount of effort they put into them . . . but we decided we couldn't get contaminated with the thoughts of others. We developed the philosophy of the Wright brothers: First things first. We did a lot of flight testing, then went back to calculations." ("We" included Peter Lissaman, an expert in bird flight—he wrote a paper once on why geese fly in V-formation—and vice-president of MacCready's firm, who designed the airfoil by computer but who wasn't around that day to see it perform.)

According to what I had read, the idea for the Gossamer Condor came to MacCready while he was on vacation, his mind "disconnected to anything else" (uncontaminated?), watching birds soar and musing about hang gliders. He made calculations on the back of an envelope (there ought to be a museum of the backs of envelopes, plus tablecloths) to the effect that if the lift of a hang glider could be tripled without changing its weight, the muscle power required to fly it was within the capability of a strong man. Those calculations led to the winning combination: an aircraft with a large lifting area (wings that were longer than on a DC-9 and wide as well) which could thus be flown very, very slowly and did not need to be very strong; the Condor's wings, like a hang glider's, were supported by thin exterior wires rather than by the heavier wooden interior ribs that previous man-powered aircraft relied on. The craft was in fact flimsy—could be repaired after accidents using tape, glue, and wire—and extremely light, weighing only 70 pounds.

Lessons learned along the way, MacCready reported, included the fact that the skin didn't have to be "supersmooth"—"Mylar changes day to day, almost as if it's living." It could have dents and bumps as long as they didn't keep the airflow over the wing from breaking up. Also, the wings behaved in the opposite way to standard airplane wings; that is, the craft turned *toward* the wing with the lowered trailing edge instead of away from it. "There had never been a plane with a wing like that before," said MacCready. "It was an educated guess."

What now? he was asked. "First, we're going to have some fun," he answered. "Everybody associated with the project is going to fly the plane. Then we can horse around with it, maybe build a version with an extra wing. Or see if we can make one without a tail." As he went off to the hangar to call the Royal Aeronautical Society in London, he passed the Gossamer Condor. "About as substantial as the airplane," he said, indicating the shadow of its wing on the ramp, "and even more beautiful." By then the wind had picked up, so several people rolled the plane back into the hangar, where Allen was talked into climbing into the cockpit again and posing for pictures. I noticed his ring was back on his finger, a large turquoise-and-silver one, not lightweight. He sat staring ahead, his feet strapped in, a thoughtful look on his face.

Meanwhile Tyler, his attention already shifted elsewhere, was lunging about the hangar with a two-foot-long hunk of Styrofoam floating in the air above his head. He would lunge, then run crookedly about, slow to a walk, step sideways, forward, then back, and lunge again, all the while keeping his face tilted upward and his eyes on the piece of Styrofoam. It was a "walkalong" or "runalong" glider, and he'd designed and made it himself. Brilliant! I thought. The whole family had the touch. All the kids, I'd been told, including eight-year-old Marshall, could make flyable objects out of nearly anything—paper, cardboard, Styrofoam from the Gossamer Condor—and in nearly any shape—a Z, an S, a helix, a penguin. Tyler showed me how his glider worked. You threw it out like a paper airplane, ran and got your head under it, kept it aloft with the cushion of air over your head, like ground effect over a runway, made it climb by moving your head forward in relation to it, which forced the nose up, made it lose altitude by pulling your head back, which forced the tail up, caused it to turn by placing the palm of a hand in the air under one wing, which made that wing rise. He let me try it but the thing kept shooting away from over my head, like a bar of wet soap. Nevertheless, I bought it from him, for $2. Across the hangar Marshall was sitting on the eleventh version of the Condor (the twelfth being the winning one), pedaling in place, seemingly as un-bowled over by the day's events as his brother. When I asked for one he gave me a piece of pea-green Styrofoam from the penultimate Gossamer Condor, and I walked around collecting signatures, starting with his. Was I the first human-powered groupie? I wondered. One signer wrote the initials "N.Z." after his name, explaining that he'd come from New Zealand on vacation, stumbled on the project, and stayed to work on it because he liked the people.

Nobody was in at the Royal Aeronautical Society when MacCready phoned except the librarian so he left a message. If that was a letdown for him he didn't reveal it. "There are no measurements where you wonder," he had said earlier. "It was well over the mark." Before long he and his wife and Tyler and Marshall climbed into their Volvo and drove off toward Pasadena, looking no more excited than a family setting out for a picnic. I, however, was still quite thrilled and looking to party, so when I saw a young man come in the other side of the hangar I went over and found him standing next to . . . another human-powered airplane! He told me he'd built it for a class at the California Institute of Technology, and he had intended to try for the Kremer Prize with it. The "Icarus HPA," he called it. It seemed far more substantial than the Gossamer Condor, with a long fuselage, low wings, and a greenhouse canopy of red, blue, and clear plastic panes. "I can fly it myself and I'm in lousy shape," he said cheerfully. He appeared not to be at all disappointed at having lost his chance to win the prize. I had seen him on a bicycle chasing the plane that did win it, wearing a ponytail and flip-flop sandals, carrying a young woman on his handlebars, the quintessential Californian.

When even this young man had drifted off, I went back, reluctantly, to my plane. It seemed a long time since I had left it. As I was doing my preflight, still astonished by what I'd seen, a couple of yellow butterflies flitted around the plane. My, but they made it look easy!

Old Howard DGA15 with straw in inspection holes, at Creve Coeur.

Artwork for the airborne: Farmers' fields.

Waiting for mom
to fill the tanks
at Wall.

Dogs find a welcome at little
airports, too.

Bemused Mr. Smith, at Oljato trading post.

Tied down (and grounded) in Monument Valley.

In his 80s, a citrus rancher still flew his Staggerwing "beautifully."

The rich canvas of earth, which pilots spread out beneath them every time they take off . . .

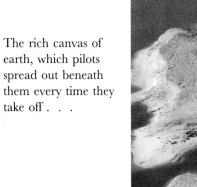

Bryan Allen pedaling the Gossamer Condor into history.

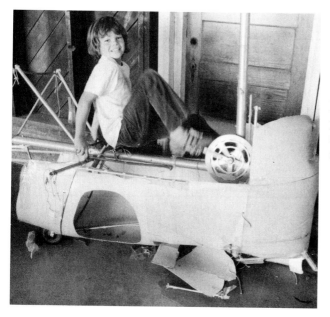

Marshall MacCready pedaling a chunk of an earlier Condor, for fun.

Paul Imeson with son
Sparky's "only" ram.

South Dakota Badlands,
from 1,000 feet.

Fantasist Steven at the controls of a real plane.

America's small towns: What are people *doing* down there?

Mr. Christie, a dark, stubborn spirit from the old days.

Back at Spring Valley, after 10,000 miles, with 11 bags, 2 boxes, and a chair.

San Francisco · Tahoe

To get fuel I had to taxi to the other side of Shafter. That end had real planes on it, with fat, round, hard bodies you could thump, doors that couldn't be seen through, big tires to kick. Three Stearmans were parked together in a line down there, alike except for their N numbers, all of them unpainted silver with yellow wings and tails. The yellow was that shade you see on old taildraggers as well as school buses and taxicabs, all machines with a stake in being seen from a distance. A slightly sour, or ocherish, yellow. The old taildraggers it was usually seen on were Piper J-3 Cubs. When Cubs were first made, in the late 1930s, they were painted a more lemony yellow, but as they sat outside the factory in Pennsylvania waiting for buyers, sometimes for months at a time, soaking up cosmic rays and chemicals from paper plants nearby, they turned a darker shade of yellow, even before they left the lot. So company president William T. Piper decided they should be painted that shade of yellow to begin with. "See and be seen," he said of it, making the best of things. At that time the need for see-and-be-seen wasn't nearly what it is today, when there are more airplanes in the state of Florida alone than there were in the whole country then. Nevertheless, you don't see much of that eye-catching yellow on planes anymore. They tend to be painted a cloud white, a hazy-day white, a blinded-by-the-sun white instead.

Hear and be heard. As soon as I took off from Shafter, proud to be even a small part of an enterprise that included scenes such as I'd just witnessed (that long struggle upward!), I put on my earmuffs. The muffs consisted of two cushioned plastic cups connected by a metal band, like a radio headset except not wired for anything, just meant to dampen engine noise. An audiologist once told me when he found out I was a pilot that I'd probably already lost some of my hearing in the upper registers. Engine noise, he explained, if it was loud enough and lasted long enough, could damage the delicate hair cells of the inner ear, causing them to lose their ability to absorb oxygen, or their tension, or something (nobody knew for sure then). It was back in the days when people didn't look after their bodies as assiduously as they do now, and the pilots I knew, including myself, didn't give much thought to their inner ears. After I saw the audiologist, though, I started wearing earplugs, and now that I was flying my Luscombe— supposedly one of the noisiest of all single-engine airplanes—almost every day, I decided to wear earmuffs as well as plugs. Through both layers I could hear and monitor the engine, but it sounded the way bicycles used to when boys attached playing cards to their rear spokes with clothespins, puh puh puh puh, a muffled beat.

Smell and be smelled. As I headed up the San Joaquin Valley toward San Francisco, a powerful stench suddenly filled the cabin. Peeyoo! Manure! Even in the air you couldn't get away from the smells of earth; they rose up to smite you at 1,000, 2,000, even 3,000 feet. Not just extended, regional smells, like factory exhaust or smoke from forest fires, urban pollutants so thick they could turn the sky over a city pink by midday, but concentrated, local smells too. Once I was flying over a town where I caught the unmistakable odor of bacon frying. Another time while airborne the aroma of soap floated up to me. Still another time, when I was up near Hannibal, Missouri, I clearly smelled cornbread cooking. It wasn't just my imagination either, although I had had Mark Twain on my mind at the time, and minds can conjure up smells as well as sights and sounds. On long air trips there were times when, after days of eating in the chain restaurants that predominate around airports and airport motels and worrying vaguely about bad blood and vitamin deficiency and other hazards of the constant traveler, I found myself daydreaming about fruit—*craving* fruit—and while flying the Idea of Tomato would suddenly come over me, flood my senses, and I not only thought I could taste tomatoes *in absentia* but smell them as well.

In this case, there was no wishful thinking involved, of course; I was flying over a cattle feedlot. From 1,500 feet it looked like a dirty window with flies crawling over it. Some of the "flies" were crawling around faster than others: cowboys on horseback. Poor guys. If the smell dispersed up through 1,500 feet of air was like this, what must it be like at the source?

The valley of the San Joaquin was wide and deep and bountiful, with everything seeming to grow with a machine-like precision, all members of the same crop and trees in the same orchard reaching the same height and width, each row of equal length and straight as a hoe handle, but among the highly ordered fields there was one with a maverick, rakish look to it. It had worn grass on it, through which grayish lines weaved around, forming loops, ovals, and teardrops, widest at the sharpest curves, so when seen from above the whole swirling pattern resembled a big silver brooch, all of a beautiful piece. In other places around the country I had seen fields like this one, some of them even more densely webbed, with even sharper turns and more loops, so I knew, even without watching a motorcycle retrace the sinuous lines, what had created it.

Where I left the valley, about 150 miles up it, the fields took on the look of a man's wardrobe. Or rather fabric from a man's wardrobe. One of the fields was pale brown with wide dark-brown stripes, one was a light gray ribbed like corduroy, another a dark-green, lumpy cable-knit, still another a brown pinstripe upon a plain green ground, and running diagonally across them all, setting them off like a shiny silk necktie, was a canal of peacock blue.

While listening to weather on the radio I learned that Half Moon Bay, an uncontrolled airport on the coast, where I intended to land shortly, was closed because of fog. Fog out that way seemed more solid to me than ours back home, cohesive, stiff even, with well-defined edges beyond which the air could be totally clear and blue. None of those creeping cat feet . . . To my left I could see fog lying on a range of mountains, the last before the sea, looking like surf that had tried to pass over the peaks but become frozen at the top of its swell, the foam whipped into points by the wind. However, Palo Alto, a controlled field only 20 miles from Half Moon Bay, was wide open, so I decided to go there. When I radioed in, the controller told me to "report over the twin bridges," and I was relieved. Even someone from New York could find twin bridges. On my way to them I crossed one of the most gaudy "natural" sights on earth: mile after mile of colored ponds, brick-red, lilac, olive, chocolate, ocher, milk-white, and dark green, side by side, separated only by narrow dikes. I found out later that they were salt-evaporation ponds, the colors determined by the different lengths of time that salt water had been standing and evaporating in each of them, producing different concentrations of salt, which in turn attracted and sustained different plants and animals.

The ponds with the least salt, for instance, where the water had been standing the shortest time, maybe only one or two years, were full of algae that turned the water green, yellow-green, or brown. The ponds where the water had been standing longer and contained more salt to the cubic inch—up to seven times as much salt as ordinary bay water—contained bacteria that turned the water yellow, or a darker green, or a different brown. The ones with the most salt, where water had been standing for up to five years, were filled with red bacteria, which turned the gray brine shrimp that lived in the ponds and ate the bacteria red too.

I came to the Palo Alto area to see old friends who lived in Menlo Park, also on the bay. They had a house on Lemon Street with a redwood tree in the back yard and bougainvillea in the side yard. They lived there with their two daughters, Lucia, 7, and Lizzie, 5. The whole family loved the outdoors, went bicycling together, picnicking often, swimming in Half Moon Bay. They never watched TV, didn't even own a set. What had made them decide to get rid of the set they once had was something Lucia said when she was about four years old. Her father was staying home from work because of a cold, and after watching him drag around, sniffling and blowing, she went up to her mother and gravely offered her prescription. "Put meat by-products up his nose."

Lucia thought of herself as a poet and had written a fair number of poems on her own. Two words she loved above all others: "sneeze" and "fur." Just saying the word "sneeze" made her laugh. *"Silly sneeze,"* she'd say. Even the mention of fur would entrance her; she'd smile as if a pelt were already lying soft in her hands. One day she had come home from school and told her mother that her first-grade teacher had worn a fur collar that day but *acted as if she didn't have it on.* That is, presumably, the teacher didn't rub her cheek against it or let her fingers wander to her neck during recess or blow on the collar to ruffle the little hairs. Clearly, Lucia would never be guilty of such cold-blooded behavior. One day she hoped to have it on her license plate: *California FUR 1.*

She, Lizzie, and I played a license-plate game as their parents drove us around sightseeing, the game where you get so many points for being the first person to spot a license plate with the letters X or Z in it, so many for being the first to see a white horse on your side of the road, so many for a purple car, etc., etc. At five, Lizzie was too young to be a contender, said her mother, but she surprised us all. Intense and unrelenting, she was on the alert for possible points even when they didn't count and she knew it. One morning when we were out riding bikes we passed a family of four going the other way, on foot, and Lizzie turned on her bicycle seat and stared after them until they had vanished around a corner. "I wish," she said, with a fierce look on her face, "people's bottoms had license plates on them!"

Her "search images," as the wildlife researchers call them, stayed with her for five days and she won first prize, a cookie the size of a dinner plate with a purple car in the icing. I understood the power of the search image, even when misplaced; once after a morning of bird-watching in Central Park I went back to the streets and as a yellow cab passed, "Wilson's Warbler!" flashed through my mind (there was a black call sign on top). Another time as I was exiting the park the sight of a diagonal line on a mailbox had stirred me for a millisecond: Wingbar! My friend Cynthia, who went back to Africa to study elephants with her wildlife scientist, told me that she so keyed her scan of the landscape to large, gray, rounded, lumpy masses that she could pick out one half-submerged in swamp grass 300 yards away yet not be aware of the shaggy, yellow-brown shape of a lion in shorter, dry grass 20 yards away, until she stepped out of her Land Rover to relieve herself.

While I was in the San Francisco area I visited another wildlife researcher, one who carried a different picture in her head, which she matched to the long curves and smooth brown coats of elephant seals. Harriet had been studying elephant seals on the Farallon Islands off the coast of California for eight years, with particular interest in cow-calf bonds. Three weeks of every month she spent on the Farallons, the fourth week on the mainland; this was the fourth week. She picked me up at the bus stop (along the coast north of San Francisco there was not a single airport for 75 miles), and we drove straight to a lagoon where she had once spent a summer observing long-billed curlews. At that time it wasn't known for sure what long-billed curlews ate on their winter feeding grounds (their winter, her summer) so every day Harriet would paddle out to an island that had a curlew roost on it, wade ashore through marsh grass and pickleweed, gather pellets the birds had regurgitated (at the rate of one pellet per curlew per day), still damp and consisting mostly of indigestibles like carapaces, take them back to a lab, and study them under a microscope. What she found was that in winter long-billed curlews ate (1) mud crabs, (2) blue mud shrimp, and (3) ghost shrimp, all creatures that lived in sand burrows which, as nature would have it, are curved just as the birds' crescent-shaped bills are.

At the lagoon, we saw not only curlews but other waterbirds, heads and legs wobbly in heat waves rising off the water: godwits, killdeer, cormorants, pelicans, dowitchers, kingfishers, egrets, yellowlegs, gulls, willets. We also saw, painted in large, white letters on the face of a cliff on the other side of the lagoon, ECOLOGY! As if exposure to the word itself, a branch of science, bionomics, would get visitors to pick up their trash and not throw stones at the birds. Not the sort of graffiti we were used to in New York.

Before dinner, we sat on Harriet's deck, sipping mint juleps and looking out at the ghostly line of the Farralons, 13 miles offshore. After a while she went in to get a rabbit ready for dinner, returning once, briefly, to throw a pan of bloody rabbit rinse-water off the deck onto her flowers. That part of California was in the middle of a severe drought and evidently she didn't want to waste anything wet. An ornithologist from the Point Reyes Bird Observatory joined us for dinner. I managed to eat only one piece of rabbit but the two wildlife researchers gobbled the bunny up (ecology!). They talked about birds for a while, saying which ones they liked best and which ones they thought they most resembled.

Harriet decided she was a common murre. "They're short and squat and easily agitated," she said. The ornithologist felt more like a sooty shearwater. "They're footloose and spend a lot of time away from home." His favorite birds, however, the ones he most admired, were the snowy petrel and Arctic tern. "Good flyers, long migrators," he noted. Once he'd seen a snowy petrel face into a 75-knot wind and *move forward.* Like most seabirds, they were long-lived. "If seabirds get past the first two or three years, they can live 15 or 20 years, maybe even 35."

A Farallon, Harriet explained to me, was a weed that grew only on those islands and only in winter, when there was lots of rain, fog, and wind. She had spent many winters there (the seals pupped in December and January, mated in January and February). The researchers had no telephone, no TV, and a radio only for emergencies. Yet she didn't find the place bleak. "Earth water rocks sky," she said. "I have never been bored." Life was both familiar and changing, and nearly always simple. "Different birds arrive and depart," she said. "The pups grow a day older. A bull dies. All the eggs in a particular colony disappear." She had been away from the islands only six days but was already eager to go back. It was time, she said.

For me too it was time (earth water rocks sky, as seen from a cockpit). For two weeks I had had almost constant companionship and was eager now to be on my own. Yet a couple of mornings later when I was standing on the ramp at Palo Alto ready for takeoff, I was a little nervous. A briefer had reported a "broken" ceiling (meaning the sky was more than half covered by clouds; "scattered" means less than half covered) at 1,300 feet, winds 15 gusting to 25 near my next airport, Nut Tree, and light-to-moderate turbulence north of that. Nothing particularly daunting, but I almost wished somebody were coming with me. It seemed that being in prolonged close association with friends had rendered me dependent in some way I regretted, not quite sufficient on my own; it had weakened my flying nerve.

So as I climbed out of Palo Alto, rocking my wings for Lucia and Lizzie, who were jumping rope back at the tiedown, I was a little more apprehensive than the situation called for—fretted while working my way out of the area, trying to stay clear of clouds, the Terminal Control Area, other planes, other airports, and the hills on the far side of the bay. The hills turned out to be browned by drought, smooth, and almost shiny, as if they'd been handled a lot, fondled, passed back and forth by gloved hands. North of them, 40 miles away in Suisun Bay, I spotted a flotilla of Liberty ships, cargo vessels left from World War II, being kept on hand in case of another war. Anchored side by side, their bows pointing in the same direction, they looked from the air like bullets on an ammo belt. I felt better already. The great Earth Show had begun again!

I had been working up to—"up" was the operative word—the next part of my trip. To me it would be the big adventure—the stroll through the strangle-vine jungle, the dhow ride along the coast of Zanzibar. I was born and brought up in a part of the country where Pleistocene glaciers had planed the earth flat as plankboard, and mountains were as exotic to me as . . . well, glaciers. In our suburb of Columbus, Ohio, which I rarely left, my father being a doctor who liked to look in on his hospital patients every day of the year, there was nothing on the horizon higher than an elm tree, or chimneys at the high school. Nothing loomed where we were, nothing brooded over us. Nothing diminished our little concerns with suggestions of larger, darker ones. Occasionally we'd take a bus downtown, where there were five or six buildings over ten floors, and now and then we'd visit my grandparents' town in southern Ohio, surrounded by 200-foot hills. But I was 22 before I saw a mountain. After that, I saw a fair number of them, while traveling around, yet they remained outside my normal sphere, unfamiliar items of topography, remote to my understanding of how the world worked, exotic still.

I had flown over mountains in my plane, including some on this trip, but the ones coming up were really big-deal, the Sierra Nevada of California, for example, the Sawtooths of Idaho, the Grand Tetons of Wyoming. I'd be making things easy on myself where I could, following roads (they sought the low route), flying over valleys and through passes and across plateaus, yet there was no getting around the fact that these were the central Rockies and their Western cohorts. The problem wouldn't be getting over them; even my small, old, low-powered plane could do that (probably). The problem, if there was any, would be handling the things the mountains might throw my way because of what they did to the air I'd be passing through: speeding it up, thinning it, making it tumble, sucking it down or shooting it up, switching its direction of flow, turning it to fog or ice showers. I bought a book called *Mountain Flying*, which could give anybody high anxiety about entering mountain country, but particularly "Flatlanders," as the author, one Sparky Imeson of Jackson Hole airport in Wyoming, calls people who live in places like central Ohio. "Have you ever bitten into a cherry pie," he asks in a section on flight visibility (cherry pie being clouds 2,000 to 4,000 feet higher than the ones at the nearest reporting weather station), "where someone forgot to pit one of the cherries and caught you unawares? You may lose a tooth," he says sternly, "but if you try to fly through an area where the clouds are stuffed with rocks, you can lose your life."

Elsewhere in *Mountain Flying* he warns, "The only thing to be sure about mountain weather is that it will change—shortly, and probably for the worse." Also: "Beware of ceiling fluctuations . . . ceilings have been known to drop as much as 2,000 feet per minute in certain sections of the mountain west." And: "Expect the wind direction and velocity to be constantly changing." In addition: "Be always alert for power lines strung across canyons." As well as: "Watch for any movement or rotation of cloud edges. Updrafts and downdrafts in excess of 5,000 feet per minute have been encountered in the area of rotor and roll clouds." Scattered throughout: "Beware of low stratus and fog in narrow canyons . . . snow showers at the head of canyons . . . interior valley fogs . . ."

Whew! As a pilot you are to take all this information calmly, however. "Fear has no place in mountain flying," Imeson chides. A "phobic reaction" to the hazards of mountain flying can produce in the "unconfident" pilot (who might *that* be?) "tenseness, muscle tremor, sweating, palpitation, nausea, insomnia, frequent sighing, fatigue, and depression." Any of which (frequent sighing!) can get in the way of good flying. Instead of fear, Imeson suggests "constant vigilance," *"caution,"* and "everpresent . . . wariness."

My first hands-on lesson in mountain flying this trip came sooner than I expected, a slap with a sour rag just as I was opening the door. After lunch at Nut Tree, a restaurant in the Sacramento Valley featuring "Western food" (which I thought would be in the line of beefsteak or rattlesnake but was actually nuts, vegetables, and fruits), I phoned my next stop, Truckee-Tahoe, to ask about conditions. The airport was 60 miles east of Nut Tree but nearly 6,000 feet higher, with the Sierra Nevada mountains providing the lift. Air is of course less dense at higher altitudes than it is at sea level, and at 6,000 feet it is only four-fifths as dense, which means engine power is reduced by a fifth, takeoff rolls are longer, requiring two-thirds more runway, and stall speed is *increased* by a fifth, meaning the plane quits flying earlier than usual and takes longer to stop. In that respect airplanes are not very different from the pilots who fly them; both are sensitive to the amount of oxygen circulating in their systems. Air that is high or hot or full of moisture also tends to be low on oxygen, and a plane passing through it will perform sluggishly, just as a pilot will if his blood is short on oxygen.

Truckee-Tahoe airport was not only high but hot when I phoned, 85 degrees F, or 48 degrees higher than standard temperature for that altitude. So my airplane, if it had the consciousness I sometimes attributed to it, would *think* that it was landing on a runway a few thousand feet higher than it actually was, or 9,000 feet high instead of 6,000, with a further dropoff in density and performance. Also when I phoned, the wind speed at Truckee-Tahoe was 15 to 20 miles an hour (two things about mountain flying make it different, writes Imeson: the air is thin, and "this thin air is *moving*"), not that much of a challenge to a plane that wasn't performing sluggishly but maybe to a plane that was.

I left Nut Tree in late afternoon, to give both wind and temperature a chance to drop, as they tended to at the end of the day (the sun being an agitator). The climb into the Sierra Nevada was uneventful, unimpressive even. In light haze the mountains appeared flat-sided and greenish gray, and I was almost through the infamous Donner Pass before I realized what it was nowadays, a four-lane highway in a plain brown gorge. Lake Tahoe, though, was radiant, several shades of blue glowing within a ring of mountains. I made one high circuit of it before dropping down into the pattern for Truckee-Tahoe.

The plane ahead of me was told to land on One-Nine, but when it came my turn the operator said Two-Eight. I could see the windsock at the junction of the two runways swinging back and forth, like a dog's tail wagging, favoring first one runway and then the other. On my downward leg the air was rough but not bad, on base leg it was bad but not anything I couldn't handle, or hadn't handled before, coming in over all those dumps and dropoffs back home, but on final approach the process took on a new dimension. As Zero Three Bravo slid toward the threshold, it suddenly sank, so rapidly that it seemed to have been hurled from a far greater height, and before I could get the throttle in, the wheels had hit the runway, with such force that the plane bounced, in a way I had never known it to bounce before, even in my most botched landings; it leapt, *bounded*—a frightened deer, a jumping horse, a fleeing hare, with all the power in its hind parts— described a long arc over the runway, then slammed down again, bounced up, sank, hit, bounced, again, and again—each bounce as high as the last, it seemed—not dissipating any energy in the bounces; they went on and on, while I clung to the stick and pedals as if to the reins and stirrups of a runaway horse—a frightened deer, a running hare, with strength, will, and energy of its own.

Somehow it settled, but immediately, perversely pulled left and headed toward the grass at the edge of the runway. A headline flashed before my eyes, "GROUND LOOP!" and in the story under it was my name. I stomped on my right rudder and gave the engine a quick shot of power and just before the wheels would have left the runway they rolled back toward center stripe. Astonished to find any runway left, I let the plane roll to a stop, didn't brake, then with all deliberate slowness taxied back to the turnoff. Four men were standing along the edge of the taxiway, all wearing, it seemed to me then, identical light-blue jumpsuits, and as I inched past them they stared at my plane with somber expressions. They weren't talking or laughing, just staring. Their faces were eloquent. What had I *done?*

I asked the same question, with only a little whine, of the man behind the Thrifty Rent-a-Car desk in the airport office. He too was a pilot, but one from around there, who presumably knew mountains. "The air was thin so you had a higher landing speed than usual," he began, "and the bounces went on and on. You should have added power and let the plane bang down if you had to [but I thought that would make the bounces even higher and maybe skewed as well!?]. Or if it was slow enough you should have held the stick back [I *had* it back], so far back it was *buried.*" A pilot listening in then told me what was probably the most consoling thing he could have under the circumstances. "Oh, they scrape three or four planes a *month* off that runway! The wind can be blowing three different directions on it at once. I've seen the sock at the threshold lined up straight with the runway at the same time that the sock in the middle was pointing 30 degrees in another direction and a sock at the far end was pointing 30 degrees in another direction. [Three socks!] I've seen socks sticking straight out and *circling.*"

That evening I played nickel slots in a casino on the Nevada side of the lake, and one of my eyelids started twitching. It kept twitching, off and on, for the rest of the evening, a reminder to me of the frail hold I had on life's events, the unexpectedness of things. Overnight the temperature around the lake fell to 31 degrees, according to a weather report on TV the next morning, making Lake Tahoe the coldest spot in the nation. By noon it had risen to 76 degrees, and I and other hard-core tourists took the plunge. Swimming in the lake was like swimming in vodka; the water was clear yet tangy with cold, and I drank it as I swam.

That night the temperature around Lake Tahoe fell to 32 degrees, making it the coldest spot in the nation for the second time in a row. The next morning when I got to the airport I found frost on my airplane's wings. The man at Thrifty had told me that Tahoe was in the middle of a severe drought (presumably the same one that had prompted Harriet to throw bloody rabbit water off her deck) and fire conditions "the worst in the basin since 1923." That fact was hard to appreciate as I stood on the ramp and watched frost melt, bead, roll across my airplane wings, and drip to the ramp. Or as I remembered something I'd read in a promotional brochure for Lake Tahoe, that as much water evaporated from the surface of the lake in one day as the entire city of Los Angeles used in *two* days. So here was this large, deep body of water which threw off around it every day an enormous cloak of dampness, which at night, when temperatures fell, turned to frost, then when day came melted, beaded, rolled across airplane wings, and splashed to the ground.

Reno · Elko

More than divorce, gambling, or cattle, Reno meant, to me and probably most other pilots, air racing. Not the cross-country kind of air racing, as in the Bendix transcontinental of the 1930s and the Powder Puff Derby up to the 1970s, but the closed-course kind, where planes stay in the vicinity of the airport and fly on an aerial "track" around pylons at speeds up to 500 miles an hour, passing within 20 or 30 feet of other planes doing the same thing while spectators watch from nearby bleachers, all aflutter and agog. I had been to the races in Reno (or Stead, a field ten miles north of Reno) a couple of years before, as an agog spectator, having driven, not flown in. This time when I got there, after a flight from Tahoe which lacked the galloping drama of the one into Tahoe ("Plan early morning flights," *Mountain Flying* advised, "to take advantage of early morning air. [T]he air tends to get 'bad' around 10:00 A.M., grows progressively worse until around 4:00 P.M., then gradually improves"), the first of the qualifying heats was still nine days away so I wouldn't be seeing any races, but there *was* a little action on the field as it was being set up for the big show. (Big meant 25,000 extra people—pilots, mechanics, officials, vendors, and ticketed spectators plus an uncounted number of visitors in the parking lot, sitting on deck chairs and camper roofs, watching the races through binoculars and beer haze, for free. But before and after the races, according to an FBO whose hangar sign was peeling so badly it looked like old birchbark, the airport was so neglected he called it "Tobacco Road.")

In "headquarters," a modest white wooden building which could have been an operations shack when Stead was a World War II air base, a teenage boy was sweeping beer cans off the floor. They were last year's beer cans, he said. As soon as the races were over, headquarters was locked until the next year. Outside, another teenage boy, in a cowboy hat, was rolling yellow paint over dark-green bleacher seats, which he said had been borrowed from the Rose Bowl. Three teenage girls were standing on the ramp, painting a Coca-Cola booth bright pink. Two grown men on stepladders were stringing a banner over the entrance that said RENO CHAMPIONSHIP AIR RACES in official race colors, which not surprisingly, considering that half of the competing planes would be ex-military, were red, white, and blue. Back inside headquarters with the sweeper were two electricians, testing a bank of telephones they'd be installing outdoors in a few days, on the judges' tables, where there was nothing now but dirt and sagebrush.

In a hangar back of headquarters were the chief race props, the pylons. They had just been painted and were lying on the floor, drying. The pylons were 45-foot-long aluminum poles with cylinders on one end (the top end), the ones with magenta-and-white-striped cylinders being for the "Unlimited" race and those with orange-and-white-striped cylinders for all the other races. Gone (except for a single one being kept as home pylon) were the tall, black-and-white, pyramid-shaped wooden pylons from the "golden" days of air racing, in the 1930s, when Jimmy Doolittle zipped around them in the Gee Bee ("flying death trap") and Roscoe Turner cut a pylon but still lapped the competition twice, both winning Thompson Trophies and setting speed records.

A race director came in the hangar to check on the pylons. He was a retired Air Force colonel with the rather soldierly name (World War I anyhow) of Jerry Duty. Duty complained about having to design a new Unlimited course this year. Developers had built houses all over a hill under the old course since last year. "If they keep doing that," he said, in a tone that indicated he was sure they would, "we won't know where to go next." The Unlimiteds were the undisputed stars of the Reno races, World War II airplanes, Mustangs, Sea Furys, Bearcats, and Corsairs mostly but an occasional B-26, P-38, Wildcat, Warhawk, or P-39. By definition Unlimiteds could carry any horsepower (as long as it was achieved with piston engines) and be modified in any way their owners could think of to make them go faster: rivets made flush with polished skins, wings shortened, canopies lowered to within an inch of the pilots' crew cuts, engines boosted to two or three times normal power.

"Tremendous hammers throwing all that fuel!" said Duty appreciatively. "The pistons are trying to go out the bottom of those engines!" Some years, he pointed out, half the contestants had to drop out of the race because of engine trouble. "It looks like a demolition derby. There's not a winner but a survivor." Last year a man lost three Rolls-Royce engines, "one right after another. It must have set him back $125,000." The public, though, came less to see winning performances than "for nostalgia," Duty insisted. "We did a survey and found out there's more sentiment for the old war birds than true competition. Some purists even want to know how many *rivets* there are on these things, something us slobs who've flown them [he was a pilot in both World War II and Korea] wouldn't know!"

Having checked on the pylons, Duty decided to check on the sites for the pylons. "I worry," he fretted, "did I make the turns easy enough?" He drove out in his pickup truck with me tagging along. He stopped at a spot well out on the field which was indistinguishable from any other spot except it held an impressive pile of jackrabbit pellets. Duty looked around and burst out laughing. A couple of years ago, he explained, during a T-6 race, a coyote had stuck his head out of a hole about where we were standing. When he heard the T-6s coming, "he ran all the way across the field—just in time to catch them overhead on the back course!"

I laughed too but was thinking the coyote had the right idea. Vamoose! During races at least three officials stood at the base of each pylon to make sure no planes flew inside an invisible line extending upward from the top of the pole—*not* a place I'd like to be standing. The year I saw the races but the day before I got there, a T-6 caught one of its wingtips on the first pylon during the first lap of the first race and, according to the newspapers, went cartwheeling off, flinging the pilot out minus two arms and a leg, then exploded in front of the crowd, which included his mother and three daughters watching from a maintenance pit. "Mayday" calls went out on the radio and yellow flags went up so the rest of the pilots would know to climb to 500 feet, but the race went on. "You don't stop air races easily," said Duty, who had been in charge that day. "If you do, you do it gently, like making love to a porcupine."

Fifteen minutes after the crash, Duty sent a wingwalking act up, to calm and divert the spectators, some of whom were crying, throwing up, leaving the stands. The act featured an inverted ribbon pickup in which a Stearman was to fly upside down above the runway and a wingwalker, attached to the upper wing and therefore upside down as well, was to grab a ribbon that had been strung across the runway between two poles. A nice touch had the wingwalker's wife holding one of the poles. As the Stearman approached the ribbon, it sank slightly (the papers mentioned a gust of wind) and the wingwalker necessarily sank as well, his head making contact with the runway and scraping along it until, said Duty, "there was nothing left above his shoulders except the back of his neck." More spectators cried, threw up, and left the stands, but most stayed put. So did all of the pilots in all of the races that followed. "They took it in their stride," said Duty. "Pilots know what to expect. 'That's the name of the game,' they say. 'You pay your money and you take your chances.' "

This sort of macho cool was another thing the public was nostalgic about and came to Reno expecting to see a lot of. The Unlimited and T-6 races involved elements widely perceived as being in the male domain—speed, noise, large equipment, danger, mechanical know-how, muscle power, big money, grime, physical punishment, one-upmanship. So far no woman had flown an Unlimited plane at Reno, a fact the public was reminded of every year when the pilot of the pace plane, whose assignment it was to lead the Unlimiteds around the track and get them lined up for a racehorse start, released them by radio with the traditional phrase, "Gentlemen, you have a race!" The public would also be reminded of that fact while perusing the race program. The year I was there, fully a third of all the entries in the warplane classes, T-6s as well as Unlimiteds, had names with "Miss" in them, thus perpetuating the time-honored concept of pilot as master and airplane as mistress. "Miss Candace," "Tipsy Miss," "Miss Janice Lee," "Miss Foxy Lady," "Mis-Chief," "Miss America," "Miss-Behavin'," "Midnight Miss," "Iron Mistress," "Miss Everything." That same year, as well as each of the preceding four years, the winner of the T-6 race was a pilot from Texas who had printed on his fuselage, above a hand cupped with the palm facing up—as if to grab a man's balls, presumably the balls of the pilot left behind in a turn—GOTCHA! It was the sort of locker-room gloat that some women might find it hard to participate in. And at the end of each race, when it came time for the winner to receive his trophy, it was an air-race "hostess," chosen from among a dozen or so pretty Air West stewardesses to reign over the meet, who gave it to him.

There was a class of planes at Reno meant to emphasize craft and cunning over power and budget: the midgets. The midgets had engines of no more than 100 hp and could weigh as little as 500 pounds. They tended to fly in zippy, insect-like ways and have names like "Fang," "Boo Ray," "Li'l Quickie," "Stinger," and "Gnat." So far a couple of women had flown Midgets at Reno (a privilege they had to fight for). The fourth class of racers was called "sport biplanes." Biplanes were of course the first air racers of all; in the early days of aviation almost anything that flew had two sets of wings. Pilots were eager then to test their crafts by racing anything, the clock, cars, trains, each other. The first plane my father ever saw was one that flew over his house in Kankakee, Illinois, in 1911. It was racing a train to Chicago. The train won.

Closed-course races didn't last very long—a typical Unlimited heat was over in 15 minutes—so there had to be lots of other action to keep the ticket-buyers happy. There were aerobatic acts, in everything from antique seaplanes to baby jets; flybys by helicopters, military jets, "historic" planes, and new corporate twins; balloon "float-bys" (an elephant was scheduled to ascend this year); parachuting exhibitions; model-airplane demonstrations. Almost anything that could go aloft at Reno did. It was a real *air* show. Which made it hard to stop the freeloaders. The stage was too large. There were no walls.

"See that mountain?" Duty asked, pointing at one (people out this way seemed always to be asking, "See that mountain?"). "They call it 'Tightwad Hill.' People sit all over it and watch the show for free." He pointed again, in the opposite direction, and asked if I saw that hill. It was little more than a rise, with, I knew, a depression on the other side. "Bob Hoover disappears behind that every year," he said, referring to a pilot announcers sometimes called "The Flying Brain Surgeon" because of the precision of his act, in which he did eight-point rolls in a standard business twin with one engine shut down and a loop starting from under 1,000 feet with *both* engines shut down. At one point in his act Hoover flew so low that he disappeared behind the hill, and he stayed back there so long that people thought that this time, surely, he had bought the farm. Always, though, he emerged, one time dragging a string of power lines behind him.

Back at the ramp, Duty introduced me to the "painter girls," Shannon, Sue, and Sonya. "They're high school," he confided loudly.

"High school are more accurate. You get college graduates and they mess up." That night at his suggestion I slept on a cot in the hangar where the pylons were kept—lay canted at the same angle to them as, in another nine days, the polished blade of a Mustang prop would, as the fighter flew knife-edge, screaming beside them—lay within their charged field, their zone of influence, their aura of the quick and the dead, conscious of the sounds they would soon be drawing to them— exploding pistons, propwash blast, wind whistling over flush rivets, the growl of hundreds of horsepower straining to pull thousands of pounds of metal, fuel, and human flesh behind it—lay in the already vibrant air, on my poor cot, a twig in the path of a storm.

The field was quiet when I woke up. Even the sock seemed to be in a doze, hanging limp against the pole. The pole was surrounded by oil drums which were painted the same electric orange the sock was, all lying on their sides, in a circle, half buried in the dirt. Outside the circle were more half-buried oil drums, arranged to form a sort of swastika. Some of the arms of the swastika were bent left, some right, so that pilots flying over the field would know which way to enter the pattern for each runway. It struck me as a good thing, with the war machines that would soon be flying over, that the swastika was at least part left-handed, a Navajo type, one that the gods of Wind and Rain could stand on the arms of, instead of a Nazi *Hakenkreuz,* with all arms bent right.

There was no question of getting breakfast. The only place I could walk to, Louis's Brave Bull Cocktail Lounge, famous for its lethal burgers, wouldn't be open for hours, so I had to make do with what I had in the cockpit, namely an overripe banana on the hat shelf and some leftover iced tea in the Thermos. On flying trips, breakfasts were my best meals, when I could get them. If a worrisome flight was coming up, I'd be extra good to myself at breakfast, French toast *and* eggs *and* sausage *and* hash-brown potatoes, plus regular toast if it came automatically. In the morbid tone I sometimes fell into before flights that concerned me, I'd tell myself this might be the last one and eat up. Comfort food, even at breakfast, however, tended to be fattening, and hash browns were a particular hazard. They came even when you didn't ask for them, and weren't a regional specialty either, like some items that arrived, flourished, and, as I flew on, vanished from my plate—hush puppies, grits, and that slice of spiced apple on the side. Hash browns kept coming and, with an important flight ahead of me, I never could refuse them.

When I left Reno the sun was so low it shone in my eyes on takeoff. Shadows on the ground were ample, and hills appeared more rounded and sensuous than they would later on, the folds in their sides dark, obscene even, some of them, with a sort of hairiness, of sage and juniper, in the cracks. The shadow of my plane trailed far behind it, the shadow squarish and shot through with light, like an ice cube.

To get to Elko I flew first east, straight for the sun, then northeast, southeast, east, south, east, and northeast. "A straight line is not always the shortest distance between two points," Imeson wrote in an endorsement of the practice of "meandering" or "doglegging" in the mountains. I followed a bundle of roads, railroad tracks, power lines, pipelines, and rivers, which wound among a series of short, chopped-off mountain ranges, showing me what I assumed was the low route. On the second dog's leg, I passed the largest alkaline sink in the country, Carson Sink, which looked from the air like a big mistake, old spilled soup (my mind easily straying to thoughts of food). The river that fed it from the north was opaque and a *milky*-green, with *pea*-yellow grass on either side, and beyond the grass bare ground spreading out in all directions a *porridgy* grayish-brown.

After a couple of hours of easy, early-morning cruising around the mountains, I refueled at Winnemucca, where I didn't find breakfast but did find something. "My mother-in-law made them," the FBO said of gingersnaps wrapped in plastic and lying in a box on the countertop with a sign saying 25¢. I dropped in 75¢ and carried three snaps out to the ramp to eat while the FBO was pumping fuel. "A Luscombe!" he had exclaimed when he saw my plane. "Guy on this field has a Luscombe," he said, pointing across the ramp to a red-and-white model 8A, "and he's just learning to fly it. When I see him I'll be sure and tell him that a lady was in here with a Luscombe, and if *she* can fly it *he* surely can!"

The man was all smiles, hadn't a clue. Which reminded me of all those times I'd climbed out of my plane at little airports and caught unguarded expressions on the faces of men hanging around the ramp, as if I were a dog that had just flown in from over the Pole, solo. It also reminded me of an ad I had seen in an old *Vanity Fair* for a Spartan C-3-165 (in 1930 personal planes were evidently marketed like cars). "The rapidity with which large numbers of young women learned to fly is testimony to the fact that it is not difficult to pilot an airplane," said the ad. "Every spirited woman has the qualifications of a pilot, because . . . flying is a science easily mastered."

By reading the engine and aircraft log books for my plane I knew that it had once belonged to another woman. Her name was Lenora K. Eaton, and she lived in Glen Burnie, Maryland. At first she wrote down every time she flew (most owners confine their entries in the plane's logs to repairs, annual inspections, etc.). I liked to think of her thoroughness as enthusiasm. She flew often to begin with, sometimes every day. Some of the flights lasted only a half hour, some only 20 minutes; I figured she lived near the airport. Glen Burnie sounded like a grassy place, and I pictured her taking off early, when there was still dew on the ground. One time she had the right tank drained for water, and I wondered if that was because the plane had lost power when she was aloft, and if she'd been frightened. One time she did aerobatics, and I envied her that (I considered the plane too old for them now). In 1968, after owning the Luscombe only four years, she sold it, and I wondered why. Did she lose that enthusiasm? Or buy another plane? (Unthinkable!) Run out of money to maintain it? I thought of calling her, but when I checked there was no listing under her name in Glen Burnie. Maybe she got married and changed her name. Maybe her husband didn't want her to fly. What was she like, and what did Zero Three Bravo mean to her? Are you out there, Lenora K. Eaton?

As soon as I landed at Elko I hurried into town for breakfast. I was given a table next to one where a man was sitting with two women. I thought they might all be attending a convention. The women were looking at the man adoringly. He was tall and dark, with features that mimicked those of a handsome man (something was missing). He told them how he'd awakened one morning with a sunburn and bleeding from one nostril. "Mother thought I was in a fight," he recounted. "She began to nag me. 'Aren't you worried? Such a silly name,' she said. 'Bunky, Bumpy, Bunny.' " As he talked the women kept on looking at him devotedly while I, a few feet away, consigned as I often was, a single traveler, to other people's conversations, was, in reaction to this one, planning a particularly brutal assault on some hash browns.

After breakfast I went to the Elko County Fair and Horse Show across town. The temperature was 96 degrees and I was wearing my warm-weather flying outfit: loose, short-sleeved, cotton Indian shirt, short shorts, sunhat, and sandals. Almost every other person at the racetrack was dressed for another season altogether, or another metabolism. On and off horseback, in the bleachers and beside the track, women as well as men were wearing long-sleeved, close-fitting Western shirts tucked into the tight belts of their close-fitting denim jeans, cowboy boots (with socks inside?), cowboy hats (some of them of *pressed fur*), and (many of them) scarves tied tight as chokers around their necks. Nobody seemed to sweat, or mind. Rarely had I felt so much the alien, the outsider, so obviously *foreign,* even when traveling abroad.

After a couple of races I went into an exhibition hall to get out of the heat. Everything there was the work of amateurs, crafts made by non-craftsmen, produce grown by non-farmers, pastry cooked by non-chefs. There were macraméd chandeliers on display, framed insect collections, candies made to look like fruit in tiny baskets, sofa throws crocheted by Elda, Lorene, Earlene, and Sefia, vegetables grown by Elva, Vera, Jourine, and Orene. There were jars of lemon cucumbers and chokecherry jelly, and cakes shaped like hats, moths, and bows. All of the baked goods had wedges taken out of them, presumably by judges, who passed over a favorite of mine, the "ghost" cake, which had two eggshell halves lying on top of white icing, the insides of the shells facing up (membranes already turning brown), each half-shell holding, like a pupil in a demon eye, one colored jelly bean.

On the way back to my hotel, I cut through a graveyard. It was on a hill with a couple of shade trees but not many flowers. The stones in it were simply carved, the information on them simply stated. Around the turn of the century a woman and man had three children, "Baby," who died at age one and a half, "Ivy" who died at age 15, and "Pearl," who died, unmarried, at age 40. "Mama" passed away three days after "Papa." That was it. Earlier on this trip, near Fairhope, I had visited another cemetery, a very different sort of place. It was lush with flowers, most of them of the everlasting variety, plastic daffodils and poinsettias, waxy daisies and birds-of-paradise. Flowers in bouquets shaped like hearts, anchors, stars, and crosses with ribbons and pearls strung through them, flowers in wreaths set on tripods, flowers in ceramic planters made to look like booties, wagons, and clowns. One grave had 20 decorations on it, including a large and beautiful seashell (it was a young man's grave). The stone on another grave had a ship carved on it in full steam, the "USS *Sailing Home,*" with the words, "Bon Voyage, My Darling." The stone I liked best marked the final resting place of one Robert "Bud" Cochran, who died at age 56. It showed a tough but appreciative spirit. "We Had Lots of Fun. Edna."

While flying around I had seen a lot of cemeteries, although not as many as you might expect, considering all the dead Americans. One in eastern Texas gave me the willies. On typical rough, dry, scrubby, cowboy countryside lay a formal, dark, neat rectangle, with more dark, neat rectangles within the larger one, all formed by lines of slim, immaculately shaped, needle-topped, green-black trees, escapees from the Italian countryside, gloomy Gothic spires, so that the final resting place of a few dozen East Texans was in an excessively melancholy setting, the graveyard equivalent of a dark Victorian parlor, under trees some may never have seen during their lives.

Elko turned out to be a good place for pilots in at least one important respect: Hours there were more equal than elsewhere. Because it was a gambling town, people in Elko didn't pay as much attention to the commands of nature as they did in other places, where the sun and moon pulled them out of bed at 6 or 7, sent them to trains by 8, to bars at 5:30, to bed by 11. Buses from San Diego and Houston would pull into town at 2 or 3 o'clock at night, and passengers would stumble down the steps and head for the red-lined, brilliantly lit, windowless casino rooms to begin their days, their afternoons, their nights. When I asked the desk clerk at my hotel, which had its own casino, for a ride to the airport at dawn, something I was often refused in other places since there usually wasn't anybody up and willing to drive me at that hour, he didn't even glance up from the paper he was reading. By manner and expression he indicated, "Of course. Any time. Why not. What do you mean *early?*" I played slots that evening in the hotel casino until I had lost five dollars, then tried Keno. As I was standing up filling out a Keno card with what turned out to be 15 losing numbers I felt something . . . *undefinable* . . . at my back. I turned quickly and caught three men in the act, all drunk and laughing hilariously, throwing pennies at my butt. Maybe, I thought, the moon, through the red-flocked windowless walls, had had its way after all.

Crosby · Birds

Elko wasn't a great place for pilots in every respect. The chief pilot told me how guys would fly in, park their planes, go into town and pass a couple of days drinking, eating, dancing, and gambling, spending more than they wanted, losing more than they expected, then come back to the airport and try to sneak off without paying. "We see 'em ducking below the windows of the FSS," he scoffed. Now he made them pay up before going into town. "Our motto is, 'Take the money, honey.'" When not taking the money, I discovered when he took mine before allowing me to get breakfast, he flew helicopters, which seemed good for just about anything around there. He flew skiers to the top of "virgin" mountains by helicopter and picked them up at the bottom ("We guarantee 100,000 vertical feet of snow per week"). He took fish-and-game officials on mountain-goat and mountain-lion censuses by helicopter ("They never see the lions; they just count their tracks in the snow"). He carried meteorologists by helicopter to mountain slopes so they could count the exposed stripes on poles set at various altitudes and thus measure new snowfall. He rounded up wild horses, searched for cattle trespassing on government land, ferried gold from mines to banks, put out forest fires, and rescued horseback riders who'd fallen over cliffs, all by helicopter. He had flown helicopters in Vietnam, I found out, and I wanted to ask him whether flying them in Elko had kept the Vietnam experience alive for him in a way that was painful, and if he wouldn't rather be doing something else if he could, but he went off to get the money, honey, from somebody else and I never got the chance.

With all the variations on the bovine theme to be found in Elko (including the name of my hotel, the Stockman, which sold postcards at the front desk showing its former building being consumed by flames), I got a hankering to see a cattle ranch. I had never seen one outside a movie. I looked over the chart and noticed an unpaved air-strip about 50 miles north of Elko called "Stevens Crosby" and re-membered that Bing Crosby had once owned a ranch. He was long gone, of course, yet I wondered if this could be the one. I asked a briefer about it. Yes, said the briefer, that was Bing's—he called him Bing—ranch. Years before Bing died he sold it to two Italian-American brothers from California, and for some reason they never changed the name. (Stevens was a surgeon who owned a neighboring ranch and died of drink, the briefer said.) The briefer suggested I phone the ranch ahead of time, since the airstrip wasn't near anything and if I just dropped in I might be stuck there. I got the ranch manager on the phone, and he turned out to be from New York too (well, Syracuse) and offered to show me around a little if I came up. Taking off, I wished the Luscombe still had those old saddle seats . . .

On the wide-open, uncomplicated valley floor—few fences, minimal vegetation—I expected to find the strip easily. I thought it would stand out, like a straight scar on a smooth cheek. But where according to the chart it should have been, I didn't see it. I circled the target spot, widened my circle a couple of times, even made a foray in the direction of the foothills, but still couldn't find a strip. I went back to the spot and circled it again, scanning the valley in all directions, and still there wasn't anything. So I decided to be super-methodical, to use the most minuscule clues on the chart—bends in streams and not just the streams themselves, taking into account half-mile, even quarter-mile differ-ences, as if the chart were a map for buried treasure. Ordinarily I didn't have to do that because ordinarily airstrips were so grossly *there*.

First, I went back the way I'd flown in, down the valley to a point well south of the putative strip, then turned and flew north until I came to a pinhead circle on the chart (the town of North Fork) and from there traced a thin, blue line (unbroken and therefore a perennial, if slight, stream) leftward until it forked, whereupon I took the right fork and, as it angled more north than west, roughly parallel to the road, there, just short of the place where another road branched right off the main road, between the right fork and the main road, the air-strip should be . . . but . . . wasn't. *Now* what? I wondered. While making a few desultory passes over the unforthcoming spot I saw some-thing on top of a ridge—what was it doing on a ridge, with all that space on the valley floor?—a dirt strip, a mere widening of a road that ran up onto and down off the ridge, a double-duty 4,000-foot stretch of ground; no wonder I missed it. A white pickup truck was parked beside the road-strip. Custom I knew was to buzz the ranchhouse for a pickup, but with all the slopping around I'd done in the sky I guessed the ranch manager had gotten the message.

He didn't have much the look of a cowboy to me. He was wearing brown lace-up shoes (not cowboy boots), a black engineer's cap with large white polka dots (not Stetson), a mauve shirt with tracings of flowers in the weave (not Western-cut), chinos (not jeans), and eyeglasses with thick, dark rims. He introduced himself, Fred Voorhees, and his fat dog, Bourbon. After chocking my wheels with rocks, he ran—trotted, really—back to his truck, a habit he said he picked up delivering milk back in Syracuse. We got into the truck and drove down off the mesa, the wheels churning up a broad band of dust behind us. Everything in front, though, was in brilliant focus. I remarked on that and Voorhees said, "Most times the air's so clear around here there's nothing to break the rays of that sun. In winter when it's 10 or 15 degrees below zero, you can be in your shirtsleeves and not even know it's cold!"

On either side of the road as we moved along, pigeons and starlings were pecking at the dirt, looking quite out of place, not on their accustomed sidewalks, lawns, benches, and trees, as if they were tiny actors. After a while we pulled up to "headquarters," a cluster of five houses, two barns, and a totem pole. The pole was about 25 feet high, carved with beaks, eyes, and tongues painted orange, yellow, and green. "Some tribe in Oklahoma gave it to Bing," said Voorhees. That was back in the days when Indians did such things, initiated popular entertainers and politicians into their tribes, placed war bonnets on their heads, gave them gifts and honorary Indian names (could they do better than "The Groaner"?), and invited the wire services to take photos. Except for the totem pole, there wasn't any feature at headquarters that would suggest Movie Star, or even Big Money. Crosby had been a "very serious" rancher, said Voorhees. He put the spread together from 22 former homesteads and tripled the size of the herd. He insisted his sons work the cattle themselves, and spent a minimum of two months every year at the ranch himself. Apparently not at all the dumb dude he played in a couple of movies, milking wild cows and crooning lullabies to bulls.

By contrast, the brothers hardly ever came. Two or three weekends a year they showed up, without their families, to fish. "They're just building up equity for their grandchildren," explained Voorhees. They owned several ranches besides this one, including a 20-acre "mini-ranch" near Carmel, California, which featured a horse jumping arena lined with mirrors and a patio with retractable sod roof.

The back of Crosby's house had been turned into a store. In summer the cowhands had to work on the ranch almost all day, almost every day, so they didn't get into town much and Voorhees's wife went in instead, picked up cigarettes, shirts, toothbrushes, shaving cream, etc., brought them back, and sold them in the store. Next to the store was a bunkhouse, where 35 men could sleep but only eight did now, and next to it was the cookhouse, which Voorhees let me see. The dining room had eight small, round tables, each covered with a red-and-white-checked tablecloth on which was set a grouping of salt and pepper shakers and napkin holders, just like in a small-town diner (I had pictured long, communal tables where everyone passed and reached). On one wall hung old ranch equipment, as decoration: ox yokes, leather singletrees, old bridles, headstalls, and branding irons. (With the real ranch visible just outside the window, sharing the sunlight that warmed the panes, the nostalgia seemed somehow inappropriate, self-conscious—and I hoped premature. How much of the past it celebrated was really gone forever?) One of the branding irons, a Px, belonged to Crosby. The brothers' iron wasn't on display, but Voorhees described it as "an ox bow floating over an open heart." In Nevada, that was. In California the exact same brand, $\widetilde{\heartsuit}$, was known as "a Flying M."

Voorhees went out to the truck and we drove off—not, I was glad to see, in the direction of the airport. There was a midday hush on things, and little except the pigeons and starlings seemed to be moving. The only sounds were the whirr of the truck's wheels manufacturing dust and the hum of its engine. Then I thought I heard music. Slow, churchlike. *Choral* music. What? Ahead I could see a wooden fence with a blue pickup truck parked beside it. The door of the truck was open. Maybe a cowhand had his car radio on while he worked, I thought. But choral music? As we drew closer to the fence, the sound grew louder, and it soon became clear this was no radio.

On the far side of the fence were a couple of hundred head of cattle, all milling around, crowded together, wild-eyed, agitated, switching their tails, crying and calling—calves for their mothers, mothers for their calves—some running as they cried, a couple of them mounting other cows. "Sometimes," said Voorhees, "a cow will get so excited she'll ride clear across the corral on the back of another cow." From the fence the sound seemed less like a chorus and more like a band tuning up, with the calls coming in a variety of keys and tempos and an occasional sliding irregular horn-like note breaking through.

Why are they so unhappy? I asked. As far as I could see, they weren't being prodded, branded, roped, injected, or sprayed. "Oh, cows just hate confinement," said Voorhees. He added, "They hate being alone too." Herefords and Shorthorns, some were descended from Crosby's old herds. All summer they'd been grazing on government land in the mountains and now were being brought down and sorted according to their fates. The young bulls would be taken to another pen, sprayed, and "semen-checked," with the "worn-out" bulls going to the slaughterhouse. The older calves would go directly to the slaughterhouse, and the younger calves, as well as the cows, would be counted, then returned to the mountains for more grazing, until another roundup in autumn.

Four men on horseback were in with the cattle. All had leathery faces under wide straw hats. "Mexican," said Voorhees. "My best help has always been Mexican. Otherwise we get the poorest quality of people, drifters running from the law, running from their families, stopping to get a little money before taking off again. Mexicans *want* to work. Most other guys just want to be cowboys, ride horses and work cattle, but Mexicans will do anything you want them to. They'll get down off their horses and fix a broken fence while with the other ones you've got to send a separate crew out."

One of the cowboys was holding a whip made of green-and-white plastic and another had on aviator sunglasses, but besides that they looked to me like cowboys of the old Western-movie West, with big leather chaps and checkered shirts and pointy-toed boots and lassos dangling from their tooled-leather saddles. At one point all four of them rode out of the corral and headed off down the valley, to flush stray cattle out of a willow stand. "Cattle are real smart," said Voorhees. "Smart as hogs. They hide in the willows because they know it's hard to get a horse in there.'' The cowboys rode together, at a leisurely pace, four abreast, backs straight and bottoms swaying in gentle synchrony with the swaying of the horses' bottoms, and as their figures grew smaller and smaller against the backdrop of the mountains, and three skinny brown dogs darted around the feet of their horses, I felt the same uplift as I did at the movies watching the hero ride out of town after rounding up a gang of outlaws; a rough good was loose in the world. These men could be counted on.

One of the dogs ran into the willows. A minute later it ran out, a cow and calf running flat out in front of it. Two of the cowboys galloped after them. After about 100 yards, the cow and calf wheeled and ran off in another direction. The cowboys turned and followed. The cows changed direction again and the cowboys did the same. It was a real *chase*. One of the Mexicans raised his arm and waved it toward the calf. The calf went down in a blur of dust. ''Roping is the test of a true cowboy,'' said Voorhees, watching this. ''You get a lot of drugstore cowboys riding around here with shotguns in their pickup trucks, but those guys couldn't rope a calf if it stood and stared them in the face!''

Lassoing wasn't just a rodeo skill these days, then, and roundups and chases weren't just the stuff of movies. Before Voorhees became Crosby's ranch manager, he had been Stewart Granger and Jean Simmons's manager. They had a ranch in Nogales, New Mexico, which they called Yerba Buena. ''Much fancier than this,'' said Voorhees. ''All white fences, heated pool, beautiful guest house, big modern main house. Quite a showplace. Everything real nice. They invited only a few friends, like Laurence Olivier and John Wayne and Liz Taylor. They wouldn't give the time of day to directors. Mostly they partied with neighbors and local people.''

We heard a sound, something between a buzz and a rattle. It was so penetrating the cow band was reduced to backup. I traced it to a single gold-and-black grasshopper sitting on the top rung of the fence. As I was admiring it I could hear behind me Voorhees talking to his wife on CB radio, telling her he was bringing me to lunch. My heart leapt up—with all the flying around I'd been doing, I didn't get much chance to eat home cooking. As we drove away in the truck, the cows crooning behind us, I wondered vaguely if we'd have beef.

We had lima beans with ham chunks, lettuce salad with bacon, cottage cheese with chives, pickles, applesauce, iced tea, and iced water. Voorhees and I both had seconds but his wife, Rose, just picked. She was tiny, looked as if she weighed less than Bourbon. "The biggest thing about ranching is trying to find a woman who enjoys the life," said Voorhees, with a fond note in his voice. "In summer what with all the haying and putting cattle out and rounding up and shipping and calving, there isn't much time to socialize, and in winter there's so much snow we don't get to see other people, so it can get real lonesome." They lived in a house about five miles from headquarters, built by a retired shipowner who apparently wanted to live the end of his life in some very dry place. Ranching was a good life, though, and a good preparation for another life, Voorhees insisted. "Goldarn it, before young people make up their minds what they want to do, they ought to put in a year or two on a working ranch. You get to know how to doctor animals, how to doctor people, how to overhaul equip-ment—everything."

It was while he was working for Stewart Granger and Jean Simmons that Voorhees learned to fly. They were building up their herd and he was going to cattle auctions in different states. Yerba Buena didn't have its own airstrip, though. Granger was afraid if people discovered the strip belonged to movie actors they'd find a way to sue (run their planes off the end or something). Why, I asked, was Crosby willing not only to have a strip but to put his name on it and leave it open to the public, since he could be considered an even bigger star? "I told him somebody might need it someday and that was that," said Voor-hees. Nowadays he "flew the fences" for the brothers, making sure a gate hadn't been left open or hunters hadn't cut the barbed wire to get their cars through. During roundup he flew to Idaho Falls to pick up parts for mechanical swathers and after roundup he flew around the mountains looking for cattle left behind on government land.

"A plane comes in quite handy on a ranch," he concluded. "Pretty near every ranch has a couple of strips, one near the house and one or two in the summer range. You can't find them if you don't know where they are, though" (or even when you did, I was thinking). Most ranch strips weren't marked on the chart, and most of those that were had an "R" on them (for "Restricted," not "Ranch"). The owners, even when not movie actors, didn't want pilots dropping in and run-ning off the end of the strips, or hunters flying in and shooting up the place.

Climbing out of Stevens Crosby was like rising through gravy. It was the hottest hour of a very hot day, and the functioning altitude of the air a few inches above the runway must have been a couple of thousand feet higher than the runway itself, or at least 8,000 feet. The plane was still close to the runway when the runway disappeared under it, fell away to a sloping ridge face, while the climb needle was quivering only a gnat's-width above zero. Whew! But the engine must have gotten hold of something, because I had 1,000 feet by the time I reached the road. From there I looked back toward the strip and saw Voorhees's white truck still sitting beside it, receding as I advanced, shrinking to a point. Then I saw the point move on its own, infinitesimally, trailing a tiny worm of dust.

What followed was mostly gray. Gray rock, gray-brown soil, grayish bushes, and gray asphalt road running through it all. An occasional colored car moved up the road, and I passed a mountainside that resembled damask, with rich golds and greens interwoven on it. Otherwise, the landscape was drab almost to harshness, dour and unwelcoming. A backdrop, then, for what was to come. About 50 miles into the flight I saw, to the left of my plane and slightly in front of it, and about 100 feet below, four long, white, wavy lines. They were coming toward me in casual groups of two. Mated pairs? I wondered. They were white but the ends of their wings were black. The wings were beating slowly and their necks drooped below the mean line of their bodies, giving them the wavy look. They sailed by just like that—*four whooping cranes!* I was as astounded as if a unicorn had galloped by. I had never dreamed, even in my most indulgent moments, that I'd be flying around in the sky with whooping cranes, sharing space so naturally, so casually, with them, all of us going about our business, passing like cars on a street. They hadn't seemed at all skittish as we passed, the tempo of their wingbeats not altering, although I might be considered a brutish fellow sky traveler—large, rigid, featherless, and noisier than all their kind left on earth honking together at dusk. What did they think I was, a treetop, a mountain peak? I longed to turn and follow them, get another look. I could throttle back, do some S-turns, keep a respectful distance, whatever that might be. If they hadn't minded one close encounter, why not another?

Although I had never dreamed about whooping cranes, which were nearly extinct, I had thought about passenger pigeons, which already were. Several times when I was up flying I had tried to imagine what aviation would be like if the passenger pigeon had survived. The last one, Martha, died in a Cincinnati zoo in 1914, a year when planes were already capable of going 127 miles an hour and climbing to 20,000 feet. The last flock in the wild may have been spotted as late as 1908, in a southern woods, by none other than Theodore Roosevelt, but such holdouts never got in any pilot's way. Less than a century before, however, everyone knows the story, passenger pigeons were the most common birds in existence, outnumbering all other species of birds in the United States combined, and making up a quarter of all the birds in the world. They "darkened the skies as they passed" and a flock could take three days to pass. Their roosts sometimes covered the earth for 30 square miles, and tree limbs broke under their weight (one man estimated two billion birds in a single roost in Kentucky). When the pigeons were shot, poisoned, flayed, roasted alive, trapped, and clubbed, it was in such numbers that there weren't barrels enough to hold them, and piles of carcasses were left to rot in the sun.

So I tried to imagine what it would be like flying today if the pigeons were still around. Against the horizon, a dark spot appears. It spreads slowly, like an ink stain. It keeps on spreading, in the direction I am flying, in every direction, until it covers the sun and most of the sky. A shadow sweeps over the earth, as if a blanket were being pulled over it. Then I can't quite decide what would happen. Would all the birds be flying at the same level, and would I therefore keep flying beneath them as under a low cloud deck, in which case would guano fall like rain from the dark and twittering cloud? Or would the birds fly at several different altitudes, unpredictably, and as soon as the spot appeared would I go down and wait out their passage, as I would for a thunderstorm?

For the unwelcome fact is that not only can airplanes, with their flesh-slicing props and club-like wings, destroy birds, birds can destroy airplanes. Airborne they become rocks, cannonballs, or missiles, depending on how heavy they are and how fast the plane that hits them is going. They can tear holes in wings, twist tailfins, snap control cables, clog engines. A seagull can bring down a jetliner. I heard about a guy once who on his first solo had a vulture crash into his windscreen and get stuck in the broken Plexiglas so he had to go around in the pattern and land with claws and bloody feathers waving in front of his face (how's that for an omen?). As pilots we do our best to avoid hitting birds, but sometimes they are there almost before we know it, appearing out of the blue, so to speak, like something the clouds have thrown off.

Mostly we share the air companionably, if warily, with birds. They are after all our inspiration, our teachers, our fellow travelers. Now and then one will soar along with us, briefly, off to one side or another, then turn on a wing and as we overtake it zoom backward, as if flung. Once in Texas I was airborne on a day of sunshine so strong that the shadow of a bird on the ground was almost as dark and sharp-edged as the bird itself, and bird and shadow moved along together, drawing close to each other as the bird sank or the land lifted, moving apart as the bird rose or the land fell away. Another time, I watched an old man take off in a Piper Cruiser from a small airport in Louisiana on a flight to a nearby swamp "to see if the swan's off her nest." When he returned an hour later, making a landing of such care it could only be described as tender, he reported that the swan was indeed off her nest but he couldn't spot the chicks. "The varmints," he said softly, "prob'ly got the young'uns."

So I let the whoopers be. These meetings, between birds and bird-men, should be ones of respect. The white, wavy lines kept on going south, toward Texas, without me.

Mountain Home · Stanley · Old Baldy

Voorhees told me just before I took off from Stevens Crosby, too late for me to do anything about it, that Mountain Home probably wouldn't have fuel. The FBO up there had pulled out a couple of months ago, he said. Since I was on flight plan for Mountain Home I went anyway, in case Voorhees was wrong, and not long after I broke out of the mountains and saw spread below me the vast floodplain of Idaho's Snake River—much of it covered with a white chalky-looking substance which, on higher ground where it concentrated, looked like snow—I radioed the airport. After all, there might be a new FBO, I figured; at some airports FBO's came and went like tapdancers at an audition; one would get started with high hopes, then a year or two or five years later sink under the standard weight of airport woes, to be replaced soon enough by another hopeful who believed that this time things would be different. After crossing the Snake River I radioed again, then again from closer in, and from right overhead (I could see several planes on the ramp but there weren't enough of them to tell me anything; people parked on closed fields). I didn't get an answer to any of my calls. Still I landed, to be sure Voorhees wasn't wrong, but when I pulled up to the pumps nobody came out of the little white building I assumed was the office to give me fuel, so I assumed he wasn't. Still I walked up to the building, to be *really* sure, and opened the door. Opening that door was like turning on a TV set, instantly a teeming picture, women and men crowded into the room, all talking and laughing, gesturing, moving around, smoking—there was a lot of smoking—one woman kneeling and running her fingers up and down a long bundle of cords, holding each cord carefully, as if it weighed more than it possibly could have.

She was a skydiver. They were all skydivers. A skydiving club had taken over the field and was running it instead of an FBO. Judging by the bright chatter and flushed faces, they had already been up that day (and down) and had a great time of it. I felt a little shy with them, their energy and physicality filling the room. They were braver than I was, I knew. Brave, brave, brave, jumping from planes!

The first plane flight I took after soloing in Africa was in a Beech 23 with the right door taken off so a man I didn't know could jump out of the opening onto a plain 6,000 feet below. I sat behind him, zipped into a nylon jumpsuit to keep off the chill of the slipstream coming through the open doorway. He didn't say anything as we made a long, winding climb to altitude, then he turned to the pilot (Mr. Stewart) and said something brief and so low I couldn't hear it, at which point Mr. Stewart throttled back and the man undid his seat belt, placed both feet on the doorsill, stared downward for a long moment, then, without speaking, leapt, didn't just leap but cast himself, in terrible abandon, I thought, arms and legs held out and uselessly away from his body, back arched and belly exposed—not only exposed but presented, as if he were offering it for impalement—as if he were seeking death, choosing it, *inviting* death—a samurai falling onto his sword, a suttee widow flinging her still-living body onto the pyre.

After the man was well away from the plane, Mr. Stewart banked it in the direction of his fall, so abruptly and so steeply that I thought for an instant I too might fall through the opening even though I had a seat belt on, and together we gazed down the length of the lower wing at what was already only a spot, a dark spot growing smaller and smaller, falling away from us toward a large, brown, and indifferent earth.

I decided them that jumping wasn't for me, but I did like to watch other people do it. On days when the wind was light and the clouds high and scattered, if there were any clouds at all, and some of us were standing around Spring Valley trying to think of places to go (a major challenge for weekend pilots, thinking up places to go and reasons for going to them—eat homemade pie at Orange County? chili at Blairstown? fetch spare parts for Spatzi's Champ at Middletown? see the rebuilt Storch at Warwick?), somebody would suggest going to Stormville and watching the jumpers. At Stormville, we'd stretch out on the grass beyond the runway, jackets under our heads, and gaze up at the sky, trace on it the small dark cross of a plane circling to gain altitude, squint as it approached the sun, listen as the pitch of its engine rose as it rose, watch as the cross grew fainter and fainter until, pale almost to invisibility, it slowed and the sound of its engine dropped, or ceased altogether, and we could see, we *thought* we could see, specks issue from the plane and scatter, as if tossed like seeds, drift away from each other and one by one burst into blossoms—red, yellow, green, black, lit from behind by the sun—then bend out of shape as they touched the ground, collapse, and disappear.

Occasionally I'd be tempted to try a jump myself but would quickly think better of the idea. Once at Stormville while we were watching, a man making his first jump froze with fear and didn't pull his ripcord after exiting the plane as he was supposed to, and from the grass below my fixed-wing buddies and I heard the ground instructor crouched nearby with a walkie-talkie shout into it with increasing urgency, "Pull! Pull! *Pull!*" as the man plummeted; then we too were on our knees and feet shouting into the open air, beseeching him, "Pull! Pull!" as he nonetheless stiffly plummeted until at the last awful moment he pulled. Shortly after that a woman spiraled down to a very hard landing in a parachute that had crossed lines because it had been packed wrong, and not long after *that* a man turned his ankle landing close to a parked car, and shaking our heads we climbed back in our planes and flew home to Spring Valley, committed to staying in our own cockpits behind closed doors. Brave, brave, brave, those who jumped from planes!

Before leaving Mountain Home, I sat through a slide show the jumpmaster threw up on a screen as I passed through on my way to the bathroom, pictures of parachutes gone wrong: a "cigarette roll" (parachute so tightly rolled it could be used like a club), "Mae West" (shroud line crossing the chute and dividing it in half so it looked like a big brassiere), and "squid" (chute opened partway and bulging at one end). By the time I actually took off, there were three hours of daylight left officially, which seemed enough since the flight I had in mind to finish off this day should take a hour and a half, I figured, giving me an hour and a half to spare. (You always had to have something to spare in aviation; it was an exercise in contingencies.) At the last moment, the jumpmaster gave me some advice, about flying, not jumping. "Learn to work the ridges," he said, "starting with the foothills. A Cessna 150 can't make it to Stanley without working the ridges," he insisted, referring to a plane with ten more horsepower than mine. If after working the ridges I still didn't have enough altitude to carry me through the high passes, he said, I should "get right down to the road and fly through in ground effect" (ground effect being the cushion of compressed and therefore denser air under both wings when they are near the ground). I laughed—nobody would get down there with the automobiles, *right?*—but later wasn't so sure he didn't mean it. With people who jumped for fun, you couldn't be sure . . .

As I left the navigational certainty of the road for the foothills of the Sawtooth mountains, which were as lumpily indistinguishable as bumps on the human brain, I kept looking back over my shoulder at the mountains behind me, 50 or 60 miles to the west. With faint alarm I noted that the sun was hanging low over them, and the closer it got the faster it seemed to fall, as if the Old Fireball really *were* an object in our heavens, subject to the pull of our gravity. The air around me was all lit up, but the foothills were already in shadow, and it wasn't long before I had to admit that I wasn't going to make it all the way to my destination airport. Stanley was an unlit, unpaved strip 70 miles up the Sawtooth Valley between 9,000- and 10,000-foot peaks; I'd need daylight clear to touchdown to reach it. "Bear in mind the rapidity with which dusk closes in at the end of the day," *Mountain Flying* advises. "Allow yourself an extra half hour . . ." *Half hour?* As I entered the pattern for Friedman Memorial, an airport at the entrance to the valley Stanley was in, I saw that a couple of the automobiles on the highway running next to the field had their *headlights* on already. Whew! again. More like two hours, thank you, Sparky.

Friedman was near Ketchum, Idaho, which made it Ernest Hemingway, not Bing Crosby, country. I asked about Hemingway when I came back to the airport the next morning. Had he flown out of that airport much? Judging by what I'd read, he continued to love flying even after the two airplane crashes in Africa that messed up his spleen, liver, and kidneys. The people I talked to said he didn't fly out of there much (it was a grass strip back then). He went up a couple of times in a Piper Cub to shoot coyotes from the air, and twice during his last illness he was flown by twin Comanche to the Mayo Clinic, but that was about it. Evidently he carried so much gear with him when he traveled back and forth—guns, ammunition, fishing tackle, game bags, bear rugs, books, dogs, liquor, food, manuscripts, etc.—that he took the train. I asked if it was true, as I had read in a biography of Hemingway, that on one of the flights to the Mayo Clinic he had tried to jump out of the airplane but someone caught him undoing his seat belt and stopped him? Or that during a refueling stop on that same trip, according to the same biographer, he tried to walk into the moving propeller of a plane but the pilot saw him coming and cut the engine just in time? At Friedman they didn't credit these stories of attempted suicide-by-plane, or rather they didn't credit the biographer.

The secretary in the office lent me her truck so I could see Hemingway's grave. The grave was in a cemetery down the road from the airport and easy to find. A stone slab ran the length of it with Hemingway's name and dates on it. A large upright marble cross stood at the foot and a small evergreen on each side of the head. Someone had laid a sprig of red clover on the stone; it wasn't droopy yet, I noticed, so whoever it was must have been there quite recently. I laid a few wildflowers on the slab myself, to make my celebrity-watching post-mortem more acceptable, to myself at least, and as I was standing there, thinking about the cross—how I hadn't expected to find one, ("ghostly comfort," Hemingway called religion)—a young man entered through the gate on the far side and started walking over. He was carrying a bouquet of yellow flowers, which looked as if it had come from a florist's. Without acknowledging my presence in any way, he knelt and placed the bouquet next to the wildflowers and the clover, then stood and stared fiercely at the slab. He was about college age, athletic-looking, and casually dressed. I wanted very much to ask him if Hemingway's books were assigned reading in school anymore, and what he and other people his age thought about Hemingway's bull-fighting, big-game hunting, womanizing, and writing style. But he kept staring at the stone, seemed to be asking his own questions of Hemingway, having his own heart-to-heart.

Earlier that morning, I had visited another memorial to Hemingway, a bronze bust, on a pedestal, in a woods, beside a stream. A plaque on the pedestal was inscribed with lines that Hemingway delivered in this very cemetery, while burying someone else (a Sun Valley publicist). ". . . Above the hills," went the last two lines, "the high blue windless skies. Now he will be part of them forever." By this Hemingway didn't mean flying, but for a respectful moment I pretended he did (just as the plaque pretended the lines were about him), envisioned him floating large and free in the sky, having a lusty laugh at our solemnity and the business with the flowers. The sky he was floating in was a pale and innocent blue, with only a few brushed clouds in it. And there was no wind.

It was noon when I set out again for Stanley, so the sun was about as high above the mountains as it could get. I worked the ridges, or tried to, but the mountains remained inscrutable to me. Where I thought from the terrain and wind the air would be rising, all too often it was static or even sinking. And in places where I expected that little would be happening, the updrafts might be pumping. Working my way up the Sawtooth Valley I felt not unlike a blind explorer, discovering mountains of air only as my plane was being shoved up them, finding valleys only as I was being dragged down into them. Fortunately, mountains of air outnumbered valleys on that expedition, and I made it over the high pass without having to find space between the cars.

In the directory Stanley was listed as having a Unicom but also as being "unattended," a combination I thought odd. When I radioed in, a woman answered. "No reported traffic," she said. "Take a look at the windsock north end of the field." I understood when I flew over why she had left it to me. There was nothing inside the airport fence besides the strip and windsock except one parked plane and a shed too small for a person to stand in, so she had to be in town, but the airport was on a hill so she couldn't possibly see the sock or anything else from down there, even with great binoculars. What, I wondered, could she do for us in town, sightless, that we couldn't do for ourselves, by announcing our intentions and positions on Unicom? Send up taxis? Book rooms? On the evidence of that one plane, there wasn't much traffic, so she must have been doing something else when I called. Making out a mine payroll? Sorting pan lids? Had she ever heard a cry of alarm from some Flatlander caught in the valley as the sun was dragged toward the mountains?

At Stanley I flew a fairly tight pattern because the mountains around it were intimidatingly large, but that wasn't really necessary, more like backing off from a tall person. Seen from the airport the town had a pleasant sort of Northern bleakness to it, mostly rust, green, and gray houses scattered in the middle of a large basin, which it didn't begin to fill. I walked down the hill into town and frittered my day away there, visiting the gem shop, where I bought my mother a picture-jasper brooch with rusty streaks in it suggesting hilltops in drizzle; drinking a Kahlúa-and-cream in midafternoon at the Rod 'n' Gun Bar, where a man with watery eyes rose from a table of people celebrating a friend's birthday and sang with the bar's live country-Western band in honor of his friend, a surprisingly affecting tribute; drinking tea and eating banana cream pie while swinging on a red swing on the front porch of the Sawtooth Hotel and Cafe. The hotel was at the very end of the main street, farthest from the airport, and beyond it was empty basin, then the Sawtooths, with their ragged tops. The swing didn't face that breathtaking view, though. It faced the street. The hotel owner had probably had enough of looking at those mountains and thought his guests would want to see, as he did, what was going on in front of the bar, gem shop, post office, and laundromat.

After dinner, I sat on the swing again, then when there was just enough light left to walk by headed back to the airport. As I was walking up the hill, thinking for some reason about sheep, how pleasant it would be to nudge a few along right then, a peaceful close-of-the-day scene, a truck drove up from behind and stopped. The driver leaned his head out and asked if I wanted a ride. I recognized him: the owner of the gem shop. Also mayor of Stanley. A white-haired man with craggy features, in the Abraham Lincoln mold. A woman was sitting beside him; I recognized her too. The mayor's wife, who ran the laundromat. I said I was going only as far as the airport and didn't need a ride; then I changed my mind. It would be nice to have company, even for a few minutes, I thought. I climbed in and they drove me the last few hundred yards to the airport, kept on driving across the field until their headlights were shining on my plane, so I could see to walk to it. By then the sky was almost dark, and there was no moon.

Politely, sort of ex officio, the mayor asked why I had come to Stanley. Friends in California had told me the Sawtooths were beautiful, rugged, and great for hiking, I said, and didn't have grizzly bears or rattlesnakes, the usual drawbacks of wilderness. Maybe it was the mention of "wilderness" that set him off because he started talking about how the federal government had turned 1,250 square miles of the Sawtooth Mountains into a National Recreation Area, despite the fact that almost everybody who lived around there objected to it. "They could care less what we was content with out here," he grumbled. The hearings had been a joke; "I knew we was getting railroaded when they gave me three to five minutes to talk for everybody out here while the Sierra Club from New York got 15 to 20 minutes," he said. "When I complained they said the Sierra Club represented more people!"

He switched off the engine and lights and settled in. "We've got these loop roads on top of the mountains, and you can see a long ways from there, like you can in your plane," he said, "but the Government won't let anybody up there anymore, except on foot. Now, you take senior citizens and cripples, *they* can't see the country on foot. You got to let everybody have a recreation area, not just one or two backpackers!" Equally riled, his wife put in, "We own an acre of land in there [the recreation area], but the Government won't let us build on it or sell it to anybody except them and they won't give us near what it's worth either. They won't even let us cut firewood for our own use!"

They talked on, about many things but really one thing. The freedom to log in the parks ("People can't do what they've been doing for 50 years"); to mine in the parks ("It's a fine thing when you can't use your land as you see fit"); to ranch in the parks and carry a gun ("We're wide open out here, the sheriff's 50 or 60 miles away, we got to have a gun"). They talked with great feeling, and openly, as people often do at night, in darkened automobiles. Listening to them, I squirmed inwardly, having always been on the other side of all their arguments, in favor of setting aside as much wilderness as we could possibly get our hands on, of keeping commercial interests out of the parks, of banning handguns, shotguns, any kind of guns not used for hunting and maybe some of those. I was a Sierra Club member and from New York City. But now that I was sitting shoulder to shoulder with the opposition, I was beginning to get an idea what it was like to be on the receiving end of some good environmental moves. I was surprised to hear from them that 75 percent of Idaho's land already belonged to the federal, state, or local government. "Trouble is," said the mayor, "Idaho's got two senators and two representatives in Washington, but California's got 40 and back East they got *hundreds.*"

In response all I could do was assure them how grateful we were back East for the sacrifices they were forced to make on our behalf and how much it meant to us knowing the wilderness was there even if we never saw or used it. Later I got to thinking that perhaps they and I weren't so far apart after all. *Should* the backpacker have all the rights? I asked myself. Shouldn't pilots be allowed to fly over wilderness areas occasionally, unchastised, even if now and then they disturbed the purity of the backpacker's experience, since the view from the plane was likewise special and unduplicatable and enriching?

The headlights snapped on, outlining the Luscombe's spinner aggressively against the dark, and they drove off. I made up my bed by flashlight. I made it up in the usual layers, but instead of putting the space blanket on the bottom, I put it on top, thinking there might be dew. When I was finished I pulled the whole thing out from under the wing so I'd have a wider view of the stars. No need that night to be right next to my plane; there'd be no heat-seeking rattlesnakes or meat-seeking grizzly bears coming around. No crazed Manson druggy types either, the locals apparently wholesome. And, judging by the clarity of the stars, there'd be no rain. I did hear coyotes howling somewhere in the distance but figured they wouldn't be showing up. Too far away. Their high-pitched howls sounded rather pleasant from the airport grounds, like a delicate bedtime tune.

I was right about the grizzlies, rattlesnakes, rain, locals, and coyotes but wrong about the space blanket. When I woke up I discovered dew under the blanket instead of on top, the very principle, I realized too late, for collecting water when you've crashed in a desert and have a plastic sheet and the pep to scoop out a hollow in the sand. Not only was there dew under the blanket but ice—several shards of ice!—on my sleeping bag. I couldn't believe it! I didn't remember ever feeling so cold. The top of my head, sticking out of the bag, was being scraped raw by the cold, but the rest of my body, still inside the bag, was suffused with a dreadful damp chilliness which had already sucked nearly all the blood-warmth out of it. I lay there in the near-dark, unable to choose between getting out of my bag and freezing and staying in it and freezing. It was the polar opposite of the frying-pan-and-fire dilemma.

At last, facing the fact that nothing was about to change soon, since the sun hadn't even appeared over the horizon, I leapt from my bag, issuing a cry that would have startled a coyote, and ran to the plane (another reason, one I hadn't thought of, for sleeping right next to it), madly pulled out bags and boxes and went rummaging through them, looking for the few scraps of clothing that might, if worn all together, pass for winter gear—two cotton T-shirts, cardigan sweater (thin), cotton jacket, cotton slacks, cotton socks, cotton neckscarf (folded wide), and sneakers—then pulled them on, all of course as cold as the air around them, and ran down the hill toward Stanley, my teeth clacking like a set of Halloween dentures.

In the Sawtooth Cafe, which at that ungodly hour was already open and half full, I lifted a mug of hot tea not to my mouth but to my nose, so the steam would rise up my nostrils, which seemed a more direct route to my frozen core. I managed to make breakfast last an hour and a half, during which time, as at Lake Tahoe, the sun vanquished winter and produced what to innocent eyes might seem to be a summer day. I walked back to my plane, filled a daypack from the scattered bags and boxes, then walked through Stanley again and out to a road on the other side which led to a mountain with marked trails. I faced traffic and composed my face and body. For the large campers, with what I assumed were families in them, I stood tidily erect and kept a serious look on my face—a schoolteacher on vacation, perhaps, out collecting ferns. For the smaller vans and cars, more likely to have young adults in them, I loosened my stance a bit, wore a little smile, made sure they saw the backpack—alone because I wanted something calm after all the surfing.

There wasn't much traffic that day but what there was went right by me. People didn't even seem to be glancing in my direction. I stood, trying to look appealing or at least harmless, for almost an hour and a half, then began to feel the way the drivers apparently saw me, like a marginal, oddball loner of a creep who might foul their car or frighten their children. Then I got mad, at the big shiny campers with enough space in them to carry the cast of a Broadway musical, all barreling along, their drivers (husbands, fathers) sitting up high on their seats, not deigning even to look at me, less than a stone by the road. But the VW's and old Volvos went by just as fast, just as inevitably. I wanted to shout at them all, "Hey! I'm just as good as *you* are! I'm respectable! *I own an airplane!*"

Just as I was thinking that the only hiking I'd be doing would be back to Stanley, a beat-up car with Minnesota plates pulled over to my side of the road. A pale woman sitting next to a pale man said in a soft voice that they were on their way to Redfish Lake to fish and would that be far enough? I spent most of the time it took us to get to Redfish Lake wondering why it was these two—pale, soft-spoken, subdued, timid-seeming Northerners—among all those who had seen me on the road that day, who had been the ones to pick me up.

The hike turned out to be worth the psychic wounds of hitchhiking. Some bush was putting out a sweet scent which wafted over the trails as I walked. Small, brown birds burst out of the shrubbery ahead of me, darting off left, right, as if doors were being opened. All around I could hear the metallic chirps of gray squirrels; one was lying on a giant log in the sunshine, its legs clinging to the sides, as if it might roll off in a moment of bliss. All day I came across only one other bunch of hikers; I had three lakes all to myself. One was so still its surface duplicated perfectly the frame of yellow aspens growing around the edge.

Yellow: more evidence, as if I needed any, of how the mountains cut the sun's tenure short. A tougher lesson than temperature shifts, though, the toughest so far in the mountains, was coming up. When I got to the airport in the morning, after a cozy night at the Sawtooth Hotel, the air was as still as it had been over the mountain lakes. During preflight, I felt a faint wash over my hands and face—not much, just a touch. By the time I was ready to go, the touch felt more like a shove. On climbout I encountered a few lumps, and just before the high pass one heavy whack, but these were smiles of a summer night compared to what was waiting for me after the pass. Emerging, the plane went berserk, shot up, dropped down, lurched, tilted, rattled, rolled, did a dance of the criminally insane, the demon-possessed, beat against invisible walls and floors. I broke out in sweat so heavy I had to put a Kleenex under my hand to keep a firm grip on the stick. Worried that the Luscombe might come apart in the turbulence, I pulled back on power, although what I wanted more than anything was to hurry on out of there. There was nothing to do, though, no chance of escape, no rescue; I had to ride it out, alone. You are never so alone as in an airplane, more alone even than in a boat, and definitely more alone than in a car, nobody but nobody can get to you (forget those old movies where pilots jumped off wings into other people's cockpits), you are separated from all other people on earth by a sea of uncrossable air—a condition that I often aspire to. But this sea was roiling, tossing, making me sticky with fear.

The wild ride lasted all the way to Friedman, where the sensation of wheels contacting solid runway felt like a big bear hug to me. An instructor in the office was telling her student when I walked in, "If it's this bad in the morning, forget it!" She too had been surprised by the turbulence. She was a tiny, wiry, gray-haired woman who radiated a formidable amount of no-nonsense energy, and after the student left I asked her what I might do with this extra day I'd been handed by the demons of the mountain (I'd already done Hemingway, I told her). Without hesitation she said, "Climb Old Baldy," referring to a mountain a few miles up the valley, which might or might not have given me a punch as I passed. If I did climb Old Baldy, I reasoned, it would be the second day in a row I'd be using legs and feet not accustomed (recently) to doing anything more demanding than pushing on a couple of rudder pedals. (Aviation, despite its tough-guy image, is pretty much a sport for non-sportsmen.) But she put me to shame with her can-do peppiness, so I got another daypack together and hitched a ride with her to the base of Old Baldy.

On the way there she told me she did her instructing in a Cub, and mostly on skis. In winter there was always snow in the valley, and she liked to "bushwhack" around, landing on farms, pastures, and unplowed taxiways. One time she put down on the Sun Valley golf course but couldn't get off because the snow was too deep. The plane sank a foot or foot and a half in the snow. "When I tried to blast it off with power it wouldn't go," she said, "so I taxied it back and forth ten or twelve times to pack the snow and make a little runway." Another time, "the snow was so new it was still on the trees" and so deep it hid a fence running across the field she was aiming for, and as she passed over the fence a post ripped open the belly of her plane. She got some duct tape out of the back, taped the belly shot, and "flew it like that the rest of the winter." So there, Hemingway.

From the base of Old Baldy, a wide path had been cleared through the trees for skiers. I hiked up that and, as I did, tried picturing the skiers swiveling down in their padded jackets, goggles, and Martian boots, but they seemed no more likely creatures to inhabit this place than British redcoats with muskets. Sunlight beat down on the dusty moguls, grasshoppers catapulted out of the dry grasses, thistle and clover crunched under my sneakers. The path was steep; within minutes I was panting for breath. I started moving on the diagonal, like a novice skier. Joggers ran past me, effortlessly, upward. A boy and his dog rocketed by, disappearing into the woods within seconds. I made it to the halfway point, stopped, and sat on a rock, ostensibly to eat my lunch but really to quit. By then I was about 2,500 feet off the valley floor, an altitude I often flew at. The view seemed grander somehow than it would have from a plane, or more sweeping. Maybe it was because I wasn't looking at it through the usual frame of struts, cowling, and wings, I thought. Or maybe it was because I had put so much effort into achieving this view—"stereognosis," you perceived better what your body had experienced. Or maybe it was because I was linked to the view physically, my feet touching the ground, which ran downhill and across the valley and up the other side until it formed another peak, a mile away but still connected to me, in one long, unbroken swoop. Or maybe it was only that I was sitting on solid rock, wet with the sweat of exertion, not fear.

Southern Butte · Rexburg · Jackson Hole

And now for something completely different, or so I thought. Between the foothills of the Sawtooths and those of the Grand Tetons lay a long, flat, high stretch of ground, 100 miles or so of what looked on the chart like beard stubble, a fine gray stippling with a single word printed on it over and over: *lava*. Lava lava lava lava lava. The lava desert of the Snake River plain. A few farms were clustered at the mouth of the valley Friedman and Stanley were in—"huddled" might be a better word because beyond them the earth was almost unremittingly gray and barren. As I set out across it, on an eastward heading, the surface grew increasingly jagged, pocked, and ropy, increasingly *wicked*-looking. Phrases from my childhood kept popping into my head: "Giants' footprints." "Mud pies." "Witches' brews." "Dragon skin." With all its cones, crags, pits, bombs, and sinkholes, it wasn't a place to run out of gas or throw a rod any more than mountains were, I concluded. It might be flat on the large scale but definitely not the small.

Reasoning along those same lines, the State of Idaho had built six emergency airstrips on the lava plain, I was told, scattering them around so that a pilot making the crossing and running into trouble might be able to reach one of them. On my own crossing, I became curious about the emergency strips, wondering what they were made of, how rudimentary they were, and decided to try landing on one. I was using Big Southern Butte, an old volcano cone halfway across the flats, for navigation, just as stagecoach drivers and fur trappers on mules used it on their long cross-country treks, and since there was an airstrip beside it that's the one I chose. The strip was easy to spot, each corner outlined with a neat L of whitewashed rocks. The surface was a mix of grass and gravel and the length 2,600 feet. Not bad, I decided, and dragged it, looking for holes or rocks. Not seeing any, I came around in a standard pattern, as if I were at a busy airport and taking my turn.

As the wheels touched down I heard a clanking—rocks after all! I braked, jumped out, and checked the prop—no nicks. Then I checked the strip. There were larger rocks than I expected but mixed in with them were other, darker nuggets, about the same size and almost as hard: sheep droppings. How long, I wondered, did it take for sheep droppings to turn hard as stone? Or, to put it another way, how long ago had sheep grazed on this runway?

Certainly there were none around now. The place—in fact the whole area—looked deserted. At least 70 yards off was a fence, an empty corral, and 20 or 30 yards past it was a wooden shack missing some of its boards, and 100 yards or so past that was a decrepit barn. Widely separated from each other, the three structures looked just plunked down on the long, empty, flat stretch of plain, with nothing connecting them visually, such as a path, pole, or bush. It was a mournful sight to me, an Easterner. All that space for the wind to howl around!

Since I was on flight plan I had to get moving again, but before I took off I decided to peek in the shack. The bottom third of the front had been ripped away, yet the door was shut, as if that would make a difference. It must have made a little difference to me because I hesitated a second or two before opening it. Inside there was a single room with spare furniture, a wooden table, straight chair, and metal cot with holey mattress on top. The only other thing in the room was a piece of paper tacked up on one wall. It had handwriting on it.

"This cabin is for your convenience," it said. "Please don't . . ." Then I noticed a smaller piece of paper tacked up below the first, also with handwriting on it. "It's too bad some people don't take responsibility for what's been trusted to them," it said. "They take advantage and don't leave . . ." I heard something. A creak. A loud creak. Out there in the middle of nowhere and I heard a creak!

It couldn't have been wind; there was no wind. I froze in place, didn't move, then felt something press against my leg, oh my God—I whirled around and saw, on the floor, body wriggling, ears flopped forward, eyes directed up at my face, a long-faced, short-haired little *puppy!* I wasn't relieved, though; I was spooked. Was someone between me and my plane who didn't want me trespassing?

The dog leapt up, hit my thigh and fell back to the floor, leapt again and bounced off my thigh, fell to the floor, took one of my pants legs in his teeth and yanked on it, let go and leapt again, fell to the floor. I just stood, watching from some odd inner distance. The only sounds in the room were the thud of his feet as they hit the floor, and the rush of his breathing—and mine, both excited.

I noticed something under the table I hadn't on the way in. It had a hoof on it, and hair, and dried blood. It was the leg bone of some large animal. Then I moved, fast, out of the door into the sunlight, the dog following, diving at my ankles. Nobody stood between me and my plane; the place was as empty as before. I walked briskly to an outhouse behind the shack, and while I sat on one hole the dog jumped onto the rim of the other, and from there onto my lap, and from there at my face. Every time I lifted him down he jumped back up and squirmed against my chest, his whole body wagging.

Hungry, of course, I thought. There couldn't be much meat left on that hairy leg bone. I went back to the plane and found some cheese and crackers, carried them to a spot halfway to the shack, and laid them on the ground. As soon as the dog bent over them I started walking toward my plane. I got within 20 feet of it when he looked up and started running, leaping at me again. Maybe he doesn't like cheese, I thought, and dug through my things again and came up with a granola-mocha-nut bar I'd been saving for emergencies, brought it to the same spot and laid it down with the cheese and crackers. Slowly I worked my way back toward the plane and this time got within ten feet of it before the pup came running, then I too ran and made it inside and closed the door just as he leapt at the doorway. He fell to the ground and stayed there, sitting by my left tire, looking up at the window with big, beseeching eyes. He began to wail.

Oh what a sound! I felt like a worm. What did he want from me anyway, except attention? If somebody was looking after him (that hairy leg bone), why was he so crazy-lonesome, so needy, so *wild?* I had never seen a dog so importunate, so determined. And why would someone keep a puppy in a deserted sheep station anyway? Not for protection, surely; there was nothing to protect here now. Besides, he was too small for that job. Had somebody dumped him here with a bone for a last meal? But who would do such a thing, knowing he couldn't live off the land like a coyote? Was someone training him to be a sheep dog, perhaps? But why in a place that didn't have sheep and hadn't had any for a long time?

The wail became a keening, but the dark, glistening eyes stayed fixed on me. Of course I couldn't take him with me. He'd bounce off the walls of the cockpit, get mixed up with the stick and pedals, jump at my head. Besides, he wasn't mine to take . . . Or was he? I looked out at the face under the floppy ears and felt sick at heart. "Clear!" I yelled (procedure hardening my will), pulled on the starter, glanced out again to make sure the dog hadn't moved ahead into the prop arc, did a quick pre-takeoff check—gas (left tank on), instruments (oil pressure in the green), controls (stick forward indicating full travel, right, left, back)—*what?* I couldn't get full back stick! The elevator was stopping halfway! I looked out again, toward the tail, and saw to my immense distress that the pup was standing on his hind legs with his front legs up on the horizontal stabilizer. He was shifting his hind legs, clearly trying to get them up on the tail too. *He wanted to come along!* He knew what planes were for, then, that they went places, were vehicles, like automobiles. So had a pilot dumped him here? But what pilot would do such a thing?

I nudged the throttle in and the plane crept forward; then, looking back, I saw that the pup's front legs had slid off the horizontal stabilizer and he was down on all fours but still at that same spot, watching the plane. I shoved the throttle all the way in and went rolling down the runway, broke ground, and climbed away. I didn't turn and look back until I'd reached 500 feet, and then what I saw was a small, stationary light-brown triangle at the very spot where I had shaken the pup off, which meant that he was sitting, looking up, not eating, watching me go.

Oh, what had I done? *Doomed* him? Was I his last, accidental hope? Maybe he belonged to some hermit, I thought in an effort to console myself, an old guy who lived back of the butte and would swing by now and then and toss him a bone. But why would even a hermit do that, keep a dog where he wasn't company? And if somebody was looking after him, why was he so frantic, so imploring? I should have tied him to the top of my boxes, let him squirm and howl for the next 80 miles, and hoped for the best. He'd have loved me for life. He had done everything to win me. I kept on going, though, toward Rexburg airport, with nothing more in my cabin than his frenzied spirit.

At Rexburg I told the FBO right away about the dog. He had nothing to say, and I couldn't tell from his expression if he thought the situation odd or not. He didn't say it *wasn't* odd. I realized I had hoped that he'd be roused to instant pity by the story and offer to send somebody—a student on a cross-country, perhaps—to stage a rescue, in an act of local caretaking. He didn't even offer me an explanation, based on a knowledge of sheepherders which had to be superior to mine. He just looked off and said, "Hmm." There *was* something he wanted to talk about, though. He took me into a hangar next to the office and pointed to a blurry green-brown line on one wall about level with my throat. "This," he said, "is how high the water got the day the dam broke." From his expression it was obvious that he hadn't thought he'd have to answer the question, What dam? The *Teton* Dam, he said. It was on the Teton River, about 15 miles northeast of the airport. "We knew something was going on when one of the guys flew over before breakfast and saw a bulldozer pushing dirt into a hole," he said. "By the time the announcement came over the radio at 11 o'clock we were already flying planes out." He led me over to the office door. "I was standing right here when a wave came rolling down the runway, in about a five-foot crest."

That was almost a year ago, on a Sunday. On Tuesday the *Blackfoot* (Wyoming) *News* put out a special edition on the flood, which the FBO showed me a copy of. A schoolteacher on vacation with his family had been standing on a lookout taking photos of the nation's largest earthen dam when he got a big surprise. The *News* printed two of his color photos. The first showed a slope with a hollow in it and a bulldozer lying on its side in the hollow and a man standing above the hollow looking down into it. The second photo showed a dark patch in the hollow and water pouring through (bulldozer and man gone now) with enough force (judging by the cloud) to generate steam.

"Wet spots" had appeared in the dam the night before, the *News* recounted, a not unusual occurrence, and as usual the spots had been plugged with packed earth. This time, however, they didn't stay plugged. They grew larger and more of them appeared until at 10:20 the next morning the schoolteacher saw a "whirlpool of water" burst through the dam with "a roar . . . like at the bottom of a waterfall." Behind the waterfall came a quarter million acre-feet of stored water, which poured into the river and overflowed its banks, ripped up cottonwood trees on either side of it "like matchsticks," rushed out over beet, hay, and potato fields and turned them into boiling lakes, formed a tidal wave which drove cows ahead of it until they were stopped by fences, at which point it drowned them, whirled a couple of teenage fishermen off a bank and bore the lifeless body of one of them 17 miles downstream while ramming the still-living body of the other against a pile of floating logs, breaking his ribs in the process, then pushing him into a tree, to which he clung, shouting to no one who could hear him, "I'm dying, I'm dying."

Floodwaters rolled into the riverfront towns of Sugar Hill, Shelley, Wilford, and Rexburg, knocking out a church wall and shoving a piano and organ through the hole "like toys," scooped up sewage from a treatment plant and distributed it around town and countryside, snatched a pair of men's pants off a chair in the upstairs bedroom of a house in Wilford and whisked them away, never to be seen again, at least not by the man who owned them, who claimed he had left $3,600 in cash in one of the pockets.

Meanwhile, at Rexburg airport, water swept a hangar off its foundations and bore it along until it was stopped by a line of light poles, tore open a wall of a second hangar and slid two airplanes out, broke up and then carried off more than half the runway and taxiway asphalt. When the water receded six hours later, a farmhouse was sitting on one end of the runway and logs from an upstream mill were lying on top of the crushed fuel pumps. The golf course on one side of the airport was littered with the bodies of dead cows and the trailer court on the other side hadn't a single trailer left in it. One of the planes that hadn't been flown out in time but had been tied down was discovered a mile away, sitting in a farmer's field, right side up.

In a manner that showed the irony was appreciated, the *News* reminded its readers that the Teton Dam had been built for flood control in the first place. The federal government, which may not have appreciated the irony, was in the process of rebuilding it for flood control, using the same earthen construction. I changed my flight plan to Jackson Hole to approach from slightly farther north so I could take a look at the dam on the way. Nearly a year after the flood, it was still represented on the chart as a solid black line with blue water backed up ten miles behind it. When I saw it from the air I was reminded of what a waitress at the Sawtooth Cafe had told a couple of construction

workers at breakfast the morning I came to warm up. She had visited
the dam soon after it was built, and it looked to her then as if "somebody was playing in a sandbox and pushed the sand into a pile, like a
little kid." It still looked that way, I thought, except the kid had gotten
mad and kicked the sandpile. Bulldozers and trucks were parked here
and there on the slope and workmen were standing about, but if anything had been altered I couldn't see evidence of it. More than half
the slope was gouged out, in a vicious-looking way, the gouge black
with shadow at midday, and jagged at the edges.

"Happiness is a Luscombe on a clear day in Jackson Hole," wrote
Sparky Imeson in my copy of *Mountain Flying*. From his office windows
he could see my plane parked out on the ramp, the three Tetons ranged
like a frieze behind it. A half hour earlier I had flown in through the
8,431-foot-high Teton Pass, wary *and* cautious *and* vigilant, but the air
in there was so silky I just slid on over, with the leisure to note the
interesting charcoal-rubbing effect of dark conifer trees against the
steep, gray rock face. In person Imeson seemed almost as stern as he
sounded in the book—he had hooded, appraising eyes and never
seemed to smile—but the appearance of the office suggested otherwise.
On one wall was a rack with more than 20 coffee mugs on it. When I
commented on the high number, he said, "We have jam sessions
during storms," and I pictured a warm scene of huddling pilots,
exchanging hangar stories as lightning flashed outside. Hanging from
the ceiling beams were shirttails that Imeson had decorated himself,
and they were the most celebratory I had ever seen. Most had drawings as well as writing on them, in different-colored inks, of smiling
airplanes and shocked birds, Superman chasing "Superpilot,"
Snoopy in helmet and goggles with feet revving into a blur, a mustachioed man in a long, black cape whispering spy-like behind his
hand, "It's No Secret; I Soloed." Some of the shirttails had joke
nicknames on them ("Amelia Chickenheart") and some had slogans
done in shadow lettering ("Fly Taildraggers!"). Suspended like that
in long rows from the dark, wooden ceiling beams, each square with
its individual legend, they might have been banners displayed in a
medieval hall, the ragged escutcheons of knights who'd gone forth
at dawn to do battle with the enemy, the enemy in this case being

clouds stuffed with rocks, interior valley fogs, and winds racing down canyons.

On the wall with the mugs, in addition to a framed Indian head in profile Imeson had made entirely of spent bullets, was the stuffed head of a Bighorn ram. It wasn't mounted on a shield or anything so it looked as if it had just burst through the plaster wall from the next room, to sniff the air of the office. "That's my ram," Imeson said of it. He meant it was his only ram; he wasn't going to shoot another. "I *got* my ram," he said. He had got it in Crystal Creek Canyon; Bighorn sheep, he explained, didn't come around the airport. Other animals did, though. Antelope, for instance, drank from the irrigation ditch off the approach end of One-Eight, and "except for running across the runway every now and then, they don't bother you," he said. During hunting season moose fed under final approach for One-Eight. "They're very smart. They seem to know when the hunting season is on. They even sense when there's an *extended* season and come in." But sage chickens! They didn't seem to sense anything, even an airplane bearing down on them. "You have to land about a thousand feet long to keep from hitting them," said Imeson. "They congregate on the north runway and won't hurry for love or money. One night a Convair was on the taxiway and they never budged and the pilot didn't see them and afterward he had to get his engine changed. Those chickens weigh eight to ten pounds each."

The mountain-flying school at Jackson Hole was the only one in the country approved by the FAA, according to Imeson. He and his father, Paul, ran the school. Their students were encouraged to take at least one hour of aerobatic instruction (the idea being presumably that if they knew how to do rolls, loops, hammerhead stalls, etc., they'd be better able to handle what the FAA calls, rather coyly it seems to me, "unusual attitudes," which mountain air could throw them into). Students were also required to read Sparky's book and to take at least five hours of instruction in tailwheel airplanes, since taildraggers are the aircraft of choice for high-mountain strips, which can be short, rough, and eccentric.

"Kinky Creek at Darwin Ranch," Sparky said, describing one, "is 100 feet higher at one end than the other, so no matter how the wind is blowing you have to land uphill and take off downhill. First you have to chase the cattle off the runway." At Howard Lew's, he went on, "you land at the bottom of a dip, but from there you can't see the other end of the runway so you roll uphill and turn left and you try to stop because the runway goes down again and it gets hard to brake without nosing over."

Approaches to mountain strips could be quite eccentric too. (Says *Mountain Flying,* "The pattern must conform to terrain vagaries.") At "Maytag," a strip so called because of the vibration its corrugated surface induced in any aircraft managing to squeeze onto it, "final is in a canyon which runs diagonal to the runway so you can't turn to line up with the runway until the last moment," and at Box Y Ranch, "you're over a mountain on downwind, in a canyon on base, and between two trees on final, and to get between the trees you have to do a steep slip since the plane's wingspan is wider than the space between the trees. That's better than going in the other way, though; there's a cliff there."

The Imesons did other things with mountain flying besides teach it. They rescued lost climbers, searched for fires in the Bridger-Teton Forest, dropped supplies to sheepherders confined to high plateaus in summer, took scientists out to track radio-collared elk, and flew "air ambulance." An air ambulance was a plane with the back seats taken out to make room for a stretcher. The usual person on the stretcher was a man with a heart attack. Heart cases they took to Fremont County, Wyoming, bone-break cases to Salt Lake City, and eye cases— "like a steel splinter in the eye"—to Idaho Falls. By land it took 6½ hours to get to Salt Lake City, by air less than an hour. They could always get through without shaking up the patients, no matter what the weather, Sparky said. When I expressed skepticism he insisted, "There's always a smooth layer. It may be at 17,000 feet, it may be at 7,000 feet, but it's always there. All you've got to do is find it."

Sparky didn't go up in a plane until he was 22. The summer before he was going to enter dental school, his father took him along on a flight to check on an elk-hunters' camp. After they came down, he gave up dentistry (although he seemed to have retained an interest in the hazards posed by cherry pits). While we were talking, Paul came into the office, took a cup off the rack, and filled it with coffee. He was a chubbier, more peppery man than Sparky. He too had a lot of things to say about mountain flying, although he'd never written them down. "Always a challenge," he noted, "never the same day to day. Some days there's no lift in the canyons and the air's so dead you get pushed down to the treetops—I've had to track elk from right over the tree-tops—then when you do get lift you can't be sure where it'll come from. Sometimes it turns out to be the opposite of where you assume from the prevailing winds it's going to be [amen!].''

The worst turbulence Paul ever encountered in the mountains was on a day when there shouldn't have been any. "It was 20 degrees below zero out," he recounted, "and usually when it's 20 degrees below zero the air's real still, but this time the air suddenly started pushing the J-3 [Cub] up and down, up and down, so fast it almost passed me out. I thought these old *wings*'d fall off. I was so scared I don't know what I did. I thought, 'They're going to come looking for me.' The whole thing lasted four minutes, beginning to end, then it was almost like sitting in this chair, the air was so still." That same day a friend of his was up flying and did get knocked out. He hit his head on a cabin brace, and "when he opened his eyes he was ready to hit the rocks at the bottom of Bull Canyon, but he wasn't spiraling or anything, the way you'd think. It was like he was on a long glide for landing, nice and easy."

Minutes later I heard Sparky telling his father how he was going to make a flight in a couple of days to check on a tented camp they'd outfitted, and with some trepidation (he still seemed stern) I asked him if I could come along. I could if I got to the airport by 6 A.M., he said sternly. Two days later, while the sky was still rosy, I climbed into the back seat of a Citabria, behind Sparky. We took off, both of us wearing earplugs, so there was a lot of yelling back and forth. "We're looking for trumpet swans!" he yelled as we circled a pond near the airport. Without pointing out any swans, he flew on to the next valley, Crystal Creek Gros Ventre, so I assumed he didn't see any. Fog lay in patches on the valley floor, looking like puddles after a good rain. I had made up my mind not to be nervous on this ride; I'd trust the man who wrote the book and not second-guess him. Thereby I could relax and enjoy flying where I would not have flown myself, which was down in the valley, below the level of the peaks, our wingtips pointing at rocks, not sky.

We flew up the left side of Crystal Creek (going up the center "puts you in a poor position to turn around should you . . . find that the terrain climbs faster than the airplane," *Mountain Flying* warns). Gesturing toward a spot two-thirds of the way up a steep slope, Sparky shouted, "This is where Mom shot her ram." Her only ram? I wondered. The spot looked inaccessible to any human being, particularly his mother, whom I had seen briefly in the office, pale and meek beside her two ruddy men. There was nothing there now, but farther along the slope we could see white dots zigzagging upward: a ram (whose ram would it be?) and several ewes and lambs, all hightailing it up the mountainside, white rumps bobbing up and down, each flagging the others—and us, in the air beside them.

I noticed Sparky making a lot of control changes, adding power, taking off power, lowering flaps, raising flaps, adjusting almost constantly to changes in currents and terrain, some of which must have been quite subtle. In this way we passed smoothly from Crystal Creek Gros Ventre to Swift Canyon to Open Door Mountain to Granite Creek to Shoal Creek to Hoback Canyon, where we saw some cows. Four cows were standing on the grassy slope of a mountain, one beneath a tree, two near a crevice, one out in the open. I found it disorienting, seeing them as mountain creatures, since I'd nearly always encountered them standing foursquare on flat farmland—as if they had a secret life and I'd caught them at it.

Coming up on Taylor Mountain, Sparky yelled back, "As soon as it snows we usually find at least a dozen moose here." This was August and we found one moose. It was standing stock-still, its back to the mountain, facing the valley, like a sentinel. From our altitude it was only a spot, but we could tell it was a moose because of its color, a dark, bitter-chocolate brown. An elk would have been lighter, a tan-colored spot.

Sparky buzzed the tented camp, then started home. On the way a hawk passed on our left. "I hit a hawk the other day," he said, turning to explain: "Hawks usually cut to their right when you come at them— all predatory birds do that, I don't know why. So when we see a hawk we cut to the right too, only this one didn't and we were in a right turn when we hit it."

The rest of my stay in Jackson Hole I got around by car or on foot. One day I walked to my own hot spring. I was staying in a ski condominium at a racquet club which one of the linemen at the airport had a share in; when he found out I came from the same airport in New York as an old roommate, he invited me to stay. One of his new roommates told me about the spring. Besides the famous hot springs in Yellowstone National Park, Blue Grotto, Marble Arch, Old Faithful, etc., there were countless smaller, nameless ones, and people who lived around there knew where many of them were but kept the locations of their favorites secret. They thought of them as "their" springs, and in winter they'd ski in to the larger ones, take off their clothes, and float or swim in the pools, surrounded by snow. It all sounded so wonderful that, although there wouldn't be any snow, I begged the roommate to tell me where one of "his" springs was, swearing not to tell. Finally he gave in and told me how to get to one, not his "best." He drew me a map, and the next day I left my car by the side of the road and set out.

About where one should have been according to the map I found a stream and started following it, jangling my car keys for the grizzlies. The grass on either side of it was long and damp, and where there wasn't grass there was mud, or downed trees, or boggy patches, all of which made for heavy slogging. When I came upon feeder streams I'd check them by dunking my hand in the water to see if it was warmer than the water in the main stream, but it never was so I kept on walking, slipping along the wet banks, detouring around logs, jangling my keys, sweating away. After more than an hour I realized I'd probably missed the spring, but I didn't know where else to look for it so I kept walking. After a half hour more I was sure I'd missed the spring but wasn't willing to give up so I kept tracking the main stream, putting my hand in feeder streams from time to time until at last I found one I *thought* might be a *bit* warmer and decided to give it a try. I followed the rather unimpressive flow away from the main stream and every time I put my hand in, the water seemed . . . probably . . . warmer. Meanwhile the stream was definitely getting narrower, and soon became a trickle, then a pool, then disappeared in a patch of swampy ground.

Orange-brown, the pool was no more than a foot wide and maybe an inch or two deep. It had insects hovering above it and turned muddy when I stirred it lightly with my fingertips. Yet it was warm. *Quite* warm! And it was mine, not the roommate's! Lewis or Clark couldn't have been more pleased. I had to do something to make my claim, I felt, and since I couldn't swim or float in "my" spring (nothing could except maybe a minnow with minutes to live), I took down my shorts and underpants, looked around to clear the area, slowly lowered my backside into the open-air bidet until it came to rest on the squishy bottom, then sat with my knees up in the middle of a national-park forest, warm liquid infusing my lower parts, liquid that had seeped up from inside the earth, liquid as warm as my own body, or the fluid already in it—blood, urine, and tears.

Lander · Thermopolis · Black Hills

The air wasn't dead to the treetops the morning I left Jackson Hole, but it wasn't exactly lively either. The plane climbed foot by draggy foot, an old woman going up stairs. To make sure I had the altitude I wanted (11,500 feet) when flying over the Togwottee Pass (9,658 feet), I worked my way up to altitude first, before leaving the valley. At 11,500 and not yet to the pass, I had a mile and a half of air under me and didn't much like it. That far from the ground, I felt uncomfortable, unanchored, aloft in a leaky boat. The scaffolding of earth had been removed and left me dangling. I wasn't safer flying low, I knew, but I *felt* safer, and no amount of sensible thinking so far had changed that. Even at more middling altitudes, 4,500 or 5,500 feet for instance, I've sometimes felt uneasy. Once while cruising along at some such in-between height I had the sense that if I tilted the wings more than 15 degrees the plane would tumble, like an uncaged gyro. I'm not alone in this, I've found. Some cropdusters, accustomed to flying a few feet off the crops, feel peculiar higher up. A man once told me that his father, a duster in upstate New York, "couldn't keep the wings level" when he flew above 3,000 feet. An ag pilot I met at an airport in Maryland showed me photos he'd taken at night while going across the country in his own plane, and from the pattern of the lights it was clear that he was cruising at several thousand feet. "I felt like I was flying on the point of a pin," he said. "I felt like I was going to fall off the end of the earth."

At Jackson Hole I needn't have bothered giving myself that spacy feeling; the pass turned out to be another silk sheet, another waxed floor, and the plane slid right on through. On the far side, where I dropped down, the valley opened up as from the point of a V, and on the left side of the V, well in the distance, was a range of mountains topped with snow. Above the snow, as if by affinity (little white brothers), was a cluster of tiny clouds. As I headed down the widening valley, the clouds started moving out into it, growing larger, and riding lower, and some of the larger clouds developed bluish bands under them, which gave the sky a striped look. I wasn't sure how wary to be by then. Were all the stripes weakened daylight, I wondered, or could some of them be rain? *Mountain Flying* had made it perfectly clear: Weather out here was not to be trusted. I soon realized that I had been slightly easing the throttle in, not-quite-consciously trying to hurry the plane along with this tiny forward motion of my own. I also realized that in the center of one of the blue stripes was a narrower, opaque, gray-white one, like a dirty marble column, holding up a large, dark cloud.

"Beware!" Sparky spoke from those clouds. If they kept advancing at the rate they appeared to be, they might intercept my flight path before I got to my next refueling stop, Riverton, Wyoming, so I shifted my route 30 degrees to the south, which put me in line for another airport, in Lander, Wyoming. On my way there I looked back over my shoulder at the area around Riverton, expecting at any moment to see it engulfed by clouds, but what I actually saw was a squarish shape to the left of the airport shining brilliantly, and I determined from the chart that it was a lake, silvered like a mirror, from all the sunlight bouncing up off it. "Flatlander!" Sparky spoke from that brilliant lake.

The sky over Lander when I landed there was light blue with only a few yarn-tufts of cloud floating in it, and I was trying to decide whether or not to feel sheepish about running scared when a man with a short white cook's apron tied around his waist ran up to my window, obviously excited. "I couldn't *believe* it!" he said even before I shut down. "An 8F in my window!" He told me he'd been in the kitchen of his drive-in restaurant down the road from the airport (under down-wind for Two-One), washing dishes, when he heard the sound of an engine he recognized. "Luscombes got their clatter," he declared. "No other exhaust system comes through like that, ka-put ka-put ka-put!" He had looked out the window and seen flying by a Luscombe *of the very same model as the one he had just bought,* and which he had never seen another example of. He jumped into his truck, drove to the airport, and arrived just as I was taxiing in.

He took me across the ramp to show me his "new" Luscombe. It had scratches and dents on the cowling and rough spots on the wing. He said he'd bought it from a man who was learning to fly it "but his instructor let it get away and it went up on its nose." When he and his partner heard the bad news they "drove straight to Idaho Falls and made the man an offer." They were going to take the radio out and restore the second glove compartment. "Originally Luscombes had two glove compartments," he pointed out. What, I asked myself, give up a radio for historical fidelity? Also, they had found some flannel that resembled the original linen on the headliner and were going to cover their headliner with that. They wanted to make the Luscombe as much like the original as possible.

When we crossed back over the ramp to look at my Luscombe, a man was fueling it from a stepladder. From up there he must have had a view of the boxes on my passenger seat because he called down to us, "You can load an extra hundred pounds in one of these things." He told us he had owned a Luscombe too once, and added, "You can't overgross a Luscombe. It's the perfect vagabond airplane!" I noticed the cook was smiling broadly at that, and I must have been too. The perfect vagabond airplane! The perfect *anything!* The two of us stood there on the ramp, not saying anything, savoring the moment, beaming away, like parents of a kid who's just won a prize at school.

In the spirit of confusion about what constituted worrisome mountain weather, I decided to fly on that day but not too far. After the cook left I had heard a throat-clenching cough of thunder somewhere in the area and noticed a wide swath of gray over mountains west of the field. So I asked the office secretary if she knew of any interesting places to fly to close by. "Thermopolis!" she said warmly, and pulled a stack of photos out of a drawer. She looked for a moment at the top photo, then passed it to me. It was an aerial, in pastel colors and imperfect focus, taken of a bend in a river. "Beautiful," she sighed and handed me the other photos one by one. They were all aerials, in pastel colors and imperfect focus. One showed several white squares on a green background. They were the bathhouses, she said. "People from all over the country come for those baths."

Thermopolis it was, then. En route to it the only weather I ran into was a one-minute drumming of rain as I passed over a ridge. Clouds had lined up on top of the ridge like troops along a fortified wall, and as I squeezed between them and the ridge they let go a little rain; after that, the way was clear. I could see a city when it was 15 miles ahead of me and 1,500 feet below. I'd have known it anywhere, cupped in the bend of a river. The hills on two sides of it were pinkish in late-morning light, with tops blending to pale gold. A setting worthy of a city of pilgrims, with a name that invoked the ancients.

Thermopolis airport was a typical small one, except that it had big airplanes on it, seven DC-3s and four Constellations. One of the "Connies" appeared in the movie *MacArthur,* a mechanic told me, explaining that General MacArthur flew around the Pacific in one when he was Supreme Commander, Allied Powers, Japan. Another Connie was *the very one* that General Eisenhower flew around in when he was President. Both the DC-3s and the Connies were used now for the usual things small planes were used for, but in a big way. For instance, the Connies could spray 3,000 gallons of insecticide on grasshopper-infested countryside in one go, and the DC-3s could carry 14 "smoke jumpers" plus their chain saws, shovels, and axes out over the forest they were to leap onto and fight fires in.

The mechanic was also a pilot, of both DC-3s and Connies, but the large planes cost so much to rent they weren't rented all that often and he had to do other things at the airport to earn his pay. During a break from repairing a DC-3 engine he smoked a pipe. I realized, watching him puff away, that you didn't often see pipes at airports. They didn't seem to go with airplanes, the way cigarettes did. They were too . . . bookish, contemplative, woolgathering for aviation. He told me his name was Pat and that he'd learned to fly in Australia. He'd gone over there a lumberjack and come back a pilot. "In Australia everybody flies," he said. "It was inevitable." He'd come back with an Australian wife, Marita, and they started driving from the West Coast of the U.S. to the East, where he hoped to get a job as a pilot. They got as far as Thermopolis. He stopped at the airport to have a look around and somebody offered him a job. He seemed not to have questioned whether this was a place they would have chosen, a place they'd like. "We're used to living in the outback," he said simply.

I walked into Thermopolis for lunch. It was a town the Music Man would have loved. White picket fences, wash on a line, buckle galoshes in a store window on Broadway. Teenage girl and boy on school steps playing a duet of "Anchors Aweigh" on plastic flutes. Old man on a bench holding up a single finger as I passed: "Hello," it meant here.

Lunch in the Pink Tea Room, where the waitresses moved with the speed of cold ketchup. Toward evening I had drinks with Pat and Marita at the trailer park where they lived. We sat on folding chairs in front of their trailer drinking beer and sangria and watching people from other trailers pad by, in slippers and robes, on their way to the baths. The baths were actually a swimming pool fed by a hot spring, at the end of their row of trailers. Most of the people going by were elderly and, said Marita, from out of state. They came for their arthritis, or bad backs. "They love it," she said. "Some of them stay for years."

Later we drove to a park, where we saw a herd of buffalo grazing quietly, silhouetted against the sunset, and to the Bighorn River, where we stood on a swaying footbridge 500 feet above the water and watched the head of a beaver appear, disappear, and reappear in the swirling rapids. Then we had dinner at the American Legion Golf Course Restaurant, next to the airport. Pat told how farmers would fly in to the airport, tie down their Cubs, pick up golf clubs they'd stashed in the hangar the last time, climb up to the golf course, play a round or two of golf, eat in the restaurant, climb down, stash their clubs in the hangar again, and fly back home. These weren't gentlemen farmers either, but with their own little strips and own little planes they could enjoy the country-club life.

It was midnight when we got back to the trailer park, full of red wine and Surf 'n' Turf. Pat and Marita wanted to swim, but I thought the air was too cool. They kept insisting so I pulled on a suit, ran to the pool, and jumped in, intending to get the whole thing over with in a hurry. Several truck-tire inner tubes were floating around in there, and I climbed aboard one and started paddling with my hands. The closer I got to the end of the pool where the springwater entered, the warmer the water got, naturally enough, and, suspended as I was between the warm water and the cool air, I began to see what the point of it all was. A sexy confusion of sensations, body near-weightless and (wine-soaked) mind near-weightless too; the temperatures giving out mixed signals; a softening, obscuring mist rising off the water; the boundaries blurred between things—water and air, heat and cold, body and inner tube, states of hanging and floating—it was as close to the feeling of flying as anything I remembered doing (publicly) for a long, long time. No wonder they stayed for years!

. . .

Overnight, my wristwatch quit working. I'd been using the watch as a flight instrument of sorts ever since Santa Monica, where somebody stole my clock. Whoever stole my cockpit clock also stole my Swiss Army knife, screwdriver, scissors, and fancy computer-navigation watch someone had given me. One day I had stopped by the airport to check on my plane and found the left window standing wide open, although both doors were locked. Inside there were buckled mounds of unfolded flying charts lying on both seats. The radio tuner had been wound as far left as it would go, and the trim tab had been wound as far back as *it* would go. Clearly the work of a kid thief, I deduced, not only because of all the horsing around but because of the port of entry. The window was only ten inches high by 24 inches wide, bisected vertically by the hinge, and four feet off the ground. I hadn't gotten a new clock yet—I was looking for a windup—and meanwhile had been using my watch to figure ETA's, fuel reserves, etc. I couldn't take off without a timepiece, so I went to a hardware store, the one with galoshes in the window, and bought a $15 Timex.

Thus equipped, I took off into the kind of countryside that made all too manifest Wyoming's claim to the lowest population density of any state in the contiguous U.S. From Thermopolis to the Black Hills, a distance of 250 miles, the land looked on the chart to be nearly devoid of habitation, with even the highway which ran east, and which I intended to follow, passing fewer than half a dozen towns. And except for the Bighorn range, the Mountain West's last fling, there weren't many land features either (the chart showed only intermittent streams). To get to the highway at the point where I wanted to intercept it, I flew across 35 miles of naked plateau, which had not a single landmark to tell me if I was on course or not. I knew, though, that I was coming up on the highway when I saw something glint in the distance, like the flash of a metal button. It had to be a car, I figured, since there was nothing else around to glint—no windows (no houses), no farm machines left standing in the sun (no farms).

The Bighorn Mountains had a few splashes of color on them— mustard-orange trees, yellow hay fields, rusty grass, mud-brown ponds—but on either side, leading up to and away from them, the earth had the look of dead leaves: pale yellow and pale brown, and veined like dead leaves, with the marks of dried-up (the down side of intermittent) streams all over it. Once past the Bighorns, which produced only a couple of farewell taps, I gave myself over to the meditative side of flying. The wind was light, the clouds were innocuous, air traffic was zero, and navigation was the road. With the terrain undemanding as well, I could contemplate the view almost without distraction. For, despite the emptiness of the countryside, the view was worth contemplating. It nearly always is; the simplest landscape has its rewards. As I drifted eastward the ground would heave now and then and the highway would slice through the raised parts and expose deeper soil, which was the color of rouge, that warm reddish-brown-powdery-pink of women's makeup, attractive against the sallow tan soil. The same shade appeared, a couple of times, on top of rocky knolls, calling attention to them, like blushes on cheekbones.

With no thermals to rev it up, the engine kept to the same even note, a hypnotic drone. My thoughts floated out and over the scene and made their own marks upon it. Thus passed a dreamy hour over the state of Wyoming, with only one practical interruption in the woolgathering, to eat the Turf left over from last night's Surf 'n' Turf, which I'd laid on the hat shelf along with my bathing suit, still wet from last night's swim. The first hint that all this wouldn't go on forever and ever came after a couple of hundred miles, when I saw up ahead some bumps on the horizon, looking the way a neighboring kingdom might to a poor boy who was riding toward it ready to try his hand at slaying the giant and winning the youngest princess's hand (always the youngest), but the bumps turned quickly into dirt-colored cones, then into low, scattered hills, then were gone, with no others arising to take their place. The spell, however, had been broken, and other changes crept in. In places the ground color shifted from pale brown to dusty green, and in the middle of one such place a farm appeared. Gradually, other farms appeared, with long spaces between them but all with something in common: bold colors, or bold patterns, or both. One farm was made up of maroon and yellow stripes of equal width, with the maroon stripes shifting to bronze as I flew past and the nap of the crop and the angle of the light shifted. A cream-colored farm had been worked by plowlines into an intricate laciness, and a charcoal-gray one had a jagged line of white running through it, like a crack in a granite block.

So caught up was I in this unexpectedly rich display that I missed seeing the Devil's Tower. After I landed at Black Hills airport in South Dakota, a woman asked how I liked it. What? You passed it on your way in, she told me. I had seen photographs of the Devil's Tower, sticking up from flat land like a big fez, one of the Seven Natural Wonders of the World; how could I have missed something like that? I pulled out the chart I'd been using—CHEYENNE—didn't find it there, pulled out the next chart north—BILLINGS—and there Devil's Tower was, only 20 miles north of the highway, but that put it one mile off the CHEYENNE chart, so it might as well have been in the Yukon.

When she asked me about the tower, the woman was sitting at a picnic table in the hangar, slicing tomatoes. That domestic touch (making lunch for her kids) was only one of the things that made Black Hills airport seem homier than most. It had been built in a valley of white barns and yellow haystacks, between gently rounded, green hills, something I hadn't seen since I entered the Sierra Nevada. On one wall of the office was a photo taken the day the airport was dedicated, July 22, 1934, a day of apparently brilliant sunshine, when men as well as women were wearing light-colored hats, and a team of horses and stagecoach were drawn up next to the aircraft, many of which were biplanes, and pilots in jodhpurs and knickers were standing around in poses of consequence. A table down the hallway from the office had a pot of hot coffee on it, and across the hallway from it was a men's room with a shower, which women as well as men were welcome to use (Eighth Wonder!). "We thought that we'd like to make our airport like one we'd want to find ourselves if we were flying cross-country," said the woman. By "we" she meant her husband, a former Air Force major, and herself. They planned to build a lounge with a bed in it so pilots could stay overnight and avoid the high summer motel rates. It was a plan almost dizzying in its reach.

"We" also meant their four kids, who helped out at the airport after school and on weekends. "It's good for them," said the woman, as affirmatively as if she'd planned it that way, but later she admitted, "We couldn't afford to run the airport without them." Her husband, overhearing this, said rather sourly, "We couldn't afford to run the airport without my retirement pay either." He added, "This place isn't a money-maker. In fact, general aviation's not a money-maker." The old refrain. Mouths all over America forming the same set of words, a muttering chorus.

I did my share to help the family out by renting a car at the airport so I could drive to Deadwood, South Dakota. The leading citizens of Deadwood seemed still to be Wild Bill Hickok and Calamity Jane. There were posters of them in coffee shops, dioramas depicting them in souvenir stores, and drinks named for them in saloons. I saw a Wild Bill Hickok Ski and Specialty Shop and a Calamity Jane Pants Shaque. Tourists trudged up the steep slope of Mount Moriah to stare at the graves where they lay side by side, as they probably never had in life.

In the municipal museum, though, I didn't see anything to suggest either of them except for the knife, razor, and sharpening stone found in a booth the night Hickok was shot while playing cards, holding a "dead man's hand," all aces and eights. Otherwise, like most town museums, Deadwood's seemed to operate on the principle that anything interesting had a right to display space. On exhibit were, among other things, a petrified turtle, a petrified peach, a "beaver killed in a fight with a porcupine," a pheasant-feather corsage, unborn twin fawns, a "freak" calf, buckeyes with "curative powers for . . . rheumatism [when] carried on the person," Chinese coins which had been legal tender when Chinese men were building the railroad, a red satin shirt that belonged to Potato Creek Johnny (no explanation thought necessary of who Potato Creek Johnny was), and the usual beaded tomahawks, mounted mooseheads, and clothespin dolls. On one wall I came across a framed snapshot of "the first airplane flight in western South Dakota," which took place, or rather terminated, in 1911, when one Art Smith "landed in a mountain meadow."

When I got back to Black Hills, it was dark, and the woman and her husband were just leaving after thirteen hours at the airport. She was sorry the lounge wasn't ready yet, she said, and offered the office sofa instead. All I had to do in return was plug in the coffeepot when I got up so the coffee would be ready by the time they got there. As soon as they drove off I headed for the shower, where I found a carefully lettered placard: "If you can't aim [this was the men's room], SIT DOWN. [Signed:] Mom and Patsy." Before settling down to sleep, I flipped through a pile of aviation magazines on the coffee table, looking for something to read. In among the magazines I found a copy of *Bambi* (Patsy was eleven). I stretched out on my sleeping bag and started reading it. From one of the baseboards I could hear a cricket chirping and from across the room the rumble of a Dr. Pepper machine. It was all so reassuringly wholesome that I fell asleep within minutes, just after Thumper watched Bambi take his first wobbly steps.

When I woke up I saw another animal. It was a gray horse, grazing just outside the office window. Well, all that grass, the airport was a meadow (only slightly messed up), why not? Black Hills wasn't different from other little airports in that respect: most of them are located outside of towns, or at least at the edge of towns, and have grass between, around, and even on their runways, not to mention marshes, ponds, or woods farther out on the property, and dunes, lakes, hills, farms, mountains, or oceans next door. Even small airports can take up a lot of land, to make room for runways a half mile or mile long, sometimes two or three runways running in different directions, and usually there is plenty of land left over, not being used for anything except to ensure separation, and that land carries on, much as before, naturally.

Once during an approach to an airport in Texas at dusk my lights caught a bunch of jackrabbits standing on the numbers; they were frozen with listening, bodies held so rigid I couldn't tell at first that they were creatures. They looked instead, all together like that, like some plumbing device, a complicated set of pipes. I was considering doing a go-around when the device blew apart and the jackrabbits ran off.

Not only rabbits but antelope and moose (Jackson Hole), wild ponies (Ocean City), domestic horses (Black Hills), and cows graze at airports now and then. I've been told that cows like the dope on fabric airplanes and will eat the paint off to get it. In Georgia someone told me about a farmer who had his own strip and his own Cub but also his own cow, which could often be seen (not by him, presumably) standing next to the Cub, contentedly scratching herself on the horizontal stabilizer.

Mice, too, have their uses for airplanes. Tipped off once by the presence of "dewdrops" on the seat, a friend of mine discovered a mouse nest under the floorboards of my plane, at the top of the landing gear, and we determined, from the shredded evidence, that it had been made entirely of material found inside the plane: bits of firewall sound-proofing, tiedown rope, waxing rag, sneaker shoestring, and Blue Angels souvenir sunshade (bill only).

And birds: Intrepid (stupid?) sage chickens aren't the only ones seen lurking around airports. At dusk at my home field, as we sit beside the runway drinking screwdrivers and waiting for the last of our buddies to come in, we hear them squeaking and pipping in the air around us, swallows and sandpipers mostly, swooping among the parked planes. During the day we see sparrows perched on tailfin blades, surveying the field from seven feet up. Occasionally a flock of starlings will roost overnight on our wings, or so we deduce as we flick wads of guano off the leading edges in the morning. Pigeons, on the other hand, prefer hangar rafters, where they make terrible messes of planes parked underneath. Some birds—I don't know which kinds because I've never caught them at it—try to build nests on airplane engines, which must seem pretty appealing to them, all those cavities and crevices around cylinders and plugs to cradle the nest, a cowling to keep off rain, air-intake openings for easy access. If we want to fly we have to harden our hearts and throw out the nests, or even the mere beginnings of nests—strands of grass and paper—since the heat of an operating engine can set them afire.

Bugs too: There are even more places on planes for them to take advantage of than for birds: fuel-cap breather tubes, static-air holes, control-cable openings, ram-air tubes—particularly ram-air tubes, which stick out and down from the leading edges of wings like long, curved straws. Mine has a hinged cover, which seems to add to the appeal; I'm never surprised when during inspection I lift the cover and see the telltale thread of little legs . . .

As for plant life: Taildraggers, being low in the hierarchy of planes needing service at busy airports, are often relegated to tiedowns far out on the field, where the grass is not always well mowed, so we have the pleasure of parking among clover, daisies, black-eyed Susan, chicory, and Queen Anne's lace. Along the taxiway there may be beard-tongue, pale-spike lobelia, teasel, or moneywort, and farther out bouncing Bets, swamp roses, slender ladies' tresses, and purple loosestrife. One time I stepped out of my plane at an airport near the Massachusetts-Vermont border onto a mat of wild blueberries, so many of them that as I was unpacking I could lean over at any time, scoop up a handful, and pop them in my mouth. They were at their peak of ripeness, too, the sweetest blueberries I ever tasted.

So at Black Hills airport, I wasn't all that surprised to see a horse eating the grass. I watched the horse for a while, then when it didn't do anything got up and went down the hallway to turn on the coffee-pot. On the wall above the pot was a poster advertising airplane rides, over "the world's richest 100 square miles . . . both in wealth and scenery." The wealth had to be the town of Lead, I figured, since there was a gold mine there that produced more gold than any other mine in the country a century after the first claim. As for the scenery . . . well, I'd soon find out.

Wall

If the richness of the scenery could be determined by the number of bugs in the air (increasing by the cube root of lushness?), then the Black Hills were the wealthiest 100 square miles I had ever seen. Within minutes of takeoff bugs were hitting the windscreen like raindrops, splatting and spreading in the slipstream. It occurred to me as I looked out between their gauzy juice-spots that it wasn't so much a question of there being a great many hills in the Black Hills which happened to have trees on them, but of there being a great many trees in the Black Hills, which happened to have hills under them. Or rather *something* under them. From the air the countryside as far as I could see looked as if a green coverlet had been thrown (loosely) over the forms of sleeping giants lying this way and that, knees up, or arms flung to the sides, some over on all fours, some lying on top of others (humping, suffocating others), a few wide awake and sneaking games of cards under the covers, slowly passing the decades.

Forty miles into this was Mount Rushmore (giants' heads popping out?), and I went looking for it. The monument was on the chart, so I knew about where to look for it but not what to expect when I found it—how it would present itself from a distance, on what scale, if it would look unnatural from the start. I hadn't seen it before except in photos, which meant close up, the heads filling the frame, as in a class portrait. The way it first presented itself was as a white patch on one of several gray knobs that protruded through the blanket of trees. The patch gradually took on form as I advanced until it became recognizable as a head, but only one head until I swung left in a wide arc to approach from the front and saw Jefferson, Roosevelt, and Lincoln follow the Father of our Country into public view. The heads, in the flesh so to speak, seemed abnormally close to each other, almost cheek-to-cheek, too intimate for the office. Still, they were impressive, especially considering that the sculptor probably didn't often get the view I was getting in order to check on his work-in-progress. Several miles farther south, I flew over a rocky outcropping where the same thing was being done for Chief Crazy Horse, only even more ambitiously. He was being carved out of rock—down to his waist—sitting astride his horse—down to its shoulders—and when finished, his head would be larger than the four presidents' heads combined and his outstretched arm as long as three football fields. His statue wouldn't be finished for decades, though. After eight years of work the top of the head—headdress?—still looked from the air like a lumpy sofa.

Past the Black Hills ground level dropped fast, to consistently below 3,000 feet for the first time since Nut Tree. Ahead, the horizon was long and swept clean; underneath there was grass, not trees. The mountains were behind me but so now were the hills, with plains and prairies stretching eastward almost to my hometown. On that long roll of flatland, there would, however, be a glitch, a peculiar elaboration, a pocket of singular weirdness—something that must have knocked the early settlers, riding around looking for a better place to plow, right off their buckboards. What's *this?* the men must have said, scratching their sideburns. Icicles, spires, and undulating walls of pink, green, black, and pearl-gray stone, rocky "castles," "pine forests," and "thatched huts," voluptuous, petrified ooze. On the flat stretches between them, I could see as I flew over, were large mineral splotches of olive, rust, and white, and upon and between those the black-and-white of an occasional cow. The cow: *It* was the universal animal, the Great Occupier. Wading up to its knees in the Mississippi, standing nailed to a mountainside in the Tetons, parked foursquare on the farms of Ohio, chewing its cud amid the phantasmagoria of the South Dakota Badlands.

There was another pocket of weirdness on a highway running north of the Badlands, one the settlers never saw but might have taken a shine to, since it reflected a pioneering, pushy, bootstrap American spirit. Wall Drug Store, by its own reckoning known around the world, mostly for not being much of a drugstore, offered 70,000 souvenirs and 190 displays in 18 rooms to 10,000 visitors a day (also by its own reckoning). I landed at a grass strip in the town of Wall, five minutes late on my flight plan because of the extra time I'd spent looking at the Badlands. A briefer had already started checking around for me. He had phoned the airport, and when nobody answered phoned the owner's house. The owner wasn't in but his wife was, and she said she didn't have the keys to the airport but her son at the high school did and she'd drive over and get them. It was the first time being late got me anything; I wouldn't have thought I had a right to call somebody at home, or have even known where home was; at airports you usually take what you get. A half hour after I called the briefer, the wife showed up in a pickup truck, two small towheaded boys on the seat beside her.

"A woman in a taildragger!" she said when she saw my plane. "It's a *first* here. I've got to tell Monty when he comes in." Monty was her husband, she explained, and he was up spraying crops now. She gave me a conspiratorial little smile, as if between us we understood how endearingly single-minded our men could be, saying, "Monty eats, drinks, and sleeps flying." To fuel my plane, she used a stepladder, balancing herself with one sandaled foot on a wing strut. Below her, one of the boys, about four years old, stood leaning against a leg of the stepladder, his cheek pressed against it, an arm draped through a rung, eyes staring into space. Later she told me that he hadn't spoken a word in two years. She and Monty had had another son, in addition to these two and the one at the high school, "but he was run over. Ever since then he [the one leaning on the ladder] won't talk. They say it was the shock that did it."

She and I rolled my plane to a tiedown spot, which was so far from the pumps that it would have made more sense for me to taxi it there, but she insisted we push it. I guessed that with little boys underfoot she thought the less driving around the better. Spinning props and long wings sweeping the air a few feet above the ground did make airports less-than-perfect playgrounds, but the boys at Wall took what they could get too. When I left for the drugstore, one of them had turned the circular concrete fuel island into a little track, riding around and around the pumps at the center on his tricycle.

At the drugstore I bought a shot glass, after looking at a mere 1,000 of the 70,000 souvenirs (steer skulls, place mats, jumpropes) and a half dozen of the 190 displays (five-foot-high replica of Mount Rushmore, cluster of taxidermied squirrels, rabbits, and weasels wearing tiny suits and dresses, "Chuck Wagon band" with life-size dummies "blowing" horns and "strumming" guitars, and 1908 Hupmobile). The glass was on a table with hundreds of other shot glasses, all carrying the same red buffalo on the side and the name of some state. Mine said "South

Dakota." I had been looking for one that said North Dakota, having been reminded of what an art teacher in college told all us students, that there was no such place as North Dakota, it was something map-makers invented to fill the gap that opened up when the Mercator Projection was introduced. "Well," he'd ask, "have you ever met anybody from North Dakota?" "No," we'd answer. "See?" he'd say. "You *see?*" I searched and searched, but among all the shot glasses on that long table, each with some state's name on it, there wasn't one that said North Dakota. "See?" I heard a whisper somewhere back of my neck, "You *see?*"

When I got back to the airport, Monty was there. He'd quit spraying early because the wind was blowing so hard and the air was so rough his head kept hitting the side of the cockpit. I noticed when I faced into the wind now my shirtsleeves and slacks were glued to the front of my arms and legs, and they were pulled out behind like little flags, flapping. But it was the howl of the wind as it rounded the corners of the hangar that made me decide I should stay down with Monty and wait for the wind to drop. He was in the hangar, and we sat talking for a while. There was a Cub in there with a large orange rectangle painted on the tail and the number 37 on the rectangle, in black letters. It was his hunting license, he said. He and his brother shot coyotes "plus a fox or two" from the air, for money, not sport. "The sheepherders give us $25 for one coyote, the state gives us $5, and the fur people give us $50," he said. "One week I made $2,500 just on coyotes. If things go right, you can get seven coyotes in three or four hours."

They did their hunting in winter, when there was snow on the ground and they could see the paw prints. A day or a day and a half after a blizzard or heavy snow, they'd go up. "I do the flying, and my brother does the shooting," said Monty. "We're doing 60 miles an hour 15 feet off the ground and the coyotes are doing about 20. You don't shoot ahead of them like you do with ducks. You fly to one side and a little in front and aim behind them, a negative lead. Unless of course they cut, which being smart they usually do after the first or second time, in which case you shoot ahead of them and below. One coyote was so smart we never could get him. He was darker than the others, and I got so I recognized him. Every time we flew over he managed to get under the plane, where it's impossible to hit anything."

After hitting a coyote, they'd land on skis next to it and pick up the carcass. Some guys skinned the coyote on the spot, but Monty let "the fur people" do it. "King here [he indicated a German shepherd eating hard candy out of a dog dish] almost ate up a guy who skinned his own coyotes. Came in with the stink on his hands."

The wind didn't drop that afternoon, and neither Monty nor I went up again. I hadn't seen anybody else coming in or out all day, even before the wind got bad; those 10,000 visitors must all be drivers. Still, Monty, his wife, and the boys stayed at the airport until after dark. She told me I could sleep on the office floor; there wasn't any sofa but there were rag rugs she'd made herself, she said hospitably. As soon as they'd gone I drew the office curtains shut, and as I did my hand grazed the butt of a rifle; I recoiled, as if the thing had gone off. It was on a rack over the window, half hidden by the curtains. As I was locking the door I found another rifle, propped against the jamb. I wondered, Was there something to shoot *at* from the office (Monty had insisted I lock myself in)? Were the guns only for killing coyotes in winter (in summer why keep them so close at hand with little boys around)?

Before settling down to a defenseless sleep, I decided to investigate a light coming through a hole in the ceiling. I climbed some steps through the hole into an attic lit by a single, bare, hanging bulb (why leave a light on up there all night anyway?). There were the usual nondescript boxes and bags on the floor, but at one end of the room, suspended from a crossbeam, was something dark and furry, with a strip of white at the bottom which caught and reflected a few watts of bulb light. Teeth, I realized. Teeth revealed when lips were pulled back in a grimace. Poor coyote, not one of the smart ones.

I hurried back down the steps and into my sleeping bag. I had bought a bag of cookies at Wall Drug Store, and as I lay on the rag rug reading, I would reach over my head from time to time and take a cookie out of the bag, and on one such reach I happened to notice, inches from my hand (thus my head), a mouse, very, very dead. Its skinny legs were sticking heavenward, and its pointed face was frozen with jaws open, revealing tiny, white teeth. It had died quite recently; the body was perfectly preserved. I pulled a flying magazine off a table and, using it like a broom, nudged the little carcass across the floor and under a bookcase (I'd tell them in the morning), I didn't sleep at all well that night; the wind kept howling around the office, mingling with the cries of mice and coyotes and foxes, little boys who had been run over, and little boys who could not speak for fear.

Overnight the wind dropped by about five miles an hour, according to the office Wind-O-Meter. Five miles wasn't much but would have to do, I decided. Another pilot was already on the field when I went out, wiping bugs off the windscreen of a Bonanza (from the Black Hills?). I was doing my preflight when I got the idea of using one of those tips that flying magazines are always putting out (for instance, drop 20 degrees of flaps at the end of your takeoff run when there's a fence or other obstacle just beyond it and the plane will pop right over; make turns when all else fails by opening one of your doors—I tried that once). The tip I had in mind now was to start your takeoff roll in a corner of the runway instead of in the center, point the nose at the opposite corner of the far end, and thus gain an extra ten degrees or so of angle into the wind.

Monty arrived and I told him my plan, but he didn't say anything about it, good or bad. He just watched as I taxied around checking the condition of the strip and spacing of the runway lights, then pulled into the left-hand corner of the takeoff end of the runway, pointed the Luscombe's nose at the right-hand corner of the far end, laid right aileron into the wind, pushed the throttle in . . . fine, fine, the plane was rolling along just fine, but before I knew it a runway light was coming at me, *too soon,* oh too soon! I couldn't turn sharply enough to avoid it safely so I pulled on the stick and the plane jumped over the light but fell immediately to the ground, not having attained sufficient flying speed, which put me past the runway light but also past the runway, on grass for the moment but not for long, I pulled on the stick again and the plane jumped up but fell again, jumped up and fell, then jumped up and stayed up. My heart was beating like bone on hollow wood.

First female in a taildragger at Wall Airport, *ha!* Two witnesses: Monty and the Bonanza pilot. As I climbed away a terrible sadness washed over me, a staggering sense of loss. I began to weep. I would never get on top of this thing called flying; what I loved to do most I could not do; trying and caring mattered hardly at all. I wept as I flew into the Badlands, the sight of the exquisite pinnacles and the enduring cows bringing me no comfort. I flew on, and on, through the Badlands and out of them, weeping as if my beloved had died; weeping, weeping, couldn't stop.

Omaha · Earhart · Kansas City

Well, if anything could give a person perspective it was Wounded
Knee: *there* had been something to cry about. I mopped up and looked
the place over. I found it, or what I was pretty sure was it, or part of
it, by flying south out of the Badlands across Medicine Root Creek
and Porcupine Creek to Wounded Knee Creek, near which ran a
short, S-shaped street with a dozen or so houses built along it. All the
houses were new-looking and one of two kinds, either light green with
a gray roof or red-brick-and-stucco with a brown roof (government
issue, I presumed). I hadn't had any idea what Wounded Knee would
look like before I started out but was surprised anyhow. This symbol
of Native American resistance and suffering had all the character when
viewed from the air of a Sunnyview Acres or Bubbling Brook Estates outside Toledo or Albany. The main part of the village was probably somewhere else—I didn't see a cemetery or meeting hall—although the chart
put Wounded Knee here, and as usual there was no way to ask.

The setting for Wounded Knee seemed benign enough, with only a
few boulders scattered about, like tailings washed downstream from the
Badlands, and some farms, small ones, with cows. As I flew eastward in
the direction of Omaha, however, I realized just how benign country out
that way could be. Farms grew larger, greener, and flatter, with fewer
stones, more cows. Some fields which had been watered by rotary sprink-
lers looked like big green phonograph records tossed on the ground. One
round field had several different crops planted on it, in sections running
from the center out, like pieces of pie. One quarter of it was yellow, one
eighth rose, one eighth green-and-yellow-striped, and one half brownish
yellow with lines of a lighter brownish yellow on it. A living pie chart,
illustrating something—proportion of GNP devoted to soybean produc-
tion, cattle, etc.? Percentage of farm children who stayed on the farm,
bought another one, joined the Army, moved to Florida?

In an old-fashioned, straight-edged field, two tractors were plowing rows right next to each other, churning up a double plume of dust. The plumes rose only a short way before they were blown apart; the wind was still going strong. It probably always was out here—short grass, clover, cows, what else was there to slow a breeze down? I kept the wind clearly in mind when it came time to refuel and chose an airport with three runways since chances were that the wind would be blowing more or less down one of the three. "Twenty-five and gusting," a woman said when I radioed in. I remembered reading that when wind blows at 25 miles an hour, telegraph wires start to whistle, whitecaps are blown into spray, and windsocks stand *straight out*.

Sure enough, the sock at Ainsworth stood straight out, but it was aligned so precisely with Runway Three-Five that my landing was not only easy but short; the plane might have had a drag chute. I taxied to the pumps very slowly, so as not to push any extra air over the wings, which would give them a bit more lift, which would in turn make the whole plane a bit lighter in weight and therefore easier for the wind to shove around. When parking at the pumps, I positioned the plane so the wind wouldn't get under a wingtip and pick it up, and I chocked the wheels so the wind wouldn't set them rolling on their own.

The wind not only made takeoff (oh, that takeoff!), landing, taxiing, and parking more challenging than usual but made staying airborne with any comfort more difficult as well. Past Ainsworth the land was nearly flat, with only a gradual downslope east, one foot per mile on average, yet the line my plane was describing in the air as it passed over that land was anything but flat. It spiked, plunged, leapt, sank, rose, fell; hardly a minute passed without some change in altitude. At one point I stuck my head out the window to cool off but soon had to pull it back in because my head kept hitting the frame. Later I put both feet on the rudder pedals on the passenger's side, something I often did on long flights, to unkink my knees, but after a couple of minutes I had to pull them back too because it was hard from that angle—one leg too short, one leg too long—to make all the rudder adjustments necessary in that rough air. Finally I resigned myself to being hot, stiff, and all shook up, for almost two more hours. Much of the time flying was like that: You sat crouched in a space the size of a home freezer, being shaken like dice in a cup, either too cold or too hot, knees locked, rear end numb—just grinding on. Nearly always, though, no matter what the body suffered, there was something to soothe the eyes. Past Ainsworth it was the haystacks, which were so varied field to field that they might have been produced by different cultures. Some were pale and round, like French knots, others long, yellow and loaf-like, still others small and dark as chocolate chips.

Most of the fields had windbreaks made of lines of trees, but the trees rarely went all the way around. They'd be planted, for instance, only on three sides of a field, or only on two sides, or just at the corners, or just in *parts* of some corners, or at the corners plus a side or two. As I went spiking along I tried to picture what the landscape would look like from, say, 15,000 feet up: like one of those hedge mazes, the horticultural puzzles so popular on old English estates, except that out here the only thing trying to find its way through was the swift, unrelenting wind.

I was flying to Omaha to see a friend, a biologist at the University of Nebraska. He had moved to Omaha only recently from New Mexico, where he had studied Mexican freetail bats, elephant shrews, and roadrunners. Ken wasn't sure how long he'd be staying in Nebraska, though. He didn't know if he could come to feel the same about the ecosystem of the plains as he had about the ecosystem of the desert. He'd have to get used to a whole new set of plants, animals, insects, birds, land forms, and climates, and whether or not he stayed on at the university depended largely upon whether or not he could learn to care about these things. From the way he talked on the phone, it was still too early to tell.

For one thing, he missed bats. He hadn't seen a bat since coming to Nebraska. A couple of weeks earlier, a fellow biologist had told him about an abandoned rock mine 30 miles or so south of Omaha which had bats in it. Ken was so excited by this communication that when I phoned to say I'd be passing through Omaha in my plane he arranged for us to go to the cave as soon as I landed (he knew I liked bats, sort of). By the time I did land, however, hot, stiff, and all shook up, seeing bats in an abandoned rock mine wasn't what I most had in mind. I was thinking more along the lines of a white-tablecloth restaurant with chilled white wine, watercress salad, and strawberries with cream— something like that. But Ken showed up at the airport carrying four rubber boots and a specimen bag, his face glowing with anticipation. So I extracted two packs of lemon cookies from the airport vending machine and swallowed those, a small martyr to science.

The mine's entrance was covered with chicken wire—to keep cows from falling in, said Ken (those cows! probably make themselves right at home down there). We slipped through a rip in the wire into a "room" where the concrete ceiling had partially collapsed and slabs of the concrete were lying on the floor at crazy angles. Where we could, we stepped on those, and where we couldn't, we waded through mud and water in our boots. The air in the room was cool, "like air-conditioning," said Ken, who flashed his headlamp over the walls and ceiling, lingering on the corners, cracks, and drill holes. Not finding anything in the first room, he went into a second, darker and smaller but not as quiet. Squeak! A noise like a wire being plucked. Ken ran his beam around and stopped it on a drill hole. "There!" he said, his voice thick with pleasure. I stared at the hole but couldn't see a thing in it, kept staring until I could make out two shiny spots back in the hole: eyes. "Big brown bat," Ken said, when all I could see were the spots and a sort of tremor, as of something breathing. Something *frightened* breathing, I guessed. He flashed his light into a corner. "My-otis," he announced. This time the faces and bodies were right there for anybody to see, tiny, bunched together—and moving. "Every-body's shifting," he said delightedly. "One guy flinches and the rest flinch. It's like a little wave!"

When we left the mine the specimen bag was empty. Ken's catch for the day was a few squeaks, several shifting bodies, and some eyes in a hole. Nevertheless he looked thoroughly happy, and I wondered how much a handful of bats in an old rock mine would contribute to the equation when he was trying to decide whether or not to stay in Omaha.

His eight-year-old son, Keith, seemed to have decided already. In his bedroom Keith kept live spiders, moths, wasps, flies, beetles, but-terflies, caterpillars, bees, and worms plus dead spiders. During dinner two neighborhood boys came to the front door and ceremoniously pre-sented him with a "bug" they'd found by their garage. It was a fly, but Keith accepted it graciously. That night I slept in their basement den, where Ken kept a jar of dermestid beetles he used to clean spec-imens. Dermestids are such ravenous meat-eaters that they can strip the flesh off anything—mice, birds, bats (squeak!)—in a matter of min-utes. A vatful can, unaided, transform a full-size horse into a skeleton, leaving bones as clean as if they've been scrubbed. The jar was on a shelf 20 feet from the head of my bed. Before I went to sleep I begged Ken, "Please check the lid."

The next day he "put up" a ring-tailed lemur at the university and I watched. The lemur had been dead five years and kept in a freezer at the zoo ever since. Recently the zoo donated it to the biology department, and Ken was preparing it for the department's study collection. He planned to mount the hide—fuzzy head, bushy tail, leather palms, and all—on a sheet of Masonite, then drop the rest into a container of dermestid beetles and wait for the skeleton to emerge.

To remove the lemur's hide, Ken had to nick the underside of its skin with a razor blade and tug until the skin pulled away from the underlying tissue, but this lemur had freezer burn, so only a small bit of skin came away each time, and he had to nick the skin again and again, and tug again, nick and tug—the sound of ripping went on and on. The hide on the head turned out to be particularly resistant, and Ken made eight or ten cuts at the back of the neck, with the lemur's head flopped forward, as if in supplication, a sight I found particularly distressing. At one point as he was slicing at the same spot on the neck over and over a bit of newly thawed sticky five-year-old blood oozed up from the spot, and I decided to go somewhere and have a cup of tea.

I bought the tea in a student cafeteria and carried it out to some bleachers beside a football practice field covered with AstroTurf. A dozen or so men were standing on the AstroTurf, doing exercises. All of them had on the same kind of white shorts, high white socks, football jerseys, and helmets which hid their faces. All of them had the same build, same legs, arms, and shoulders. All of them exercised in unison, clapped in unison as they jumped in unison, chanted in unison, even whooped in unison whenever they finished a routine. Whoop! Whoop! Clearly a species. I wondered how much the University of Nebraska football team would weigh on the scales when it came time for Ken to make up his mind whether or not to stay.

There had to be an airport named for Amelia Earhart *somewhere* in the country, I knew. It turned out to be in Atchison, Kansas, the town on a crook of the Missouri River where Amelia's grandmother lived and where she herself was born and went to school up to the fifth grade. On my way to Kansas City to visit my cousins I stopped in at the airport, to have a quick look around. I made a smooth touchdown on the single runway and the first turnoff—a landing any woman could be proud of. There was an elevated area on one side of the field with an obelisk on top and three pines planted in a row, so I went up there before the office. The obelisk was gray stone with a bas-relief carving on one side and a bronze plaque near the top. The carving was done in the convention of ancient Egypt, more or less: A woman, apparently nude, was kneeling with her torso facing front but her legs and head turned sideways. She was holding out to either side what looked like the stumps of arms: tapered wings. Clouds were billowing behind them on both sides. The clouds on her right were labeled Atlantic, those on her left Pacific. It was the Pacific side she was looking at.

The plaque noted that Amelia Earhart was "the first woman to fly the Atlantic (1932)," "the first woman to fly the Pacific (1935)," and "the first woman to receive the distinguished flying cross." Also, that she was "lost on Pacific flight July 1937." Before all these firsts (and last), however, in even bigger letters and at the top of the plaque, was, "Amelia Earhart . . . a courageous Zontian." Zontian? It had a definite sci-fi ring to it (first woman to have a close encounter?). Later I found out that a Zontian was a member of Zontia, an organization of "executive women in business," and Earhart had qualified because, as a pilot, she was "her own boss and exercised decision-making in her profession."

Inside the office were several large framed photographs on one wall, of Earhart sitting in the doorway of her Lockheed Electra, Earhart standing in front of the prop of her Electra, Earhart sitting by a fireplace, writing. Other than the photos and the obelisk, there didn't seem to be anything at the airport that had anything to do with her. I asked the FBO if that were so and he said he'd *thought* about holding a fly-in using her name as a draw but hadn't gotten around to it. When I phoned my cousins in Kansas City to let them know when I'd be landing, I mentioned where I was calling from. My cousin Joyce said her mother used to live in Atchison and had gone to kindergarten with Amelia. When she asked her mother what she remembered about her famous classmate, "We had an ugly teacher with a mole" was all her mother would say.

Joyce was a pilot too, but she hadn't flown in over 25 years, not since getting her license. It wasn't that she was afraid of flying or couldn't afford it, she just found flying "boring." She had taken flight lessons in college only because her father insisted on it. He was convinced that piloting would be an essential skill in the postwar world, something a lot of other people believed back then, including airplane manufacturers, who turned out "family" aircraft as fast as they could, two- and four-place planes that could go 100 miles on a few gallons of gas ("A plane in every garage!" was the idea). But of course it didn't happen. It quickly became clear that the airplane was not going to share garage space with many automobiles, but by then Joyce already had her license and so did her two sisters, who never flew again either.

The only member of Joyce's family who'd had even a remote connection with general aviation recently was her thirteen-year-old son, Jim. Jim had spent 150 hours that winter building a radio-controlled model airplane which had a five-foot wingspan and was painted bright orange. One Sunday in spring he took it to a field near Wichita that belonged to a model-airplane club; the field had a mini-runway (mowed strip of grass), mini-taxiway (ditto), and system whereby each flyer would attach a distinctively colored clothespin to his radio aerial so the others would know what frequency he was on and avoid it. A friend of his father showed Jim how to get the plane airborne, then set him to work practicing box patterns. On one long, straight-and-level leg the engine suddenly speeded up and the plane went into a sharp dive. Frantically Jim worked the stick but the plane kept going down, out of control, and smashed into the ground. "It was terrible," said Joyce, who was watching, "terrible for everybody." The motor lay in a hole eight inches deep, and pieces of the rest of the plane were strewn across the grass. People rushed over; a man with a bad leg hobbled over. When the man saw that Jim's aerial had a red clothespin on it, as did his, he realized what he'd done—overridden Jim's signal. He was close to tears, and Jim, stuffing pieces of his plane in a plastic sack, had trouble holding back his own.

My cousin Jack, Jim's father, picked me up at Fairfax airport, in the northwest part of the city. The lineman there had taken a few minutes to decide where I should tie down, since all the spots for visitors were taken. Finally he let me park in a local pilot's space, which was available only because four days earlier the man's plane had been torn from its tiedown ropes, lifted up and carried over four rows of parked planes, and dropped, upside down, on top of another plane. In the tiedowns immediately around the empty one there were other signs that all had not

gone well that day: a squashed spinner, a twisted tailfin, a nosewheel strut
with no nosewheel, several bent wings (the tip of one high wing touched
the ramp). Elsewhere on the field the planes looked just fine. It was only
around the empty tiedown that something nasty appeared to have happened. Rolling my plane into that spot gave me a slightly creepy feeling,
as if I were climbing into a bed where someone had recently died.

The lineman said, quoting the papers, "It was the kind of storm
that happens only once every 500 years." Jack had been out in that
storm, driving home from a Royals game (called on account of rain,
not surprisingly), and by the time he got to the bridge that led to the
suburb where they lived, the bridge was under water. He left his car
on the highway, took off his shoes and socks, held them over his head,
and tried to wade across the bridge. "Dumb Swede!" he said, laughing
now as he drove me to their house. "You can't *believe* the force of that
water! You couldn't drive a 50-ton tank through it!" We passed a country-
club golf course with tree branches massed against the wood fence where
the waters had pushed them, like a second fence, then a shopping mall
where the parking lot was covered with mud and the store windows broken by cars floating through into the showrooms. "It was the heaviest
downpour in Kansas City's history," said Jack, quoting the papers. A
foot of rain fell in a single day in some parts of town. Eighteen people lost
their lives and hundreds lost their homes, some from fires set off when
floodwaters short-circuited electrical wires. By comparison, the whirligig
at the airport seemed no more than a bit of breezy mischief.

After two fine days with my cousins I went back to Fairfax and was
taxiing out of the deathbed slot when a man ran up and motioned for
me to stop. Over the noise of the engine he shouted something about
"a cup of coffee." I didn't think he was offering me a cup of coffee,
but what? I cut the engine and he said, "The guys in the shop are
having an argument. The foreman says your plane is a Cessna and
one of the mechanics says it isn't a Cessna. They bet a cup of coffee
and sent me to find out."

Which proved that Fairfax wasn't a *real* small airport, and not just
because it had a tower. Anybody at a real small airport, particularly a
mechanic, *particularly* a shop foreman, would know a Luscombe when
he saw one. A couple of thousand Luscombes were still flying, decades
after the last one came off the line—not in every garage exactly but
not in aviation museums either. I told him the foreman had to buy:
My airplane was a Luscombe. He'd never heard of it.

East of Kansas City the roads appeared to be laid out strictly along section lines, and my compass as I followed one of them registered a simple, unwavering E. I realized while looking at the E that although most of the adventures of my life had involved going east—to New York, New England, Europe—I felt little of the excitement aiming at E that I did at W. Even in these days of widespread disillusionment, going west still meant something, still signified, rightly or wrongly, a place to let go, be free, casual, eccentric, alone, start afresh, find yourself, hide. The land I was flying over was neither east nor west, in fact was at nearly the geographic center of the country. It consisted mostly of farms with neat borders and towns with names like Emma, Sweet Springs, Boonville, Blackwater, and High Hill, each with its own water tank, church steeple, baseball field, and six-story brick office building. I was flying under a 1,500-foot cloud deck so I got a good look.

By then it was almost dinnertime, and I wondered as I flew over one of those towns—what every pilot wonders at some time or other—what are the people down there doing? Could they be cooking dinner (all those tiny spoons whirling around tiny pots)? *What* are they cooking? (Tiny beans in tiny pots.) Are they maybe drinking beer and watching the news on TV before dinner? Or might they be at the table already, passing corn, biscuits, pickle relish? Was anybody down there making love at this moment? In which house? Was there even one kiss being exchanged? What were the people feeling as they gathered together toward the end of the day—satisfaction? Sorrow? Fatigue? That the day had been good? (All those hearts down there beating at once, no bigger from here than pellets!) Inside their wood and brick houses, were the people of Emma and High Hill content? What was life for them out here in the center of the country, and did they ever yearn for the big E, the big W?

Creve Coeur · Lexington

It was past everybody's dinnertime when I got to Creve Coeur, landing in the near-dark. The office was still lit up, though, with a teenage girl moving pages in and out of a loose-leaf binder, a man shouting into a wall phone, and a woman resting her plump elbows on top of a display case. Another Mom-Pop (or Mom-Pop-Child) operation. And only ten miles from downtown St. Louis too. Creve Coeur had a paved runway but I landed on the grass one, between two fields of corn. The cornstalks, I noticed wistfully, were pale yellow and stiff-looking. It was corn that closed out summer, in my experience, not roses, not oak leaves. I was running out of time.

When I asked about motels, Mom took my question very much to heart. She picked three, discussed them with Pop, and called one, but even though it had a room available she didn't ask for it on my behalf, not being sure it was the right motel after all, which one really was the best, if any of them was quite right. Seized by doubt, she equivocated, put off a decision. I felt like a kid home from school, a neighbor's kid maybe, she felt she had the responsibility to look out for. She must have noticed me eyeing the office couch. "You could sleep on the sofa," she said, "but I wouldn't recommend it. My brother-in-law slept there after a fight with his wife and he couldn't wait till morning. It creaked terribly." Creaks, schmeaks, I wouldn't have minded, but didn't insist; she had decided it would not do. Suddenly her face lit up. "Jack Oonk!" she said. "He's got that great, big house all to himself!"

As it turned out, Oonk was the very man whose plane was parked in the spot next to mine and who only minutes before had lent me a set of tiedown ropes. "Question," he had said. "How do you tie a Luscombe down?" "Answer," he answered himself. "You lay it on its back and drive stakes through its wings!" Which was a variation on "You're not through flying a Luscombe until it's in the hangar with the doors shut," both versions paying joking tribute to pilots who could handle a Luscombe (with its short coupling, heavy nose, narrow gear, small tail, and awkward brakes) on the ground, so of course I liked to hear them. "Safe," Mom said, lowering her voice. "Been around here for *years*. Never married. Lived all his life with his father and mother and three sisters. He's very close to all his sisters, particularly the oldest, but they all got married and moved out. The oldest one left three years ago, then two years ago his father died. Last year his mother died. Now he's all alone in that great, big house."

Within minutes Oonk showed up in the office, and Mom told him she'd told me I could stay at his house; he took the information amiably. He appeared to be unassuming, mild, vague even. He had pale eyes and gray-brown hair, slouched, and wore loose clothes. He seemed not to hurry about anything. His house was indeed fairly big, brown-brick, Victorian, with a handsome oval window in the front door and lots of dark wood inside. Some of the larger furniture was covered with sheets. Explaining the sheets, or trying to, Oonk said his oldest sister and her husband were about to move back in. I got the feeling, though, that the house would look in transition anyhow; he showed me around it as if he too might be visiting. He seemed not quite familiar with things, a little surprised when I pointed them out.

Of the four bedrooms upstairs, he had taken for his own the smallest, with a narrow cot in it, what might have been his mother's sewing room. I got her bedroom with big four-poster bed. The only other room in the house he seemed to use besides his bedroom was the kitchen. The kitchen table was covered with magazines, papers, envelopes, and engine parts (Oonk was a machinist). Moving slowly, as if dazed, he put water on the stove to heat for tea for me, took a bottle of beer out of the refrigerator for himself, then pushed the papers, etc., aside to make room for my cup, his bottle, and a stack of color photos.

The photos were all taken at fly-ins. Oonk loved fly-ins and would go a long way to attend a good one. So far that summer he had flown to Coldwater, Michigan, Savannah, Georgia, and Colorado Springs, Colorado, for fly-ins. Like boat meets or sports-car rallies, fly-ins are gatherings of the like-minded, usually one- or two-day affairs at some previously agreed-upon airport to which people fly from their own airports, park their planes, stroll around looking at other people's parked planes, do a lot of "hangar flying" (talking, usually about flights past, often using hands), meanwhile drinking sodas and eating hot dogs, getting a shirtsleeve tan, introducing the mate, watching a drunk-pilot act, competing in a spot-landing contest, lending a hand with the evening fish fry, applauding when the trophy is handed out to the oldest pilot and the pilot who's flown the longest distance to get there, and falling asleep under a tent draped over the wing. They could be organized by type—Bonanza fly-in, Swift fly-in, Stearman fly-in; by profession—physician fly-in, lawyer, dentist, funeral director fly-in; by activity—pancake-breakfast fly-in, 25th anniversary of the opening of the airport fly-in; by region—Upper Nyack Valley Annual Fly-in; or by the simple desire of aviators to get together with other aviators.

"Here's 'Little Butch,' " Oonk said, handing me a photo from the Coldwater fly-in. Little Butch was a Monocoupe. "And here's 'Spinach,' " he said of a dark-green Porterfield. "It used to belong to actor Bob Cummings. He was a health-food freak and painted it green to look like spinach but cracked it up." The next photo was of an Airmaster, and Oonk took a long look before handing it on. "An Airmaster's nine-tenths of a 195," he said, which explained the long look. His plane was a Cessna 195; in fact he owned two 195s. "It's the greatest airplane ever built," he said flatly. He flew his 195s only to pick up parts with which to fix them (he fixed them himself; "What else is there to do?") and to attend fly-ins.

There followed photos of an Eagle, a Waco, a Funk, and a Meyers. All the photos were of old planes. "People can't afford new planes so they're buying the old ones and fixing them up," Oonk pointed out, forgetting for the moment perhaps that I was one of those people. He knew and cared a lot not only about old planes but about *particular* old planes, who their previous owners were, what modifications had been made on them, their home bases, their crash histories, and even, sometimes, their registration numbers. He had such a strong feeling for planes as individual entities that he opposed the practice at fly-ins of giving awards for Best of Type and Grand Champion. "A guy with a beat-up Ercoupe," he said huffily, "is just as proud of his plane as anybody." Also, "there's too much emphasis on paint." I'd noticed his 195 had pretty ratty paint.

When I woke up the next morning, in the presence of his mother's flowered vases, lace doilies, and statue of the Virgin Mary, Oonk had gone to work, but he left me one of his cars so I could drive back to the airport. On my way there I stopped at the Missouri Historical Society, to visit the Charles A. Lindbergh collection. Three large rooms were filled with Lindbergh's things, although most of the things hadn't been his for long. Apparently he was so besieged with gifts from strangers after his flight to Paris that within a month or two of his return he began passing them on to the museum, sometimes before he'd seen them himself, there to be seen by other strangers. The point of the exhibit seemed to be to make palpable the excitement, longing, wonder, hope, fantasy, awe, and even love Lindbergh's flight set up in people around the world, by showing the range and nature of their gifts. The effect was cumulative:

There were poems composed by the senders ("Ave Lindbergh" started out, "Courageous viking, fearless youth . . . ," and "Slim," mailed with a knife by Boy Scout Troop #2, began "We've been singing for joy, with love for the boy . . ."); military honors (Third Class Order of the Rising Sun, Star of the Order of the Bust of Bolivar, Grand Order of the Guatemalan Army); testimonials on parchment and brass ("Eternal honour and mondial recognition to the great collaborator of international peace"; "Il Intrepido y Esforzado Aviador Colonel Carlos A. Lindbergh"); keys to the cities of Havana, Santa Domingo, and Mule Bay, Ontario. There was a Mexican dinner menu featuring a cocktail, "Esprit de Saint Louis," as well as a dance program from the Belize Polo Club in British Honduras listing both a waltz, "No Pilot E'er Was Cooler," and a one-step, "Oh Why Must My Shoulder Straps Sideslip/When I Stall in a Bank or a Spin?"

Someone, not Vachel Lindsay, had sent Lindsay's poem, "The Queen of Bubbles" ("Nay, sun is but a bubble, Earth is a whiff of foam"), while more prosaic types mailed clocks, watch fobs, jewel boxes, rings. William Randolph Hearst's gift was the two celestial spheres Lindbergh had admired in his office when the publisher was offering the aviator a movie contract (refused). Other admirers made presents of Romanian silk scarves, a piece of the Christopher Columbus family altar taken from the cathedral in Santo Domingo, a *kulac* (Hungarian drinking vessel), a greeting card in which a paper airplane moved across the Atlantic Ocean whenever the card was opened and slid backward whenever it closed, and a miniature mail sack made out of gold. In France a women's group had stitched "Spirit of St. Louis" onto a handbag in colored beads, for Lindbergh's mother.

As for Lindbergh's father, he was represented only by a quotation, as far as I could see, yet it suggested what the old man's gift to his son might have been. "Home to me," he once wrote, "is anywhere. I've gotten used to being at home where night finds me." It was a credo as useful to a pilot as to a lawyer, which is what Lindbergh's father was at the time. One night found young Charles over the Atlantic Ocean, flying blind and battling sleep, and some of the things he had with him then were also on view at the museum, in a glass case: a brown canvas flying suit, a map of the Atlantic with a course marked in pencil, a gallon-size water canteen, a pilot's license, and a stick of Wrigley's Doublemint gum, still in the wrapper. The gum, according to the label, was taken along on the flight "for the ears."

Back at Creve Coeur (pronounced locally to rhyme with "leave more"), a Cessna 150 was doing touch-and-goes on the paved runway. "A new solo," Mom said of it. Except for the sound of its engine rising and falling, the airport was quiet. On the opposite side of the runway from the office a few planes were parked near a red barn with a large willow brushing its roof. I crossed over the runway, between a go and a touch, to have a look around. Under an eave at the right-hand end of the barn sat an old Howard with straw sticking out of the wings' inspection holes (birds *in* wings?) as well as a potato chips delivery van without wheels. Inside the main part of the barn were several loose fuselages and wings, a refrigerator, a farm machine, several bales of hay, and a Tiger Moth. Under an eave at the left-hand end was an industrial-size wind tunnel, rusted, with three-bladed prop inside.

I asked a man on the ramp if he knew what the wind tunnel had been used for. His answer was, "People do their own things around here—including," he added darkly, "driving their cars on the runway." I had found him crossing the ramp with a dog padding along in the wake of his boots. The dog was named Mincemeat, he said, "because he's going to become it. He doesn't even look up when a prop kicks over his head!"

While paying up I noticed a sign above the office door inside: FLYING IS FUN, it said. Mom was again resting her elbows on the display case, which, I took the time to notice, was full of cigarette cartons for sale. On the wall over her head was a row of bowling trophies on a shelf, and next to them a poster of Snoopy in his flying duds, and near it some shirttails, neatly inscribed. One of the shirttails was a scrap of white T-shirt that had belonged to a man whose first solo took place at the airport on May 17, 1977. Besides his name and the date, printed on the shirttail was, "50th Anniversary Charles A. Lindbergh Trans Atlantic Flight." With the 150's stubborn drone in the background as the new solo went up and down, up and down, between a cornfield and a barn, I was thinking: More than a half century after all the loving cups, embroidered pillows, odes, ribbons, keys, posters, watch fobs, and verses were lavished on Lindbergh, some of our airports, and some of our airplanes, were not so different from those he knew.

Flying is still fun.

To get to the takeoff end of Creve Coeur's grass strip, I had to taxi the length of it first. As the propeller whirred over the thick grass, it churned up from the depths of it countless grasshoppers, plus a couple of bees, which fluttered up under my wings, rising like a wave just back of the leading edges, going my way for a while but gradually falling behind, to be replaced by other grasshoppers bounding out of the grass and filling the air with a quick, trembling movement. (Ah, Nature's version of the crowds at Le Bourget!)

For the next leg I didn't have a flight plan. In fact I had no plan at all except to fly east and be on the ground by dark. Home would be where night found me. Working my way out of St. Louis I had to pass under the second tier of the TCA and that took me low over a parking lot, which glowed like chain mail in the sun, then over a golf course. After that a parkway, and a farm. Then a graveyard by a pond. Some fields. A barn with the upper half painted bright red. A long, dark hedge. An aqua roof. A triangular lake. A tree in a plowed field, distinct as a rose in a buttonhole. Oh America, middle America, my own part of America, how lovely you are! And at this moment how loved!

Later, while crossing a woods, I spotted a trailer pulled up under the trees. *Aha!* thought you were alone, didn't you? I said to myself and racked the plane around for a better look. One of the less lofty attractions of small-plane flying was just this sort of voyeurism, coming upon people's hideaways and gleefully inspecting them, peering down into their hidden niches, their private nooks, seeing what their ideas of escape consisted of (a spit of sand jutting into a river reachable only by boat, the couple on it basking in their supposed secret?). Sometimes you can only wonder at how they manage. You are flying over a mountain, say. The mountain is high. The sides of it are steep. It has a lake on top. There are a lot of trees around the lake but nothing else. No road, house, car, trailer, or even horse. There is, however, a boat. A small, white rowboat pulled up on shore. Who comes? Somebody. *Somebody comes.*

An hour and a half out I passed from Illinois into Indiana without realizing I was doing it. On the chart the few scattered dashes of the state line were immersed in the Wabash River and I failed to see them. Charts generally don't make much of boundaries; to them, and increasingly to me on this trip, it was all just country. I realized I was in Indiana only when I landed to refuel and saw a sign over the office door that said so (Huntingburg, Indiana). By the time I'd refueled, drunk a can of the state cola, Mr. Bipp, and taken off again, it was late afternoon. At that hour the landscape was at its most alluring, at least to me, airborne. Shadows were long and thin—shooting—making cows look lanky. Textures were wonderfully tactile; even lawns had a nap on them. As I was heading east over the state of Indiana late in the afternoon on a day toward the end of summer, I would have liked to lower my hand to the ground—a giant's hand, capable of sensation but not of injury—and, palm down, let it brush the tall grass, graze the tops of trees, trail through a small, dark pond—hold it close to the earth and let it feel the scratch of corn stubble, the tickle of weeds. Thus caught up in stroking the surface of the land I was flying over, I passed without noticing I was doing it from Indiana into Kentucky.

I started thinking about a place to land. Briefly I considered a field called Haps, near Louisville. When I flew over I didn't see anything moving so figured it might be closed for the day, yet there was something appealing about it, snappy, like a well-run ship. The planes were neatly set out and brightly colored, most of them, and the light hit the ground in such a way that the grass seemed to glow with good health. I kept on flying, though, not quite ready to quit for the night. I felt a touch of regret, as if I'd come upon an inn on a cold, dark night with the smells of cooking drifting out and lights glowing at all the windows and had to pass it by.

In the end I picked Blue Grass airport in Lexington, Kentucky, as much because of the name as because of where it was, close by when night found me. Most little airports don't have good names; they generally don't live up to their naming potential, which is considerable. Overwhelmingly they are named for the county they are in or the closest city (Monroe County, Jackson Municipal), or else for their owners (Peterson, Evans, Brennan). A few do catch the spirit: Floating Feather, Idle Hour, Friend (air-strips *are* friends, especially in closing weather), Birds' Nest, Neversweat, ZZYZX, Possum Kingdom, Farmer's Pride, Hoodoo, Burnt Cabins, plus all the Flyings (Flying Cloud, Flying Hoof, Flying Dollar, Flying F, G, H, L, M, U, V, W) and the Skys (Sky Haven, Sky Harbor, Sky Castle, Manor, Lane, Line, Top, Hook, Way). To me Blue Grass sounded refreshing, but I should have known better since it had three runways and a tower. Instead of acres of sweet-smelling grass I found acres of oil-doused asphalt.

However, there was something refreshing down the road from Blue Grass, "the prettiest racetrack in Kentucky," someone in the office called it. In the morning I walked the half mile down the road to see it. The name KEENELAND was spelled out in red begonias in the center of the oval track; bushes along the edges of the track were so neatly trimmed they looked carved; silver balls glistened from the top of red-and-white-striped fenceposts. The grandstand boxes had bronze plaques that carried the names of track patrons: Curry, Gentry, Boone, and Quinceberry. Behind the grandstand were rows of stalls, some of which had horses in them even though the next races weren't going to be run for two more weeks. The horses' names weren't on the stalls, just the names of their sires (Colt by Glad Flame, Filly by Farewell Party) and the stables that owned them. Under a sign for Goodpasture stable, a small, leather-faced man was stroking the nose of a black horse.

He was, he said, a groom or "shit foreman," and his name was Curvin Smith. "She's nervous," he said of the horse, which was swinging its head from side to side. "That's why we put a goat in with her." In the shadowy rear of the stall I could see a white goat tied to a post, not doing anything, apparently fulfilling its purpose just by being alive, having four legs and warm blood. The horse was two years old, said Smith. "It takes 65 to 70 days to get two-year-old fillies fit," he explained. "You start them from scratch, you got to hold them back a little, keep them lazy at first. Once they're fit, though, it's hard to break them down. They've got to take a bad step.''

Did having an airport so close to the track make the horses nervous? I asked. Had the sound of engines or sight of airplanes overhead ever frightened them? ''No,'' Smith said, ''they don't pay any attention.'' Then he remembered one time. He had been exercising a horse when a plane flew over and the *shadow* crossed in front of her. ''She stopped dead and I went right between her ears!''

He laughed. He'd been thrown by horses so many times he could probably afford to find some of the times funny. ''Riding, I about broke every bone in my body,'' he said cheerfully. He had been riding since he was ''big enough to sit on the back of a pig,'' in the mountains of Tennessee where he grew up. ''I'd ride about anything—mules, donkeys, hogs, horses, cows. When the family was at church or the neighbors' I'd sneak out and ride something.'' Yet when he dropped me at the airport on his way somewhere in his truck and saw my plane on the ramp, he exclaimed, ''Why, *you're* more dangerous!'' So taken aback by the sight of my plane did he seem that I wondered if he'd ever really looked through the fence before. He told me he'd like to see my plane close up so I took him out on the ramp with me. He approached the Luscombe slowly, as if it had power to hurt just sitting there. Wide-eyed, he asked, ''You fly that yourself?'' I nodded. A minute later, he said, ''I think I'd want somebody to die with me.'' He started walking around the plane. ''Sure is a light little thing,'' he concluded. He laid his hand on the fuselage. ''Why, I could get throwed twenty times and not get hurt bad, but all it'd take is one crash in this thing!'' He pointed down the line to a Comanche. ''That one there's a *Cadillac* next to yours!''

Before driving off he told me, ''My father's the one would love to see this thing. He's back in Jackson County, Tennessee. He used to grow corn, tobacco, potatoes, pigs, and chickens but mostly tobacco. Now he's retired. He doesn't believe people really fly these things. He never did see one of them on the ground.''

Auxier

Past Lexington, I carried sentimental freight. For years my mother's father was a coal-mining foreman in eastern Kentucky, first in Wheelwright, then Betsy Layne, Whitehouse, Glo, Thealka, and finally Auxier. When I was little I visited him and my grandmother in Auxier several times. Then he had a heart attack and had to quit the mines; they left Auxier and never came back. I never came back either. Nevertheless my memories of the place were strong and strangely persistent. I could still see on the flickering small screen of my cortex the gray wooden slats the sidewalks were made of; the dark, iridescent, crunchy, loose nuggets of coal slag the streets were made of; the sunbonnets on the old women (my grandmother's lilac-flowered one); the corncob pipe an old lady down the road smoked while sitting in a rocking chair on her front porch *in full view of everybody;* the coal train that rolled by in front of their house two times a day, very very slowly, the engineer waving at me from the cab while I, standing on the porch, probably in some hairbow, deeply moved, waved back; the passenger train that came through at night, much faster, not stopping, on its way somewhere else, always waking me in time so I could get to the window to see the white rod of light thrust out in front of it and hear the devouring roar as it drew even with the house, then went whistling and clicking off, dragging a string of lit windows behind it.

The picture that keeps coming up most for reruns, though, is of the town water pump. For some reason it was in a corner of my grandparents' front yard. I would stand near the wooden platform it was on and watch people hang their buckets on the little faucet hook, bend and bob to work the handle, lift the bucket with the still restless water off the hook, and carry it away. Kids, some as small as me, would bring buckets as big as the grownups' and fill them just as full, then carry them back over the sharp coal ash *barefoot*—and never slop. When they weren't there I'd pump water into my own little sand pail, not clear to the top either, and carry it around the *yard* with my shoes *on*— and I'd slop. To me those kids were superbeings, tough and serious in a way no kids I knew were, a breed apart.

Auxier wasn't on the chart or even a road map I had bought, but Paintsville was, and Paintsville rang a faint bell; I'd heard somebody somewhere mention it so I figured Auxier was nearby (people then didn't talk all that much about places not close to home). I found an airport on the chart five miles from Paintsville, called Combs, so after Curvin Smith had driven off, leaving me with those chipper reminders of the dangers of riding my steed, I took off for Combs. The road out of Lexington that I followed was a straight, four-lane highway, but as it swung south and east into the coal-bearing hills, it became increasingly crooked and narrow. The hills weren't particularly high, but there were a great many of them and they were very close together, so close that in places the valley between them seemed little more than troughs. At the end of one valley, for instance, hills rose from either side of a house, with space beside it only for a yard with a line of wash running across it and a vegetable garden in which a woman in a loose dress was standing between two rows of greens.

As I looked out across the hills, they gave one impression, but as I looked down on them they gave quite another. Seen from the horizontal they were mountains, high, blue, distant, cold, imposing mountains, lined up in ridge behind wavy ridge, leading away in ever paler versions to an ethereal finish. Seen from the vertical, however, which meant close up since I was flying under a low cloud deck, the hills were simply that, domestic little hills, not lined up at all but jammed together, sticking out toward the road like so many fat fingers. As the road twisted around the hills, I had practically to count the turns the plane was making in order to be sure where I was on the chart. At one point a railroad pulled in beside the road, crossed over it, crossed back, did that a few times, wound back and forth over the road like a tendril; then a river joined them both and all flowed together through the valley toward Combs.

The valley the airport was in was as trough-like as the rest, and my downwind leg put me over a piece of rising, wooded ground; I flew the leg higher than usual so there'd be plenty of space between my wheels and the treetops. Turning from crosswind to base leg, I found a small hill sticking up between my plane and the end of the runway, so that for an unpleasant moment I couldn't see the end, which for all I knew could have been the takeoff and not the landing end, since the sock was hanging motionless and no one had answered my calls on Unicom. Once I'd landed I wished I had done what a pilot who came in just ahead of me in a Cessna Citation said he always did when flying into Combs: Ignore the pattern and just fly up the valley (or down) and keep dropping until you hit the numbers.

A Cessna Citation, I was thinking, was a rather heavy piece of equipment for an airport like Combs. But on the ramp with it were two Turbo Commanders, a Cessna 421, an Aztec, an MU-2, another Citation, a Heliocourier, plus a 210 and a Cardinal. What was going on? I wondered. The energy crisis, said the pilot. During the energy crisis power companies began having second thoughts about coal; with new extraction methods they could get coal out of mines seemingly worked out long ago. He had just flown a couple of business executives in to talk with mine owners in Paintsville.

Not only was there heavy equipment at Combs but plenty of light— 150s, Cubs, 172s. In fact, every parking spot was filled. Even with a limp windsock I didn't want to leave the Luscombe unsecured, so I asked an old man sitting in the office if he knew of any tiedown spots I might have overlooked. He said no, then yes. He had seen a set of rings farther out on the field once but couldn't remember now where they were. The grass out there wasn't mowed very often because nobody kept his plane there, and it had gotten pretty high. "If you can find the rings," he said airily, "you can use 'em."

The Citation pilot helped me look. In crisp, navy-blue blazer, white shirt, black pants, and black tie, he waded into the tall grass and began pulling aside clumps and looking near the roots as best he could, combing some of the low stuff with his fingers, kicking at stalks of flowering weeds. Meanwhile I was rooting around myself, feeling not unlike some Tolkien character, searching with a fellow traveler through the lush, blossom-rich greenery of a secluded valley for three much-desired yet long-lost metal rings whose existence had been predicted by a stranger of ancient and imperfect memory. After much pawing around in the golden sunlight, the Citation pilot found a ring. Then I, knowing where to look, found a second. But though we searched and searched through the dense, thick-packed sward, we never did find a third.

After connecting rings to wings, I set out walking to Auxier. I'd been told it was four miles down the road that ran by the airport. There was a tunnel-like quality to the road, with a wall on the left side (a hill with a vertical slice taken out of it to make room for the road), reeds on the right side higher than my head which allowed only occasional glimpses of the river beyond, and a canopy of tree branches overhead. Truckers honked and hooted as they passed (I had on shorts), but I didn't care; I was on my way to Auxier, of my persistent past. After three miles or so I came upon a sign by the road: "AUXIER HEIGHTS," it said. *Heights?* Why, there had hardly been an Auxier then! Two rows of little white houses ran back from the road, eight houses in all. Not far past them the road forked, and I took the right fork, as I'd been told. It led to a bridge high over a shallow, fast-moving river, and on the other side of the bridge an old man was mowing a tiny, handkerchief lawn using a power mower: Auxier.

Except for his house, which had one story, all of the houses on that street had two storys. They were essentially alike, this being a company town, long and narrow with the narrow ends to the street, and porches on all the narrow ends, and swings on all the porches, sometimes more than one swing, plus rocking chairs. The houses were all close to the street (asphalt now, the sidewalks cement) so front yards were shallow, but side yards were ample and looked well tended, with grass clipped and flowers planted in neat borders. There was one yard with no flowers, but it did have four statues of dogs, all life-size, and facing different directions—one brown dog, one white, one tan, and one gray-green. And another yard that was *all* flowers, the plants growing unchecked in that closed hothouse of a valley. Over everything, even the smell of other flowers, hung the scent of blooming honeysuckle.

A few hundred feet down the street, railroad tracks angled across it, casually, like a footpath, and a short way down them two freight cars stood, casually too, like parked trucks. Thus far I hadn't seen anybody except the old man with the mower. I turned right onto a street that ran past an empty baseball diamond, then when that road dead-ended in front of a church (the church building simplicity and purity themselves, a white box with two peaked windows and a chimney), I turned left. At that point I found inhabitant number two. She had just come out of a trailer which, like the houses, had been set narrow end to the street, only instead of a porch at the end there was a flowerbox; it was the post office. She was young, 19 or 20 maybe, and wearing a lot of makeup and a sulky expression. (Maybe she hadn't gotten a letter she wanted.) She passed within a couple of feet of me but acted as if she didn't see me. So much for small-town friendliness, and nosiness.

Past the post office was a wooden building with a roofless porch on which a half dozen men were standing, looking out. The men seemed to be communicating with each other yet were arrayed side by side, in a line, spaced like crows on a fence, each with his own little territory. One of them was whittling. Another was shifting from one foot to another in a peculiar way, swinging his head back and forth, also in a peculiar way, and looking at me out of the corner of his eyes as I stepped onto the porch. The village slow boy, I concluded, hanging out with the old men in front of the store.

Inside I picked out things for lunch—pressed ham, canned orange juice, and Ritz crackers—and while a man at the counter bagged them I asked him my question. "Do you—does anybody here—remember Alonzo Coburn? From the days of the mine?" He was my grandfather, I explained. The man told me he hadn't been around back then (the mine closed a year after my grandfather left it), but "wait a minute," he said, and went out the door. Sure enough, a minute later he came back with two of the men who'd been standing on the porch. One was the whittler, a fleshy man with buckles on his shoes. The other was a tall, thin man in a feed cap. They stood rather awkwardly just inside the door, a spittoon (empty Maxwell House Coffee can) at their feet. "Anybody with time," the thin man said softly, "remember Lon Coburn."

What I remembered was a man with thick, dark eyebrows under thin, gray hair, skin so firm on his face it shone, and false teeth that stayed put (unlike my grandmother's). I remembered a man in suspenders and collarless shirt standing by a large, brown floor radio in the house he and my grandmother moved to after Auxier and playing cribbage by himself in a chair by the piano my mother learned on. He was a quiet man who was good to us kids; we didn't pay much attention, and soon he was gone.

It took the men a while to tell me what they remembered, or perhaps simply to remember. Finally the whittler spoke. "I remember when Lon burned his glasses." He paused, went on. "We had crab motors. Lon hooked up one of the motors and a wire short-circuited. He set his glasses on the ground and the slag burned the lens. Ruined 'em." I nodded gratefully. "Lost my eye while Lon was boss," the thin man said. *Eye?* Could that have been Grandpa's fault? I worried. "Piece of steel flew up and hit the lens." The whittler added, cleaning his fingernails with the point of his knife, "It was real dangerous. Three brothers died in an accident." The thin man carried on. "We hand-loaded the coal. The machines would cut it in holes and shoot it, but we shoveled it. I got a bet once I couldn't load a ton in four minutes. We were using number four shovels. You could lift 15 to 25 pounds with number four shovels. I sure won *that* bet!"

They both laughed. By then another man had joined them. The man behind the counter, whose name was Bob, had followed him down an aisle and brought him back to where we were standing. After that every time a man of a certain age came in Bob would go after him, and the man would come back and stand listening to the others, then maybe say something himself. " 'Ducky' Wells jerked your grandfather away and kept him from getting killed." "Lon helped 'Shrimp' Daniels get his foreman's papers." "Lon would go along with anything you wanted to do." "A nice old man." (Was he so old even then? And *nice*—what was I to make of that?)

One of the men told a little story. "There was this law. We were supposed to cut out smoking in the mines and Lon was supposed to see we did it. I went to the air course one time to sneak a cigarette. There was a curtain over the air course. I pulled the curtain back and there was Lon with his pipe. He said, 'Caught one another, didn't we?' " They all chuckled. None of the men laughed loud, or talked loud, or talked fast, or moved fast. There was a muted, reserved, mild, unassuming, almost gentle quality about them (an old miners' habit of acquiescence?).

Another man told a story about " 'Grasshopper'—that was Leroy Adkins. Grasshopper hadn't been working too long when Lon gave him a place to his side. He was supposed to mark the center. You had to lie down on the floor to mark the center, and sometimes there was water down there. Grasshopper marked it off-center because of the water. He didn't want to lie in it. That put Lon in a bad spot. 'I get paid for marking up,' Grasshopper said. Lon said, 'You never got paid for marking *that* up. You ain't got sense enough!' " Chuckles all around, little snorts of amusement. Then the punch line, "He never did fire him!" Many chuckles. "Never paid for marking that up!" one man said again, shaking his head and laughing. I laughed too but wasn't sure I got the joke, the *real* joke they were sharing, the essence of it somewhere back in the mine.

All the men had worked in coal mines until they retired, which meant, since Auxier's mine was long closed, that they were living in other towns when they quit. Why had they come back to Auxier? I asked. They were slow to answer, so one of the wives, standing at the edge of the group, did. "You get rooted," she said, and that seemed enough. Of the 850 people who lived in Auxier now, according to the thin man, 750 were retired. (No wonder the girl had a sulky look.)

All the men had black lung disease, or at least brown. "I was 59 when the doctors told me I had miner's pneumoconiosis, second-and-a-half-to-third-stage," said the thin man. "They told me I had to get out of the mines. I had trouble breathing. I couldn't do nothing. The doctor told me, 'You better be getting your house in order.' Well, I didn't have too much saved. Us coal miners never had too much saved. I owed for my home. It took me seven years to get my money. Thirteen doctors had to say I was sick before the company would give it to me. A lawyer took near half of it. I got $13,000." The words may have sounded resentful but the tone did not. From the sidelines a younger man, in his mid-50s maybe, said, "I quit *before* I got black lung." He had a woman's face tattooed on one of his arms and "Sailor's Grave" on the other. "I was afraid of it."

I asked about Auxier, starting with the water pump. Everybody in town got running water now, from Mr. Music, who lived in the last house on Main Street. Did the trains still come through? There were no passenger trains anywhere in eastern Kentucky anymore. Freight trains came through but they didn't stop, just kept on going north, "carrying watermelons from Florida." How about the old lady who sat on her porch smoking a pipe? "Old Mizz Webb," the whittler shot back. Then, as if pressing a claim, he said, "My mother both chewed tobacco *and* smoked." Sensing that he'd gone too far in his claim, he added, "The pipe was only clay, though."

All the men agreed I should go see "Yeller Cat." "He knew your grandfather better'n anybody else around," one said. The whittler offered to take me over. He had an old Cadillac and drove it through town at about the speed of a float in a Fourth of July parade. On the way we passed signs hung on trees and light poles. ARVEL "MUSH" NELSON FOR SHERIFF. JAMES "JITTER" ALLEN FOR REPRESEN-

TATIVE. JOSEPH "LIGHTNING" LEONARD JR. FOR JAILER. When we came to a sign saying WELCOME TO CRAWDAD BOTTOM we pulled up in front of a *brick* house with a *wide* front porch—clearly not a company house. "Didn't used to be any houses in Crawdad Bottom when your granddaddy was here," said Yeller Cat's wife as she toed the porch swing back and forth with dazzlingly white sneakers. "It was swamp then." Yeller Cat joined her on the swing, a cheerful, cocky man with a lot of black, wavy hair and no teeth. His real name was Fred Goble. "Everybody had a nickname around here," he said. Did my grandfather have a nickname? I asked. "No," he said. "Lon was boss."

Both he and the whittler chewed, and the bushes in front of the porch shook with the impact of flying tobacco juice as Yeller Cat told me what *he* remembered. "Lon would holler at me and Palmer and 'Ducky'—that was Ernest 'Ducky' Wells—'You're going somewhere or other after dinner.' It would be some *trip*. Maybe Paintsville. If Lon was ready to go somewhere he'd get somebody to work in your place. We'd ask him, 'What are we going to do?' and he'd say, 'We're going to be on that train.'

"One time we went to Washington to see the cherry trees. Lon bought some sweetbriar whiskey that had been put up. He gave $10 or $20 for four or five pints. His wife laid back to sleep. He had an orange in his hand and he told her he was going to eat that. She didn't like him drinking. He told the conductor, 'We ain't got a drop,' but we had our pockets full. We run to the toilet and drunk all we had. And there was Lon with that orange. His wife never did find out."

In Washington, they went to a burlesque show. "There were two or three of those stripteasers. Some were all right and some weren't so hot. We just had a big time." Yeller Cat must have suddenly recalled that I was family because he said, "You know, I never did see Lon out of the way. He'd have a couple of bottles of beer in the saloon-and-shot-bar and that was about it."

There he was, then: my grandfather. A man's man, a nice old man, a man of his time and place. Sweetbriar whiskey and beer. A pipe. Burlesque, for heaven's sake. The orange trick on the train. Crab motors. Number four shovels. Marking up on a wet floor. These things didn't bring him closer so much as push him away from the house in southern Ohio where I'd known him. Where was his house in Auxier? I thought to ask them. They told me where and the whittler dropped me off nearby. At first I thought it was the tidy white house with potted flowers on the porch and a broad lawn, but that was the third house in and my grandparents' was the second. The second had gray, peeling paint, broken glass in all the windows, and a yard with vines, weeds, and grass so thick and intertwined it would take a bulldozer to clear them. There were several cracked and missing boards on the porch (clearly nobody lived there so I felt entitled to go up on it), and the front door (I felt entitled to go in) wasn't locked.

On the first floor were two rooms of equal size, one behind the other, with linoleum on the floors and wallpaper on the walls and a small boarded-up fireplace in the front room. They were both empty except for women's hats strewn across the floor and a stack of *Life* magazines, all dated 1969. Behind the rooms was a bathroom, with ivy growing through an opening in the window down into the bath-tub, plus two pairs of women's slippers on the floor beside the tub, one black pair and one red pair, and a jar on a table with false teeth in it. Behind the bathroom was a kitchen: Votive candles floated in a stopped-up sink.

Upstairs there were two rooms like those below, almost empty but not quite. A mattress lay between them with feathers spilling out of a large rip in the side and half-buried in the feathers a pair of green shoes with brass buckles. On the floor beside it was a black wool sweater with wasp's-egg casings in the folds. Hanging on one wall was a teddy bear dressed in someone's powder-blue net ballgown, the skirt cover-ing its little stuffed legs. Beside it was a red felt pennant with AUXIER written in black letters. I lifted the pennant off the wall, brushed off the dirt and cobwebs, rolled it up, and stuck it in my purse. (Was I entitled?) As I was turning to go I noticed a pile of letters in a corner. I picked one up and read it: One Patty Jane Cuppley went off to college.

Outside I went looking for the water pump. In the corner of the yard where I remembered it being I found a low, boxy structure with a patched tarpaper roof, peeling gray paint, and a door hanging crook-edly on a single hinge. Vines were growing about a third of the way up the sides. What a fall from glory! Thomas Gray in his country churchyard could not have felt more melancholy than I did contem-plating that tired little box, all that was left of what had once been the most valuable thing in town.

Bob, the clerk at the store, had told me that if I came to the school, where he taught science in the afternoons, he'd show me a picture of Auxier as it was in the days of the mines. In the school entranceway I passed two cardboard placards: "When Duty whispers low, THOU MUST, The Youth replies, I CAN. Ralph Waldo Emerson" and "God helps Them that help Themselves. Benjamin Franklin." I found Bob on the second floor, giving a lesson on weightlessness. He motioned me in and told the kids to study; they just stared and whispered. He got out a hefty book on the history of Kentucky and opened it to a double-page spread. The spread had a picture on it, which may have been a photograph and may have been a drawing, most likely was a touched-up photograph, of a town with what looked like a bridge running over the tops of the houses. "Tipple," Bob said.

He swept his finger across the right-hand page and announced, "All the people in this part of town got drinking water from your grandfather's yard." I hoped the kids were paying attention. He pointed at a rectangle on a slope. "This was common pasture," he said. "From your house you could see the cows." Click! My sister Molly had told me once that Grandpa had told her, and she believed him, that cows had legs longer on one side than the other so they could stand on hillsides. He and she must have been looking out the window together at the time, at common pasture.

There was another picture of Auxier I ought to see, Bob told me, a painting done by his uncle after World War II when he was "dreaming of home." Bob's uncle's mother had it, and when I appeared at her door she went and fetched it and propped it on a chair for me to see. What a dream of home! The painter seemed to be a few hundred feet in the air. The main street was bright orange, the trees on either side mint green, the houses yellow, and the tipple—which seemed to float— a rusty brown. Four rows of company houses went back in deep perspective to a point, actually an exquisite fold in the hills, at the far end of the valley. This Auxier glowed, for the uncle, for his mother, for me. Being literal in just this one matter, though, I said, "But Grandpa's house was white!" The old woman would not be moved. "All the company houses," she said firmly, "were yellow. *Dark* yellow."

That night I stayed in a hotel on the road between Auxier and the airport, named for a woman kidnapped by Indians. I took a glass out of the bathroom and filled it with vodka I had brought from my plane plus orange juice from Bob's, then sat on the bed and raised my glass to what must have been a very happy day for my grandfather. On his way to Washington to see the cherry trees, his mining buddies around him, sweetbriar whiskey in his pocket, his wife unconscious on the seat beside him, and, emblem of all that I still didn't understand about him, an orange—why an orange? why fool my grandmother with an orange?—in his hand.

When I woke up fog covered the tops of the hills on both sides of the valley. While waiting for it to lift I walked into Auxier again. The thin man was already in place on Bob's porch. "It's rare when the day breaks clear," he said. Actually I didn't mind having this chance for another go at Auxier. I felt . . . almost . . . *right* there. Which was odd on the face of things, because it was a town of limitations—short views, a slug's pace, hardly anything doing. Yet I sensed a buzz beneath the surface, something that hinted at freedom, the freedom of anarchy. The carefully tended yards were only a temporary holding action against the fury of growth, the relentless push of weeds and vines and blooms. Behind the houses were woods, thickets, and hollows, and what mightn't there be in them? In town there was a mood of tolerance: People without teeth spat, dogs ran loose, the dimmest boy stood in the most public place. Even neglect, of the largest public building (the company store, which after the mine closed became a sewing factory, but which after the sewing factory closed, years ago, had stood empty), felt like license, something slipping through the net of social monitoring, let live. And always there were the railroad tracks, heading away north, south. "I used to hobo a lot," the thin man said. "Whenever I felt bad, I hopped a car. Started when I was not thirteen."

To be realistic, though, if I actually lived in Auxier I'd almost certainly be wearing a sulky look and too much makeup. Besides, all this fog had to be bad for flying. From the store porch I had a good view of the sky and after a while noticed that a couple of pond-size holes had opened up in the overcast. From somewhere I could hear the sound of an engine; a plane would probably be dropping through one of the holes soon, on its way into Combs. The holes weren't big enough for me yet; still I decided to wait at the airport so when they were I'd be ready. At the airport I asked a man on duty in the office about the fog. Did it ever *not* clear? I wanted to know. Did it ever hang around the valley all day? He was a retired miner, with a bad leg and a head that wobbled around as if his neck were boneless. The question seemed to upset him. "*I* don't know anything about aviation!" he snapped.

While I waited, I looked over the shirttails. Some of them had names on them with the ring of the hills: Betty Pluncket, Zeb Campbell, Jim Cash, Byrd Preston, Peggy Arnett. There were two Gobles, a Betsy and a Joe, and I wondered if they could be Yeller Cat's kin (he hadn't mentioned them, and he knew I was a pilot). None of the new solos had a nickname, or at least was willing to have it put up on display. I couldn't help feeling they were missing out on something.

Columbus

Once the fog started to break up for good, the old miner might have said, it broke up fast. By noon the pond-size holes were lagoons. On my way out of Auxier I passed over the town and took some photos, for my mother; she never came back either. I flew dead reckoning from there, on a north-by-northwest heading, not adhering to any road, on which straight course there was almost nothing to see in any direction except hills—small, rounded Kentucky hills, close to each other as lovers' lips. They would pop up on the horizon, pass under, and disappear, hills, hills, and more hills, all the way to the Ohio River and on to the other side, until 25 miles or so north of the river they subsided at last, into softly rolling farmland. It was about there, at the point of subsidence, that I began looking for the Serpent Mound.

Even though I was from Ohio and it was one of Ohio's most famous landmarks, I had never seen the Serpent Mound. It is a 1,300-foot-long earthwork built by Indians thousands of years ago in the shape of a wriggling snake with a tightly coiled tail. The snake has an open mouth about to ingest something round—an egg, frog, nobody knows for sure (the suggestion has even been made that the round thing is the moon and the snake is Halley's comet, which the Indians had surely seen, about to swallow the moon). Now seemed the time to see it, and flying seemed the way. I found the town of Locust Grove using a road map and flew eight miles northwest (or what seemed like eight—no odometers in planes), according to directions in a brochure. I didn't see any sign of a snake around there, or even a raised area or intriguingly cleared field, so I climbed for a better view, made a few turns, then several long, parallel passes, farther and farther afield, and still didn't see anything serpentine, went back to Locust Grove and did it all again, eight miles northwest, look around, make sweeps and circles at different altitudes and distances from the target point—still no snake. I began feeling annoyed, as if I'd misplaced something, the keys to my apartment—after all, the mound had to be *somewhere* around there. I couldn't take much more time at it since my family was waiting for me in Columbus but decided to have one last go: to Locust Grove, northwest, scan, side excursions, climb. But though there were many low, smooth hills and long, narrow fields and even farms that had been plowed up into curved relief, there was nothing that turned out, on close inspection, to be the Mound.

Feeling thoroughly peeved by now, I flew away, toward Columbus. Maybe, I thought, the gods and goddesses of old southwest Ohio, looking down from their mounds of heavenly cloud, could still see the serpent, as they were meant to when it was built, facing upward, but if so I wished that they had deigned to give me, a fellow skywalker, some help in all this, a visual steer: Let the egg be covered with red blossoms, or a hundred sheep graze on the tail.

Pretty soon even the flattened hills flattened out and the terrain became like the top of a box, what I had grown up on. From a long way out I could see the towers of Columbus, eight or nine of them where before there had been one, the A.I.U. building, our skyscraper on the prairie. I was supposed to call my family as soon as I got to Don Scott airport (named for an all-American quarterback and place kicker at Ohio State University who was one of the first American pilots to die in World War II, while test-flying a B-26 in Chipping Ongar, England); therefore I was surprised to see as I taxied in a young man standing by a Cherokee 140 and waving at me. "Welcome home, Auntie!" he shouted as he ran up. My 17-year-old nephew, Steve, who, I'd just been informed, was taking flight lessons. He was grinning. "My lesson starts in five minutes," he said. "Want to go up with me?" Oh dear. About the last thing I felt like doing then was going up in another airplane; I was hot and wrung out from looking for that stupid snake, had had nothing to eat all day but a few Ritz crackers, and was sure my mother was at that very moment sitting beside the phone waiting to hear whether I had survived yet another leg. However, *this was not to be missed* . . .

While growing up, Steve had done the usual things with aviation, built the usual model airplanes, set off the usual rockets in the schoolyard, read the usual fighter adventure stories. But he and his older brother Doug went further than most boys of their time, one or another or both of them devising their own complex board games based on air battles, building a hang glider starting from a kit but changing the design according to their own interpretation of aerodynamics (too heavy to get off the ground, it made one appearance on TV), and launching into the night sky balloons made from plastic dry-cleaning bags (Swan's Cleaners' were best) held open at the bottom by two crossed balsa sticks with lighted candles on top which heated the air in the bag and thinned it so that the transparent bags with their tiny flames rose and floated over the darkened rooftops of the neighborhood like shimmering, half-materialized angels.

However, Steve's greatest commitment to aviation involved creating airplanes for the company that he founded, Bongo Blisters Inc. (motto: "Scabbing the Scummy Skies"). With Doug and a couple of friends he produced a catalogue featuring 60 original, pencil-drawn designs for "Blisters," as the craft came to be known. Most of the airplanes were to have practical uses, such as the D-DAY DIMWIT, meant to carry into combat one "fully cramped platoon"; the CRYPTO STICHMO, an obloid, copter-like craft to be built under Russian franchise for the purpose of "carrying troops out of gun range while eating"; and the STRATO CRAP SCRAPPER, with a nose that was actually an open mouth into which other planes (in trouble or manned by enemies) could be sucked in midair, compressed within the body of the plane, and expelled, like eggs from a chicken, as neatly tied bundles from under the tail.

There were ethnic Blisters, including the German STUMPPFLICH SCHMULSTIG STÖREN ("Stubby Bombastic Bomber"), which appeared

WARTSLY WATERBUG   SNOZE BLOZER

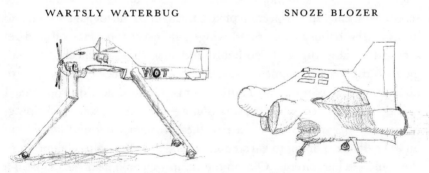

to have a mustache; the Cuban CASTROID-ASSTROID, whose nose was attached to the fuselage by a stick of sugar cane; and the versatile but confused Polish MECZJUSKIE CZLYZHEWCKI CLECKTRACKCZEVSZSKI, featuring both tank-tread gear and a filigreed tailskid. Outright failures were shamelessly included: The Italo-American FELUGY FANG "fell on its nose when untied from ground," and the TORPEDO TUB became a casualty of poor market research, having been conceived of as a "suicide plane . . . designed to re-use wings and engine but kill pilot."

So of course I had to go. I climbed into the right rear seat of the 140, behind the instructor, so I could watch Steve on the left. By then he had had only three hours of flight lessons, but already he handled the plane with an impressive authority and a light touch. The voice I had remembered as a boy's was now a man's on the radio. We stayed in the pattern and he made two landings, both of them smooth, then taxied to the ramp and let me out. He taxied out again and made a smooth takeoff. Oh CRYPTO STICHMO! little Steven!

The next week I spent eating homemade noodles and roast beef à la Midwest and Mother's peach preserves and the Jell-O salads that have such a bad name in New York but are so *good.* Since I was going to be staying in one place for so long, I decided to have the annual inspection done on my plane. I found someone at a farm strip 20 miles northwest of Columbus willing to do it, and when I asked him if I could help with the inspection, he agreed—but reluctantly. ''I usually charge extra to help,'' he said.

My mother packed me a picnic lunch—roast-beef sandwich, real tomato, potato chips, radishes, Thermos of tea, homemade butterscotch cookies—and I took off. Packer was grass and named for Richard Packer, the mechanic. He was also a cropduster, and when I flew over I could see his Ag Cat pulled out onto the ramp to make room for my plane in the hangar. As soon as I landed he went to work, or we did. While I unscrewed hubcaps and inspection plates, unsnapped the luggage screen and loosened the battery caps, pried wing-spar inspection plugs off and removed the cabin rug and floorboard and stick cuffs, he checked the engine—compression, magnetos, spark plugs. He was focused but easy. An hour passed pleasantly, two hours. From time to time I'd drop what I was doing to watch what he was doing—the real reason for helping. Meanwhile his wife, Sue, was across the hangar putting new fabric skin on a Tri-Pacer, hoping to earn enough money for a trip to California so she could see her parents. Out on the ramp we could hear the clunk of a paving stone—what seemed to me a dangerously large one, considering that there were soft-skinned planes around—being tossed by their six-year-old son Rich, who was playing fetch with Princess, their German shepherd (the breed of choice at an airport, it seemed).

When it came time for lunch I got out my roast-beef sandwich and took a delicious bite, then laid it on the floor beside me while I finished shampooing the cockpit rug. The next time I reached for it it wasn't there. It was in Princess's mouth. ''My roast beef!'' I screamed, close to pain, but the Packers all laughed merrily. *Not funny,* I thought, glaring at them, then at Princess. "Don't hit her!" said Richard cheerily. "She'll bite back." Sulking at their lack of sympathy, I ate the remains of my lunch, and a half hour later there appeared on the floor beside me a hamburger in a bun. Without saying she was going to do it because that would have spoiled the fun, Sue had quietly gone into the kitchen of their house, which opened onto the hangar, and cooked me a replacement.

As the day went on the hangar got increasingly hospitable. Neighbors and friends dropped in—first a doctor on a motorcycle, which he drove right into the hangar and stayed on the seat of while he chatted with Richard. After a while, acknowledging my presence, the doctor remarked, "I'm blind in one eye and myopic in the other, which is why I drive a motorcycle instead of an airplane." Next, a flight student of Packer's came by, a short young woman who a couple of weeks before had run a Cessna 140 off the grass and into the corn beside it while trying to land in a crosswind. Rather jovially she reminded Richard that she'd gone through *two* rows of corn. He seemed as tickled by the story as she, despite the fact that it was his 140 that got banged up and his corn. Next, a "firefighter" who sometimes rented Packer's 182 showed up, and after that a neighbor who owned a Luscombe stopped in. I was surprised to hear he kept the Luscombe at Packer's, because I hadn't seen it. I went out and discovered it in the yard in front of the house, a nice black-and-red 8A.

Except for the doctor, who never left his motorcycle seat, they all sat around a table in the hangar and had a good time. They joked and told stories and drank beer from a refrigerator the Packers kept at the back of the hangar. Now and then one of them would get up and go see what Richard was doing, maybe hold something for him, and now and then he'd go over and sit with them. At one point Sue held a windbreaker up for the firefighter to see, and he burst out laughing. It was his windbreaker, which he'd accidentally left behind at the airport a few days before. Then it had been a plain light-blue windbreaker; now it had writing on the back. The writing said in big, white, iron-on letters, FLY A TAILDRAGGER—PACKER AVIATION. "Anybody leaves a jacket here," said Sue, waving the windbreaker in mock menace, *"that's* what happens to it. We've done three jackets and a shirt so far." Moving carefully, so as not to attract attention, I stuffed my safari jacket out of sight on the Luscombe's hat shelf, beneath a box of screws.

For the neighbor, who hadn't heard it yet, the student told her corn story again. This time I detected a note of regret in the telling. Maybe it wasn't quite as funny to her as she had let on. Probably the neighbor heard the same note because he said, "Oh, there's too much emphasis put on landings anyway. You can fly the whole flight perfectly, takeoff and cruise and navigation and weather, but if you don't squeak the landing, you're a bum." He wasn't just being kind, he was being truthful. Landings were the final exam plus the term paper. You were expected to make them not only safe but seamless.

Richard told a couple of stories of his own, about cropdusting. One time a woman who owned a campground next to a farm he was spraying telephoned the police to report that he'd killed all the fish in her lake. " 'Have you got any dead fish?' the man from Agriculture asked her. (The rule is you've got to show dead fish.) 'No-o-o,' she said. 'Well, have you *seen* any dead fish?' 'No-o-o.' 'Then how do you know the spraying killed your fish?' 'Used to be better fishing here than it is now!' "

Only last night a man had phoned and accused Richard of "wrecking" his garden. "Maybe I did," Richard admitted. "The chemicals we're using these days are so strong that if the wind shifts they can drift over and get a garden. DDT you could eat a carload, but this stuff hits like frost. It kills the chlorophyll. I'll call the guy today—that's the mistake you make, not calling them—and tell him his garden will come back next year. 'God giveth,' " he was actually planning to say in consolation, and I imagined how this would go down in New York, " 'God taketh away.' "

Inevitably, the subject of New York City came up. All the others shared Packer's view of it. He had been to New York once and didn't like it and didn't understand how anybody could live there. From the beginning of the inspection it was clear that he considered it his duty, his *obligation,* to find something wrong with my airplane. Doing so would confirm his view that the mechanics who looked after my plane in New York (representing the rest of the population there) weren't nearly so great as they thought they were. When he found something wrong he'd call out triumphantly, "No cotter pin on the rear attach point of the left gear!" as if that proved once and for all the inferiority of the East Coast life, the inadequacy of the big-city mentality.

After a while the doctor rolled his motorcycle over to my plane and, staying on the seat, told me, "You know, I always thought people from New York were different. Had pointed heads or something." I recognized this as a friendly remark, meant to convey the idea that I was not so weird after all. The way I was standing at the moment, bent over with my rear end sticking out, trying to get the bolts off a gear fairing, I must not have looked particularly sophisticated, effete, rude, Communist, *or* criminal. I defended New York City vigorously to all of them while privately dismissing their attitude as small-town chauvinism, born of ignorance and isolation. But later, thinking about the mood of the hangar, I concluded that there might be something to what they were saying after all.

Times were, in places like this, small-town or even rural settings (most little airports were small-town, in feeling if not in fact), when I felt a decided lifting of tension, a palpable comfort, as if someone had laid a soft hand on my face, as if I had entered, briefly, a clear space, a sort of balloon of warm, roseate air, in which these people lived and moved every day, a matrix of goodwill—friends and neighbors who knew and for the most part cared about them, greeted them, kept track of them, wished them well—and whenever I came upon it, as here, I relaxed in it and felt calmed by it. How simple it all seemed . . .

In the end Packer charged me less than the annual should have cost because he felt sorry for me "having to live in New York City." That made us both happy. The following day I had planned to leave Columbus, but visibility dropped to two miles, in haze. Earlier that week I had read an article in the *Columbus Dispatch* about a recently released report comparing the average visibility at several big-city airports in the U.S. with the average visibility at the same airports ten years earlier. At Columbus International, for instance, visibility over the last ten years had declined more than ten percent; that is, on an average day in Columbus now a person could see ten percent less far than he or she could have on an average day only a decade before. In some cities the decline was even more marked: 25 percent in Phoenix, Arizona, Lexington, Kentucky, and Ely, Nevada, 40 percent in Salt Lake City and Cheyenne, Wyoming. It wasn't nice news for anybody, but particularly not for pilots. Increasingly, it seemed, we were taking off into great bowls of porridge, looking around for a horizon and finding instead a brownish smear, or gazing at the ground through a pearly film drawn over the earth like a snake's eyelid.

Maybe the day would come when "blue sky" would be as outdated a phrase as "cracker barrel" and "horse and buggy," I mused. "Horizon" would be a theoretical concept, not confirmable by direct observation. Or maybe blue skies would exist but only in pockets, which tourists would travel miles to see, above the Sahara (between dust storms) or the islands of the Galápagos, something to be photographed along with other endangered pieces of nature, the last of the giant tortoises.

Thundershowers came through the very next day and took some of the haze with it and visibility climbed to five. Mother and Molly came to the airport to see me off. On the drive there Molly told me she and Doug had both had dreams of airplane crashes that night. (Oh, thanks.) In Doug's dream, a large plane was heading for a field where he and some other people were standing with their belongings. The people ran to get out of the way of the plane and dropped their belongings. After the plane crashed and burned, they went back and picked up the belongings. In Molly's dream, two airliners came from behind the plane she was in and passed on either side, closing to a V in front. At the point of the V they burst into flames and fell to the ground. It wasn't my idea of a rousing send-off, family dreams.

In all the years I'd been flying, I realized, I had never dreamed of an airplane crash, even when I was worried about a flight coming up or had just had a lousy one. What I *had* dreamed about, several times in fact, was making, or trying to make, landings in odd places, such as on the ledges of hillsides, under power lines, or in garages. One time I dreamed about taking off in a roadster, a handsome brown-and-cream Bentley-type car, which when it got to a few feet of altitude seemed to become aware, as I was, that something wasn't quite right and sank gracefully to its place on the road. Another time I dreamed the opposite, that I was driving around the streets in an airplane, changing lanes, keeping an eye out for wide-hauls. Still another time I watched as a Cherokee 140 taxied slowly into a winner's circle after a race, an actual white circle painted on the ramp, and was pleased to see two matronly women in housedresses climb out of the cockpit and stand in the circle together: the winners!

My favorite flying dream, though, was one where I was in my Luscombe high over the plains of East Africa, able to see a great many miles in every direction, and the shadows of clouds were making giant blotches on the ground, like Andy Warhol blossoms, and standing on the blotches as well as in the sunny places between them were elephants—hundreds of elephants. My sister was in the passenger seat, looking out with me over this wide world, sharing it with me. It seemed to me then that in this dream were all the elements it took to make a person truly happy.

Luray · Wings · Spring Valley

It wasn't enough that corn should signal the end of summer on the ground, it rose to remind me of it in the air. On climbout I had crossed the spire of the Pontifical College of Josephinium, which was the only institute outside Italy under direct authority of the Pope and which had, for what earthly purpose I never found out, its own airstrip, then the reservoir where Doug sailed the boat he bought with his paper-route money, then the outer beltway and the first farms, when I saw moving along below me at about 2,500 feet some pale, dry cornhusks. I had never had a visitation aloft before (although I had read about storms sucking frogs out of ponds and sending them into orbit) and was astonished, particularly by its altitude. In the elegiac spirit produced by a closing season I turned south and followed a road my father used to drive us down as children and young adults to visit our grandparents in the town they moved to after Auxier. It was another place of worked-out coal mine, close-packed hills, train tracks in front of the house, town pump and privies (then), and population top-heavy with retirees. It wasn't a whole lot bigger than Auxier but had several more churches, many more stores, and at least two saloons plus an American Legion hall that served beer. Still, it wasn't on the chart either, so my mother made a dot for where I could find Murray City (I was going to fly over but not stop), midway between Glouster and Carbon Hill.

The road to Murray City was wide open until I got to within five miles of it; then it disappeared under trees. I had to work to catch glimpses of the gray asphalt through breaks in the greenery to make sure I was on track. With trees growing so thick around it, Murray City seemed to me as remote, as backwoods, as out-of-the-way as I had always thought of it being when I was a kid. In the suburb where I grew up we were all pretty much alike (particularly the 80-some classmates I sat with grade after grade), and I was uncomfortable with even minute deviations from what I considered the human norm (the human norm including correct placement of scatter pins and degree of dirtiness of saddle shoes—my parents did not conspire in this). To me people in Murray City deviated more than minutely. They spoke differently, dressed differently, walked differently, even sometimes smelled different (the women powdery, the men—was it tobacco? sweat?). I liked them fine but they were foreigners, mostly. One of the most terrifying nights of my life was spent at a picnic with a group of Murray City kids. The boy across the train tracks invited me, and my mother, thinking How Nice, all those children her age, made me go. So toward sundown one day, several dozen teenagers and near-teenagers set off from the edge of town for the wooded hills, and from the time we entered the woods my seventh-grade heart never stopped racing.

First we did little-kid things like play Ring-Around-a-Rosy around a bonfire, while I scoffed to myself at this backward behavior; then after a while we left the cozy light of the fire and went off into the dark of the woods to play Hoot-'n'-Holler, a game altogether too grownup for me. The rules for Hoot-'n'-Holler were that one team would go out and hide somewhere, usually on a hillside behind trees (while choosing a place to hide, our team flushed a hobo from back of a tree, his clothes the color of dirt and his eyes wide and frightened, caught in our flashlight beam), and once settled the team would give out periodic hoots or hollers while the other team would try to find it by tracing the sounds or catching sight of clothing or movement against the hillside. Actually the whole thing, as I began to understand it, was a setup for boys and girls to do whatever they could manage with each together in the excitement of waiting and the darkness, and the only thing that saved me from a fate worse than death at the hands of a taxi driver from Nelsonville who was ten years older than I and who had latched on to me, an obvious newcomer of unsurpassed innocence, and was cunningly helping our team win by covering the paler parts of my clothing with his grownup hands, was the fact that the boy across the street who'd invited me kept hanging around, poking at me, stealing my cap, wouldn't give up.

Abruptly the trees over the road parted and houses and streets appeared in the gap. I throttled back into slow flight and took note: several blackened buildings on the main street—there'd been a big fire.

Edie and Edna's old house had a new roof. Sunday Creek was that same rusty-orange color. The elm tree in our back yard was gone. The railroad tracks were gone but not the raised bed; it ran like a dike between rows of houses. Johnny's Saloon was there but was it open? The depot was there too but definitely not open, hadn't been for ages. I thought of Old Mode Lewis sitting in there with his plump, manicured hand cupped over the telegraph key, moving the hand slightly now and then to depress the key, lifting it when the clicks started to come back . . .

When I was going for my pilot's license, I tried to learn Morse Code so that I could recognize the three-letter call signs VOR stations put out over the radio, such as --•• --•• •••- (ZZV) for Zanesville, •- •• •-• (AIR) for Bellaire, - -•-• •-•• (TCL) for Tuscaloosa, to help pilots trying to fly to one station not to track by mistake to another station on a nearby frequency. It wasn't really necessary to know it by heart, since the dots and dashes were printed on the chart next to the stations that broadcast them, but I thought it might be useful in case sometime in some light I couldn't read the chart, or I crashed, survived, and wanted to signal a search party with something more informative than ••• --- ••• (SOS). It was while trying to learn the code that I began to appreciate what it must have taken for Mode to make sense of all those corn-popping sounds. I discovered that I needed to translate, either in my mind or on paper, the audible dots and dashes into visible ones before I could figure out what most of them stood for—that is, go through an extra step—while Mode had understood them as De Gaulle understood French, directly in the ear. I suspect Morse Code doesn't play a part in the running of railroads anymore, but I am glad that it still has this small part—made even smaller by the fact that most VOR's give out the station's name by voice as well as by code—to play in aviation.

In West Virginia, I picked up the 120-degree radial of the Parkersburg (•--• -•- -•••, PKB) VOR and tracked it away from the highway over the otherwise trackless hills. The hills in West Virginia seemed just like the hills of eastern Kentucky except there were maybe even more of them in view at once, squeezed into even smaller spaces. Gradually, though, the hills began to coalesce, line up and form ridges which ran parallel to each other and so far in either direction I couldn't see the ends of them: the Allegheny Mountains. While picking up the radial I had called Parkersburg Flight Service, and a briefer there told me to expect "moderate turbulence" on my planned route of flight. ("Moderate" when applied to air turbulence, it has to be said, is not a mealy word; the usual definitions of "calm," "sparing," "temperate," and "abstemious" don't convey the proper sense of things.) He suggested I'd be "more comfortable" flying above the clouds, which had tops to 7,000 feet. Since I like seeing mountains rather than inferring their presence under clouds, I didn't take his suggestion but should have kept in mind just how uncomfortable things could get over mountains, even ones only half as high as the fiendish Sawtooths.

At first there was nothing but the usual cradle-rocking over hills, and I paid attention to the sights, particularly the ponds—a turquoise pond, two pumpkin-colored ponds, and a pond the color of blood, shaped like the heel of a shoe (chemical companies in the area, I presumed). As I was following the 105-degree radial out of the Elkins (• –•– –• EKN) VOR, things got moderate in a hurry. From perfectly level flight the plane suddenly shot up and shook hard, as if someone had hold of a naughty puppy. He-e-ere it goes, I thought. But just as suddenly the shaking stopped, a naughty puppy let go; the control stick didn't so much as wobble afterward. Within minutes it was all happening again, the shooting up, the shaking, the sweating of the pilot, followed by total calm and abstention. All the way to Luray Caverns, 60 miles that felt like 600, the plane was repeatedly whacked, clubbed, booted, and left to fly away as if nothing had happened. I minded the waiting almost as much as the pummelings, never could predict when they would start, where on the undulating line the Alleghenies were describing under the plane (upslope, peak, downslope, valley) they would strike. It was like being in some alley and knowing there were bullies and muggers lurking in the shadows and not knowing when they'd make their move. They wouldn't try to kill me—not like the psychotics I'd dealt with in Idaho—but they sure were giving me a beating.

After one final uppercut in the pattern, I landed at Luray to find the airport deserted. Local pilots probably knew better than to fly on such a day. There wasn't even a car in the parking lot to suggest somebody was up and had yet to come in. There wasn't a phone booth on the field either, so I couldn't cancel my flight plan or call a motel. I was standing beside my plane trying to decide whether to walk to the little white house I could see a couple of miles down the road and ask to use the phone when I saw a car coming down that road in the direction of the airport. It pulled into the parking lot and a man got out; he had blond hair and a face that reminded me of mine. He said he'd been on his way home when he heard the sound of an engine overhead, "so I came back." He explained that he was the airport manager. "I thought you might need something."

I told him I needed a place to put my chair for the night. In Columbus I had bought a chair, a country Windsor I found in an antiques store I went to with my mother and spent a long time looking at from every angle, growing fonder and fonder of its birdcage back, bamboo-turned legs, and old dark stain until it set up such a glow in my heart I decided I couldn't do without it, and splurged. Clearly, it wouldn't fit in the plane's baggage compartment, not with all the bags and boxes already in there, forming an almost solid wall behind the seat, so I put it in upside down on the passenger side, seat on top of the boxes, legs sticking up in the air. From the other seat I could see out past it okay, although there was a modest jailhouse effect with all the legs and rungs. Also, the crest of the chair was wider than the boxes and crowded my throttle arm slightly, but that wasn't much different from flying with a hefty man, just keep your elbow in.

While the manager took the chair into a back room of the office to find a place to stow it for the night (ever the New Yorker, I was afraid somebody might see it through the window of the plane and like it as much as I did and make off with it), I stayed in the front room and looked over the snapshots on a bulletin board. One was of a baby in a green snowsuit sitting on the cowling of some plane. Another was of two house sparrows, hunched in the snow under the tail of a tailwheel plane. Another was of a group of men and women picnicking under the wing of a Cessna 172, on what looked like a fine summer day. Life not only in but on and under the family airplane.

I told the manager I also needed a motel room, so on his way home for the second time he dropped me at a motor inn, where I got a room for $6 off because the TV was only black-and-white. By the time I strolled into town for dinner it was almost dark out and the air had turned cool. I climbed the streets of Luray—it was on a hillside— looking at houses that had been converted into law offices and craft shops and at houses that were still houses; stared past porch posts into front rooms and around corners into back yards; watched light pass from the sky to lamps, and for a moment forgot where I was. This could be any town, I thought, the way it looked: a Southern town, a Western town, a Hill town, a Farm town, a Tourist town—all towns seemed mashed together here, came together in this one small town— Any Town. Behind a lowered blind in one house a lamp was on and light from the lamp shone through the blur of slats and of bottles standing upright on the sill—glowed yellow-orange behind the glass, like blood passing behind membrane, like serum, the yellowish-orange pulsing against the shadow-blue frame of the window—*living tissue!* On this trip when I had needed the warmth of human contact I had usually found it, in the large extended family of little airports, and the towns they were usually in.

After passing up a Japanese restaurant called Pickwick, I ate in a Chinese restaurant called Brown, where there was a chain-link curtain over the kitchen doorway made entirely of bent beer-can tabs. Larry Gatlin's "Every Time a Plane Flies Over Our House" was on the jukebox, and I played it, twice. Before I left the motor inn I had called Molly, and she told me that Stevie had just soloed! If I had known that was about to happen, or if he had, I'd have stayed an extra day in Columbus. Molly had gotten to watch, from the tower. Her heart, she said, was pounding. Steve, though, was supercool. As he stepped out of the cockpit onto the ramp to accept the hugs of Molly and his sister Kathy, "a little turbulence on the second landing" was all he said. At Brown's I ordered a glass of pink champagne with my egg roll and pecan pie (having lost all sense of menu propriety) and toasted with silent but heartfelt praise nephew Steven, whose idea of airplanes was the far-out and fantastic, now solo pilot of a workaday Cherokee 140.

In the morning before going back to the airport I visited Luray Caverns. The justifiably big draw there was two limestone "fried eggs," authentic-looking down to the slightly-browned-bacon-grease look of the yellow yolks. Another draw was an organ with stalactites for pipes. The stalactites were in different parts of the caverns but connected by wires to a console in the main hall, on which a man was playing a haunting "O Shenandoah" as we passed through. So far, according to our guide, 162 weddings had been performed in the caverns, to the accompaniment of that sound.

When I got to the airport, the manager asked me about my trip. I realized that he was the only person, except for the FBO in Reno with the peeling sign, who had done that, shown much interest in what I was up to. With *his* camera he took a photo of *me* with *my* plane, after which I took a photo of him with his fuel pumps. He told me he wished he could fly around the country in a small plane as I was doing, but he had a family. He used to be a high-school teacher but quit to take the airport job because it paid more (not many occupations pay less than airport jobs, but teaching might be one). While I was engaged in my last preflight, another man came over and displayed a similar interest. "I didn't know there were any Amelia Earharts *left,*" he said generously. Portly, bald, and wearing thick-rimmed glasses, he moved neatly from one aviation pioneer to another. He had wanted to fly "back when Lindbergh flew" but didn't get his "ticket" until four years ago, at the age of 53. What kept you from it? I asked. "Wars," he said. "Four children." As he kept talking about all the flying he'd done since getting his ticket, it became clear that every hop he'd made thrilled him, was an adventure he cherished, and he seemed surprised that he had been able to pull it off. Which got me to thinking of all the men at airports around the country who, like him, were flying airplanes for the first time in their lives, or for the first time in a very long time, or owning part of an airplane for the first time—50 and 60-year-old men for whom the burdens of family and work and country had lifted a little, making them feel lighter, disposed to float a bit, try their wings.

From Luray, the Shenandoah River meandered north, like a long curl unwinding. It was the color of tank paint, dull and unreflecting under a brilliant blue sky. I followed the river as far as Harpers Ferry, where (transformed into the Potomac) it veered northwest and I northeast, toward home. *Home.* The word sent a pulse of excitement through me. At the moment there was nothing around the plane except farmland, but before long I could just make out on the horizon to my right five sprocket-like projections: a city. It had to be a fairly large city, since it was quite far off. Probably Baltimore, I figured. But not New York. *Not yet.*

From other flights I knew what to expect when coming up on New

York City, how it might look when I first caught sight of it from the air. It could of course look quite different on different days, from various distances, angles, and altitudes, in different kinds of weather and light, at different hours of the day. For example, when I was far enough out that the skyline filled no more than a degree or two of the earth's arc, so far out I could hardly be sure that that's what I was seeing, New York was a speck of ivory, an intricately carved bric-a-brac, elephants in a bean. Closer in but not truly close, and viewed under the light of late day, New York was an old, old city, of worn, red-brown brick, some of the buildings already turned to rubble. From approximately the same distance out but on a day of light haze, New York could be a city of glass, insubstantial, a visionary's metropolis, a pale rendering of a city-to-be. From the distance I most often saw it, thirty miles away, since that's how far midtown Manhattan was from my home airport and I looked in that direction almost every time I took off, New York was a collection of gray, stone slabs, one slab per side of a building, uninhabited, the population fled, evacuated, gassed, something, except occasionally the sun would strike a building in such a way that one of the slabs would seem to ignite, turn brilliant orange, as if somebody were in there after all, setting seditious fires; then the orange would slowly recede and the slab turn back to stone as my plane moved off the line of reflection.

The site of the final filling of the tanks was a small, busy airport north of Philadelphia called Wings. It deserved a medal, I soon realized; a sign there called it the oldest airport in Pennsylvania. I asked the man behind the desk if they'd ever gotten an Our Lady of Loreto medal from a visiting pilot. No, he said in such a harsh, dismissive manner that I was convinced he'd thrown it in the trash. Earlier I'd been treated to an example of his sneering style, so I should have known he wasn't the type to be sensitive to the nuances of history, despite that sign. He had been looking out the window at what I assumed was my airplane being fueled on the ramp when he remarked, to nobody in particular although four of us were within hearing, ''You know, the Luscombe used to be *the* cross-country airplane [pause to prepare everybody for the really funny part] *because it was faster than the Cub!*''

Guffaws all around except from me, of course, not nice laughs but derisive, patronizing ones, as if the FBO and the other men were all superior human beings for flying bigger equipment. So what did *they*

know? The attitude seemed particularly inappropriate since Luscombes were once manufactured a few miles from the airport, in West
Trenton, New Jersey, known as "the birthplace of the Model 8." So
what did *they* care about *that?* Before Jacqueline Cochran became the
first woman to fly faster than the speed of sound, in an F-86 Sabrejet
fighter, she had flown a Luscombe on a speed course and set a lightplane record in the process (105.6 miles an hour). The feat had dignity
then. Why rob it of dignity now? No reason to look down on a plane
just because the world around it had changed.

When I paid my fuel bill a woman was behind the counter, and she
must have read "Luscombe" on the bill because she volunteered that
she had worked for Don Luscombe at the factory in West Trenton.
After a few years the factory went bankrupt, but later she worked for
him again. Not in an airplane factory, though. "He ended up making
playground equipment," she said, sounding sympathetic, not sneering. "Went broke making that too."

Out of Wings I made a noise-abatement takeoff, which meant I
honored the sign beside the end of the runway: No DEPARTURE TURNS
BELOW 1200 FEET. As I climbed straight out I watched small houses
slide past on either side and wondered how the people in them (who'd
obviously complained) were perceiving the noise I was making, as a
gentle buzz in the ear, I assumed, a hum back of the air-conditioner.
A few clouds had materialized in the sky by then, but they were min-
imalist; any smaller and thinner and they couldn't be counted as clouds.
Some were so thinly striped they looked like fingerprints against the
blue. I took a couple of minutes to go over the chart again, noting all
the roads that would soon be crossing my flight path, the towns that
would be spreading their yellow tentacles in its direction, the inverted
V's (obstacles, like TV towers) that would be popping up. When I
looked up from the chart, a Skylane was only a quarter mile off my
right wingtip. As it happened, on the entire trip I had seen no more
than a couple of dozen small planes airborne when I was, except in
the vicinity of airports—that is, in the process of arriving or departing.
Away from the honeypots of large cities and airports, it was hard to
come to the conclusion, as so many people had, that the skies of America were crowded. However, I was coming up to the Biggest Honeypot
of all, so it behooved me to think of the skies as crowded and spend
more time scanning them.

Soon I noticed a smooth white bump on the horizon, dead ahead.

Oboy! From there on I didn't need a chart. I sat and watched the bump grow, lose its smooth outline, split into sections resembling teeth, then upright tablets, kept watching as two of the tablets separated from the rest and came slowly into focus as . . . the ends of a bridge. The Verrazano! I heard a voice on Unicom say, "Say your active"—an Eastern phrase!—then another voice, a woman's, calling an airport. Another nervous pulse went through me. It was my airport she was calling!

Passing through the steel swag of the Verrazano Bridge and up the eastern shore of Staten Island, what struck me was not the intimation of urban life to come but the liquid setting for it, the vast reach of water—bays, rivers, sound, and sea all coming together and rendering everything upon and around them—tankers, shorelines, bridges, piers, skyscrapers—merely ornamental; even the Statue of Liberty, with its arm raised in welcome (for which I had to admit I was as grateful as the next traveler, the dust and sweat of the journey still on me), seemed diminished by the enormous lay of the water. After circling the statue a couple of times and taking pictures, I leveled the wings of my plane and took aim at the island of Manhattan, at which point the dominion of the water began to wane and that of the metropolis to wax, spectacularly.

The congregated towers of Wall Street, the World Trade Center, the Woolworth Building—how could anyone belittle New York? You skeptics out there, think again! BIENVENIDO, BIENVENUE, WILKOM-MEN! blared a sign at the end of a pier in letters large enough to be seen from cruise ships, for which the greeting was intended, although I chose to accept it. In the Hudson River corridor—1,100 feet high and as wide as the riverbanks—created by the FAA especially for planes not in contact with controllers, I was flying at 600 feet, about level with some of the skyscraper windows. From that altitude I could sight down the trenches of Manhattan's crosstown streets, strung with bright red dots: car-brake and stop lights in crowded perspective. The Empire State Building! The Chrysler Building! I was almost bashful, the small-town girl in the big city again. Rockefeller Center! Suddenly the cockpit was filled to the brim with the smell of coffee so powerful it was as if the burden of thousands of office workers taking their breaks simultaneously had exceeded the capacity of the air to contain the aroma; then I noticed on the New Jersey side of the river the neon Maxwell House Coffee sign, an immense cup tilting to drip one last good neon drop of coffee into the river.

My office building, still there, with the time on top, then the 72nd Street boat basin and, counting the streets past it, my apartment house (not burned down yet!), Soldiers' and Sailors' Monument, Riverside Church, Grant's Tomb, George Washington Bridge, after that the lower, more scattered, boxier buildings of Yonkers, woods, railroad tracks, estates—and New York City was behind me. I looked back to the right and saw gray stone slabs. I looked left too, toward the west, the way I had come: Other places were behind me as well, Oljato and Thermopolis, Shafter, Creve Coeur, and Tallulah, Gallup and Elko; lakes shaped like horses' hooves and grand pianos; terrain that rose and fell, in waves, as if the land were breathing; mountainsides as intricately carved as conch shells, or the inside of an ear. Creekbeds that split the earth apart like bolts of lightning, fields with islands of grass shaped by plows into Egyptian eyes, which stared up at the sun, and at my plane, passing, passing . . .

"Welcome back!" Mr. Christie growled when I taxied into my tie-down, next to his. He had a Cessna 182, and he was standing by it wearing the same baggy dark-gray pants and shirt I'd always seen him in. Mr. Christie—it was always Mr. Christie or Christie but never John—was said to be 60 but looked older. His broad, flat-topped, nearly hairless head was often bent, in grievance or discontent. Someone once described him as "rancid," but others used such words as cantankerous, ornery, crazy, lonesome, and sad. For almost 40 years he had owned and run a grass-strip airport ten miles north of this one, called Christie, but recently he'd sold it to developers and now hung out at Spring Valley, grumbling about this and that in the world of aviation. We had all heard stories about Mr. Christie at his old airport, how he'd pick fights with pilots for offenses only he could perceive and abruptly order them off the field or refuse to sell them gas. He held grudges for years, not only against people but against airplanes, even types of airplanes (he couldn't stand Navions, for example, considered them arrogant). We had also heard stories about his flight instructing, how he would sock students if they made mistakes; one was seen climbing out of his cockpit with a bloody shirt. He kept photographs in a cigar box to show students when they got too confident, or confident at all, it seemed. All of the photos were of airplane wrecks; he let me see them once, while he chuckled wheezily over each one. His favorite photo was of a plane with a large hole torn in the side and a woman's leg protruding from the hole, a high-heeled shoe dangling from her foot.

I liked Mr. Christie anyway, convinced that his churlishness covered something awful in his past which he couldn't swallow. We knew that he had been married once, in the 1930s when he was trying to make a go of his little airport, but his wife, he would say in a mock-snooty voice, "read *Hahpuh's Bazah* all the time." Evidently she wanted to live in "the city" instead of where she did, on the grounds of a grass-strip field 40 miles away. One day she gave Mr. Christie a choice, the airport or her. "I lost my wife to aviation," he was fond of saying. I thought of him as a dark, stubborn spirit from the old days of aviation, which he was in continual mourning for. He often spoke about the time author Ernie Gann flew into his airstrip in a Ford Trimotor.

"Hi, Mr. Christie!" I called back, disoriented by the familiarity of the setting. "What happened while I was away?" An arm rose slowly and a bent finger pointed at the hill where the coffee shop was. Or had been. "That's been turned into a *fahn-cy* bar and restaurant," said Mr. Christie, adding gloomily, "Oh the whole airport's going to go. It's just a matter of time." He said he planned to sell his Ryan and move to Texas. For years he had been talking about fixing up that Ryan (the make of plane Lindbergh flew to Paris, much modified) and selling it to a collector for big bucks, but no one thought he'd get around to it. "I'm going to spend what I have in Texas," he announced. "Down there they respect aviation." He looked a little gray in the face to me; I'd heard that he had cancer. No one thought he'd get around to moving to Texas either.

While we were standing between his plane and mine talking, a low-wing plane pulled into the tiedown on the other side of his; it was a Piper Arrow. The door swung open and a small woman with a big head of frizzy hair stepped onto the wing and looked around. She spotted us, jumped off the wing, and ran over. "My heart's *pounding*," she said, breathing fast and holding out her trembling hands for us to see. "But I'm not scared. I'm elated!" She started dancing around and crooning, like a happy child. "Outrageous!" she yelled. A man followed her out onto the wing; I recognized him, a local businessman who always seemed to be flying off somewhere, in golf clothes, ski clothes, sailing clothes, usually with a woman on board. He had dark, wavy hair, dimples, and puppy-dog good looks. She gazed over at him adoringly. He had just given her her first ride in a small airplane, she said. They had flown to Orange County airport, for pie and coffee, and back. She would never forget it. "The only thing more fantastic," she said, smiling and waving her arms, "was when I gave birth to my two kids!"

Even Mr. Christie had to smile, the twisted smile of a man who shared the woman's excitement about flying but was too ill-natured to express it himself. "Only way to go!" she yelled. The pilot didn't pay much attention to her, just went around closing up his plane, apparently quite blasé about the whole thing, except that as he passed from the front to the rear of the plane he laid his hand on top of the fuselage, absent-mindedly, as someone might the back of a horse he was fond of. While I was unpacking my plane I did a similar thing—good Luscombe! In all I took out eleven bags, two boxes, and a chair and laid them on the grass in a row, gave the woman my camera, and asked her to take a picture of me and them. Then she (laughing like a child), the pilot (apparently still blasé), and Mr. Christie (head bowed and grumbling) helped me carry the bags and boxes up the hill to the new bar (fahncy because booze was served in Mason jars), where I telephoned a friend. I stood waiting beside the road for my ride, on a bench next to the airport picnic table where I had once seen men and women from the Russian Orthodox Church across the street sitting after a funeral, drinking vodka out of a bottle and weeping. The sky was still blue but the clouds had grown slightly, in size and substance. They were too low to be cirrus clouds yet were long and brushed, like the thin feathers of cirrus. No, I thought, more like wings.

A Note on the Type

The text of this book was set in a digitized version of a type face called Baskerville. The face itself is a facsimile reproduction of types cast from molds made for John Baskerville (1706-1775) from his designs. Baskerville's original face was one of the forerunners of the type style known to printers as "modern face"—a "modern" of the period A.D. 1800.

Composed by Creative Graphics, Inc.,
Allentown, Pennsylvania

Printed and bound by Arcata Graphics/Fairfield,
Fairfield, Pennsylvania

Designed by Robert C. Olsson